T0364823

Dumbarton Oaks Colloquium
on the History of Landscape Architecture

XXI

Perspectives on Garden Histories

edited by Michel Conan

Dumbarton Oaks Research Library and Collection
Washington, D.C.

Library of Congress Cataloging-in-Publication Data

Perspectives on garden histories / edited by Michel Conan.
p. cm.
"Dumbarton Oaks Colloquium on the History of Landscape Architecture XXI"—P. preceding t.p.
Includes bibliographical references and index.
ISBN 0-88402-265-X (hc.) — ISBN 0-88402-269-2 (pbk.)
1. Gardens—History—Congresses. 2. Gardens—Historiography—Congresses. 3. Landscape architecture—History—Congresses. 4. Landscape architecture—Historiography—Congresses. I. Conan, Michel. II. Dumbarton Oaks Colloquium on the History of Landscape Architecture (21st :)
SB451.P45 1999
712'.09—DC21 98-30313
CIP

Contents

Introduction

Michel Conan

Gardens are places of contested meanings, and history a discipline of contested purposes. The symposium "Perspectives on Garden Histories" at Dumbarton Oaks could neither refuse to celebrate the achievements of garden historians who had contributed to intellectual encounters on its grounds, nor silence challenging voices calling into question the purposes of garden history itself. The collected papers of this symposium offer a source of very useful references on the main achievements of garden history in several domains (Italian and Mughal gardens in particular), and they may contribute in a significant way to a self-critical examination of this emergent discipline.

The contributions build up a reflexive discussion about the conditions under which contemporary studies of gardens have developed. Taken as a whole, they yield a picture of ongoing issues that could not be properly captured by any single paper.[1] Four approaches to the collection of papers can be suggested as a first description of its complexity. Each one suggests a different life-world, with its own actors, conflicts, and passions. Each one is duly sketched and suggests both deep shadows and Caravagesque chiaroscuro in the ongoing debates as it highlights some events. First, we shall review the development of garden history as it has been reflected through the years at Dumbarton Oaks, show how it seems to call forth a paradigm shift, and reflect upon the contribution of these historical accounts of scientific progress to cast some doubt upon the model of paradigmatic shift itself; second, we shall argue that garden studies have moved into a historiography starting from problems rather than style; third, we shall focus upon political uses of garden history that seem to cause some paradoxical biases in its development; and fourth, we shall examine how garden history may inadvertently contribute to a naturalization of Western culture and further its hegemony over everyday life in other cultures.

The Coming of Age of Garden History

Elisabeth Blair MacDougall was a noted garden historian when she became the first director of Studies in Landscape Architecture at Dumbarton Oaks. Her research on the origins of this program is revealing. It illuminates our understanding of the conditions

[1] Readers will find an index at the end of this volume that may help them find their own reading entries into this collective discussion. Tracing the uses of one or a few words by different authors may help reach a sense of both explicit and implicit debates in the field.

under which the new discipline of garden history became established and found some support at Dumbarton Oaks despite the strong reluctance of professional organizations, schools of landscape architecture, and academia. It provides an introduction to the history of Italian garden studies to which she had eminently contributed. The first symposium on garden history took place at Dumbarton Oaks in 1971, one year before she started her directorship. It was convened by David Coffin, whose contribution to this volume analyzes the state of art in Italian garden studies at that time.

By the end of the nineteenth century, English and American wealthy families had grown more and more interested in Italy and its gardens. This created an audience for books that offered design models and accounts of travel through Italian gardens. It spurred interest among English and American landowners in the restoration and reinvention of Italian gardens, which in turn stimulated more studies by architects or amateurs oriented toward design. The climax in this kind of interest came in 1931 with the Florence exhibition, which the Fascist regime intended as a political move to capitalize on the interest of American visitors by using and praising the documents produced on Italian gardens by the American Academy at Rome. World War II put an end to the Anglo-American presence in Italy and to these studies. Historicist garden design came under the fire of modernist architects in the 1950s, preventing a redevelopment of attention that landscape architects had given to Italian garden precedents for their own works. However, in the 1960s an interest in Italian garden studies was revived by the arrival in the United States of German art historians. These historians' American students availed themselves of scholarships paying for travel and stays in Italy. They brought to fruition a new wave of Italian garden studies, providing fresh approaches centered on garden meanings rather than garden design. Academia saw for the first time a well-trained group of professors and researchers, with firmly established aims and methods, who rallied under the banner of garden history, started publishing scholarly books, developed courses, and directed a new generation of students. This change was not heartily welcomed by landscape architects and students of gardens of previous generations, but they could not stop it. These developments are documented in the papers by Coffin and Mirka Beneš. They testify to the impressive achievements of the first generation of scholars and of their students who have become professors in turn and are training a third generation of garden scholars.

Even though the word is never used, it can be seen that these scholars have succeeded in establishing a research paradigm. In so doing, they are pursuing a normal course of scientific progress, a course reflected in Beneš's image of the brick wall to which each scholar is contributing in turn, as Thomas Kuhn described in *The Structure of Scientific Revolutions*[2] many years ago. Let us summarize this briefly. Gardens are to be studied as complex works of art, and art as a self-contained phenomenon that gives rise to different fields of creation. Two of these fields, architecture and sculpture, are of direct importance for garden studies, while other visual arts may provide useful information. Methods of study demand an extensive gathering of primary sources. They allow the reconstruction in an authenti-

[2] Thomas S. Kuhn, *The Structure of Scientific Revolutions*, Chicago, 1969.

cated manner of successive stages of the garden at well-known dates, and documentation of the historical context as well as of the figurative, discursive, and ideological sources of the works intended and produced. Each reconstruction of a garden, at any stage, is accounted for in narrative form, allowing the garden to be described as a succession of places as it would be in a very thorough guidebook. Actually, this pattern seems ideally suited to Italian gardens since it follows the pattern of Renaissance guidebooks. Despite its great successes, this approach to garden studies did not remain unchallenged. Neo-Marxist Italian scholars and German historians joined forces in studying the economic and agrarian context of villa development in the Veneto, proceeding from this standpoint to an analysis of landscape appreciation and garden design as an ideological superstructure. Far from allowing gardens to be studied by themselves and for their own sake, they proposed viewing them as an outgrowth of agricultural production processes, of interest because of their contribution to the social domination of the rural population by garden patrons. This amounted to a competing paradigm. Although it failed to take over, it created a sense of an impending paradigm shift among scholars of the second generation. Consequently, these scholars have attempted to broaden their domains of interest and to incorporate new questions that had no place in the paradigm they inherited. This has created a sense of uneasiness with the universal value of the paradigm, which is presented in the last art history section of Beneš's paper. She exposes a paradoxical feature of the development of an American school of garden history. Garden historians in the United States have been dominating the scene of garden history in the world since the establishment of this school of garden studies in the 1970s, and at the same time they seem to have grown more and more isolated from larger changes in the world of historical research at large. Other historians have been confronting all other social sciences in attempts at putting their research into an anthropological perspective.

John Dixon Hunt, the second director of Studies in Landscape Architecture at Dumbarton Oaks, raised during his tenure the question of the purpose of garden history, suggesting that a new direction had to be discovered. His contribution to this volume echoes this concern and offers some perspectives toward the development of a new paradigm. His argument does not stem from a direct criticism of the art historian perspective developed for Italian gardens, but from the indictment of another tradition, the historiography of English gardens, since its inception in the eighteenth century. The defense of a "more perfect perfection" achieved by the English discovery of the landscape garden by Horace Walpole is taken as the original model after which garden histories have been patterned, enabling them to avoid any question about causes and effects, development of social processes through time, or accounts of cultural or political conflicts. This criticism engulfs all other garden historiographies written since the eighteenth century without entering into any further discussion of particular ones. Michael Leslie has further documented the deliberate manipulation of historical narrative by Horace Walpole and the precise political condition under which it took place in Great Britain. His contribution puts the relationships between politics, gardens, and garden history at the center of the picture. Gardens are not inconsequential objects indulged by wealthy patrons that can be studied in and for themselves as a mere luxury item. On the contrary, they turn out to be battlegrounds where elite factions confront one another in their attempts to establish a symbolic language conveying what they consider the most appropriate ideology to the lower and middle classes. Garden history turns out to be a helping hand, a tool for these great symbolic deeds. Neither gardens nor their history can be studied independently of the contested ideologies that they express and of the social movements that give prominence to these ideologies. Thus we may see, from a critical perspective bearing upon the English scene, garden designs and their histories as battlefields of social importance. This derives from their usefulness in naturalizing arguments exchanged in ideological conflicts about directions of a society's future.

James Wescoat offers a number of practical directions that could be pursued once the necessity for a political decentering of garden studies has been acknowledged as a condition for allowing relationships between garden making, garden history, and politics to come under scholarly scrutiny. Even further, he shows the existence of a growing effort among researchers to pursue garden studies in a comparative perspective, by drawing upon the resources of different academic disciplines and by pursuing in a variety of ways comparisons between gardens in different times and countries. The idea of comparative studies is fraught with difficulties. In a preliminary period it was restricted to questions of filiation, dealing with transmission of formal features across different gardening traditions. But this limited approach of comparison is being superseded by attempts to set both similarities and differences in a theoretical framework. It should be stressed that this presses in favor of a theoretical framework that has yet to be developed and tested in actual research. Wescoat shows how studies of gardens in lands that have been at some time under Muslim rule have made varied uses of comparative studies. But he also stresses a rather dismaying observation: Garden studies seem to proceed either from broad political concerns or from short-term economic interests, of the tourist industry in particular, rather than from practical and cultural concerns about or from people who are living in their vicinity or who may be their primary users. Of course this is a political question, and it can be a haunting one in any perspective that would stress political implications of garden histories. This would call for new approaches.

Demands for yet another paradigm shift are coming from an altogether American perspective, as presented by Kenneth Helphand. He suggests that the growing interest for gardens of the past and for public parks stems from a reaction against ill effects of technological inventions and their democratization, and of the automobile in particular. While the impact of these technologies led to dispersion in homogenized local environments and to individual enjoyment, it has spurred an interest in revivals of local history, natural idiosyncrasies, and public space for common encounters. Thus garden history, protection, and restoration should be seen as an outgrowth of large social and cultural changes in America. These changes are driven by a dialectical encounter between national cravings for mobility and for land-based community. Thus garden studies cannot be made into a self-sufficient domain of inquiry; gardens cannot be accounted for by a functional or a teleological explanation of their forms, meanings, or changes because this would deny the dialectical nature of the larger phenomena of social and cultural change in which they participate. Hence gardens should be studied as *explanans* rather than *explanandum*, and narratives of garden history in America should explore the embeddedness of landscape culture in American culture. American studies provide descriptions and analyses of characteristic features of American culture and of social processes that contribute to its changes. Thus they stress a number of definite perspectives for further cultural studies, calling attention to categories of thought, such as the idea of Nature, or cultural complexes embodying a dialectical relationship, such as the idea of the "everywhere community" that embodies the tension between calls of mobility and of stable community integration. Gardens offer specific fields of study for the understanding of different outcomes of these tensions, allowing scholars to unravel how, for instance, individualism, community, and mobility meet one another. This affords gaining a new perspective on garden development, and on the role professionals or public officials could play in a way that would be meaningfully American.

Joachim Wolschke-Bulmahn, the third director of Studies in Landscape Architecture at Dumbarton Oaks, has also developed a political criticism of garden history. It echoes concerns voiced by Hunt and Leslie that garden history may be used as a tool in political attempts at social and cultural domination, but he adds a twist that highlights difficulties that had also been signaled by Coffin. This author shows how historiography of Italian gardens had been rescued from the narrowly defined interests of designers in the 1960s. Wolschke-Bulmahn takes issue in a broader way with the purpose of garden history: Should garden historians provide justifications for claims to professional autonomy for landscape architecture, or should they provide accounts of links between social development at large and practices and ideas of landscape architects? He shows how garden history in Germany has been written and slanted several times in order to legitimize a particular course of professional development and to provide it with moral authority. He proceeds then to show how questioning the attempts by contemporary garden historians in the United States to divorce landscape history from a broader political history has led him into polemical debates that have not yet subsided. Beyond any final adjudication of accounts of acrimonious exchanges, we come to see the importance for garden historians of a study of the role of gardens in symbolic communication. Gardens can be used to foster some ideologies. Yet attempts at manipulating social and cultural ideologies developing through positive discrimination of a gardening culture may backfire! The creation and uses of garden allotments for the working class in Sweden provide a well-documented case in point. This example is developed by Michel Conan as one of several cases of studies of vernacular gardens that aim only at contributing to an understanding of a specific kind of social agency. He suggests the possibility of a social anthropology of gardening that would be "a study of an art that turns an environment into places encapsulating intentions and representations about man's relationship to nature" (this volume, p. 204). It breaks away from studies of gardens as objects for consumption, or as symbolic texts used in ideological warfare only, by stressing the unique domain of social agency that they provide. It would divorce garden studies from commitment to any political or professional interests, helping development of public debates about gardening and landscape.

Of course, gardening is not the domain of action of landscape architects alone any more than health is the domain of action of doctors and nurses alone. Thus garden studies cannot be seen from the sole perspective of landscape designers, even if such a perspective may have developed an elaborate system of categories that take the layman's experience into account. This point is further stressed by Stanislaus Fung. His call for a paradigm shift is most radical. He shows first that the introduction of European concepts used by professional landscape architects, while it provided for the possible development of a Chinese landscape architecture grounded in a modern interpretation of Chinese garden making tradition, also defaces memory and renders incomprehensible aspects of Chinese culture that were accessible only through self-involvement with gardens. Thus comparative research itself might be self-defeating if it exports European concepts into other cultural contexts, barring access to differences it had intended to study. When suggesting that such limitations could be linked to European visual culture or to the ontological status of space and time in Western thought, Fung underwrites the importance given by Kuhn to beliefs and metaphysical assumptions in the grounding of scientific paradigms and makes a case for a radical shift in the approaches of garden studies. It should be stressed that he does not provide an ideological critique of Western discourse about China, in the way Edward Said expertly debunked Orientalism and its scholarly output. In an extremely concise manner he reaches for another level of deconstruction of Western culture, moving away from Derrida. His analysis explores fundamental differences in sensual experiences of the world through vision and experience of time and place that result in a different train of thought to be explored by discourse. This is not to claim a primacy of figurative language over written language which could easily be deconstructed, but to stress that in any comparative endeavor, garden studies should proceed from a knowledge of the dialectics of figurative and discursive language that can account for gardening as a field of social action.

At first sight garden history seems to be a lively academic field in which successful research paradigms are assailed by contenders that cry out for some paradigmatic shift. It seems to follow the pattern of scientific revolutions described by Kuhn: a paradigm of art history applied to Italian garden history had been able to establish a course of development of "normal science." It is assailed by many challengers, and their efforts are ushering in a scientific revolution in garden studies. Should we accept this metaphor of intellectual warfare as a valid reflection upon the conditions of development of the field?

In this view, scientific paradigms are a set of instrumental features necessary for description of scientific production processes. They comprise theories, methods, and beliefs shared by a group of scientists and enable them to agree on purposes and courses of action in scientific research. Such large domains of agreement allow scientific progress to proceed in a "normal" way. It is the most usual situation, and it results in accumulation of knowledge rather than in conceptual changes. It enables researchers who take part in a successful research paradigm to reap some social rewards. However, since such rewards as stipends, research facilities, and tenure are limited resources, researchers adhering to different paradigms are competing with each other. It can be observed, according to Kuhn's theory, that some paradigms achieve social dominance and provide their supporters with a very large share of available rewards. This stimulates competition in the form of other researchers attacking some fundamental aspects of dominant paradigms and introducing conceptual debates about methods and purposes. Such debates are focused around scientific issues and pit groups of researchers against one another in discussions about the conceptual framing of scientific questions and of scientific results. Thus scientific production processes are seen to result from the interactions in which many mutually contending groups are engaged. These groups may fight each other in order to appropriate a larger part of resources and rewards available in their field. Defeat of a dominant group allows scientific revolution to take place and new scholars to enjoy a privileged position.

Let us show that some elements of Kuhn's theory are present (a variety of competing groups of scholars, a dominant paradigm, attacks on the directions it proposes and beliefs upon which it rests) and yet that the debates in progress do not reflect the process described by his theory. This volume presents several groups of scholars who are engaged in garden history: a group interested in Italian gardens, another one in English gardens, a third one in Middle East and southern Asia; a few more kinds of places, such as American vernacular gardens, are defended by isolated contenders. Members of these groups are certainly very much engaged in discussions about purposes of garden studies, and in questioning of beliefs or assumptions underpinning research done by many of their predecessors. Yet it is striking to observe how little they engage in mutual criticism and how much they seem to be confronted each with their own contenders outside garden history. The only polemical debate that was registered during this symposium resulted from an attempt to conduct comparative research between Germany and the United States. It certainly referred to a larger polemical debate about nativism and developments of environmentalism in landscape architecture, but this debate itself did not extend to a discussion of concepts. We shall come back to this question later.

The contributions by Coffin and Beneš account in a richly documented and convincing way for the establishment of a scientific paradigm for studies of Italian gardens deriving from iconological studies in art history. They show how purposes, methods, and sources for Italian garden studies were a matter of common agreement among a very productive group of American scholars who benefited from several fellowship programs. They did produce new and cumulative knowledge about Italian gardens. Despite a few competing groups of researchers, they were never engaged in any polemical defense of their approaches, and they seem to offer a very good example of "normal" research in progress. In view of this, it may be slightly surprising that criticisms of this paradigm should come from within the ranks of its followers rather than from other groups of researchers engaged in garden studies. Moreover, art historians studying Italian gardens do not engage in intellectual intercourse with English historiographers as much as they do with Italian architects involved in restoration projects of historical gardens. And even this relationship does not seem to amount to any intellectual contest. To a certain extent these architects are carrying on work that could have been initiated by art historians, but neither do they pursue the same kinds of results nor do they claim the same types of rewards. So they provide new material to be used as starting points for different pieces of work by garden historians, which may come to reflect in the long run the domains of interests specified by the Italian heritage industry. Thus we may wonder about the role of social and economic patterns in the developments of garden studies. Wescoat shows in some detail how Constance Mary Villiers-Stuart wrote *Gardens of the Great Mughals*[3] in an attempt to contribute to the acceptance of British rule among Indians, and he notes that "studies of Mughal gardens, undertaken by designers more often than by classically trained scholars, also emerge from practical and comparative interests. In recent decades those interests seem repressed, unvoiced, or underexamined" (this volume, p. 138). He notes with some distress the competition with the tourist industry when restoration of Mughal gardens is at stake. In a somewhat different vein, Hunt notes that garden studies remain in a marginal position in academia because of the difficulties of attaining tenure as a garden specialist.

To make a long story short, these developments of landscape studies seem to be constrained by the particular interests of three groups of people—landscape architects, preservationists, and tourists—rather than solely by ongoing intellectual warfare between groups of garden scholars. It must be stressed that these different social groups that have a stake in garden studies may also develop ways of studying gardens. This is certainly true for landscape architects, or for architects doing restoration of villas and their gardens. But they do not compete in the same course of excellence, or for the same symbolic or material rewards, which prevents these intellectual encounters from developing into a field for scientific revolutions as described by Kuhn. Outsiders' influences seem to bear mostly on the choices of gardens that may receive attention and even on the garden elements that deserve careful historical research. They proceed from social agenda rather than from scientific or conceptual questions.

Yet this volume also reflects another kind of debate that seems to have weighed upon the development of the field. MacDougall vividly describes difficulties encountered by Mrs. Mildred Bliss, the founder of this program at Dumbarton Oaks, in obtaining academic support and approval of a program in landscape studies. The ensuing developments indicate how a subdiscipline of art history reached academic status. The Dumbarton Oaks program in landscape studies may have played a role in establishing garden history as a field of scholarly work and as a course topic in schools of landscape architecture. Yet Hunt points out that this field of research is not yet fully established and accepted in academia and that many young researchers are discouraged from pursuing doctoral research on gardens lest their future career suffer from such choice of topic. In short, garden studies seem to be looked down upon for their lack of concern with theories that are developed in a number of disciplines at the margins of which they are growing. But on the other hand one may watch another criticism leveled at them by landscape architects teaching in university departments who are interested in design-oriented knowledge and wary of too much abstraction in garden studies. Thus garden studies tends to be treated in academia as a domain of applied research for scholars who are already established in their own discipline rather than as a discipline in its own right. This situation is prompting many scholars who are

[3] Constance Mary Villiers-Stuart, *Gardens of the Great Mughals*, London, 1913.

approaching garden studies from very different perspectives, and with quite different field work experience, to search together for possible groundings of the discipline. Hunt offers a set of principles for the discipline; Wescoat suggests systematic comparisons over long periods of time and different places in an interdisciplinary spirit; Helphand proposes to establish garden studies within the context of American studies. Obviously there is a debate, and there are contending positions, but they are not motivated by internal competition for the appropriation of established rewards, but rather by external competition in search of academic legitimacy in a divided academe.

Yet there is little doubt that garden studies have achieved great changes during the last 30 years, and that they are broadening their interests and moving into new directions in using new methods in search of an adapted theoretical framework. So we should simply conclude that the model of scientific revolutions proposed by Kuhn does not apply in this domain and that to gain an understanding of changes in garden history one should take a fairly broad view of its social and political context. This volume, however, offers a striking view of changes that are taking place.

From Period Gardens to Cultural and Social Problems

Any reader discovering this book may wonder why, on the twenty-fifth anniversary of garden studies at Dumbarton Oaks, medieval gardens, French formal gardens, ancient Roman villas, Persian gardens, or picturesque gardens were not given as much attention as Italian gardens or Mughal gardens. This may be felt as a weakness of the whole volume. MacDougall in her introduction indicates that she "hoped eventually to organize symposia for all national styles and periods" (p. 25). And readers might feel eager to learn how historiography of each of these subdomains of garden history has evolved over the last 25 years. The question is certainly an interesting one. Yet addressing only this question would give a false picture of changing scenes in garden historiography.

Clearly garden studies received a great impetus from the support given by Dumbarton Oaks to encounters between scholars interested in national styles and period gardens. It has allowed garden historians to confront their own work with scholarly interests in neighboring fields or disciplines. Beneš shows how her generation of garden historians have discovered the kinds of questions that were raised by Marxist scholars and how the questions led to different framings of garden research. She also invites a broader intercourse between garden studies and other domains of historical research.

Actually the national style approach of garden history is crumbling. This is not to say that studies of Italian gardens are on the way out, but simply that the political agenda of research purporting to link garden style and nation has become one of the critical issues coming under scrutiny in garden studies. This is an important point to which we shall return, but it is certainly not the only one. Helphand in his attempt to propose future perspectives for research provides a very interesting example of a search for meaningful contemporary issues that lead to garden studies. The reversal from the previous historiography, which started from a few arbitrarily selected gardens to search for questions that could be addressed by research, is worth noting. His questions relate to American society and

American culture. They take as a starting point some deep cultural contradictions in the relationship between Americans and nature, and they develop into a search for relevant material, places of study, and sources. He notes, for instance, that "the impact of [transportation] technologies has been simultaneously centrifugal and centripetal, spreading things and people apart and pulling them together, creating dispersed concentrations," and goes on to suggest how this may invite a study of Lawrence Halprin fountain environments as a way of seeking the solace of the traditional in a defensive way; or a study of the resurgence of park interest as a response to a trust in "nature" coupled with a hope for a new public life.

The same approach starting from some cultural issue common to a large number of societies might be used to construct research topics over different places or time spans. Hunt goes as far as proposing a set of guidelines that would avoid falling into the most common pitfalls of past garden historiography. It can be summarized like this: (1) rule out teleology as a principle of judgment; (2) beware of worn-out categories that go in pairs, such as formal versus informal, or gardens versus ecology; (3) pay attention to countertrends when studying trends, to margins when studying a central theme; (4) establish a specific domain for your historiography, one related to other kinds of history such as social history or history of *mentalité*; (5) engage in studies of garden reception; (6) always keep the question "what is a garden?" in front of you; (7) seek the universal in man's dialogue with nature and culture that results in gardens. These seven rules set a difficult challenge. They posit gardens as historical manifestations of a transhistorical human endeavor that mirrors the human condition between an ever changing culture and a nature filtered by social and cultural constructions in a world without finality. Wescoat demonstrates a number of different ways of setting up problems for research: discussing the diffusion and differentiation of garden models; or attempting to integrate different disciplines in order to examine relationships between two structures, one cultural and individual—the structure of vision—and the other political and social—the structure of power inscribed in Cordoban space. In several of his examples one may recognize that the problems raised stem from a criticism of unstated assumptions of previous garden historiography. This is undoubtedly different from Helphand's approach, and it leads to very different problems to be studied. Conan describes briefly a small number of problems that have stimulated garden studies. His first examples start from problems raised in the social sciences: establishing the functional rationality for a horticultural society of a seemingly irrational system of beliefs about gardening described by Malinowski. He also suggests that comparisons between different societies may give rise to dilemmas that can serve as a starting point for future research, noting, for example, that among horticultural societies that all indulge in beliefs about supernatural beings there is no explanation of why some practice garden magic and others scoff at the idea. And most intriguing problems have been raised by Fung when noting that garden research assumptions by Westernized scholars may detract from any possible understanding of the objects they are studying and may contribute to changes in the cultural value or existence of these objects. Then we can see that fundamental concepts, even some of the *a priori* concepts of the mind posited by Kant, are the source of problems that cannot be clearly expressed, because this would require altogether new concepts at a deeper level.

A search for concepts and conceptualized questions to be addressed is noticeable in many of these efforts. It has not yet reached any great success that could have been presented during the symposium. Yet there is a deep lesson that is coming through. We have noted earlier that the only polemical debate that we were fortunate to hear about during the symposium did not reach into discussions of concepts. Actually it was not a debate about research theories, but about ideological implications of research assumptions! The debate was external to the field, not internal, as would have been expected according to Kuhn's theory. It is no surprise then to observe that efforts toward conceptual progress are sought through interaction with already well established disciplines in the social sciences. This was the way the Ecole des Annales had contributed a rejuvenating of history. The guidelines proposed by Hunt give clear indications about developing new concepts and new theories and refrain from attempting to provide conceptual foundations for an encompassing paradigm for garden history. He warns against pitfalls such as uncritical use of traditional categories of description of judgment, against confusing domains of observation, such as gardens, with conceptual objects of enquiry, and he recommends linking history of gardens with history of social or cultural change, which implies at least using a few concepts and assumptions from these domains, and eventually borrowing or reformulating some theories.

Nevertheless this parade of new approaches points to all sorts of directions, and one may feel at a loss because no central focus or set of problems has been found to catch most attention. Instead of the orderly procession of studies devoted to period gardens, one watches a disorderly crowd of studies that span time and space according to the needs of each issue. Can a discipline survive such a centrifugal movement? If we follow Beneš's intuition that the Ecole des Annales has something to teach to garden studies, it could be simply hoped that in the future this problematization of garden research would be promising. There has never been any method, purpose, or paradigm common to all historians who were published by the Annales. They were united at a different level, moving away from narratives that made historical research a handmaiden of national consciousness and of the reconstruction of times past, toward studies of theoretical problems in the social sciences that could benefit from studies over long time spans when temporality itself was subject to discussion. Some researchers took demography as a source of problems to be raised; others started from economics. They were extremely successful because of the concepts and quantitative methodologies they could rely upon. But many other approaches borrowing sociology, psychoanalysis, or cultural studies have been used as well, providing different concepts and approaches and depending very little if at all upon quantitative methods. A lively field of historical research that has captured the interest of contemporary audiences for history has resulted from this eclecticism. Cultural or social issues, paradoxes, and theoretical questions are a number of ways of establishing a problem to be analyzed as the focus for historical research on gardens.

This new direction for garden studies remains, however, veiled in some obscurity because research has not always explicitly addressed such practical concerns as the kind of materials, archives, methods of observation, and methods of analysis to be used. Furthermore, one might wonder whether any problem is as good as any other as a starting point for research. A possible answer might be that problems that are stated within a clearly established theoretical perspective are most likely to provide such useful guidelines. Social history derived immediate benefits from borrowing questions from demography. It offered theories, methods, and concepts that attracted attention to parish registers, which had been ignored until then as a useful source, and it allowed transposition of these questions into studies of book publications and readership, two populations that called for adaptation of the conceptual apparatus. This may suggest how garden studies after having borrowed from existing disciplines may enrich them. A few examples of this have been alluded to in the contributions by Wescoat and Helphand. The discussion by Conan of recent studies of family garden allotments in Scandinavia offers a snapshot of several problems raised by a succession of authors: Lena Jarlov, E. N. Anderson, Werner Nohl, Mark Francis, and Magnus Bergquist. The last author adopts an interactionist perspective in order to analyze the outcomes of municipal policies, a surprising and interesting move, and calls upon life histories of the gardeners as well as upon accounts of social interactions in the gardens or at home, and of gardening practices. This provides an unexpected presentation of relationships between popular gardening and developments of contemporary myths in Sweden, which certainly contributes to a deeper understanding of both Swedish gardens and Swedish society.

Politics and Garden History

Out of all these problems, a few seem to grow out of various manifestations of contemporary difficulties in moving toward multicultural societies everywhere in the world. They call into question abilities to construct self-identities in a culturally decentered world. And since gardens provide symbols for individual or group identities, these problems may lead to garden studies and to political confrontations around such innocuous things as flowery gardens and their histories. Wescoat provides a fascinating example in his account of the first major study in English of Mughal gardens, Villiers-Stuart's *Gardens of the Great Mughals*. He shows how her very sensitive study of Indian garden-craft aimed at fostering a new policy for the British Empire in India that would allow "peaceful domination" and Indian loyalty: gardens as opium for the Indian people! Her garden history was meant to carry a political message, and the suppression by later scholars of any mention of her intent does not improve the truth value of a historical vision guided by ideological concerns with the time of its writing. It contributes, willingly or not, to the diffusion of some of her preconceptions about Indian society and to the confusion between preaching and describing. This volume shows to a surprising extent how deeply garden history is still bound to political discourses.

Garden history can be used like any other piece of art history for nationalistic purposes, as in the Italian Fascist government's use of American historical research of gardens that is briefly noted by Coffin. This certainly deserves attention, but it is not specific to garden history. All art history has been used for propping up nationalistic regimes in search of internal as well as international legitimacy. Hunt points to a specific kind of relationship.

He shows that the naturalization of a political message that was written down in the model for garden historiography proposed by Horace Walpole in the eighteenth century has been a major conceptual block to the development of garden history: England was pictured as the first country to have discovered the "only true mode of gardening," so the very beginning of garden history was only its end, since it was true to eternal nature. It implied that the same was true of the English political regime that had brought the most perfect system of liberties to its people, as Leslie has argued with great acumen in his own paper. Instead of accepting this false ingenuity in the use of the concept of nature, which contributed to a nationalist narrative by naturalizing it, garden historians might attempt critical reviews of the different ways of constructing the idea of nature in the context of their own research.

The model of historiography proposed by Walpole has been very well received by many students of garden history because it is very difficult to avoid believing that nature proceeds from an eternal essence rather than from a cultural construction, and to evade the argument that acts of reason should be true to this essence. A garden art that claims nature as its source of materials and its mode of expression lends itself to such beliefs, and to passing facile judgment in the name of an idea of nature on other approaches to garden art. Thus the identification of garden art as a quintessential expression of national identity may serve as a political instrument in attacking contending political regimes as essentially wicked since they are acting against nature. This argument may seem to apply first and foremost to English garden history. It is the merit of Wolschke-Bulmahn's paper to have broadened the study of the interdependence between garden history and broader social and political issues. It is meant to show how garden history can be rewritten in order to legitimize a particular course of professional development, and to provide it with more authority so that it becomes part of political propaganda. The paper proceeds from a study of the development of landscape architecture in Germany under the Nazi regime that had been presented at previous symposia at Dumbarton Oaks to an account of the polemics among garden historians that he stirred when questioning some political implications of ecological landscaping in the United States. It certainly illustrates the difficulties of a critical analysis of political aspects of garden history that would avoid the pitfalls of ideological polemics. According to Wolschke-Bulmahn's argument, the interdependence between garden history and broader social and political issues would stem from a conjunction of three factors: (1) the reappropriation of political ideas by landscape architects in order to provide their profession with positions of authority; (2) the willingness of garden historians to write history in such a way that it supports the claim to authority of contemporary landscape architects; (3) the ethical context of political ideas upon which landscape architects rested their professional orientations. Under such conditions writing garden history would become entangled in ethical debate, at the same time pushing garden historians to realign their interpretations of garden history with changing political ideas.

This certainly cautions garden historians against the temptation to act as beacons in contemporary debates and to provide further legitimacy to any direction sought or achieved by the profession of landscape architecture. More importantly, this argument raises a difficult issue: What is the impact of an appropriation of political ideas by landscape architects upon public debates, or upon the "public space," if we may borrow the words of Habermas?

What is the symbolic efficacy of landscaping? One may fear that controversial ideas in human ethics, when applied to plants in the name of ecological correctness, may become familiar arguments inviting many people to accept contested ethics as laws of nature. Thus one might fear that landscape architecture might have a symbolic efficiency that would amount to no less than political alienation. This is typically a problem for garden research.

Such a claim can be examined empirically. It demands a study of the role of gardens in symbolic communications. Conan, describing Scandinavian research on garden allotments, provides examples that illuminate another aspect of such a discussion. Bourgeois philanthropists who advocated garden allotments in Europe were hoping that gardening and garden experiences of family life would curtail revolutionary impulses of the working class. Yet gardening is not a discipline in the Foucaldian sense of a method for subjugating people under a self-imposed power. Most working-class leaders never bought into the idea of gardening, and success of garden allotments in Sweden did not prevent social-democrats from wresting political power from the hands of the bourgeois establishment. One should add that working- and middle-class gardeners who cultivated these allotments have created ways of life in the garden allotments that do not match the expectations of their initiators. This example only shows the need for a deeper understanding of conditions under which garden experiences resonate into everyday life and political life outside garden limits. A reflexive analysis of the mutual embeddedness of political rhetorics and discourses about nature demands empirical studies of landscape and garden reception, as well as an effort to propose theories of communication, and of cultural development through rituals of garden making.

Toward a Critique of Universalism in Western Culture

Wescoat in his reflections upon the place of garden history within narratives of world history takes the discussion in a slightly different direction. He shows how various authors who have written on Mughal gardens have chosen a different cultural perspective on their topic: Anglo-imperial with Villiers-Stuart, Eurocentric with many European travelers, Islamicate with Marshall Hodgson, Indian with K. N. Chaudhury, American with a few contemporary researchers. It becomes apparent from such a survey that the indiscriminate use of garden history as a guide for conservation or reconstruction of ancient gardens may underwrite a particular culture to the disadvantage of others that are equally concerned with the same gardens. This concern illustrates in a new way the need for research on symbolic efficiency of gardens, and for reception of gardens by users belonging to different cultures. It also shows how much garden historians in spite of their aspiration to truth, method, and reason cannot avoid building up their narratives upon deep-seated beliefs about men, society, and the part of the world where they anchor their own identity. This line of thinking echoes the deep skepticism of deconstructive analysis of metaphysical bases of rational discourse in Western cultures. Such concerns, voiced in this volume, have called into question fundamental beliefs that are the building blocks upon which description of gardens are resting.

Conan calls attention to garden studies conducted by social anthropologists and by sociologists that have attempted to account for the gardeners' perspectives on garden experiences without imposing the observers' categories of thought. It reveals how much delusion may grow out of trusting ideas and interpretations derived from visual experience. In his work among the Achuar Indians, Philippe Descola accounts for similarities between forest growth and garden growth. Both of them comprise three layers of vegetation, and gardens, being much smaller than the forest, look like miniature forests to Western eyes. To the Indian's eyes the situation is reversed: forests are gardens tended by supernatural spirits, and this similitude derives from their interpretation of kinship relationships rather than from our interpretation of the layering of vegetation. Two different cultural systems lead to diametrically opposed evidence offered by the naked eye. These examples suggest critical methods that may help us avoid the pitfalls we might encounter if we relied solely on our own visual experiences when studying gardens and their meanings and uses. Fung takes the reflection upon cultural encounters one step further, from critical philosophy into uncharted territories.

Fung's argument grows out of a critical reading of Chinese garden historiography. It leads him to broad epistemological questions about the truth value of visual evidence. Descartes would have loved that! In a word, seeing is believing according to a cultural habitus, and describing the sight offered to the eye is falling prey to cultural bias, to the fallacy of primary visual evidence. He recalls how a Japanese scholar, Oka Oji, produced a major history of Chinese gardens that introduced a visual interpretation according to the criteria of Western landscape architecture, and provided a model for developments of Chinese garden historiography as well as sources of the recently growing practice of landscape architecture. Thus garden history appears as a contribution to the Westernization of China. By providing new ways of seeing, experiencing, and relating to gardens of the past these garden histories may give a sense of reappropriation of a forlorn culture even as they obfuscate the past.

The history of gardens is very seldom mentioned in ancient Chinese texts. Fung mentions only one text, by Chen Jiru (1558–1639), that calls "garden history" a poetic record of particular events in a garden. He insists on the fact that gardens are experienced and that experiences are ephemeral. Traditional Chinese writings thus do not seek to define general characteristics of the physical aspects of gardens that could be subsumed under physical components, or visual qualities; rather, they see them as parts of life processes.

Fung suggests that this could be linked to the ontological status given to space and time in modern Western metaphysics. This is a very interesting line of thought that could be pursued by asking how contemporary historiography is retroprojecting our ideas of time and space upon previous Western cultures. Should we write the history of gardens of antiquity in the light of Renaissance ideas about time and space?

His criticism of the cultural validity of methods and concepts used when defining visual sources of information—or texts, or professions—invites a thorough reflection on the invisible limits of scientific categories that make claims to universality. What is the experience beyond the object that we are describing? This is the fundamental question that

Fung raises. It demands that we question the implicit assumption of much garden history that making a garden is an intentional activity that finds its conditions of satisfaction in the realization of a place that can be thoroughly experienced in a visit. Should we consider historians as scholarly tourists traveling through time, and garden history as a subclass of travel accounts, or would-be itineraries for armchair tourists? Or would it make sense to acknowledge that there have been many ways in the past of making sense of garden experiences, some of them in allotment gardens, or native gardens in horticultural communities depending upon gardening and garden making (albeit in a way that is not similar to the Chinese), and others making sense out of public interactions, others out of intimate moments? We would then have to acknowledge that any experience has to be grasped as part of a larger number of experiences in order to yield its own cultural significance.

Yet the paper by Fung is raising another very significant question about the kinds of outcome that we may expect from such acknowledgments of differences between our own culture and the culture of other social groups, be they or not our predecessors in any sense. Should we see contemporary garden history as part of a modernization of the present culture or as an effort at distancing ourselves from the present? In other words, should we study history as a way of legitimizing a conservation of past objects, or as a way of discovering in past experiences new ways of thinking about our own?

Prelude: Landscape Studies, 1952–1972

Elisabeth Blair MacDougall

This occasion marking the twenty-fifth anniversary of the year that I came to Dumbarton Oaks to assume the post of director of Studies in Landscape Architecture is both a happy and a sad occasion for me. I am happy for the opportunity this gives scholars to assess and review the status of the history of landscape architecture today, sad that these 25 years have passed so swiftly. I was invited to address "the development of the program during my time as director of studies." But the events of those 16 years are well documented and the results widely disseminated; I find it difficult to expand on the record. Perhaps I can sum those years up with: "I came, I saw, and I'm not sure who conquered." I shall, instead, turn to the virtually forgotten fellowship program established by Mildred Barnes Bliss in the early 1950s and use that as a springboard for a review of the state of landscape architecture history in the years before 1972.

I believe that Mrs. Bliss's intention to establish a fellowship program at Dumbarton Oaks grew out of her plan to create a center for study in the Dumbarton Oaks gardens; the idea of a fellowship program developed as her ever more ambitious project for the study center evolved into what we now call the Garden Library. The idea of creating such a center first emerges in 1947 in some letters between Mrs. Bliss and Beatrix Farrand, the designer of the gardens and her friend and confidant.

Starting with her letter of May that year, we can trace a rapid evolution from her first suggestion of creating a center, as a service to the community, where garden visitors could read about plants, gardening techniques, and design, to the concept of a "specialized small library . . . on landscape gardening and design."[1] Mrs. Farrand had written that "the cultural and intellectual basis on which [the gardens] have been developed should be at hand for gardeners of various ranks of ability and also for students of the art." She speaks of "a small . . . collection of really first rate books on the development of the art of gardening. This second group would appeal to students rather than to . . . the exclusively delphinium-minded Garden Club member. [It should include] the foundation books and prints underlying garden philosophy and design."[2] Mrs. Farrand's reply tells of her "rejoicement that

[1] Bliss to Farrand, 12 June 1947, Garden Library Archive, Dumbarton Oaks (hereafter cited as DO).

[2] Farrand to Bliss, 26 May 1947, DO:

> It seems increasingly clear to me that the gardens and their influence on the community is as potentially strong as the other and historically scholarly side [sc. Museum and Library]. . . . The

[Mrs. Bliss] wants to leave at Dumbarton Oaks as scholarly a garden library as that you have for Byzantium and the middle ages . . . ";[3] this is the first appearance of what later becomes a leitmotif—keeping up with the Joneses, i.e., Byzantinists. Later Mrs. Bliss states that her "desire for the garden library at Dumbarton Oaks is of two kinds: a) thoroughly useful library for consultation by botanists, horticulturists, arboriculturists, etc., b) the old books on garden design with . . . the bibliophile items on materia medica etc."[4] Finally, in 1950, Mrs. Bliss writes to Mrs. Farrand, "we are in the midst of phrasing and rephrasing a communication to the Corporation [i.e., the President and Fellows of Harvard College], and I prefer, I think, to have it called the Dumbarton Oaks *Library* as the word center has social service connotations which may not, I believe, be conducive to responsiveness on the part of the Corporation."[5]

The proposal apparently was accepted (the official text has not been located); a formal acquisition record book was started, and its first entry—Jacquin's *Plantarum Rariorum*, purchased despite Mrs. Farrand's advice to avoid "pure botanical books"[6]—sets the pattern for the next 20 years. Acquisition records and annual reports made by Robert Woods Bliss to the Dumbarton Oaks Administrative Committee show that Mrs. Bliss collected flower plate books, incunabula, and horticultural and early taxonomic treatises in addition to the old books and prints on design to which she referred earlier. In 1952 the Garden Group, as they were called, numbered 745 out of a collection total of more than 2,500.[7]

> physical gardens should, as we agree, be kept up well, . . . but alongside them and a part of the cultural and intellectual basis on which they have been developed should be at hand for gardeners of various ranks of ability and also for students of the art.
>
> This implies more than the actual gardens—it means a reading room where current . . . books may be freely consulted, a small but well chosen collection of really first rate books on the development of the art of gardening. This second group would appeal to a student rather than to . . . the exclusively delphinium-minded Garden Club member. [It should include] the foundation books and prints underlying garden philosophy and design.

[3] Farrand to Bliss, 17 June 1947, DO. The letter continues, "You will have I know a reserve alcove where the rare books, such as the Kip, LeRouge and the rare botany books (Loudon, the great Iris book, etc.) should be a part of both collections."

[4] Bliss to Farrand, 7 July 1947, DO. This file also contains an undated list of books "purchased by Mrs. Farrand for Mrs. Bliss."

[5] Bliss to Farrand, 25 July 1950, DO. This contradicts her earlier statement of her desire to be of service to the community.

[6] Farrand to Sweeney (Blisses' librarian), 28 February 1944, DO: "As to the three volume Jackquin [*sic*], that book belongs to a botanic library and is definitely nothing that even the most ardent garden student would need at Dumbarton." Another example is in Farrand to Bliss, 2 August 1950, DO: "Regarding the Ventenat [proposed by Mrs. Bliss as a possible purchase] would you agree with me that temptation should be stoutly resisted to adding pure botany books, and to apply energy to books on design, horticulture and the history of gardening . . . it seems as though prints, books such as Kraft, Pückler, and MusKave[?] and many (to me at present unknown) 18th- and early 19th-century monographs were more important."

[7] Report no. 1 of the Co-founders to the Dumbarton Oaks Executive Committee on the Founders' Rooms and Their Contents, Correspondence of the Dean of the Faculty of Arts and Sciences, 1951–52, Dumbarton Oaks File, Harvard University Archives (hereafter Dean Cor.). "The collection is housed in the Founders' Room, formerly the Drawing Room, and the Oval Room. . . . The total number of volumes in the Collection is 2560, of which 745 belong to the 'Garden Group.' " The Bliss Collection at this time included

In 1951, the first surviving discussion of the establishment of a fellowship program appeared in a memorandum to the Corporation describing the use the Blisses desired for their proposed new endowment to be named the Dumbarton Oaks Garden Endowment Fund.[8] The income was to be expended not only on maintenance of the gardens and enlargement of the Garden Library, but also for the "Support of the Garden Information Center [and] for the establishment of Visiting or Exchange Fellowships for the individual study of garden design, ornament and Horticulture." Mrs. Bliss's letter to Mrs. Farrand of August 1951 reiterates the title she has chosen for the program, "Garden Design and Ornament."[9] The evident purpose of the fellowships was to supplement and improve on the education of landscape architects. The proposal was clearly not happily received by those who would be involved, including the administrators of the Faculty of Arts and Sciences, the dean of the Graduate School of Design and other educators, and prominent practicing landscape architects. You might say it put the cat among the pigeons, for a prolonged discussion with and between many different constituencies ensued. Concerns about administration of funds to support the fellowships were voiced; contention arose regarding methods for selection of the fellows, the fellowships' purpose, and even the title of the fellowships. Eventually the problems were resolved, but the discussion took years. Even though income for the fellowships was available from 1952, the first research garden fellow was not appointed until the spring of 1956.[10]

Four major problems had to be resolved: the title of the program; its financial administration and the reluctance of some of the Harvard officials to approve its establishment; the method by which the fellows were to be selected; and the site. The question of the site was the easiest. Despite suggestions that the fellow or fellows be resident in Cambridge, Mrs. Bliss was adamant that the program be "centered on Dumbarton Oaks."[11] Mrs. Farrand

---

a collection of eighteenth- and nineteenth-century *belles lettres* and a large number of "association items," i.e., autographed first editions and gifts from authors and friends. A list of some of the "Garden Group" titles was included in the report.

[8] Dean Paul Buck to Jack [John] Thacher, director of Dumbarton Oaks, 10 March 1952, Dean Cor. "Mr. and Mrs. Bliss have addressed a revised letter to the President and Fellows of Harvard College. This replaces their original memorandum dated July 10, 1951 and was drawn up on February 14, 1952." See the appendix.

[9] Bliss to Farrand, 17 August 1951, DO:

> You will be glad to know that a separate Endowment Fund for the Gardens is an accomplished fact and is being built up bit by bit, and the letter creating it states in unequivocal terms what the money may legitimately be used for. I have had a long and satisfactory talk with the Provost [Dean Paul Buck] who is interested in Dumbarton Oaks and has enough vision to understand what we are trying to do. . . . We will be sending out a request for candidates for the first Fellowship in Garden Design and Ornament.

The original donation to the Endowment Fund was about $375,000. It was added to annually until Mrs. Bliss's death in 1969. At that time the fund's value was $2,823,318, and Mrs. Bliss's will directed that that amount be increased to $4,000,000.

[10] The text is published in J. Wolschke-Bulmahn, ed., *Twenty-five Years of Studies in Landscape Architecture at Dumbarton Oaks: From Italian Gardens to Theme Parks*, Washington, D.C., 1996.

commented sympathetically that Harvard officials' "obsession as to centralizing at Cambridge is a steep stile to climb."[12] Mrs. Bliss wanted the fellow(s) "to eat live and work with the Byzantine Fellows" and did not agree with Dean McGeorge Bundy's suggestion that the landscape fellow would be in too much a minority and hence uncomfortable with the Byzantine fellows.[13]

Questions were raised about the administration of the funds; the Faculty of Arts and Sciences appeared reluctant to undertake the responsibility, and Reginald Isaacs, chairman of the Landscape Architecture Department, Harvard Graduate School of Design, was willing to take it on only if the school was involved in the selection of fellows and their residence in Cambridge was guaranteed.[14] Some non-Harvard possibilities were investigated; at one stage, the Blisses proposed donation of funds to the Hubbard Educational Trust, a foundation recently established "to further understanding and appreciation of the art and science of landscape architecture and to foster general education in that field."[15] It could not have been more appropriate, and the directors of the trust were willing to undertake the role. Finally, however, Mr. Bliss informed Leon Zach, chair of the Garden Advisory Committee, in a letter dated 25 June 1955, that he had spoken with President Nathan Pusey, and the question of the administration of the fellowship funds by Harvard had been settled satisfactorily. The tone of the letter suggests that "old boys'" (i.e., fellow Harvard graduates') solidarity prevailed and an agreement was reached.[16] Thereafter income for the fellowships was handled in Cambridge like all the other Dumbarton Oaks endowment funds.

Methods for selection of fellows and their supervision were also of great concern. Selection methods used by the American Academy in Rome were proposed, with some talk of the academy jury for landscape architecture assuming a role in the selection. Reactions by the several organizations suggest that the responsibility was thought inappropriate and the value of the program questionable. The Education Committee of the American Society of Landscape Architects (ASLA) was deemed the most appropriate. However, the

[11] Notes on Conference with Mr. and Mrs. Robert Woods Bliss, 1 February 1955, Leon Zach File, DO. McGeorge Bundy, dean of the Faculty of Arts and Sciences at Harvard, had suggested the landscape fellows should live in Cambridge. Zach's notes report that "the Blisses will have no part of such an arrangement and insist that the Fellow be centered on Dumbarton Oaks."

[12] Farrand to Bliss, 2 August 1950, DO: "The Harvard situation is a very Prickly one. They are totally insensible to anything relating to landscape art or the beauty of plants, and their obsession as to centralizing at Cambridge is a steep stile to climb."

[13] Notes on Conference with Mr. and Mrs. Robert Woods Bliss, 1 February 1955, Leon Zach File, DO: "The Blisses intent was that this Fellow would work, eat and live with the 'Byzantine Fellows.' . . . Dean Bundy does not feel it would work; that the Landscape Fellow would be in too much of a minority; and that, therefore, he should be 'centered in Cambridge.' "

[14] Although Dean Bundy's reservations about the program and the problem of its financial administration are clear in the correspondence of Zach and others, his files in the Harvard Archives do not contain correspondence about the problem. Possibly they were voiced at meetings of the Dumbarton Oaks Executive Committee, to which I have no access.

[15] *Hubbard Educational Trust,* pamphlet, n.p., 1969, 3.

[16] Bliss to Zach, 25 June 1955, Leon Zach File, DO. Bliss reports to Zach that he has discussed the problem with President Pusey and "that they had been able to work things out satisfactorily."

directors of ASLA feared this would overburden the Education Committee. Eventually a special committee, its members drawn from the Dumbarton Oaks Garden Advisory Committee, was created and given the responsibility of selecting the fellows.

For our purposes, however, the discussion of the title of the fellowships is the most significant. Mrs. Bliss had used the words "Garden Design and Ornament" in the original donation document.[17] Letters asking for comments were circulated to deans and chairmen of accredited landscape architecture programs in the United States; response to the idea of the fellowship was lukewarm at best, for the educators saw no need for or value in such a fellowship.[18] Objections were voiced to the use of the word "Garden" in the program name; "Landscape Design" or "Landscape Architecture" was preferred; there was little support for the use of the word "Ornament" in the program title. Such objections reflected a sense that professional practice now was almost entirely devoted to governmental and industrial work; the study of "garden design and ornament" was no longer relevant.[19] A letter from Bradford Williams, president of ASLA, to Leon Zach notes that even John Thacher, director of Dumbarton Oaks, agrees that "Garden Design and Ornament is too limited a subject to attract any serious students, and that there isn't enough at Dumbarton Oaks to justify any great amount of time spent in the study of the place itself."[20] Despite the unfavorable reactions by members of the profession, Mrs. Bliss prevailed both in the selection of the title and the definition of the program. The first announcements appeared in the ASLA journal, *Landscape Architecture*, in 1955, and the first fellow was appointed in 1956.

A description of the fellowship as established is contained in the booklet *Twenty-five Years of Studies in Landscape Architecture at Dumbarton Oaks*, published in 1996. Three types of fellowship were envisioned. Two of these were similar in character to the Byzantine fellowships (those Joneses again), i.e., a senior research fellowship in garden design intended for mature persons who have a creative research project they wish to develop, and a junior fellowship for recent graduates of landscape architecture schools. A third category, a summer fellowship for students, single males only, required residence at Dumbarton Oaks for one month in the summer, including actual physical work in the gardens, and a month touring of the offices of selected practitioners.[21]

A memo of Leon Zach's dated February 1955 and prepared as an aide-mémoire for a meeting of the Garden Advisory Committee shows that Mrs. Bliss wished the program to

[17] See the appendix.

[18] An idea of the nature of their objections can be gathered from some correspondence in 1960 analyzing causes of the problems incurred in the fellowship program. See the appendix.

[19] "Our profession, hardly dry behind the ears then [in 1920], has already experienced a reversal from 90 percent private residential work to 90 percent government and industrial work. . . . We studied [in the 1920s] with the anticipation of spending most of our time creating beautiful estates and lovely gardens for clients of fastidious tastes and fat incomes." R. Griswold, "A Letter from Rome, Life at the American Academy by a Returning Fellow," *Landscape Architecture* 40, 2 (1950), 125.

[20] Williams to Zach, 14 November 1953, Leon Zach File, DO.

[21] Minutes of the First Meeting of the Garden Advisory Committee, 22 March 1956, Dean Cor. The committee discussed the fellowship program at length, defining the three types of fellowship: landscape architecture fellow, a mature professional, by invitation only; landscape architecture junior fellow, to be selected through competition; and gardening student, a student of an accredited school of landscape architecture.

concentrate on aesthetics and history, not on technology: "Mrs. Bliss does not see the Fellowship in any sense as a continuation of normal school studies but rather as a spiritual experience and inspirational journey . . . his fellowship will not result in his producing a stronger concrete retaining wall, but a more beautiful one."[22] Inspiring as this sounds, I believe her project was an expression of her wish to preserve and perpetuate the kind of design methods that created Dumbarton Oaks and other great gardens in the late nineteenth century and the first quarter of the twentieth. Not only were their layouts based on historical styles—Italian, French formal, English landscape (often including Persian, Japanese, or Chinese styles)—but their ornaments (fountains, pavilions, benches, etc.) were copied from historic precedent or were actual imported decorations.

Designers drew heavily on historic precedent and maintained design resource notebooks. For example, an album of the English designer Harold Peto in the Garden Library contains annotated sketches of perennial borders, photographs of actual garden ornaments, and even postcards of paintings by Holman Hunt and other pre-Raphaelites, the latter with "Roman" garden furniture and fountains. Mrs. Farrand's records for the design of the Dumbarton Oaks gardens contain sketches and photographs of ornaments she had seen in her travels. Mrs. Bliss therefore expected that designers in the 1950s, both fellows and visitors, would want to avail themselves of "those noble calf-bound books containing steel engravings of the great garden designs of the 16th-, 17th- and 18th centuries," and the many volumes with plates of ornaments from the past that she collected for the Garden Library.[23]

What she didn't understand or refused to acknowledge was that the world of great estates no longer existed. Ralph Griswold, the first landscape senior fellow, commented in 1950 that during the past quarter century "our profession . . . has already experienced a reversal from 90 percent private residential work to 90 percent government and industrial work."[24] Although practicing landscape architects realized that lessons of organizing and articulating large spaces could perhaps be learned from the past, they could not see the value of studying historic ornament or garden, i.e., domestic, design. Their practice consisted primarily in the management of urban open spaces, highways, public parks, and residential developments.

If we review the history of the subsequent 13 years until Mrs. Bliss's death in 1969, we can see that the criticisms were justified. Projects of the early senior research fellows, some on an aspect of landscape history, some on design problems, were left incomplete. In 1965 Leon Zach wrote Grady Clay, editor of *Landscape Architecture Journal*, "we would prefer not to give out a list of research titles because only one out of nine research projects to date has ever been published." Although he implies that some projects are still being considered for publication, others are unfinished, and two fellows, he complains indignantly, "used their stipend for travel exclusively; never wrote anything to amount to anything."[25]

[22] 1 February 1955, Leon Zach File, DO.

[23] Bliss to Farrand, 7 July 1947, DO.

[24] Griswold, "Letter from Rome," 125.

[25] Zach to Grady Clay, editor of *Landscape Architecture,* 14 December 1965, Leon Zach File, DO.

In 1960, when there were no applications for the junior fellowship, educators in the field were consulted as to reasons for "the failure of the Junior Fellowship." Although economic difficulties were considered a barrier, most telling, for our purposes, was the perception of these educators that landscape architects, whether students or graduates, were not trained to carry out research or prepare treatises. All the responders emphasized this point. Hideo Sasaki at Harvard said, "the desire to do scholarly study is not strong as yet in the group to which this scholarship applies." Robert Vaughn, University of California, claimed that "research is done by scholars. . . . Landscape architects are accustomed to gathering and analyzing for the purpose of problem solving. They are not accustomed to . . . communicating their results in the form of a research treatise."[26] Their opinions were borne out by the fact that no publications ensued from the fellowship projects until the requirement that fellows be landscape architects was apparently dropped in the mid-1960s. Even then, members of the selection committee preferred design projects, and the award winners were landscape architects.[27]

This then was the dilemma of the garden fellowship program and, I might add, the Garden Library. Created as a resource for the exposure of landscape architects (as "Garden Designers" had by then been exiled to roadside plant nurseries) to the historic past, their intended beneficiaries saw no contemporary use or need for them. In addition, members of the profession emphasized that neither their training nor what I might call their propensities prepared them for historical research. On the other hand, no other kind of program was training potential landscape architecture historians. While all accredited landscape architecture schools were required to include a course or courses in history, the material presented was limited. It was usually perfunctory and delegated to junior members of the department whose own training was skimpy. Norman Newton appears to have been the exception.[28]

Additionally, even though the study of the history of architecture had spread from the professional schools to art history departments—a recent phenomenon in America—landscape architecture was included peripherally at best. To my shame, I will admit that I inserted some garden history in a course on seventeenth- and eighteenth-century European

[26] Memorandum to the chairman and members of the Dumbarton Oaks Garden Advisory Committee, 29 May 1960, Leon Zach File, DO: "The following reasons for the failure of the Junior Fellowship and recommendations of its revision have been extracted from the four letters received by Leon Zach." Note the meager response to the request for advice.

[27] "Aside from the fact that Dumbarton Oaks is on the way to being fed up with historical research (our Senior Fellow and two overlapping Junior Fellows all have historical subjects and what we are looking for in our next Fellowship program is a creative design project). . . ." Zach to Norman Newton, Professor of Landscape Architecture, Graduate School of Design, Harvard, 22 June 1965, Leon Zach File, DO. Michael Rapuano, chair of the Garden Advisory Committee, wrote to Zach regarding reconsideration of Masson and Abbé Fellowships, "[Georgina Masson] is a very fine garden historian, . . . but here again we are getting into the historical aspects in lieu of design. If Miss Masson could direct her studies somehow so that her work would generate an interest in design, then I think she would be worth considering." 20 July 1965, Leon Zach File, DO.

[28] N. Newton, *Design on the Land*, Cambridge, Mass., 1971.

architecture, giving it the title "Frivolous Friday." I will add that it became the most popular part of the course. I know of no specialized seminars or lecture courses offered then. In a list of doctoral dissertations in the United States before 1972 only three appear: David Coffin's on the Villa d'Este in 1953, F. Hamilton Hazlehurst's on Boyceau and the French formal garden in 1956—the first time the word "garden" appears in a thesis title—and mine on the Villa Mattei in Rome, which I started in 1960.[29]

What about publications? The literature of the relevant 75 years can be summarized as follows. A vast bibliography of general books on garden history exists. I listed more than 40 titles in the Dumbarton Oaks library, all published after Marie Luise Gothein's general history, English edition, in 1928 and Julia Berrall's *The Garden: An Illustrated History* in 1966.[30] These publications were aimed at a nonspecialized audience; indeed, they often seem to have been written for Mrs. Bliss's "exclusively delphinium-minded Garden Club member." Most were organized by national styles and periods: Italian Renaissance, French formal, English landscape, even (though rarely) American colonial. Non-European history—Chinese and Japanese—was treated as a kind of exotica. The texts are descriptive rather than analytic and based on previously published material, often perpetuating myths and unfounded traditions. The gardens and parks are treated as isolated phenomena, without reference to the social or literary climate of the period. I am speaking primarily of English-language publications, although a similar literature appeared in other languages. Of course, this is not the whole story. More specialized writings began to appear in the 1950s, devoted to one national or even regional style, or one chronological period. English and French publications of this type seem to predominate.

So this was the situation that confronted me in 1972 when I came to Dumbarton Oaks. I do not recall being shown the 1969 statement by the Garden Advisory Committee recommending a focus on the history of landscape architecture history for the fellowship program (published in *Twenty-five Years*) but my memories of that hectic and confusing first year are quite dim. The only charge I recall, to compile and publish a catalogue of the Garden Library, I had neither the tools nor the desire to accomplish. In the face of a great deal of skepticism from scholars in the other programs, my internal goal was to establish the validity and serious scholarly aims of studies in landscape architecture in the eyes of the Joneses and even the Smiths, since by now the Pre-Columbian program was well established.

Beyond that there was the marvelous library which was, you might say, "a closed book" to me, and a largely invisible fellowship program—that year the senior fellow, Marcia Allentuck, a literary historian, was not even in residence. The first symposium—or, as it was called at the start, "colloquium"—had taken place in 1971, and two others were planned: the "Picturesque Garden and Its Influence outside the British Isles," organized by Nicholas Pevsner, and the "French Formal Garden," organized by F. Hamilton Hazlehurst.

[29] See P. Kaufman and P. Gabbard, "American Doctoral Dissertations in Architectural and Planning History, 1898–1972," in *The Architectural Historian in America*, ed. E. B. MacDougall, Washington, D.C., 1990.

[30] M. L. Gothein, *History of Garden Art,* London, 1928, a translation of the original German text *Geschichte der Gartenkunst,* Jena, 1914; J. Berrall, *The Garden: An Illustrated History*, New York, 1966.

For the symposia a standard had already been established: to invite scholars already active in the field of the chosen topic and to establish links with other arts, primarily literature. This was more difficult than we can imagine now—specialists were very thin on the ground and the fields in which they delved very limited. It became my aim to use the symposia not to reexamine standard garden history but to establish a solid factual and interpretative foundation usable as a basis in general and popular publications and as a *point de départ* for more specialized studies. It was impossible to determine a fixed succession of symposia, although I hoped eventually to organize symposia for all national styles and periods. Some came about almost accidentally: "Islamic Gardens" grew out of conversation at a dinner party with Richard Ettinghausen, curator of Islamic art at the Freer. Some were proposed and organized for me—"Ancient Roman Gardens" and "Ancient Roman Villa Gardens," led by Wilhelmina Jashemski, "Prophet with Honor"[31] on Andrew Jackson Downing, organized by George Tatum. Two of these in particular reflected concerns important to me. One, the conference on preservation and conservation of historic gardens, was planned to introduce Americans to standards and accomplishments of historic garden preservation in Europe, for we had almost no knowledge in this field—indeed, we still have very little. The other was an attempt, alas unrealized, to establish standards and recommendations for curricula for teaching history to landscape architecture students.

Let me end by observing that most of us who were working in landscape architecture had come to it with training as art or architectural historians. We brought to the new field standards and methods we had learned, even the descriptive and analytic vocabulary. In the 1960s and early 1970s architectural history was primarily Eurocentric, elitist, limited to structural and design analysis; interdisciplinary studies were almost nonexistent. Over the years, of course, all of this changed, and as the changes took place in architectural history they also occurred in landscape architecture history, as the recent symposia demonstrate.

Something much more important has changed—the way our discipline is viewed. Educators in the profession have revised and greatly improved their attitude toward history. Proof of that appears in the papers in *What Do We Expect to Learn from Our History? The First Symposium on History in Landscape Architecture*, published by the Center for Studies in Landscape History at Penn State in 1996. It is an admirable appraisal of the present situation.

Moreover, the thinly disguised snobbery of scholars in the more established fields has given way to a greater understanding and appreciation. As evidence of the earlier snobbery I can refer to Bundy's unstated but implicit disdain for the abilities of researchers in the field. This held true in other appraisals such as rejections of papers for scholarly publications—because the subject matter was not serious or important—and remarks by colleagues. One referred to my work as "tiptoeing through the tulips." Again, there are no longer real questions about the validity and importance of our work. We've come a long way from Frivolous Friday!

[31] A disaster almost occurred when I misunderstood George's title for the symposium. I heard *Profit* instead of *Prophet*; the error was not discovered until Tatum saw proofs for the symposium program.

Appendix

[The purpose of this letter is] to initiate the Dumbarton Oaks Garden Endowment Fund, the principal of which is to be invested in the same manner as the other endowment funds of the University and the income used only: for the maintenance, operation and development of the Gardens at Dumbarton Oaks; *for the establishment of Visiting or Exchange Fellowships to or from this or other countries for the individual study of Garden Design and Ornament* [my italics]; for the publication of monographs or books on such subjects as incidental decorative horticulture; for the maintenance of the Garden Research Library already established at Dumbarton Oaks; for the support of the Garden Information Center; and for other related educational purposes.

Dated 10 July 1951, this description appears in *Endowment Funds of Harvard University*, Cambridge, Mass., 1955.

An enlarged and slightly revised statement was submitted to the president of Harvard on 14 February 1952; it adds, "the maintenance and enlargement of the Garden Library already established at Dumbarton Oaks." The donors explain in another part of the document, "It is our hope that the Dumbarton Oaks Research Library and Collection [the legal title of the entire institution] may in time attain as high a standing in its capacity as an institution for the study of garden design and ornament as it already has attained for its scholastic work and research and that the unusual potentialities may be fully realized." Horticulture is added as a field of study to the earlier fields of garden design and ornament. The document also spells out conditions of the fellowship: "It is not our proposal that Landscape Gardening, Horticulture and Botany should be made the subjects of organized class instruction at Dumbarton Oaks. It is rather our expectation that the Dumbarton Oaks Gardens may usefully serve to advance garden design, ornament and horticulture by example and through the dissemination of historical, cultural and technical information."[32]

[32] A copy of this later statement is enclosed with Dean Paul Buck to Jack [John] Thacher, 19 March 1952, Thacher File, Dean Cor.

The Study of the History of the Italian Garden until the First Dumbarton Oaks Colloquium

David R. Coffin

The first significant study of Italian gardens in their own right was that of W. P. Tuckermann, *Die Gartenkunst der italienischen Renaissance-Zeit,* published at Berlin in 1884. Certainly there had been earlier considerations of Italian gardens in relation to Italian villas, most notably Charles Percier and Pierre Fontaine's *Choix des plus célebrès maisons de plaisance de Rome et de ses environs,* first published at Paris in 1809. Percier and Fontaine as architects wished to adapt antiquity to their own time, thus creating the Empire style appropriate to the reign of the emperor Napoleon. As they noted in the introduction to their book, their purpose was "to offer useful material to the progress of the art which we profess."

Tuckermann was also an architect connected with the Technische Hochschule at Berlin, but was interested in the history of Italian gardening as a discipline in its own right. Thus the late nineteenth century presented a dichotomy in the historiography of Italian gardens between a concern for design principles and historical values that would continue through much of the twentieth century.

Earlier in 1868 Tuckermann had published a reconstruction of the Odeon of Heroides Atticus in Athens and later in 1879 a study of the literary output of the German architect Karl Friedrich Schinkel. In contrast to the later flood of publication on the Italian garden, Tuckermann's work was a very thorough investigation of the subject using a variety of sources. Unlike the later writers, he considered the geography and climate of Italy and their effect on the horticulture of the Italian garden. He accordingly identified four different Italian landscapes determined by the climate: first, the landscape of the northern lake country; second, that of the northern seacoast; third, the area around Rome; and finally, that of Naples. He was equally interested in the historical aspect of Italian gardening, unlike many of his successors. In a chapter on gardening before the Italian Renaissance, he considered Pliny the Younger's villa complexes and illustrated Schinkel's reconstructions of the two layouts, thus renewing his earlier interest in the reconstruction of ancient monuments and the ideas of Schinkel. Tuckermann also studied the medieval monastic gardens and the Moorish gardens in Spain. His longest chapter, of course, is devoted to the descriptions and history of Italian gardens from the sixteenth century to the beginning of the nineteenth, when English gardening overwhelmed the classic style. He illustrated the principal gardens with engraved vedute and some 21 plans.

Tuckermann's study, for all its thoroughness, seems to have had very little influence outside Germany. From the end of the nineteenth century until 1931 the study of the Italian garden was dominated by Anglo-American publications. In July and August 1893 the artist Charles Platt, soon to be an outstanding designer of Italianate villas and gardens in the United States, published two articles on Italian gardens in *Harper's New Monthly Magazine.* He explained his articles by claiming that there is "no existing work of any great latitude treating of the subject of gardens, the only one of importance being that of Percier and Fontaine." At the same time he signed a contract with *Harper's* to publish a book on the subject with one thousand new words supplementing the two thousand words of his articles.[1] Platt illustrated his book with some 31 of his own photographs of Italian gardens as his main sources, emphasizing that his descriptions were purely supplementary to the illustrations. Thus the emphasis of his work is almost solely on the design of the gardens. Their history is not considered at all. The only possible historical reference is a vague acknowledgment of an eighteenth-century date for the Villa Albani in Rome.

Although Platt's book was soon a popular and influential one, it was rather severely criticized by Charles Eliot in the *Nation* of December 1893, noting among other things that "Our author is not acquainted with W. P. Tuckermann's *Die Gartenkunst des Italienischen Renaissance-Zeit,* published in 1884 containing besides twenty plates, some twenty ground plans and cross sections of Renaissance villas." Platt's principal audience was primarily American architects.

The popular architectural periodical the *American Architect and Building News* ran in the 1890s a series of photographs titled "Accessories of Landscape Architecture," and by at least 1897 began to include views of Italian gardens, although the factual information of the captions was occasionally inaccurate, in one case locating the Farnese villa at Caprarola in Sicily. These were followed in February and March of 1900 by the article "The Italian Garden" by James S. Pray. This study, like Platt's, was basically on the design of the gardens, although at the end he incorporated a slight history, noting that the Renaissance garden was inaugurated by Bramante's Belvedere Court at the Vatican. He also observed that there was a growing popularity of the use of the Italian garden in he United States, which was, of course, in part due to Platt's work. In the following year the elder Professor Alfred Dwight Foster Hamlin at Columbia published in the February issue of the *American Architect and Building News* a three-page paper, "The Italian Formal Garden," which he had read at the convention of the American Institute of Architects. His dates were often quite inaccurate, claiming that the Villa Lante at Bagnaia was first built in 1477 by Cardinal Riario and then remodeled about 1550 by Giacomo Vignola or that the Villa d'Este at Tivoli was designed about 1540 by Pirro Ligorio.

[1] For Platt's book, see Keith Morgan, "Overview," in C. A. Platt, *Italian Gardens,* Portland, Ore., 1993, 97–117.

A broader audience was addressed by the appearance in 1904 of Edith Wharton's *Italian Villas and Their Gardens.* She too observed that the "Cult of the Italian garden has spread from England to America." Although she remarked on "the deeper harmony of design" in the Italian villa and its garden, her study was much more historical than those of her American predecessors. By examining the monuments in chapters devoted to different regions she suggested that there was both a geographical and chronological development of the villa and garden. Her descriptions of the individual sites are charming, but limited in their consideration of any possible meaning, so she characterizes the animals in the grotto of the garden at Castello as merely a "curious delight." She was so sensitive, however, to aesthetic values that she would designate the architect Francesco Borromini as a "brilliant artist," long before his acceptance by most Anglo-American historians. An additional factor in the popularization of her book were the illustrations by the artist Maxfield Parrish, who would soon be the most famous American illustrator. The intense blues and greens of Parrish's watercolors and their rather hard edge almost seem to foreshadow color photography.

There appeared about this time two delightful essays on the restoration of Italian gardens. Frederick Eden, the landscape painter and brother-in-law of the English gardener Gertrude Jekyll, published in 1902 *A Garden in Venice,* which is an account of the restoration of a garden on the Giudecca that he had bought in 1884. In his essay he considered in detail every aspect of the restoration: different types of pergolas, paths of seashells bordered with box or old brick, the construction of wells and reservoirs, and even the difficulties an owner may suffer with Italian gardeners, although he notes that his head gardener at age 25 was paid 100 francs a month, which he claimed was a good salary in the region. A few years later in 1909 appeared the essay by Sir George Sitwell, father of the famous Sitwell siblings, titled *On the Making of Gardens.* Later his son Osbert would assert that his father hoped that his work would rank with Sir Francis Bacon's famous essay on gardens. Certainly the extended first part of Sitwell's essay is successful in that regard, but the last part, with its detailed consideration of the psychology of the beauty of a garden (with frequent references to William James's *Principles of Psychology* and the ideas of Herbert Spencer and Archibald Alison), diminishes its literary quality. Repelled by French gardening and the English landscape style, Sir George claims that "no place is so full of poetry as the Villa d'Este," which in company with the Villa Lante at Bagnaia and the Giusti gardens in Verona he identified as the three greatest gardens of Italy from which he could educe the principles of good gardening. He also, however, examined many little-publicized gardens such as that of the Canossa Palace in Verona, of the Quirini Palace in Vicenza, and gardens in Bergamo, Cremona, Piacenza, and Brescia. He believed that through such study art could be used to perfect the beauty of nature.

Commencing in 1910 and continuing for the next quarter century the English architect Cecil Pinsent designed and built Tuscan villas and their gardens for the well-to-do Anglo-American community in Tuscany.[2] This activity encouraged a mutual relationship with writings on the Italian gardens.

In 1906 the architect H. Inigo Triggs followed his study of formal gardening in En-

[2] For the most recent information on Cecil Pinsent and his work, see the several essays in *Cecil Pinsent and His Gardens in Tuscany,* ed. M. Fantoni, H. Flores, and J. Pfordrecher, Florence, 1996.

gland and Scotland with *The Art of Garden Design in Italy.* Although other English and American works have often achieved more popularity and fame, I would judge that Triggs's book was at that time by far the most important historical account. His work commenced with an excellent long historical introduction. Engravings of Pompeian garden frescoes and a drawing attributed to Pinturicchio, and now identified as by Baldassare Peruzzi, of the plan of a town garden were even incorporated among the illustrations of the introduction. This section was then followed by some 31 chapters devoted to individual gardens or regions. In the introduction Triggs noted that Percier and Fontaine's collection of garden plans was limited to Rome and its environs; this was his explanation for his study, which contains some 27 plans. Some of the plans were created by Triggs himself, while others, such as those of the Villa d'Este or the Villa Borghese, were redrawn after Percier and Fontaine. Several plans were derived from historical documents: the plan of the garden parterre intended for Caserta is from Luigi Vanvitelli's original drawing; that of the Villa Pamphili is based on a seventeenth-century plan in the collection of Prince Doria.

Soon the English historian Julia Cartwright contributed to the subject her *Italian Gardens of the Renaissance and Other Studies* (1914). Limited to Renaissance gardens of the fifteenth and sixteenth centuries, most of which have disappeared, Cartwright's book concentrated on the history associated with the gardens and has no consideration of garden design. In fact, her book is really a collection of historical studies of the owners of individual villas.

Although there has been avoided any mention of general histories of gardens in which there is incorporated some treatment of the Italian garden, one must not omit consideration of Marie Luise Gothein's *Geschichte der Gartenkunst,* which first appeared in 1914, with a second edition in 1926 and an English edition in 1928. Although occasionally dated in its historical information, it nevertheless remains an important standard work today. The only treatise in the field of gardening contemporary with it that can rival it is Amelia Amherst's *A History of Gardening in England,* which first appeared in 1895, followed by a second edition in 1896, and a third and enlarged edition in 1910. Gothein, pointing out in her introduction that even art historians have shown only a perfunctory interest in the subject of gardens, relied on early prints of gardens, such as those of G. B. Falda, as well as photographs to illustrate her section on Italian gardens, indicating a historical orientation rather than the design concentration offered only by photographs.

A series of important articles on individual sixteenth-century Roman gardens by archaeologists and topographical historians commenced with Domenico Gnoli's article in the *Römische Mitteilungen* in 1905 on the garden of the Cesi family in Rome. Thomas Ashby in *Archaeologia* of 1908 reconstructed the collection of ancient sculpture in the gardens of the Villa d'Este at Tivoli. Christian Huelsen enlarged the subject in 1917 with an exhaustive, fundamental study of several sixteenth-century antique sculpture gardens in Rome in the *Abhandlungen* of the Heidelberg Academy, followed by Luigi Dami's account of the Quirinal garden at Rome in the *Bollettino d'arte* of 1919. Much later, in 1930, a delightful two-part article by Gnoli on the literary gardens in the Rome of Pope Leo X appeared posthumously in *Nuova Antologia.*

Contemporary with Gnoli's first article Edgar Williams, a young American landscape architect at the American Academy at Rome from 1910 to 1912, made drawings of the plan, elevations, and section of the famous gardens of the Isola Bella on Lake Maggiore which were published in the periodical *Landscape Architecture* in July 1914. This was one of the numerous sets of plans and drawings of Italian gardens produced by fellows of the American Academy between the two world wars. The academy, founded in the late nineteenth century on the model of the French Academy at Rome, was to introduce young American artists to the great examples of classical and Renaissance art and architecture in Italy, thus promoting the classical style in America already represented by the architects McKim, Mead, and White, and their artistic associates, several of whom were founders of the American Academy.

To offset the strong predilection to emphasize Tuscan and Roman gardens in previous publications, Charlotte Pauly concentrated on Venetian pleasure gardens in her *Der venezianische Lustgarten* of 1916. She claimed that because of what she described as the architect Andrea Palladio's antagonism to the "Baroque" mode, the Venetian garden would remain that of the early Renaissance until the seventeenth century. With frequent references to Gothein's history of gardening and Pompeo Molmenti's social history of Venice, Pauly devotes her last chapter to an interesting examination of the place of the garden in Venetian culture. She identifies three specific qualities of gardens with respect to Venetian life. First is the hygienic aspect caused by the climate, for which she discusses the role of summer *villeggiatura* from June 12 to the end of July and autumn *villeggiatura* from October 4 to mid-November. Second, she emphasizes the oligarchic and aristocratic quality of the Venetian garden. Finally, she describes how it fulfills the traditional Venetian concept of an art of luxurious living.

In the 1920s publication on Italian gardens became more international with the French publications of Georges Gromort from 1922 to 1931 and Gabriel Faure in 1923, the American Harold Eberlein in 1922 with his emphasis on the lesser-known Tuscan villas and gardens, and the Italian Luigi Dami in 1924 with some 351 plates, including paintings and prints of gardens as well as photographs. In 1928 the English author Rose Nichols published a very full survey of Italian gardens from Pompeian peristyle gardens to those of the twentieth century. She even printed two pages of description of the Orsini garden at Bomarzo with an illustration of the elephant group. This appeared a quarter of a century before the international fanfare celebrating Mario Praz's "discovery" of Bomarzo.

The book that achieved the most popularity and acclaim was *Italian Gardens of the Renaissance*, the work of two young British fifth-year students at the Architectural Association in London, Jock Shepherd and Geoffrey Jellicoe. Their "year-master" had suggested in 1923 that they explore Italian gardens, since he claimed that "no surveys had been made since the somewhat crude drawings of the French architects Percier and Fontaine a hundred years previously."[3] Jellicoe did the ground work, while Shepherd photographed and

[3] For an account of the preparation of the book, see G. Jellicoe, "An Italian Study, Being an Analysis of *Italian Gardens of the Renaissance* Published in 1925," in *Geoffrey Jellicoe: The Studies of a Landscape Designer over 80 Years*, Woodbridge, Suffolk, 1993, 61–157.

then drew up the plans and sections, basing his technique on the drawing style of the Frenchman Gromort. Their published work included 28 villas, the illustrations accompanied by brief descriptions in three languages. Jellicoe later admitted that at first they omitted the Villa d'Este at Tivoli "as being vulgar" and the Isola Bella "as being decadent." Tivoli was copied later in England from an "inaccurate plan." Regarding accuracy, it might be noted that Jellicoe later explained that, although they had been taught the orthodox method of surveying with precision instruments, in their hurry the measurements of their drawings were made by Jellicoe pacing off the dimensions, claiming that any errors should not exceed 5 percent. *Italian Gardens of the Renaissance* has run through at least six editions, the latest in 1993.

The climax of this interest in Italian gardens came in 1931 with the great exhibition on the Italian garden held at Florence in the Palazzo Vecchio. The exhibition, comprising prints, drawings, models, paintings, and photographs, occupied three floors of the palace in some 53 rooms. The exhibition was undoubtedly a political move to further the Fascist goal of propagating the glory of the nation. Ugo Ojetti in the preface to the catalogue of the exhibition, *Mostra del giardino italiano*, claimed that the art of gardening is "singularly ours," but has been obscured by other modes. He noted with particular pleasure that the Italian garden was being revived outside Italy and "especially in North America." No longer are Italian gardeners exported to foreign countries, but foreign designers come to study Italian gardens. He points out that the most accurate drawings and plans of Italian villas and gardens on exhibit in the show were by American artists, that is, fellows of the American Academy at Rome.

For almost the next quarter century the study of the Italian garden lost all interest. This was, of course, in part caused by World War II, which dispersed the Anglo-American communities in Tuscany and Rome. In America this lack of interest may also have been furthered by the neglect of the history of their fields by architects and landscape architects under the influence of the teaching of Walter Gropius at Harvard from 1937 to at least 1952. There seem to have been practically no publications on Italian gardens until the "discovery" of Bomarzo announced by Mario Praz in a 1953 issue of *Illustrazione italiana*. In 1955 appeared an entire issue of the *Quaderni dell'Istituto di Storia dell'Architettura* with articles by five Italian scholars devoted to Bomarzo. This opened the floodgates of publication on Bomarzo, although much of the resulting material in fact obfuscated our comprehension of the garden. Meanwhile in 1954 James Ackerman's magisterial study of the Belvedere Court at the Vatican was published, demonstrating its innovative role in the development of landscape architecture and site planning.

Soon two general works on Italian gardens were published by Camillo Fiorani in 1960 and Barbara Johnson under the pseudonym Georgina Masson in 1961. The outstanding scholarship of the latter was obscured by its popular presentation and lack of scholarly apparatus. A series of monographs and articles on individual gardens revived scholarship in the field, including my work on the Villa d'Este at Tivoli in 1960, Angelo Cantoni and his colleagues' on the Villa Lante at Bagnaia in 1961, Webster Smith's article on Pratolino in 1961, Eugenio Battisti's *L'Antirinascimento* of 1962, and Elisabeth MacDougall's Harvard dissertation on the Villa Mattei and Roman gardening in 1970. Much later, in 1979, Sir Roy Strong in the preface to *The Renaissance Garden in England* identified these studies as marking a new development in the subject, noting that "as an area of academic study, garden history is a relatively new one" and acknowledging his debt "to the pioneers in the field of Italian Renaissance studies, in particular the exemplary work by David Coffin and Eugenio Battisti."

The first Dumbarton Oaks Colloqium, "The Italian Garden," was held on 24 April 1971, and the resulting papers were published in 1972. The participants in the conference were concerned with the meeting as an attempt to revive interest in the discipline. Lionello Puppi at the beginning of his paper on Venetian gardens remarked that in the study of gardens there is "almost [a] total absence of the best qualified scholars." The quantity of negative replies that I received from my numerous letters and telephone calls to invite colleagues to participate confirms his observations. In the end I had to invite three foreign scholars to join one American for a minimum panel. At the meeting, however, one member of the audience was very aware, and probably disturbed, that the conference marked a new approach to the discipline. Angelo Cantoni, restorer of the gardens at Bagnaia, and Sir Geoffrey Jellicoe, coauthor of the 1925 collection of plans and drawings of Italian Renaissance gardens, were invited by Dumbarton Oaks to attend the colloquium as guests. Cantoni was taken ill on his trip to the States and had to return home, but Sir Geoffrey came. After the papers had been presented, Sir Geoffrey was invited to comment on the conference. Unfortunately there was no tape recorder to register his remarks, so we have to rely on my fading memory. After politely commending the participants for their papers, he added an admonition to the effect that we should always remember that the essence of the Italian garden was its design. Although the four papers at the colloquium often referred to elements of design, it was obvious that their major thrust was the meaning, the iconography, and the social context of the gardens. This, however, was not so much a generational difference as a difference in training and interests. Of the five participants in the colloquium, four of us were trained as art historians who approached the gardens as we would any work of art. Sir Geoffrey and many of his contemporaries were architects or landscape architects who looked to the Italian gardens primarily for what they might contribute to their own work, hence their concentration on design.

In the quarter century since the first colloquium there have again been many new developments in the subject, but I shall leave it to a member of the generation that has participated in those elaborations to survey them for you.

Bibliography

1884 Tuckermann, W. P. *Die Gartenkunst der italienischen Renaissance-Zeit.* Berlin.

1893 Platt, C. A. "Formal Gardening in Italy." *Harper's New Monthly Magazine* 87, 518 (July and August).

1894 Platt, C. A. *Italian Gardens.* New York.

1897, 1899 "Accessories of Landscape Architecture." *The American Architect and Building News* 55 and 64, illustrations.

1900 Pray, J. D. "The Italian Garden." *The American Architect and Building News* 67.

1901 Hamlin, A. D. F. "The Italian Formal Garden." *The American Architect and Building News* 71, pp. 43–45.

1902 Forbes, A. H. *Architectural Gardens of Italy.* New York.

1903 Eden, F. *A Garden in Venice.* London.

1904 Wharton, E. *Italian Villas and Their Gardens.* New York.

1905 Gnoli, D. "Il giardino e l'antiquario del Cardinal Cesi." *Mitteilungen des kaiserlich deutschen archäologischen Instituts: Römische Abteiling* 20, pp. 267–76.

1905 Latham, C. *The Gardens of Italy.* With descriptions by E. M. Phillips. 2 vols., London.

1906 Triggs, H. I. *The Art of Garden Design in Italy.* London, New York, and Bombay.

1907 Elgood, G. S. *Italian Gardens.* New York, Bombay, and Calcutta.

1908 Ashby, T. "The Villa d'Este at Tivoli and the Collection of Classical Sculptures Which It Contained." *Archaeologia* 61, 1, pp. 219–55.

1909 Sitwell, G. *On the Making of Gardens.* London.

1912 Le Blond, A. *The Old Gardens in Italy.* London and New York.

1914 Cartwright, J. *Italian Gardens of the Renaissance and Other Studies.* London.

1914 Gothein, M. L. *Geschichte der Gartenkunst.* 2 vols., Jena; 2nd ed., 1926; English ed., 1928.

1914 Williams, E. I. "Isola Bella." *Landscape Architecture* (July), pp. 167–70.

1915 Ponti, M. P. *Il giardino italiano.* Rome.

1916 Pauly, C. E. *Der venezianische Lustgarten.* Strassburg.

1917 Huelsen, C. "Römische Antikengärten des XVI Jahrhunderts." *Abhandlungen der Heidelberger Akademie der Wissenschaften: Philosophische-Historische Klasse* 4.

1919 Dami, L. "Il giardino Quirinale ai primi del 1600." *Bollettino d'arte* 13, pp. 113–16.

1922 Eberlein, H. D. *Villas of Florence and Tuscany.* Philadelphia and London.

1922–31 Gromort, G. *Jardins d'Italie.* 3 vols., Paris.

1923 Faure, G. *Les jardins de Rome.* Grenoble.

1924 Dami, L. *Il giardino italiano.* Milan.

[1925] Shepherd, J. C., and G. A. Jellicoe. *Italian Gardens of the Renaissance.* New York.

[1927] Damerini, G. *Giardini sulla laguna.* Bologna.

1929 Nichols, R. S. *Italian Pleasure Gardens.* London.

1930 Gnoli, D. "Orti letterari nella Roma di Leone X." *Nuova Antologia* 347.

1931 Damerini, G. *Giardini di Venezia.* Bologna.

1931 *Mostra del giardino italiano: Catalogo; Palazzo Vecchio.* Florence.

1942 Bafile, M. *Il giardino di Villa Madama.* Rome.

1953 Praz, M. "I mostri di Bomarzo." *Illustrazione italiana* 8, pp. 48–51, 86.
1954 Ackerman, J. S. *The Cortile del Belvedere.* Vatican City.
1955 *Quaderni dell'Istituto di Storia dell'Architettura* 7–9, pp. 3–76.
1956 Calvesi, M. "Il Sacro Bosco di Bomarzo." *Scritti di storia dell'arte in onore di Lionello Venturi,* vol. 1. Rome, 369–402.
1957 Lang, S. "Bomarzo." *The Architectural Review* 121 (January–June), 427–30.
1960 Coffin, D. R. *The Villa d'Este at Tivoli.* Princeton, N.J.
1960 Fiorani, C. *Giardini d'Italia.* Rome.
1960 Romanelli, P. "Horti palatini Farnesiorum." *Studi romani* 8, pp. 661–72.
[1961] Cantoni, A., et al. *La Villa Lante di Bagnaia.* Milan.
[1961] Masson, G. *Italian Gardens.* London.
1961 Smith, W. "Pratolino." *Journal of the Society of Architectural Historians* 20, pp. 155–68.
1962 Battisti, E. *L'Antirinascimento.* Milan.
1964 McGuire, F. M. *Gardens of Italy.* New York.
1966 Lamb, C. *Die Villa d'Este in Tivoli.* Munich.
1967 Von Hennenberg, J. "Bomarzo: The Extravagant Garden of Pier Francesco Orsini." *Italian Quarterly* 2, 42, pp. 3–19.
1969 Benedetti, S. "Sul giardino grande di Caprarola ed altre note." *Quaderni dell'Istituto dell'Architettura* 91–96, pp. 3–46.
1970 MacDougall, E. "The Villa Mattei and the Development of the Roman Garden Style," Ph.D. diss., Harvard.
1972 Coffin, D. R., ed. *The Italian Garden,* Washington, D.C.

Recent Developments and Perspectives in the Historiography of Italian Gardens

Mirka Beneš

In this study I wish to begin with an assessment of the state of the literature at the time I entered graduate school at Yale University in the mid-1970s and began to work on Italian villa gardens. I will then analyze the evolution of the field over the last 25 years and conclude with a view on its current state and the directions in which I believe it should go next. At the outset, I wish to emphasize that the Italian garden should not be treated separately from the villa complex of which it is part, for the term "villa" refers to the entire compound of main palace, buildings, grounds, agricultural areas, and parks and gardens (Figs. 1, 2). But for the purpose here, I shall focus on the gardens, albeit in context. I shall consider Italian gardens in the period from about 1450 to 1750, for which they have become a sort of canon, although important literature for nineteenth- and twentieth-century Italian gardens has made a recent appearance. By Italian gardens I thus mean "Italian Renaissance and Baroque gardens."

Short of writing a book on the historiography of Italian gardens, such a study as this cannot aspire to complete coverage of the topic.[1] Thus the footnotes are not intended as a full bibliography on the subject, but rather as suggestions of the milestones placed in the field during recent decades. My intent is to identify the major directions that have been pursued, and thereby to provide both a rough map and a kind of genealogical table of the events and figures that have structured the recent historiography of Italian gardens.[2]

In the mid-1970s, when I was a graduate student, my bibliography consisted of a few major interpretative works and an abundance of journal articles that simply documented

[1] A historiography of Italian gardens of the Renaissance and Baroque periods has not yet been written, as I far as I can tell. A mention of the American contribution to Italian garden history after World War II is made by Tod Marder, "Renaissance and Baroque Architectural History in the United States," in *The Architectural Historian in America,* ed. E. B. MacDougall, Studies in the History of Art 35, and Symposium Papers 19, National Gallery of Art, Washington, D.C., Hanover, and London, 1990, 170.

[2] Something of an autobiographical thread will run throughout my narrative, because along my path from college to graduate school to my 10 years of teaching the history of landscape architecture with a focus on Italian villa gardens, I have had the fortune to encounter and learn from the protagonists of this historiography. None of them was my primary teacher nor my dissertation adviser, but because of their great generosity to younger scholars I benefited deeply from contact with them, and I thank them all here. As of 1998, I have been teaching the history of landscape architecture at the Graduate School of Design, Harvard University, since 1988.

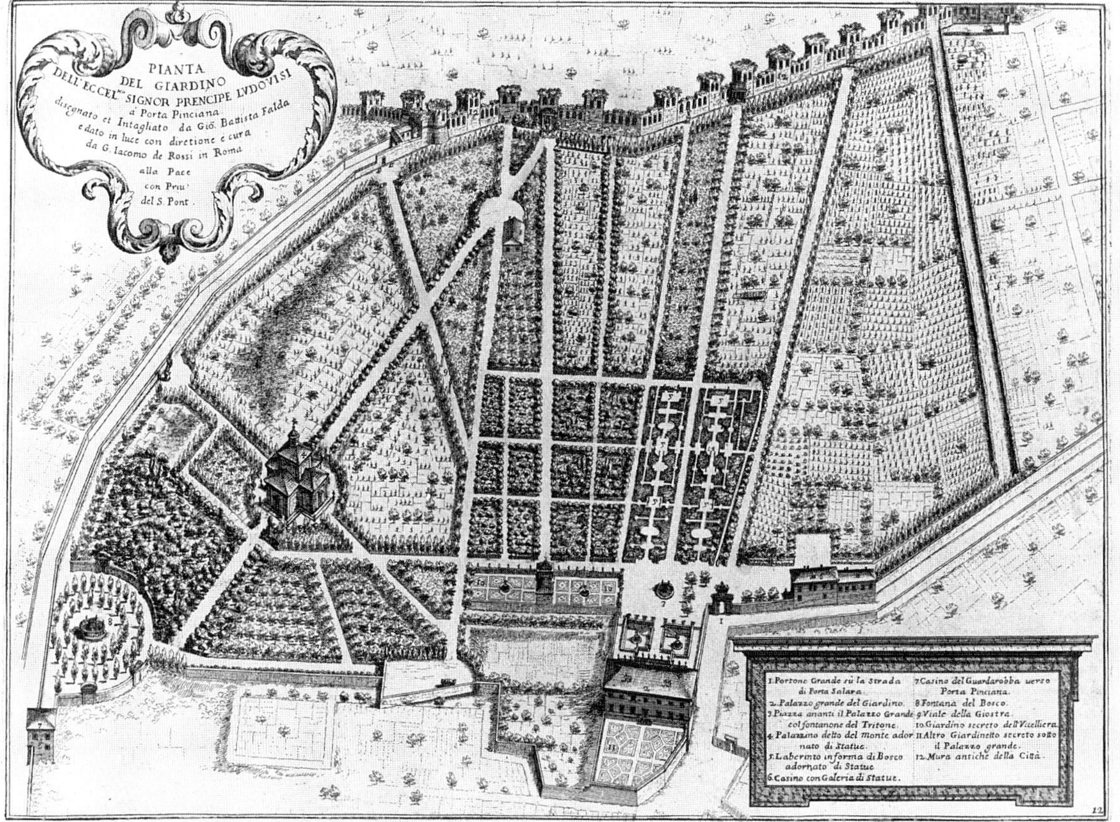

1. Rome, Villa Ludovisi, 1621–23, bird's-eye view by Giovanni Battista Falda (ca. 1675) (from G. B. Falda, Li giardini di Roma, *Rome, ca. 1675)*

individual villa gardens, in addition to the original sources of maps, drawings, and printed views of gardens. The 1950s seemed to represent a dividing line, with large changes in the literature thereafter. I did not realize at the time that this line of demarcation stemmed from the effects of World War II, which brought important art and architectural historians from Germany to America.

As David R. Coffin has shown in his article in this volume, the works written before 1950 were mainly of two types, either site surveys by architecture students and professionals[3] or compilations of photographs and short texts that functioned largely as guidebooks and belonged to that genre.[4] The studies by Marie Luise Gothein[5] and Luigi Dami[6] were

[3] A noted example of the former is "Shepherd and Jellicoe," *Italian Gardens of the Renaissance,* published in London in 1925 by the architect John C. Shepherd and the landscape architect Geoffrey A. Jellicoe. Other examples of such compendia of analytic drawings, site surveys, watercolor views, and photographs are Charles Platt's *Italian Gardens,* New York, 1894, prepared as a photographic survey two years earlier; Charles Latham and Evelyn March Phillips's *The Gardens of Italy,* London, 1905; George S. Elgood's *Italian Gardens,* New York, 1907; and Georges Gromort's *Jardins d'Italie,* Paris, 1922.

[4] An example of the latter is Mrs. Aubrey Le Blond's *The Old Gardens of Italy: How to Visit Them (with Illustrations from Her Photographs),* New York and London, 1912. Other examples of the genre are Edith Wharton (1862–1937), *Italian Villas and Their Gardens,* New York, 1904; Gabriel Faure (1877–1962), *Les jardins de Rome,* Grenoble, 1923; and Rose Standish Nichols, *Italian Pleasure Gardens,* New York, 1928. Faure's writings in the

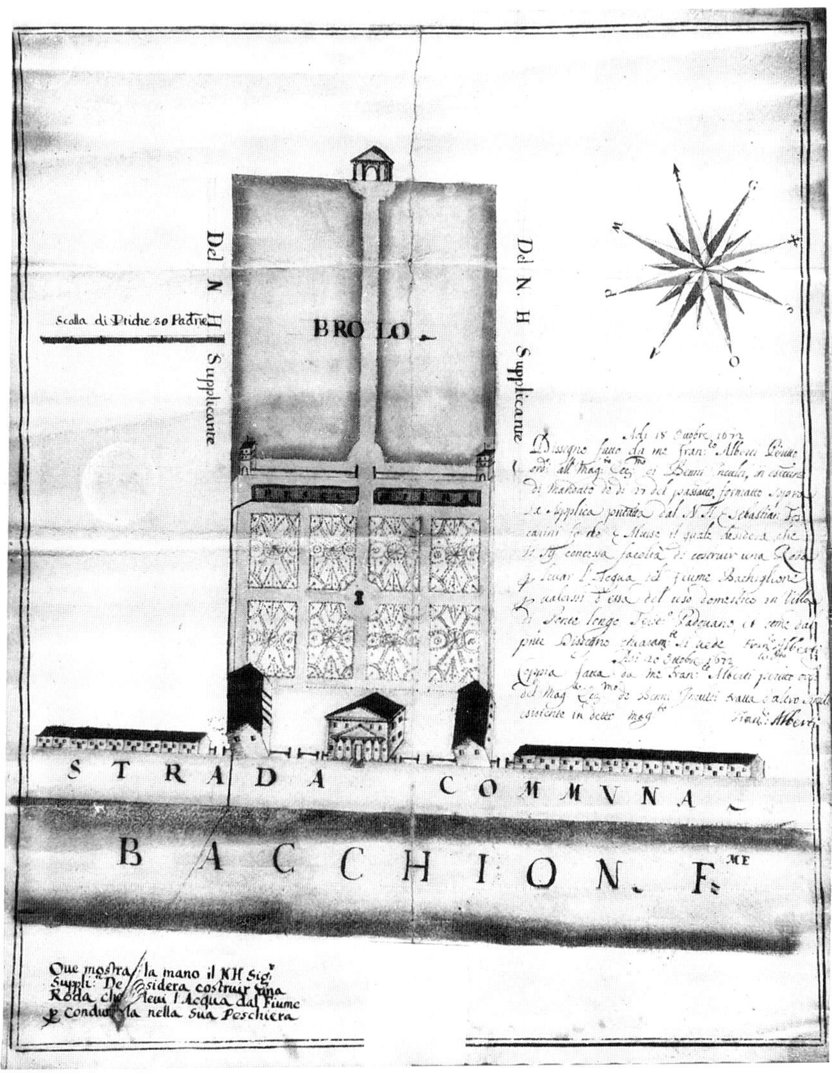

2. Pontelongo (Padua), Villa Foscarini on the river Bacchiglione, watercolor map, dated 20 October 1672. Archivio di Stato di Venezia, Venice (photo: courtesy of Archivio di Stato di Venezia)

---

travel genre include *Heures d'Italie*, Paris, 1913, and English trans., *Wanderings in Italy*, Boston, 1919; *Aux lacs italiens,* Grenoble, 1922 and 1925; *Les jardins de Rome,* Grenoble, 1923, and English trans., *The Gardens of Rome,* London, 1926; and *La route des Dolomites,* Grenoble, 1925.

[5] M. L. Gothein, *Geschichte der Gartenkunst*, Jena, 1914; 2nd ed., Jena, 1926; English trans., *The History of Garden Art,* London, 1928.

[6] Another was the superb compendium of images and bibliography produced by the art historian Luigi Dami (1882–1926) in both Italian and English: *Il giardino italiano*, Milan, 1924, and *The Italian Garden*, New York, 1925. Dami's bibliography still provides the most complete list of early printed books and views that documented Italian gardens from the fifteenth to the eighteenth centuries. His corpus of images includes not only contemporary photographs of the gardens but also drawings, prints, and paintings from the earlier centuries. Dami was a historian of art and architecture. See, for example, his *Bramante,* Florence, 1921, and *La pittura italiana del seicento e del settecento alla Mostra di Palazzo Pitti,* Milan and Rome, 1924. Especially for original sources on Italian Baroque gardens, I still refer my students to Dami.

3. Strà (Padua), Villa Pisani on the Brenta canal, 1740s, view of the stables (left), *labyrinth* (center), *and palace* (right). Veduta del labirinto nel giardino del nobilissimo Pisani a Strà, *pen and wash, attributed to Francesco Guardi. Museo Correr, Venice (photo: courtesy of the Museo Correr, neg. no. 5462)*

exceptions. Those who wrote scholarly works on Italian gardens from 1950 to the mid-1970s were mostly German and American art historians based at high-ranking research universities such as Harvard and Princeton and institutes such as the Bibliotheca Hertziana, the German art history library in Rome. Their works concentrated on fifteenth- and sixteenth-century villas and rarely touched on the seventeenth and eighteenth centuries. In terms of methodology, they approached the gardens from the point of view of art and architectural historians. The gardens and their ornaments were considered as architectural extensions of the main palace or house of the villa. The architectural approach was at first very satisfactory, for it was a criterion that had been set up by Renaissance architects themselves. However, it did not account for plantings and other nonarchitectural categories, such as groves, parks, and naturalistic features of fountains and grottoes (Fig. 1).

Nearly all the scholars of the interpretative works were the leading international figures in the study of Italian Renaissance architecture when they wrote on villa gardens, and a few were students of these major figures. They can be cited in order of the older to the younger generations. The Germans were Ludwig von Heydenreich and Wolfgang Lotz, followed by Christoph L. Frommel, Klaus Schwager, and Carl Lamb. The Americans were John Coolidge, James S. Ackerman, David R. Coffin, and Elisabeth B. MacDougall. The British author and journalist Barbara (Babs) Johnson, who wrote under the pseudonym of

4. Strà (Padua), Villa Pisani on the Brenta canal, 1740s, wooden and stucco presentation models for three garden buildings. Museo Correr, Venice (photo: courtesy of the Museo Correr, neg. no. 2251)

Georgina Masson, was the exception in professional terms, since she was neither an academic nor a university-based scholar.

Up to 1970, the following works were essential to any scholarly art historical study of Italian villa gardens. In order of publication date, they were Coolidge's article of 1943 in the *Art Bulletin* on the Villa Giulia in Rome;[7] Ackerman's *The Cortile del Belvedere* and his *Palladio's Villas*;[8] Coffin's *The Villa d'Este at Tivoli*; Frommel's *Die Farnesina*; Masson's *Italian Gardens*; Lamb's *Die Villa d'Este in Tivoli*;[9] and MacDougall's "The Villa Mattei and the Development of the Roman Garden Style," her Ph.D. dissertation advised by John Coolidge and James S. Ackerman at Harvard University in 1970.

All of these works were based on the extensive gathering of primary sources (Figs. 3, 4). These consisted of drawings and prints from museum collections and libraries; the family archives of garden patrons, which contained payments to architects, gardeners, and fountain engineers, as well as lists of plants; and, even if rare, descriptions by the patrons or their circle of the gardens themselves. The scholars also made very creative use of travel

[7] J. Coolidge (d. 1995), "The Villa Giulia: A Study of Central Italian Architecture in the Mid-Sixteenth Century," *Art Bulletin* 25 (1943), 117–225. This exemplary article is an early model of art historical scholarship applied to Renaissance architecture and gardens.

[8] See J. S. Ackerman, "The Belvedere as a Classical Villa," in his *Distance Points: Essays in Theory and Renaissance Art and Architecture*, Cambridge, Mass., and London, 1991, 325–59, chap. 11 (the article was originally published in 1951); idem, *The Cortile del Belvedere*, Vatican City, 1954; idem, "Sources of the Renaissance Villa," in *Studies in Western Art: Acts of the Twentieth International Congress of the History of Art*, vol. 2: *Renaissance and Mannerism*, Princeton, 1963, 6–18, reprinted as chap. 10 in his *Distance Points*, 303–24; and idem, *Palladio's Villas*, Locust Valley, N.Y., 1967.

[9] D. R. Coffin, *The Villa d'Este at Tivoli*, Princeton, 1960; C. L. Frommel, *Die Farnesina und Peruzzis Architektonisches Frühwerk*, Berlin, 1961; G. Masson, *Italian Gardens*, London, 1961—note her distinction of title from her *Italian Palaces and Villas*, London, 1959; C. Lamb, *Die Villa d'Este in Tivoli: Ein Beitrag zur Geschichte der Gartenkunst*, Munich, 1966.

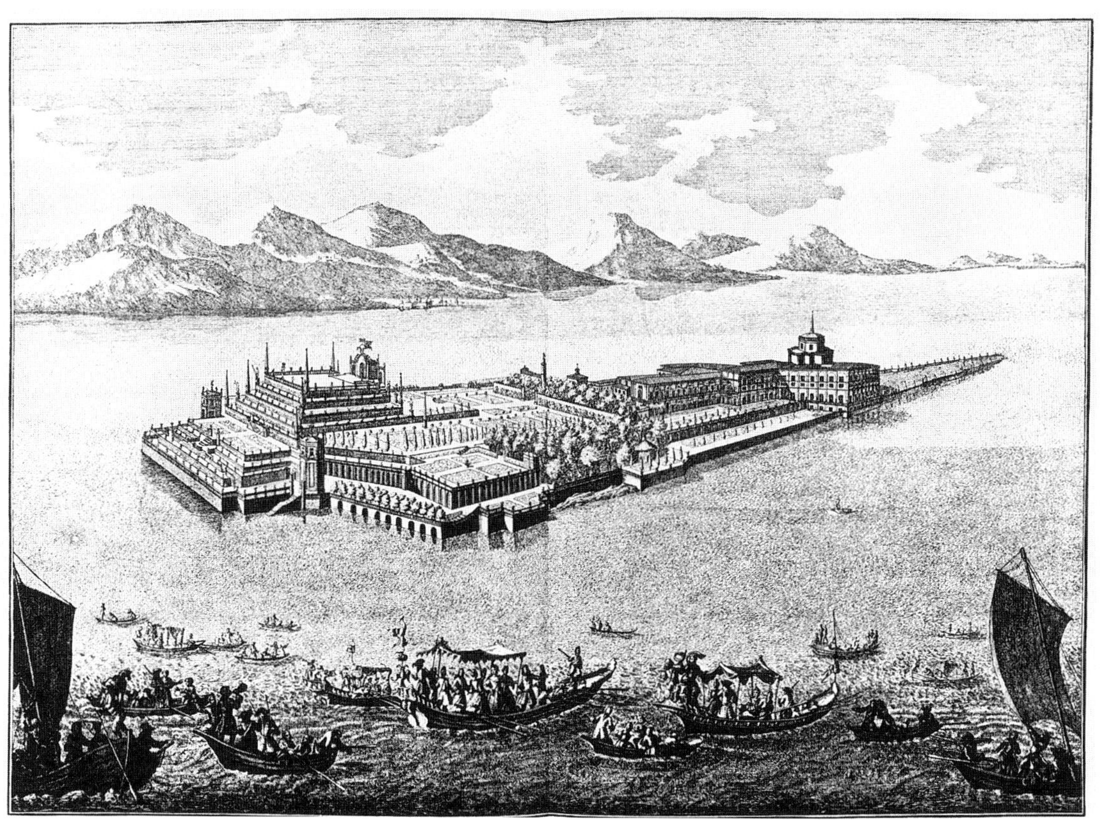

5. Isola Bella, Villa Borromea on Lake Maggiore, Lombardy, ca. 1630–70, bird's-eye view (from M. Dal Re, Ville di Delizia, *Milan, 1726)*

guides and diaries of the sixteenth to the eighteenth centuries, which texts they compared to the evidence of the archives.[10] The similar approach of these scholars is evident from their respective title pages and tables of contents.[11] In their reconstruction of the original

[10] The use of the travel guidebook for the study of Italian gardens, of which there has been a sharp increase in recent years, owes its origins to these scholars. A model for this approach is the first part of J. Dixon Hunt's *Garden and Grove: The Italian Renaissance Garden in the English Imagination (1600 –1750),* Princeton, 1986. Increasingly compendia of historical travel descriptions for individual Italian cities are being published, and these can be mined for contemporary evidence. See, for example, G. Cusatelli and F. Razzetti, *Il viaggio a Parma: Visitatori stranieri in età farnesiana e borbonica,* Parma, 1990, where descriptions are given in chronological order.

[11] The monographs by Coffin and Lamb on the Villa d'Este present an interesting comparison. Neither knew of the other's work, as World War II cut off such international exchanges. Lamb began his in 1938 in Rome at the Bibliotheca Hertziana with advisers such as Wolfgang Lotz; he halted the study with the war and completed it only in 1966, soon after Coffin's study had appeared (Lamb, *Villa d'Este,* 7). Coffin began his study in Princeton in 1945 with Erwin Panofsky. He used the art historical method of iconography, which he learned from Panofsky, to approach all aspects of the Villa d'Este, from painted interior decorations to the gardens. Lamb's method of analysis was also art historical, but he used an approach that considered the genesis of the design; for example, his subtitle, *A Contribution to the History of Garden Art,* and his own photographs and

6. Castellazzo (Lombardy), Villa Arconati, then Crivelli Sormani-Verri, ca. 1627–1700, bird's-eye view (from M. Dal Re, Ville di Delizia, *Milan, 1726)*

gardens, many of which changed drastically over centuries, they used a precise method, the descriptive model of the Renaissance guidebook for contemporary tourists, moving with their readers room by room, garden space by garden space, and fountain by fountain. This model still is sound today, and is particularly evident in German art history as it is applied to Italian gardens.

---

reconstructions (made with an architect), which illustrate the book, speak strongly to readers who are design professionals.

A summary of tables of contents for Coffin and Lamb is as follows. Coffin, *Villa d'Este*: I. Early History of the Villa; II. The Gardens and Fountains; III. The Interior Decoration of the Villa; IV. Tapestry Designs by Pirro Ligorio; V. The Villa's Symbolism and Pirro Ligorio; VI. The Later History of the Villa and Its Gardens; VII. Appreciation and Influence of the Villa D'Este; Appendices (textual sources, including D. Unpublished Documents). Lamb, *Villa d'Este*: 1. The Sources; 2. The Building History of Palace and Garden under Cardinal Ippolito II d'Este; 3. The Individual Garden- and Fountain-Complexes; 4. Decoration of the Palace and Its Relation to the Garden; 5. Pirro Ligorio in the Service of Cardinal Ippolito II d'Este; 6. Ippolito II d'Este as Patron of Architecture; Textual Sources (some are translated into German).

Although such archival work had been done previously in German and American art history, the three decades following World War II witnessed an enormous increase in the method, particularly in the case of American art historians, whose work was favored by research fellowships such as Fulbrights and the strength of the dollar.[12] Overall, scholars of this era focused on the great Italian Renaissance architects who, among their other works, also designed villas and garden complexes in Rome (Fig. 3): Donato Bramante at the Belvedere Court, Raphael at the Villa Madama, Giacomo Barozzi da Vignola and Bartolommeo Ammannati at the Villa Giulia, and Pirro Ligorio at the Villa d'Este.[13]

In the midst of these research campaigns, Italian Baroque gardens received little attention, partly because few of the famous architects, such as Bernini, Borromini, and Pietro da Cortona, designed formal gardens, and partly because there was a tendency among political and social historians to favor the Renaissance over later centuries (Figs. 5, 6).[14] In fact, starting with Benedetto Croce in the Risorgimento period, historians eschewed Baroque Italy as a subject because it was associated with the notion of a supposed decline in Italian culture under first Spanish and then Austrian rule during the seventeenth and eighteenth centuries. Historians of art, architecture, and culture since the time of Heinrich Wölfflin and Jakob Burckardt concentrated their attention on "the Renaissance villa" in disfavor of Italian Baroque villas, thus partaking of a Crocian viewpoint.[15]

For the last 30 years the studies of Roman Renaissance architects and villa gardens have set the guidelines for anyone initiating a scholarly study of Italian gardens. Even today the field remains too focused on Rome in the Renaissance, but changes are now occurring, with respect to both geography, i.e., regions beyond Rome, and chronology. Other Italian regions are now receiving greater attention—Tuscany, Liguria, the Piedmont, Lombardy, the Veneto, and Sicily—and there is a very recent emphasis on Baroque villa gardens (Figs.

[12] As Coffin notes in the preface to *Villa d'Este,* "The principal impetus to my study of Ligorio, and consequently the Villa d'Este, was given by the award of a Fulbright grant for research in Italy for the academic year 1951–1952" (p. viii).

[13] After World War II, the outstanding collections of the Bibliotheca Hertziana in Rome gave German art historians, such as Lotz, Lamb, and Frommel, and their American counterparts, the occasion to study Roman gardens and their designers. The same situation was true of the Kunsthistorisches Institut in Florence, although Tuscan villas received less study.

[14] Exceptions, in the case of Pietro da Cortona, are the landscapes of the two Sacchetti villas, at Castelfusano (1625–29) near Ostia and at the Valle Inferno (1630s–1650) near the Vatican in Rome. Because they were agrarian and their formal gardens were limited in extent, the landscapes of these villas have not been analyzed as landscape architecture. For recent studies of their architecture and decoration, see J. M. Merz, "The Villa del Pigneto Sacchetti," *Journal of the Society of Architectural Historians* 49, 4 (December 1990), 390–406, and his *Pietro da Cortona: Der Aufstieg zum führenden Maler im barocken Rom,* Tübingen, 1991; and L. H. Zirpolo, "Pietro da Cortona's Frescoes in the Villa Sacchetti in Castelfusano," Ph.D. diss., Rutgers, 1994.

[15] Croce, writing after the Risorgimento, saw Italy as a decadent, paralyzed cultural and economic system owing to Spanish hegemony in northern and southern Italy and to the loss of power by the papacy in Rome vis-à-vis other European states such as France. Recent historical research, however, has revised this Crocian view, positing Italy and Rome as very active and vital societies and showing how these vital societies dealt with conservative and repressive Counter-Reformational culture. See, among others, E. Cochrane, *Florence in the Forgotten Centuries (1527–1800),* Chicago, 1973, the title of which speaks of the redressing of the Crocian view; and L. Nussdorfer, *Civic Politics in the Rome of Urban VIII,* Princeton, 1992.

5, 6). To use as an example one region, Genoese gardens in Liguria, from the 1980s on, studies led by George Gorse and Lauro Magnani expanded the foundation work published in 1967 by Emmina De Negri and a team of scholars, namely a catalogue of Genoese villas and gardens. Gorse and Magnani added to this iconographical and social approaches that had previously been used mainly for Roman and Tuscan gardens.[16] The same kind of expansion in approaches has been done by Lionello Puppi and especially Margherita Azzi Visentini for the Veneto gardens in important publications from the 1980s on, and it is being undertaken currently by a younger generation for Renaissance, seventeenth-, and eighteenth-century gardens in Sicily and Lombardy (Figs. 2–6).[17]

In the field overall there have been two main interpretative approaches, architectural and iconographical, and they still have great validity.[18] The architectural analysis of Italian villa gardens came first: James S. Ackerman's fundamental study of Bramante's Belvedere Court in Rome revealed its significance as a great achievement in landscape architecture and site planning, and set the framework to this day for studies of Italian gardens as architectural complexes. All subsequent studies on Roman Renaissance gardens refer to Ackerman's synthetic analysis of the principles of axial relationship between building and garden, connections between terraces by ramps and staircases, and issues of monumentality in relationship to ancient architectural and landscape complexes such as the Temple of Fortune at Praeneste.[19]

Next came the application of iconography, as it was defined for Italian Renaissance painting by Erwin Panofsky and Edgar Wind, among others early in this century. In the 1960s and 1970s this approach was applied to the study of architectural decoration, foun-

[16] E. De Negri et al., *Le Ville Genovesi*, Genoa, 1967, and *Catalogo delle Ville Genovesi,* 2nd ed. with new data and bibliography, Genoa, 1980. For the 1980s on, see G. Gorse, "The Villa Doria in Fassolo, Genoa," Ph.D. diss., Brown University, 1980; idem, "Genoese Renaissance Villas: A Typological Introduction," *Journal of Garden History* 3 (1983), 255–80; L. Magnani, *Il tempio di Venere: Giardino e villa nella cultura genovese,* Genoa, 1987; and the late Donna Salzer's recent Ph.D. dissertation on the villas of Galeazzo Alessi in Genoa, Harvard University, 1992. The tragic early death of Salzer at 41 in 1992 deprived Genoese garden studies of a major new impetus.

[17] Among her other works on the Veneto gardens, see M. Azzi Visentini, ed., *Il giardino veneto dal tardo medioevo al settecento*, Milan, 1988; idem, *La villa in Italia: Quattro e cinquecento*, Milan, 1995, 221–94; and idem, "The Gardens of Villas in the Veneto from the Fifteenth to the Eighteenth Centuries," in *The Italian Garden: Art, Design and Culture,* ed. J. Dixon Hunt, Cambridge and New York, 1996, 93–126, with bibliography to date. In the same volume edited by Hunt, see Iris Lauterbach, "The Gardens of the Milanese *Villeggiatura* in the Mid-Sixteenth Century," 127–59. Recent doctoral dissertations on eighteenth-century villa gardens include one by Dianne Harris, "*Lombardia Illuminata*: The Formation of an Enlightenment Landscape in Eighteenth-Century Lombardy," University of California, Berkeley, 1996, and Erik Neil, "Architecture in Context: The Villas of Bagheria, Sicily," Harvard University, 1995.

[18] For a brief historiographical sketch along these lines, see M. Beneš, "The Villa Pamphilj (1630–1670): Family, Gardens, and Land in Papal Rome," 3 vols., Ph.D. diss., Yale University, 1989, 1:7–8, 18–19.

[19] Ackerman, *Cortile del Belvedere.* The introduction by Richard Krautheimer and Kathleen Weil-Garris to Ackerman's collected essays, *Distance Points,* ix ff., situates Ackerman's intellectual biography. In brief, he did his Ph.D. studies at New York University, completing his thesis in 1952 with Richard Krautheimer as his adviser. He taught first at the University of California, Berkeley, from 1952 to 1969, when he joined the fine arts faculty at Harvard, remaining there until he became emeritus in 1990.

tain art, and plantings in Italian villa gardens. The key leaders of this new methodology were David Coffin in *The Villa d'Este at Tivoli* and, as we shall see later, Elisabeth MacDougall in a study of sixteenth-century Roman garden style, "The Villa Mattei."[20] Coffin wrote in the preface to his book in August 1959, "It was in a seminar on Renaissance art given at Princeton in the fall of 1945 by Dr. Erwin Panofsky of the Institute for Advanced Study, that I became interested in the person and art of Pirro Ligorio, from which this study of the Villa d'Este derives. Dr. Panofsky has encouraged me ever since in my study of Ligorio, and it is obvious in this work that I am much indebted to his approach to the history of art."[21]

In addition to these two approaches, another strand in this historical web of events was developing in the literature in the 1960s and would become very important for the study of Italian gardens two decades later in the 1980s. This was a historical perspective on the Italian villa that considered its social and especially its economic aspects. This new approach diverted scholars from Roman case studies and shifted their focus to Veneto and even Tuscan villas, because the latter two were centers of agricultural production whereas the Roman ones were mostly not (Figs. 1, 2).[22] This shift would also aid the opening of scholarly eyes in future to other Italian regions, such as Lombardy, the Piedmont, the Marche, and Emilia Romagna.

The shift from Roman villas to those of northern Italy was not just a geographical one. Beginning in the 1950s and continuing through the 1970s, a group of Italian and German art and architectural historians, led by their Venetian colleagues, began to consider the pre-Palladian and Palladian villas in social and economic terms. Here Georgina Masson, the English expert on Italian gardens, was a pioneer. Her seminal article, "Palladian Villas as Rural Centers," appeared in *The Architectural Review* (London) in 1955, and because it was in a very prominent English architectural journal it was read by architects and architectural historians.[23]

[20] E. B. MacDougall, "The Villa Mattei and the Development of the Roman Garden Style," Ph.D. diss., Harvard University, 1970. Parts of MacDougall's thesis were published in important articles from 1972 to 1985, and were included with many new studies in her book, *Fountains, Statues, and Flowers: Studies in Italian Gardens of the Sixteenth and Seventeenth Centuries,* Washington, D.C., 1993.

[21] Coffin, *Villa d'Este,* viii.

[22] This was because Roman Renaissance villas generally were not farms, unlike the Veneto villas. However, in the seventeenth century matters changed, and several important villas in the Roman *campagna* and hill-towns were conceived as the agricultural centers of vast family estates, for example the Villa Mondragone (1613–33) of the Borghese family near Frascati and the Villa Sacchetti at Castelfusano, mentioned above. I have emphasized the agricultural landscapes of the Roman Baroque villas throughout my doctoral dissertation, "Villa Pamphilj," esp. 1:7–9, 144–52; 2:431–48, 450–54, 491–96, 539–69. A more recent work on the agrarian landscapes of the Villa Mondragone near Frascati expands on the approach. See Tracy L. Ehrlich, "The Villa Mondragone and Early Seventeenth-Century *Villeggiatura* at Frascati," Ph.D. diss., Columbia University, 1995.

[23] The Venetians were soon joined by the American scholar James S. Ackerman. Writing on "patronage and typology in Palladian Villas" in 1969, the late Manfredo Tafuri, an architectural historian well known for his neo-Marxist critiques of modern architecture, hailed Masson's article as "one of the first studies in which the theme of the Palladian villa as agricultural farm is addressed." M. Tafuri, "Committenza e tipologia nelle ville palladiane," *Bollettino del Centro Internazionale di Studi di Architettura "Andrea Palladio"* 11 (1969), 120–36, esp. 120 and 134 n. 1.

In this new type of study, the villa's agrarian functions, the layout of agrarian landscapes, the patrons who were city-dwellers with large economic interests in the countryside, and occasionally the gardens themselves were carefully studied, often in the light of contemporary Marxist critiques. The paper which Lionello Puppi of the University of Padua presented at the first colloquium at Dumbarton Oaks on the Italian garden (1971) exemplifies this approach to the garden. In "The Villa Garden of the Veneto" Puppi analyzed this regional type in Marxist terms, describing its cultural world as one "that fostered an ideological self-awareness in the dominant class" and "their structural conditions which created, at the superstructural level, an ideology of the countryside."[24]

Such concerns of art and architectural historians with ideology in respect to gardens arose, as in Puppi's case, from their own current political interests and engagement in the years around 1968–70. They were also supported by the international scholarship of economic and social historians, many of whom were using the tools of Marxist critique.[25] A new generation of studies on the Veneto villa was thus initiated and with it came significant implications for the study of gardens. These implications, however, would only be fully investigated decades later in the 1980s. Nonetheless, several immediate results can be singled out.

One was the publication of maps, plans, and aerial views of the garden layouts of Veneto villas in the *Bollettino* published by the Andrea Palladio International Center for Architectural Studies, founded in 1959 (e.g., Fig. 2). Because many Italian architects also did scholarly research, crossing the boundaries between professional practice and scholarship, the study of Italian gardens received new visual and formal standards, which emphasized the reading of maps and plans and the professional design processes, for example the reconstruction of how Palladio or Sansovino designed on the land.

Another was the international nature of the scholarship sponsored by the Palladio Center in Vicenza. It led over time to a much more international history of villas and gardens (as it did for Renaissance and Baroque architecture).[26] James S. Ackerman's book,

[24] L. Puppi, "The Villa Garden of the Veneto from the Fifteenth to the Eighteenth Century," in *The Italian Garden*, ed. D. R. Coffin, Dumbarton Oaks Colloquium on the History of Landscape Architecture 1, Washington, D.C., 1972, 84, and see 81–114. For earlier approaches, see G. Mazzotti, ed., *Le ville venete,* Treviso, 1954; and idem, *Palladian and Other Venetian Villas,* London, 1958.

[25] Examples of this scholarship, which affected the study of Veneto villa gardens, are the path-breaking studies by S. J. Woolf, "Venice and the Terraferma: Problems of the Change from Commercial to Landed Activities," *Bollettino dell'Istituto di Storia della Società e dello Stato Veneziano* (1962), 415–41; and A. Ventura, "Considerazioni sull'agricoltura veneta e sulla accumulazione originaria del capitale nei secoli XVI e XVII," in *Agricoltura e sviluppo del capitalismo,* issue of *Studi storici* 9, 3–4 (1968), 674–722.

[26] The editorial board of the Center mingled, in 1969 for example, the art historians Rodolfo Pallucchini from Padua, Anthony Blunt from England, André Chastel from France, Heydenreich and Lotz from the Bibliotheca Hertziana in Rome, and Rudolf Wittkower from America with modernist architects such as the Italian Bruno Zevi. The Center was and is still truly international. When its *Bollettino* was devoted in 1969 to the issue "La villa: Genesi e sviluppi," the authors included the major historians of Italian Renaissance architecture at the time, including Ludwig H. Heydenreich, Hartmut Bierman, Christoph Frommel, Marco Rosci, Lionello Puppi, Manfredo Tafuri, Erik Forssman, and Giangiorgio Zorzi (the Palladio scholar), and the economic historian Angelo Ventura, among others. See *Bollettino del Centro Internazionale di Studi di Architettura "Andrea Palladio"* 11 (1969).

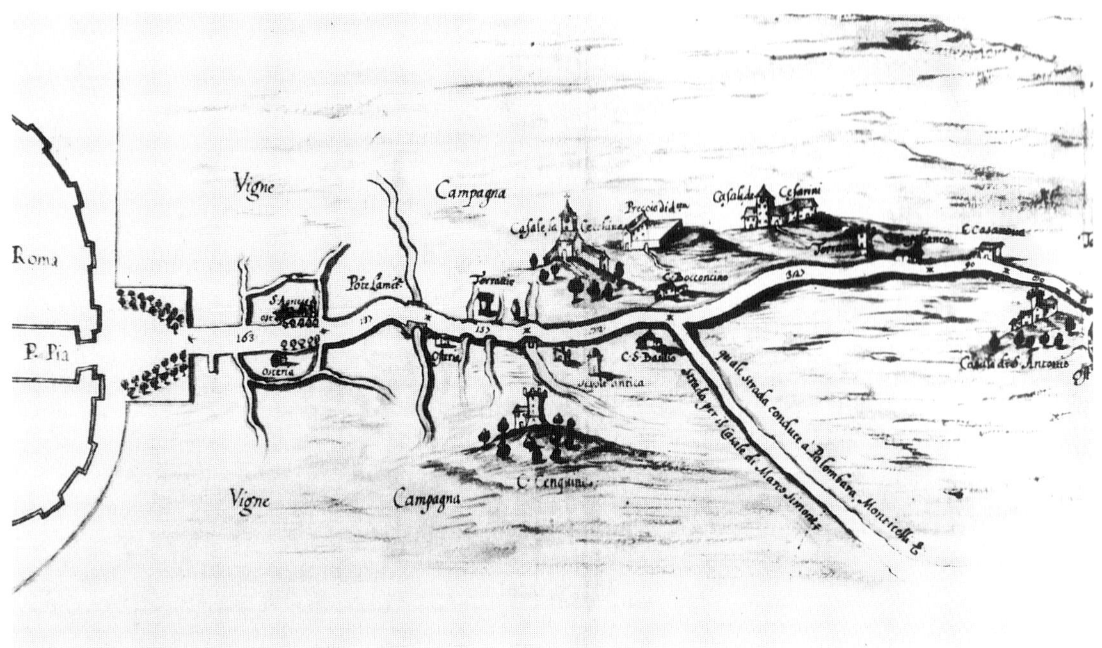

7. *Via Nomentana, Rome. Plan by Giulio Martinelli, 1661, Archivio di Stato, Rome, Catasto Alessandrino (from A. P. Frutaz,* Le carte del Lazio, *vol. 2, Rome, 1972, pl. 123)*

Palladio's Villas, of 1967, was born in the midst of this fertile exchange at the Palladio Center and in the political climate of a social history of art described above.[27]

Yet another contribution was the emphasis by the Palladio Center and its scholars and architects on interregional, comparative work, which it still upholds today. Ackerman's *Palladio's Villas* exemplifies this point. The book begins with a now famous comparison between the gardens and layout of the Villa Barbaro at Maser by Palladio and those of the Villa d'Este at Tivoli by Ligorio, thus opening up the topic of interregional comparison for Italian garden studies. However, this interregional approach did not immediately bear fruit, and in my view it remains one of the most important directions that the study of Italian gardens can take today.

Understanding the economics of the agrarian production of villas, such as those of the Veneto, required historians of agrarian economics also to reconstruct and interpret to some degree the original agricultural landscapes of the Veneto region in earlier centuries. Studies of the Italian agrarian landscape were produced by social, economic, and agrarian historians from the 1960s on and yet were not used by scholars of Italian gardens until the 1980s and 1990s.[28] A key work that was overlooked was the fundamental and remarkable book pub-

[27] For the context of his subject, see his "Gli studi palladiani degli ultimi trent'anni," in *Andrea Palladio: Nuovi contributi*, ed. R. Cevese and A. Chastel, Milan, 1990, 122–26.

[28] For the 1980s and 1990s, see further below. A few exceptions in the 1960s and 1970s can be noted here, such as an article by Philip Foster (1969) on the dairy farm at the fifteenth-century Villa Medici of

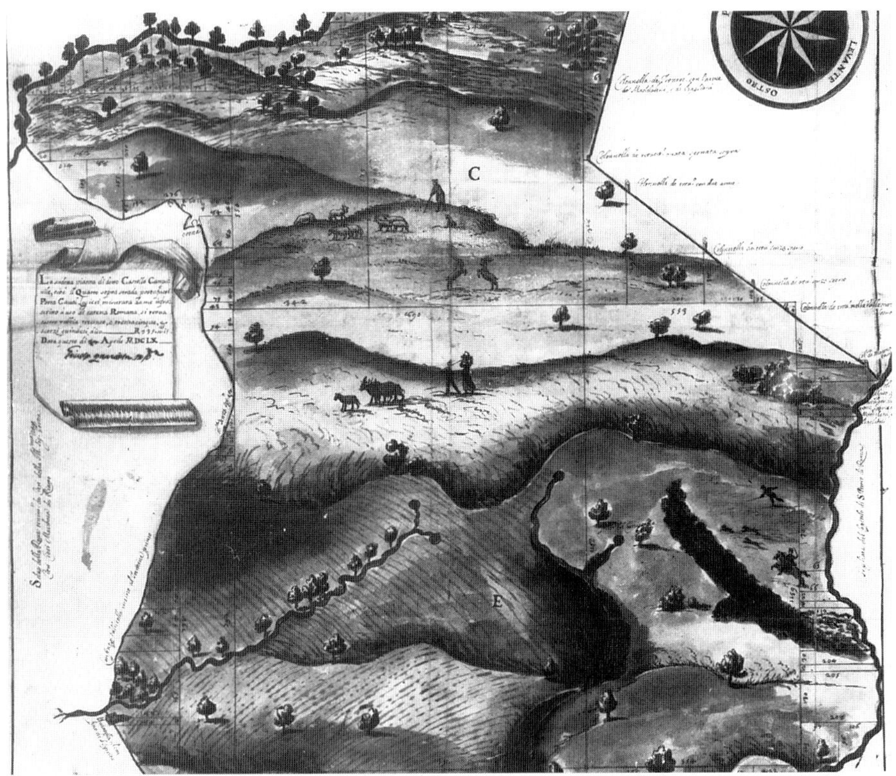

8. Casale di Castel Campanile, farm of Prince G. B. Borghese, on the Via Aurelia west of Rome, water map, dated 27 April 1655 (central portion). *Archivio di Stato, Rome, Presidenza delle Strade, Catasto Alessandrino (photo: courtesy of the Archivio di Stato, Rome)*

lished in 1961 by Emilio Sereni, the Marxist historian of Italian agrarian life and later senator in the Italian parliament, namely *Storia del paesaggio agrario italiano* (History of the Italian landscape). It has been largely unknown to garden historians until my generation, despite the fact that Sereni meticulously documented the elements of Italian agrarian landscapes from Roman antiquity to the nineteenth century. However, these landscapes were the essential material of Italian gardens, because they were the natural fabric out of which the gardens were evolved or directly carved (Figs. 7, 8).[29]

Poggio a Caiano near Florence, the subject of his dissertation, for which see P. Foster, "A Study of Lorenzo de' Medici's Villa at Poggio a Caiano," 2 vols., Ph.D. diss., Yale University, 1974, published New York, 1978; and H. Burns, L. Fairbairn, and B. Boucher, "Villas," in *Andrea Palladio, 1508–1580: The Portico and the Farmyard*, exhibition catalogue, London, 1975, 163–204.

[29] E. Sereni, *Storia del paesaggio agrario italiano*, Bari, 1961, with numerous subsequent editions in paperback. The book was very recently translated by R. Burr Litchfield, the historian of Florentine Renaissance society, as *History of the Italian Agricultural Landscape*, Princeton, 1997, with an important introduction situating Sereni's intellectual context. D. R. Coffin is one of the few historians of Italian gardens who mention Sereni; see the bibliography to his book, *The Villa in the Life of Renaissance Rome,* Princeton, 1979, 371.

Sereni's book remained outside the purview of art historical studies of Italian gardens for several reasons. Most probably it was viewed as a book about agrarian landscapes and not about gardens. In his view, research on contemporary agrarian labor and medieval and early modern agrarian landscape belonged together, as one sees in his contribution to *Agricoltura e sviluppo del capitalismo* (Agriculture and the development of capitalism), a major issue of the journal *Studi storici*, produced in 1968 at the time of the student uprisings in Europe and America. At the time that *Storia del paesaggio agrario italiano* was published, there were no intellectual frameworks available to art historians of the Italian Renaissance showing the links between the landscapes outside the villa walls and the garden forms inside them. At that time as well, environmental and ecological concerns did not yet have the relevance to the study of art and architecture that they have today. Moreover, Sereni's work belonged to the field of agricultural and labor history, and it had a leftist and contemporary political context.[30] The very recent translation of *Storia del paesaggio agrario italiano* will, I believe, have an impact on those future studies of Italian gardens which will take a social-geographical approach.[31]

In which broad directions did the study of Italian villa gardens develop in the 1970s and 1980s? First, there was a general consolidation of the field, using the two main approaches developed in 1960s, architectural and iconographical. The decade from 1970 to 1980 saw the flourishing of monographic studies of Italian villa gardens, most of them in doctoral dissertations on previously unstudied Roman, Florentine, Veneto, and Genoese villas by students of the German and American scholars discussed above. Although justice cannot be done here to their contributions, a genealogical tree for their historiography would show them rooted in the paths charted first by Lotz and Frommel, Ackerman and Coffin, and then by MacDougall who had studied with Ackerman. Thus the way that Italian garden studies developed in this decade was akin to the building of a brick wall: Once the wall had been conceptualized and designed, masons worked at filling in the bricks. In the scholarship, the result was the writing of monographs, for example, on Roman gardens such as the Orti Farnesiani on the Palatine, the Villas Mattei, Medici, and Giulia, and the Casino of Pius IV in the Vatican gardens, the Villa Lante at Bagnaia, as well as the Villa Medici at Castello near Florence, and most recently, the villas of Galeazzo Alessi at Genoa.[32]

[30] Sereni was a Marxist historian and a public figure in Italian politics, among other activities as a senator in the Italian parliament. Besides *Storia del paesaggio agrario italiano,* several of his studies are especially relevant to the study of Italian gardens and landscapes: "Agricoltura e mondo rurale," in *Storia d'Italia*, vol. 1: *I caratteri originali*, Turin, 1970, 135–252; and *Terra nuova e buoi rossi e altri saggi per una storia dell'agricoltura europea,* Turin, 1981. In Italy his work initiated studies parallel to those of Marc Bloch on French rural life and of the French historians of the so-called Annales group. On Sereni, now see A. Giardino, "Emilio Sereni e le aporie della storia d'Italia (Pagine autobiografiche di Emilio Sereni)," *Studi storici* 37, 3 (July–September 1996), 693–726.

[31] During fall semester 1997, at the time of editing this article, I used Sereni's translated text as an essential component of my teaching in a seminar on Italian villa gardens.

[32] As mentioned above, Ackerman directed the Ph.D. dissertation of Elisabeth B. MacDougall, "The Villa Mattei." D. R. Coffin's Ph.D. students included G. A. Andres, *The Villa Medici in Rome*, 2 vols., New York, 1976, and original Ph.D. diss., Princeton University, 1970; C. Lazzaro Bruno, "The Villa Lante at Bagnaia," Ph.D. diss., Princeton University, 1974; G. Smith, *The Casino of Pius IV*, Princeton, 1977, and original Ph.D.

Second, at the same time as the consolidation of the field there was an overall increase of attention to the gardens themselves among the elements of a villa complex. In 1970 a major work of synthesis appeared, which greatly influenced my generation, namely Elisabeth MacDougall's dissertation on the Villa Mattei. This work broke new ground by accounting for the stylistic evolution of Roman gardens, and it provided a framework for understanding their iconographical constructs, which was relevant for the entire sixteenth century and the early seventeenth.[33] By contrast, the approach to date had been the documentation of one garden in a monographic study. MacDougall's work appears to me to be synthetic, because it interpreted information from massive archival documentation and from every published source on four of the most significant Roman Renaissance gardens.[34] The evolution of the Roman garden style was discussed from the Villa Madama to the Villa Mattei.

This thesis broadened the discussion of iconography, to date, for the elements of the gardens, especially ancient sculptures, by reconstructing their associations with Renaissance literary theory. MacDougall presented such a reconstruction at the Dumbarton Oaks symposium on the Italian garden, and her paper, "*Ars Hortulorum*: Sixteenth-Century Garden Iconography and Literary Theory in Italy," became a classic in the literature. In terms of garden design, this thesis innovated in interpreting the changes in the heights and forms of the plantings (trees and hedges) in Roman Renaissance gardens, which occurred as the sixteenth century progressed. It began to explore how these changes affected the visitor's experience of walking through the gardens. Finally, it provided a framework for studies of Italian Baroque gardens by examining all these aspects in Roman gardens at the beginning of the seventeenth century (Fig. 1).[35]

A third new direction was inaugurated in 1970 with the publication of the first volume of the series Ville italiane (Italian villas), a census organized by Italian art historians.

---

diss., Princeton University, 1970; and D. R. Wright, "The Medici Villa at Olmo a Castello: Its History and Iconography," Ph.D. diss., Princeton University, 1976. Among the German studies in the ambit of Lotz, Frommel, and other scholars of the Bibliotheca Hertziana in Rome, see K. Schwager, "Kardinal Aldobrandinis Villa di Belvedere in Frascati," *Römisches Jahrbuch für Kunstgeschichte* 9/10 (1961–62), 291–382; T. Falk, "Studien zur Topographie und Geschichte der Villa Giulia in Rom," *Römisches Jahrbuch für Kunstgeschichte* 13 (1971), 101–78; H. Giess, "Studien zur Farnese-Villa am Palatin," *Römisches Jahrbuch für Kunstgeschichte* 13 (1971), 179–230; and M. Quast, *Die Villa Montalto in Rom: Entstehung und Gestalt im Cinquecento*, Munich, 1991, first written as a Ph.D. dissertation for Frommel.

[33] MacDougall's work on iconography and on its relationship to design in Roman Renaissance villas has been fundamental to all subsequent literature in the field. See her articles, "*Ars Hortulorum*: Sixteenth-Century Garden Iconography and Literary Theory in Italy," in *The Italian Garden*, ed. Coffin, 37–59, and "*L'Ingegnoso Artifizio*: Sixteenth-Century Garden Fountains in Rome," in *Fons Sapientiae: Renaissance Garden Fountains*, ed. E. B. MacDougall, Dumbarton Oaks Colloquium on the History of Landscape Architecture 5, Washington, D.C., 1978, 85–113.

[34] These were the d'Este gardens on the Quirinal Hill; the Villa Giulia (1550–55) outside the Porta del Popolo; the Villa Montalto (of Cardinal Felice Peretti, later Sixtus V, 1585–90) on the Esquiline Hill; and the Villa Mattei (1585 f.) on the Caelian Hill.

[35] MacDougall has always worked closely with scholars of ancient Roman gardens. See, for example, E. B. MacDougall and W. F. Jashemski, eds., *Ancient Roman Gardens,* Dumbarton Oaks Colloquium on the History of Landscape Architecture 7, Washington, D.C., 1981; E. B. MacDougall, ed., *Ancient Roman Villa Gardens*, Dumbarton Oaks Colloquium on the History of Landscape Architecture 10, Washington, D.C., 1987;

The series, which is ongoing, concentrates on villa buildings, but there is much material on gardens. In it we witness a return to prominence of Italian scholarship in the field, which had nearly disappeared before World War II and ceded to the wave of German and American studies discussed above. This return brought a new perspective to the field, which was a strong interest in conservation of historical gardens in Italy as part of the national patrimony.[36] Introductory essays on themes pertaining to the geographical and social characteristics of each region were followed by catalogue entries with excellent photographs of first the major, then the minor villas. New regional volumes are added every few years, and recent ones, *Ville Sabaude* (1990), on the villas of the Savoy dukes and their courtiers in the Piedmont, and *Ville di Firenze (la città)*, reflect the latest methodologies in their use of social and cultural history.

The cast of the series brought new blood and methodologies to the study of the gardens, because the driving force behind this census of villas came from professional architects concerned with preservation. Their thinking structures the documentation at every step; for example, one feature of the series is plans at 1:500 metric scale of the main floors of each villa building. Occasionally, site plans and surveys of the surroundings' gardens were made, but the contribution for the villa buildings revealed the need for measured surveys of the gardens, which are still lacking today for the major Roman gardens (as well as for most Italian villas). The categories of analysis derive from professional conceptualizations based on site surveys and the need for preservation.[37] Such analyses are morphological and typological. Examples include sections in *Ville di Roma* (1970): "Villa Types and Their Developments," "The Gardens," and " The Villas and the City." This approach reflected, in fact, the interest in types and typology which contemporary Italian architects such as Aldo Rossi manifested in the 1970s.[38]

From around 1980 on, this professionally motivated direction in Italian garden studies received yet another impetus from the profession of landscape architecture in Italy and in Europe in general. At that time, the design and construction of many large-scale public parks began in Europe, for example in Paris and Barcelona. In Paris, the "Grand Travaux"

---

and idem, "*Il Giardino all'Antico*: Roman Statuary and Italian Renaissance Gardens," in *Studia Pompeiana and Classica in Honor of Wilhelmina F. Jashemski*, vol. 2, ed. R. Curtis, New Rochelle, N.Y., 1989, 139–54.

[36] The aim of the series was to document Italian villas regionally by publishing a catalogue of villas of all centuries in each region. The first volume was *Ville di Roma* and the next, in 1975, was *Ville della Campagna Romana*. The main author of both was an Italian art historian, Isa Belli Barsali, a professor at the University of Rome, who set the very high standards that still distinguish this series today. I. Belli Barsali, *Ville di Roma: Lazio I,* Milan, 1970; I. Belli Barsali and M. G. Branchetti, *Villa della Campagna Romana: Lazio II,* Milan, 1975. Each volume is equipped with an impressive bibliography to date. In *Ville di Roma,* 9, Belli Barsali wrote that the first volume was timed for "Rome's centenary year as capital of the Italian state," and that it "makes its contribution to the knowledge of, and thereby to the wish to preserve, a part of the monumental heritage of the Eternal City." For the first years the volumes were in both Italian and English, which demonstrated the international character of the intended audience.

[37] See, for example, F. Fariello, *Architettura dei giardini,* Rome, 1967; 2nd ed., Rome, 1985. The book is useful for the plans and sections by the author.

[38] For the study of typologies, see, for example, I. Belli Barsali, "Tipi e sviluppi," in *Ville di Roma*, 27–49; idem, "I giardini," ibid., 49–66; and idem, "Le ville e la città," ibid., 67–87 and nn. 87–94.

for President François Mitterrand included the competition for La Villette Park, won by Bernard Tschumi, the competition for the renovation of the Tuileries, and the design over time of many new parks in contemporary style. Consciousness about contemporary park design and the restoration or modernization of historical parks was thereby raised in the design professions.[39] The debates about the theories of restoration and reconstruction generated new interest in the documentation of historical gardens. Architects, who in Italy were the main restorers of gardens and parks, needed to know the history of what they were restoring in order to make appropriate choices about styles and concepts. Italian architects began to receive commissions in the 1980s for both new parks and the restoration of Italian Renaissance and Baroque gardens; in executing these commissions, they developed a new genre of technical and theoretical literature on the restoration of Italian gardens.[40] Intellectual frameworks were provided by the art historian Cesare Brandi and the philosopher Rosario Assunto, who brought contemporary theoretical and philosophical issues of the 1970s into the debates over how the restorations should be conducted.[41]

Tourism and the Italian government's desire to increase it were factors in augmenting restoration work on gardens during the period discussed, for which the government provided funding, justifying the additional expenditures as valid in view of the investing of the gardens with the idea of national identity.[42] The Villa Lante at Bagnaia and the Villa Farnese

[39] This can be seen, for example, in several issues of design journals in 1980 and 1981. *Lotus International, Rivista trimestrale di architettura,* and *Quarterly Architectural Review* 30 (1981/2) included articles by historians of early modern gardens (e.g., K. Woodbridge and M. Mosser on Parisian gardens of the eighteenth century) and by architects and historians who were teaching in design schools, writing on nineteenth-century public parks in Paris and Berlin and on new public parks in modern Germany (e.g., M. L. Marceca on Alphand, H. Schmidt on Berlin, and M. De Michelis on Weimar Germany).

[40] I thank Franco Panzini, architect and landscape architect, Rome, for discussing the contemporary Italian professional situation and these questions with me, and for indicating relevant literature. See, for example, V. Cazzato, ed., *Tutela dei giardini storici: Bilanci e prospettive,* Rome, 1989, 50 ff., section III.1, "Dal convegno di 'Italia nostra' alla carta di Firenze (1959–1981)."

Also see M. Catalano and F. Panzini, "Documenti: Comitato internazionale dei giardini e dei siti storici ICOMOS-IFLA," in *Giardini storici: Teoria e techniche di conservazione e restauro,* Rome, 1990, 111–13; and M. Pozzana, *Giardini storici: Principi e tecniche della conservazione,* Florence, 1996. The Fondazione Benetton in Treviso, in the Veneto, has a mission to support studies in landscape architecture, both contemporary and historical work, and it publishes a bulletin on research and design. For example, the *Bollettino della Fondazione Benetton* 2 (March 1993), edited by D. Luciani, includes the sections Centro di Documentazione (Raccolte, repertori, sistemi informativi); Repertori: Scritti di Rosario Assunto; Norme per il governo del paesaggio; Scuole europee di pasesaggismo; Beni culturali: Salvaguardia e valorizzazione dei patrimoni storici; Paesaggio e giardino: Corsi sul governo del paesaggio e del giardino; and Premio internazionale Carlo Scarpa per il giardino.

[41] Franco Panzini has stressed the role of Cesare Brandi. Rosario Assunto's role is evident in his writings, which also appear in conference volumes on restoration theory. See Assunto's articles, "I giardini della parola e la parola dei giardini," in *Tutela dei giardini storici,* 1989, 30–33, and "Il problema estetico del giardinaggio: Il giardino come filosofia," in *Il giardino storico italiano: Problemi di indagine, fonti letterarie, e storiche,* ed. G. Ragionieri, Atti del convegno di studi, Siena-San Quirico d'Orcia, 6–8 ottobre 1978, Florence, 1981, 1–17.

[42] Additional funding from the European Economic Community has been allotted in recent years to restoration projects of Italian gardens and parks. For example, the EEC gave funding in 1997 for the in-depth restoration of the marvelous park at the Palazzo Chigi at Ariccia, near Frascati southeast of Rome, which was built in the medieval period and then enlarged for the papal Chigi family of Alexander VII (1655–67) in the later seventeenth century.

at Caprarola, both jewels of Renaissance garden art lying about fifty miles north of Rome, are showpieces of the government, which has long had a presidential summer seat at Caprarola.[43] Very recent research by Claudia Lazzaro, presented in "The Italian Garden and the Idea of Italy," addresses both modern and twentieth-century political uses of the cultural identity of Italy as a garden and the historical Italian garden as a representation of Italy's national identity despite its regional differences.[44] These kinds of contexts—tourism, historical patrimony, and modern national identity—structured the interests of the designers who attended to the restorations of the gardens.

In a fourth new direction, the historiography of Italian gardens began to be influenced by new developments in art history beginning in the mid-1970s and early 1980s. As noted above, Italian garden studies had originated in the discipline of art history and had generally followed art history's course. This had resulted in few, if any, connections to the methodological frameworks used in the fields of social and cultural history. Art historical methods began to be influenced by the discipline of social and political history in the 1970s, and in time the influence was felt in the study of Italian gardens. However, this influence was for a very long time limited to consideration of the political iconography of rulers and rulership, rather than the political and cultural structures of Italian society. In terms of gardens, this meant study of the political messages that were conveyed by sculptures, fountains, plantings, and coats of arms.[45] The iconography of rulership was at times studied synthetically in relation to literary and antiquarian contexts, considerably enriching our knowledge of Italian gardens, for example, in an important article of 1984 on the Sacro Bosco of Bomarzo by Margaretta Darnall and Mark Weil.[46]

Several other significant themes were developed in Italian garden studies as a result of, or in conjunction with, developments in art history. Among these were the relationships between Italian gardens and the theater (Figs. 5, 6; note the spectacular open-air theater, top left on the island, and the water festival in foreground in Figure 5, and the perspectival alignment of the hedges in Figure 6); between the gardens and the study of Roman antiquity (Fig. 1, see aedicule top center, at city wall; Fig. 9); and, in a related vein, the notion of

[43] In the 1930s, Benito Mussolini, then head of the government, asked Pius XI Ratti which villa the papacy preferred as its summer seat, Caprarola or Castelgandolfo near Albano and Frascati. The pontiff chose Castelgandolfo, to this date the papal summer seat. On Castelgandolfo, see the first part of E. Bonomelli, *I papi in campagna*, Rome, 1953.

[44] This article is forthcoming in a volume *Italian and French Baroque Gardens: A Generation of New Research*, to be edited by Mirka Beneš and Dianne Harris. Lazzaro first presented the research at a roundtable symposium at Dumbarton Oaks on Italian gardens, in honor of E. B. MacDougall, in February 1995.

[45] As examples, see R. M. Steinberg, "The Iconography of the Teatro dell'Acqua at the Villa Aldobrandini," *Art Bulletin* 47 (1965), 453–63; D. Heikamp, "La Grotta Grande del Giardino di Boboli," *Antichità viva* 4 (1965), 27–48; and Wright, "The Medici Villa." See also the studies of Genoese gardens by G. Gorse: "The Villa Doria"; "Genoese Renaissance Villas"; "The Villa of Andrea Doria in Genoa: Architecture, Gardens, and Suburban Setting," *Journal of the Society of Architectural Historians* 44, 1 (March 1985), 18–36; and "An Unpublished Description of the Villa Doria in Genoa during Charles V's Entry, 1533," *Art Bulletin* 68, 2 (June 1986), 319–22.

[46] M. J. Darnall and M. S. Weil, "Il Sacro Bosco di Bomarzo: Its Sixteenth-Century Literary and Antiquarian Context," *Journal of Garden History* 4, 1 (January–March 1984), 1–94.

9. Rome, Villa Pamphilj, view of the casino and formal gardens from west to east (photo: J. H. Aronson)

the garden as a museum or collection of antiquities, rare species of plants, and other exotic collectibles such as rare fowl and zoo animals. During my graduate studies in the 1970s, to resume the autobiographical perspective of this article, the leading studies on Italian Renaissance gardens and antiquity were mostly by the prominent scholars cited at the beginning of this article—Lotz, Coolidge, Ackerman, Frommel, Coffin, and MacDougall.[47] The

[47] For Italian gardens and the study of antiquity, see the authors cited above, as well as Darnall and Weil, "Il Sacro Bosco di Bomarzo." In particular, both D. R. Coffin and E. B. MacDougall have always devoted attention to Roman antiquity in the Roman Renaissance garden.

In the case of Coffin, his original point of departure was the archaeologist Pirro Ligorio, who collected a massive number of records of ancient art, artifacts, architecture, and coins, as can be seen in Ligorio's encyclopedic series of volumes of studies now primarily in Naples and Turin. See Coffin, *Villa d'Este* and *Villa in the Life,* to be discussed below, which contains many chapters on the Renaissance garden's relationship to ancient sites, excavations, statuary, and villa forms, e.g., chap. 4, "The Classicizing of the Roman Garden," and chap. 5, "The Iconography of the Renaissance Garden."

MacDougall's seminal works on Roman gardens and antiquity include "The Villa Mattei," chap. 4, "Influence of Antiquity: Renaissance Garden Literature," 82–103; *"Ars Hortulorum"* and *"Il Giardino all'Antico"*; and the several essays recently republished in her *Fountains, Statues, and Flowers.*

same situation obtained for gardens and theater, essentially because the ancient Roman villas, which provided models for the Renaissance ones, had been settings for theatrical forms and performances.[48] Coffin, MacDougall, and their graduate students particularly emphasized the study of Roman antiquity, as can be seen in the scholarship of my generation.[49] The notion of the garden as a museum of collectibles, both antique and modern, inert and living, was studied starting in the mid-1980s, in the midst of a larger set of intellectual concerns with museology and taxonomy in early modern European history. One of the earliest investigations of the subject appeared in a volume titled *The Origins of Museums.*[50]

The major research and publication on these themes took place in the 1970s and 1980s, but there has been some very recent work as well, and one could fairly say that these three topics are being rethought currently in respect to Roman Baroque gardens above all (Fig. 9).[51] Focus at present is on the study of ancient Roman landscaped sites, as these were

[48] The literature on Italians gardens and theater is very large. Significant works include the following. Sources and background: H. Tintelnot, *Barock-Theater und Barocke Kunst: Die Entwicklungsgeschichte der Fest- und Theater-dekoration in ihrem Verhältnis zur barocken Kunst,* Berlin, 1939; J. Jacquot, ed., *Les fêtes de la Renaissance*, Paris, 1956, and *Le lieu théâtral à la Renaissance,* Paris, 1964; A. M. Nagler, *Theatre Festivals of the Medici, 1539–1637,* New Haven, 1964; P. Bjurström, *Giacomo Torelli and Baroque Stage Design*, Stockholm, 1961, esp. 134–95, and *Feast and Theatre in Queen Christina's Rome,* Stockholm, 1966; B. Wisch and S. Scott Munshower, eds., *"All the World's a Stage. . . .": Art and Pageantry in the Renaissance and Baroque,* 2 vols., Papers in Art History from the Pennsylvania State University 6, University Park, Pa., 1990.

Theatrical forms and performances in gardens: Coolidge, "The Villa Giulia," 215–19; Frommel, *Die Farnesina*, 36–37, 114–16; MacDougall, "The Villa Mattei"; M. Viale Ferrero, *Feste delle Madame Reali di Savoia,* Turin, 1965, on court festivals in Baroque Turin; R. Strong, *Splendor at Court: Renaissance Spectacle and the Theater of Power,* Boston, 1973; M. Fagiolo, ed., *Natura ed artificio,* Rome, 1979, and *La città effimera e l'universo artificiale del giardino: La Firenze dei Medici e l'Italia del '500,* Rome, 1980; P. Marchi, "Il giardino come 'Luogo Teatro,' " in *Il giardino storico italiano,* ed. Ragionieri, 211–19; J. Dixon Hunt, "Garden and Theatre," in *Garden and Grove,* 59–72; M. S. Weil, "Love, Monsters, Movement, and Machines: The Marvelous in Theaters, Festivals, and Gardens," in *The Age of the Marvelous*, exhibition catalogue, ed. J. Kenseth, Hanover, N.H., 1991, 159–78.

[49] For other recent perspectives on the relationships between Renaissance and Baroque villas and ancient ones, now see Beneš, "Villa Pamphilj," esp. chap. 9 on the antique villa sources; P. de la Ruffinière Du Prey, *The Villas of Pliny from Antiquity to Posterity,* Chicago, 1994; W. L. MacDonald and J. A. Pinto, *Hadrian's Villa and Its Legacy,* New Haven and London, 1995; and Ehrlich, "Villa Mondragone," esp. chap. 1 on ancient Tusculum and its villa culture.

[50] The larger intellectual framework includes thinking such as that in K. Pomian, *Collectionneurs, amateurs, et curieux: Paris, Venise, XVIe–XVIIIe siècle*, Paris, 1987, esp. 61–80; A. Schnapper, *Le géant, la licorne, et la tulipe: Collections et collectionneurs dans la France du XVIIe siècle,* I: *Histoire et histoire naturelle,* Paris, 1988; and P. Findlen, "The Museum: Its Classical Etymology and Renaissance Genealogy," *Journal of the History of Collections* 1 (1989), 59–78.

On gardens as museums and collections of rarities, see the essential works by J. Dixon Hunt, " 'Curiosities to adorn Cabinets and Gardens,' " in *The Origins of Museums,* ed. O. Impey and A. MacGregor, Oxford, 1985, 193–203, and "Cabinets of Curiosity," in *Garden and Grove,* 73–82; and E. B. MacDougall, "A Paradise of Plants: Exotica, Rarities, and Botanical Fantasies," in *The Age of the Marvelous*, ed. Kenseth, 145–57. Although it will be discussed below, it is important to note here that Claudia Lazzaro's *The Italian Renaissance Garden: From the Conventions of Planting, Design, and Ornament to the Grand Gardens of Sixteenth-Century Central Italy,* New Haven and London, 1990, extensively treats notions of collecting and museology in the gardens.

[51] For recent perspectives on gardens and theater in Roman Baroque gardens, see Beneš, "Villa Pamphilj," 475–79; D. R. Coffin, *Gardens and Gardening in Papal Rome,* Princeton, 1991, 230–33, for the performance in

10. Rome, Casino Ludovisi, villa landscape with courtly figures, vault fresco on the ground floor, 1620s. Attributed to G. B. Viola and Guercino. See Fig. 1, center left pavilion, for another view (photo: courtesy of the Istituto Centrale per il Catalogo e la Documentazione, Rome, neg. no. E 62602)

analyzed by Renaissance and Baroque designers of gardens in drawings and site surveys.[52] For the theme of collecting and the garden as museum, new work by art and cultural historians on museology in early modern Italy provides a creative intellectual basis for reconsidering the garden museums.[53]

---

the Chigi garden at the Quattro Fontane in 1668; and Ehrlich, "Villa Mondragone," 281–89, for a fine discussion of water theaters in the Frascati villas and their contexts.

[52] See, for example, the drawings of Praeneste, Hadrian's Villa at Tivoli, Pliny's Laurentine Villa, and Domitian's villa at Albanum, among others in the collection of the antiquarian Cassiano Dal Pozzo (1588–1655). See the forthcoming volumes on architecture and topography in *The Paper Museum of Cassiano Dal Pozzo,* London, and the brief preview in "Topography and Architecture," *The Paper Museum of Cassiano Dal Pozzo,* exhibition catalogue, The British Museum, London, May 14–August 30, 1993, Quaderni puteani 4, Milan, 1993, 120–29, 134. On the Dal Pozzo project, see F. Solinas and A. Nicolò, "Cassiano Dal Pozzo and Pietro Testa: New Documents Concerning the *Museo Cartaceo,*" in *Pietro Testa, 1612–1650: Prints and Drawings,* exhibition catalogue, ed. E. Cropper, Philadelphia, 1988, lxvi–lxxxvi; and F. Solinas, ed., *Cassiano Dal Pozzo: Atti del seminario internazionale di studi,* Rome, 1989.

[53] See the transposition of the framework provided by J. Connors, "Virtuoso Architecture in Cassiano's

At the end of the 1970s emerged a fifth new direction for Italian garden studies, the investigation of their functions and uses. David Coffin's *The Villa in the Life of Renaissance Rome,* the most comprehensive study of the buildings and gardens of Roman villas to that date, is the first example and the foundation work for this approach. Coffin wrote in his preface, "The major focus of this study is on the concept of *villeggiatura,* the withdrawal to the country of the urban Romans, and on the architecture inspired by it."[54] The villas in the Roman countryside served three main functions for their essentially ecclesiastical patrons, as summarized by James S. Ackerman in an important review of Coffin's book: "a place for summer (1 July–1 October) *villeggiatura,* . . . escape from the plague, and expression of their eminence, taste, and wealth."[55] Coffin documented the activities of *villeggiatura* with numerous sources, for example, the instances in which villa gardens were used for outdoor dining, theatrical entertainment, hunting, and learned and leisurely conversation (an example for the Baroque period is Figure 10). This was the first time in the literature that such a large number of categories for villa life had been structured and discussed in documentary detail. For this purpose, he uncovered and interpreted an extremely rich range of documentary sources, including the diaries of papal masters of ceremonies, personal letters, biographies, and the *avvisi di Roma,* which are manuscript newsletters that reported on the activities of the papal court and Roman noble society.[56] Coffin subsequently continued the investigation of how Roman villa gardens were used in an article on the "Lex Hortorum," the rules governing access to the gardens for visitors, and in a major study *Gardens and Gardening in Papal Rome.*[57]

Rome," in *Cassiano Dal Pozzo's Paper Museum,* vol. 2, London, 1991, 23–40, into the work on gardens by his Ph.D. students, e.g., Ehrlich, "Villa Mondragone." For early modern Italian museology as studied at present, see P. Findlen, *Possessing Nature: Museums, Collecting, and Scientific Culture in Early Modern Italy,* Berkeley and Los Angeles, 1994.

[54] Coffin, *Villa in the Life,* preface. *Villeggiatura* can be roughly translated as "villa life and culture." Coffin was the first to provide a complete account in English of the construction histories, decorations, iconographic programs, and uses of the major Roman Renaissance villas, based on a vast array of both primary documents and secondary literature. Gardens were discussed in the history of each villa. J. S. Ackerman has called Coffin's work "this grand compendium of the state of our knowledge of the subject." See Ackerman's excellent review of Coffin, *Villa in the Life,* in *Journal of the Society of Architectural Historians* 39, 3 (October 1980), 242–43, which provides an exquisitely synthetic map of the field, as well as a fine reading, for graduate and advanced scholarly research. Due to its comprehensiveness and to its paperback printing from 1988 on, Coffin's *Villa in the Life* has been extensively used by scholars across the world and especially by architecture and landscape architecture students; in my own teaching it has been a key tool.

[55] Ackerman, review of Coffin, *Villa in the Life,* 242.

[56] *Avvisi di Roma,* like *avvisi* from any Italian city, were manuscript newsletters and logs prepared by agents of princes, cardinals, and nobles, who, in residence in Rome, followed the important political and social news of the papal court, and wrote back to their masters and mistresses in other parts of Italy or Europe.

Brendan Dooley, Department of History, Harvard University, is preparing a study of the *avviso* in early modern Italy. See his forthcoming works, "Political Publishing and Its Critics in Seventeenth-Century Italy," *Memoirs of the American Academy in Rome* 41 (1997), and *The Social History of Skepticism: Information and Belief in Early Modern Europe.* I am very grateful to him for sharing his studies with me.

[57] D. R. Coffin, "The 'Lex Hortorum' and Access to Gardens of Latium During the Renaissance," *Journal of Garden History* 2 (1982), 201–32; and idem, *Gardens and Gardening,* in which all aspects of Roman gardening activities and culture, from botany to entertainment, are examined. For garden uses, see *Gardens and Gardening,* chap. 13, "Entertainment," 227–43.

It would remain for the next generation of scholars to put Coffin's foundation study in the larger contexts of Roman society and culture. Ackerman, in his review, suggested two future avenues for interpretative studies: "first, an evaluation of the villa phenomenon in the light of the peculiar conditions of patronage and social custom, and its impact on the design of the buildings and the gardens; second, a comparative assessment of the Roman villa and the major counterparts elsewhere, particularly in Tuscany and the Veneto."[58] These two paths could be forged only when scholars of Italian gardens became much more closely engaged than before in the larger disciplines of social and cultural history, and could define such contexts for the gardens.[59]

The five directions just discussed and their consolidation have structured the historiography of Italian gardens to date. They still remain fundamental parameters. However, a shift in the approach to the subject that defines a new historiographical period has recently occurred, beginning in the late 1980s and continuing into the first half of the 1990s. This shift moved from viewing the gardens as discrete objects, whose aspects are to be analyzed by the criteria of art history, to viewing them as integral parts of the larger structures of early modern Italian society. Historical narrative is not considered as a backdrop to the formal and iconographical analyses of the gardens but as an integral part of the latter. The gardens are increasingly considered as part, parcel, and product of the dynamic structures that evolved in early modern Italian society.

I can give one example of this methodological approach from my own experience. Gradually, due to the very nature of the Roman Baroque villa gardens and to the documentary material itself, I developed such a methodology in my Ph.D. dissertation of 1989, "The Villa Pamphilj (1630–1670): Family, Gardens, and Land in Papal Rome," an interdisciplinary study of one significant papal villa. In it I charted the relationships between the rise of a noble family to papal rank, its landowning strategies, and the ways in which the highly innovative designs of both architecture and park of the Villa Pamphilj were the results of these very trajectories (Fig. 9). As the use of iconography as an interpretative tool did not account for the large-scale geographical and landscape features of the villa, I turned

[58] Ackerman, review of Coffin, *Villa in the Life,* 243. An example of what Ackerman proposed is the essay by D. R. Wright, "The Boboli in the Evolution of European Garden Design: A Study in Practical Function and Organizing Structure," in *Boboli 90: Atti del convegno internazionale di studi per la salvaguardia e la valorizzazione del giardino*, 2 vols., ed. C. Acidini Luchinat and E. Garbero Zorzi, Florence, 1991, 1, 311–22. As noted above, Wright was a Ph.D. student of D. R. Coffin.

[59] In practice, this occurred first mainly in studies of Roman Baroque architecture. Joseph Connors pioneered in bringing to life again, based on a sophisticated study of primary documents, the seventeenth-century Romans' views of the complex connections between architecture and society in *Borromini and the Roman Oratory: Style and Society,* New York and Cambridge, Mass., 1980; see especially the chapter "Finance, Function, Imagery," 59–79. A new generation of studies on the relationship between interior planning and social and dwelling functions, especially etiquette, in Baroque architecture has been inspired by Patricia Waddy's *Seventeenth-Century Roman Palaces: Use and the Art of the Plan*, New York and Cambridge, Mass., 1990. Some aspects of these approaches have been creatively transferred, recently, to the study of villas outside Rome by a Ph.D. student of Connors, Ehrlich, "Villa Mondragone." In my own "Villa Pamphilj" and the publications based on it, for which see the next note, I am also indebted to Connors's approach as well as to the ambit of social history of the 1970s that inspired his work.

to other contexts or ways in which to structure the study of Villa Pamphilj and the related group of Roman estatelike villas of the first half of the seventeenth century. The two obviously important contexts were society and land. I concluded that the social rise of a family, the Pamphilj, and its work over generations to gain the papacy in Rome—the process of becoming Roman for families new to the city—was inevitably embedded in the forms and in the very structure of the landscape of the papal villa, one of the key products of the family effort of generations.[60]

In the making of the Villa Pamphilj, the gardens and enclosed landscape predominated over the architectural elements.[61] Here and earlier at the Villa Borghese (1606–33) in Rome, the designers took a new approach to garden design, in which landscape components such as pine forests and farmland were transposed to the villa's parks from other geographical locations around Rome. These locations consisted of three rings of land properties around the city, namely the suburbs of *vigne* (vineyards), the *campagna* of farms, and the fief-towns surrounded by forests and agrarian holdings, and were identified in the Romans' mental map of landscapes with specific characteristics and trees (Figs. 7, 8, 11). From the medieval period on, these three rings were in constant internal evolution, in correspondence with changing patterns of ownership generated by successive waves of immigration to Rome from elsewhere in Italy. In sum, Romans read the territory around their city as a social geography of properties. When Romans and informed visitors looked at a villa such as the Villa Borghese, or Ludovisi, or Pamphilj (Figs. 1, 9), they could read in them the changing structure of Roman society during the later sixteenth and the seventeenth centuries, a period of great social mobility in the upper tiers of the patriciate. The location and the specific connotations of a property, in the landscapes inside and outside the walls of Rome, formed a sort of diagram in which the history and the current situation of power relations in the city were figured.

In my more recent work I have pursued understanding of the seventeenth-century Roman *mentalités* in respect to landscapes within the larger contexts of their culture, and considered both garden design and landscape painting as interrelated within this culture.[62] This methodology shifts the focus from gardens to the larger territorial subject of landscape in its two major cultural manifestations in Rome between about 1550 and 1700, namely villa gardens and landscape paintings, which can be shown to be intertwined phenomena

[60] M. Beneš, "Landowning and the Villa in the Social Geography of the Roman Territory: The Location and Landscapes of the Villa Pamphilj (1645–70)," in *Form, Modernism, and History: Essays in Honor of Eduard F. Sekler*, ed. A. von Hoffmann, Cambridge, Mass., and London, 1996, 187–209; and idem, "The Social Significance of Transforming the Landscape at the Villa Borghese, 1606–30: Territory, Trees, and Agriculture in the Design of the First Roman Baroque Park," in *Gardens in the Time of the Great Muslim Empires: Theory and Design*, ed. A. Petruccioli, Studies in Islamic Art and Architecture: Supplements to Muqarnas 7, Leiden, 1997, 1–31.

[61] In concluding *Villa in the Life,* Coffin noted that "the significant history of the seventeenth-century Roman villa is more a history of garden and landscape design than of architectural design" (p. 369).

[62] For discussion of social history and the notion of *mentalités* in French historical writing, see below, pp. 67–69. I am preparing a book titled *Landscape and Society in Baroque Rome: The Roles of Villa Gardens and Landscape Paintings in the Social and Cultural Concerns of a Land-based Patriciate.*

11. Claude Lorrain, The Flock Being Driven in a Storm, *etching, 1651 (photo: courtesy of the Harvard University Art Museums)*

that shared patronage and social-geographical themes (Fig. 11).[63] In this approach, paintings and views are examined not only as documents of landscapes and gardens or as models for the picturelike construction of landscape designs,[64] but with a structural focus, taking into

[63] I recognize with pleasure, now 20 years on, my conceptual and intellectual debts in this kind of approach to the work of the adviser of my doctoral dissertation, Emeritus Professor Vincent J. Scully, Yale University. In 1974–77, when I studied with him in graduate school, Scully was lecturing widely and writing on the larger geographical and territorial structures reinterpreted in the French formal gardens of André Le Nôtre, such as canals, roads, and fortifications by Sébastien Le P. de Vauban. Two of his lectures were published much later in V. J. Scully, *Architecture: The Natural and the Manmade,* New York, 1991, 221–73 and 284–92. Scully's pioneering work on the structural meanings of French gardens has very recently been complemented by the publications of Thierry Mariage, *L'univers de le Nostre*, Brussels and Liège, 1990, and Chandra Mukerji, *Territorial Ambitions and the Gardens of Versailles*, Cambridge and New York, 1997, for which see below. Mariage and Mukerji do not cite Scully, although their intellectual premises are the same.

[64] For this very different approach, fruitful in recent years, see Linda Marie Cabe, "Sets of Painted Views of Gardens, c. 1728–1740, and the Relationship between Garden Design and Painting in England in the First Half of the Eighteenth Century," Ph.D. diss., Yale University, 1988, and Linda C. Halpern (the same author), "The Uses of Paintings in Garden History," in *Garden History: Issues, Approaches, Methods*, ed. J. Dixon Hunt, Dumbarton Oaks Colloquium on the History of Landscape Architecture 13, Washington, D.C., 1992, 183–202. Views themselves of Italian, French, Flemish, and other early modern European gardens have been the

account all the relevant categories of reference, or the framework of meanings in which a society—in my case that of seventeenth-century Rome—addressed its concerns with landscape. In the case of Rome, countryside and prospects, tracts of land with natural systems such as forests, rivers, and their ecologies, land uses as basis of the food chain, landowning, and visual representations of rural life are taken into consideration and evaluated in respect to Baroque Rome's larger social and cultural concerns.[65]

Such a social mapping of landscape elements as carriers of meanings in an interrelated way in villa gardens and landscape paintings can be illustrated by a specific example of this kind of study. Pastoralist art in Baroque Rome, whether structurally embedded in landscape paintings or in the design of villa gardens, was a direct relative of the city's vital livestock economy (Figs. 8, 11). For patrician families such as the Giustiniani, Costaguti, Sacchetti, Borghese, Barberini, and Pamphilj—particularly those who were newly arrived both socially and geographically in Rome and who owed their high social rank to the papacy as either papal or cardinalate families—some of the revenues from the pastoralist economy (cows, sheep, and goats) of their farms in the Roman *campagna* paid for new types of pastoralist art, for which they as patrons were in part contemporaneously creating new demand and structuring a new portion of the art market.[66] For them, Claude Lorrain painted half of his three hundred landscapes with livestock and shepherds (the other half went mostly to French patrons), while Paul Bril, Domenichino, and the *bamboccianti* together produced hundreds of *campagna* landscapes, which these families bought in large quantities (Fig. 11).[67] And for them too, landscape architects invented a new type of estatelike

---

subject of a recent master's thesis, with complete bibliography to date, by Elizabeth S. Eustis. The thesis will see publication soon: "The First Century of Etched and Engraved Garden Views, 1573 to 1673," Master's Program in the History of the Decorative Arts, Cooper-Hewitt, National Design Museum and Parsons School of Design, 1998.

[65] A proper definition of the structures of the Roman situation will also involve comparisons with other early modern agrarian societies—France, England, and the Netherlands are those most studied to date—with different patterns of social organization, landownership, and agrarian land uses.

[66] See my forthcoming article in *The Art Bulletin,* "Pastoralism in Roman Baroque Villas and in Claude Lorrain." Studies of pastoral art have so far not considered the structural interrelatedness of pastoralist or livestock economies and the art produced by such land- and livestock-based societies. For examples of the recent literature on pastoral art, see A. Patterson, *Pastoral and Ideology: Virgil to Valéry,* Berkeley and Los Angeles, 1987; R. C. Cafritz, L. Gowing, and D. Rosand, *Places of Delight: The Pastoral Landscape,* exhibition catalogue, Washington, D.C., 1988; L. Freedman, *The Classical Pastoral in the Visual Arts,* New York, 1989; and the essays in J. Dixon Hunt, ed., *The Pastoral Landscape,* Studies in the History of Art 36, Washington, D.C., 1992.

[67] For the paintings, which have not been studied in these interdisciplinary social, geographical, and economic contexts, see, within the vast literature on painted landscapes, L. Salerno, *Pittori di Paesaggio del Seicento a Roma: Landscape Painters of the Seventeenth Century in Rome,* 3 vols., Rome, 1977–78; G. Briganti, L. Trezzani, and L. Laureati, *The Bamboccianti,* Rome, 1983; M. R. Lagerlöf, *Ideal Landscape: Annibale Carracci, Nicolas Poussin, and Claude Lorrain,* New Haven and London, 1990; and D. A. Levine and E. Mai, eds., *I. Bamboccianti: Niederländische Malerrebellen in Rom des Barock,* Milan, 1991. Primary studies of Claude's oeuvre include M. Röthlisberger, *Claude Lorrain: The Paintings,* 2 vols., New Haven, 1961; idem, *Claude Lorrain: The Drawings,* 2 vols., Berkeley and Los Angeles, 1968; M. Kitson, *Claude Lorrain: Liber Veritatis,* London, 1978; and H. D. Russell, *Claude Lorrain, 1600–1682,* exhibition catalogue, Washington, D.C., 1982.

suburban villa in Rome, exemplified by the Villas Montalto, Borghese, Ludovisi, and Pamphilj (Figs. 1, 9).

These kinds of approaches to the study of Italian gardens have been possible only due to the existence of new concurrent historical work on early modern Italian societies and economies.[68] From the mid-1980s to the present, Italian social and cultural history has effectively been reborn as a new field. This development has begun to affect the historiography of Italian gardens, and will surely be able to enrich the already strong foundations of the field.[69]

Meanwhile, in the late 1980s, a quite different contextual approach to Italian gardens, one that regarded the very materials out of which they were made, the plantings, was being studied at a very sophisticated level by both art historians and botanists.[70] The most significant work to result, across the field, has been the magisterial and seminal work by Claudia Lazzaro, *The Italian Renaissance Garden: From the Conventions of Planting, Design, and Ornament to the Grand Gardens of Sixteenth-Century Central Italy.* It is already a classic, and shall

[68] For example, I could not have developed my work on Claude Lorrain, villa gardens, and sheep farming in Rome without full structural understanding of topics studied by the likes of J. Delumeau, *Vie économique et sociale de Rome dans la seconde moitié du XVIe siècle*, 2 vols., Paris, 1957–59; J. Coste, "I casali della Campagna di Roma all'inizio del Seicento," *Archivio della Società Romana di Storia Patria* 92 (1969), 41–115; and J. Marino, *Pastoral Economics in the Kingdom of Naples,* Baltimore and London, 1988, to name very few. Nor could I have done without key studies of the Italian patriciates, such as W. Reinhard, "Ämterlaufbahn und Familienstatus: Der Aufstieg des Hauses Borghese, 1537–1621," *Quellen und Forschungen aus italienischen Archiven und Bibliotheken* 53 (1974), 328–427; idem, *Papstfinanzen und Nepotismus unter Paul V, 1605–1621: Studien und Quellen zur Struktur und zu quantitativen Angaben des päbstlichen Herrschaftsystems*, 2 vols., Stuttgart, 1974; idem, "Nepotismus: Der Funktionswandel einer papstgeschichtlichen Konstante," *Zeitschrift für Kirchengeschichte* 86 (1975), 145–85; H. Gross, *Rome in the Age of Enlightenment: The Post-Tridentine Syndrome and the Ancien Regime,* Cambridge and New York, 1990; L. Nussdorfer, "City Politics in Baroque Rome, 1623–1644," Ph.D. diss., Princeton University, 1984, and idem, *Civic Politics,* a work of fundamental importance for anyone writing on Roman Baroque society. For southern Italy and the study of Neapolitan and Sicilian villa gardens, one would find necessary, for example, T. Davies, *Famiglie feudali siciliane: Patrimoni redditi investimenti tra '500 e '600,* Caltanissetta and Rome, 1985; G. Delille, *Famille et propriété dans le royaume de Naples (XVe–XIXe siècle),* Rome and Paris, 1985; and T. Astarita, *The Continuity of Feudal Power: The Caracciolo di Brienza in Spanish Naples*, Cambridge and New York, 1992.

[69] J. S. Ackerman had indicated a direction such as this already in 1982: "An approach to architecture based on political, social, and economic history has emerged in the last fifteen years as the dominant critical-historical method in the study of Renaissance architecture in Venice and the Veneto. . . . The method has a wider application, and I believe it will in time become prominent in the criticism of architecture of all times and places for which documentation has survived." "The Geopolitics of Venetan Architecture in the Time of Titian," in *Titian: His World and His Legacy*, ed. D. Rosand, New York, 1982, 41; reprinted in Ackerman, *Distance Points.*

[70] Important work was being done at the time, and just preceding, on the history of botany in Italian gardens by Georgina Masson (d. 1982) and Lucia Tongiorgi Tomasi, for the full discussion and contexts of which see below. Also see the extraordinary volume—in terms of comprehensiveness and rich illustrations—in the exhibition catalogue of the Biblioteca Casanatense, Rome, *De arbore (Botanica, scienza, alimentazione, architettura, teatro, storia, legislazione, filosofia, simbologia, araldica, religione, letteratura, tecnologia degli alberi dalle opere manoscritte e a stampa della Biblioteca Casanatense),* Rome, 1991. The title of the 800-page tome does some justice to its contents, which can provide a major basis for the study of tree plantations in Italian gardens, complementary to Lazzaro's.

stand in the field for decades to come.[71] Lazzaro's intentions, for gardens of the period about 1450 to 1600, were "to establish a context for understanding gardens in the culture of the Renaissance . . . to clarify the most fundamental concept of a garden—the plant materials and how it was thought appropriate to organize and manipulate them" and, as well, to study "the principles of organizing plant materials, which are given expression in the subdivisions of a garden, the plants that define them, the disposition of trees, and the designs of flower beds." Her hypothesis is "that a new concept of a garden evolved some time in the second half of the fifteenth century."[72] Lazzaro's recognition, at a very broad level, that it was the organization of plantings that *most* defined Italian gardens as a conceptual category, and her demonstration of this historical fact with an exceedingly rich visual documentation, both historical representations and outstanding contemporary photography by Ralph Lieberman, advanced the field of study of Italian gardens to a new level.

Lazzaro's study tackles, as well, the philosophical and cultural categories of reference for Italian garden design, and her discussion is at a broad enough level that it can be applied to, or compared with, gardening in later centuries and in other countries.[73] Both at the physical level of the designs of the gardens and their natural-philosophical level, to use the term "natural philosophy," which early modern science was named, Lazzaro's work has broken new ground. Lazarro's third chapter, "Nature without Geometry: Vineyards, Parks and Gardens," although it deals with the Roman region above all, can be translated conceptually for use in studying other regions, providing categories in which to situate Italian gardens in all regions. *The Italian Renaissance Garden* also contributes, though it is explicitly not a social history, to the history of social uses of Italian gardens. For example, Lazzaro's definitions of the pleasure park, in contrast to the garden, which she delineates with Renaissance terms and ideas, has recently been and will continue to be a departure point for a social history of the Italian park, as is Coffin's study of the hunting park in *The Villa in the Life of Renaissance Rome.*[74] The welcome reception given Lazzaro's book among students

[71] See the review by E. B. MacDougall in the *Journal of the Society of Architectural Historians* 52, 1 (March 1993), 97–99. MacDougall understood well the uniqueness of Lazzaro's enterprise: "She starts with an enquiry, almost unique in the literature on Renaissance gardens, into plants and planting (chap. 2, 'The Planting Reconstructed')" (p. 98). Before 1990, I can think of few other treatments of plantings-in-design in major early modern European gardens, set specifically in design and cultural contexts, except for Kenneth Woodbridge's chap. 6, "The Vegetal Component," in *Princely Gardens: The Origins and Development of the French Formal Style,* New York, 1986, 97–118. Most studies, instead, deal with horticultural and botanical aspects in botanical gardens or as isolated components; for the bibliography on the subject, see Lazzaro, *The Italian Renaissance Garden,* 333–36.

[72] Lazzaro, *The Italian Renaissance Garden,* 1. Lazzaro put it directly, that she wanted "to bring the planting back into Italian gardens" (conversation with the author, Rome, 21 June 1997). She also observes that "the notions of ordering them [plants in Renaissance gardens] are instead what most differentiated this broad period from both earlier and later ones" (p. 2).

[73] This was begun 20 years ago in a much simpler way by Terry Comito, *The Idea of the Garden in the Renaissance,* New Brunswick, N.J., 1978, and has received more sophisticated treatment in several very recent essays in Hunt, ed., *The Italian Garden.* See in particular "Introduction: Making and Writing the Italian Garden" by Hunt and the essays by L. Battaglia Ricci and G. Leoni.

[74] See Lazzaro, *The Italian Renaissance Garden:* "The development from a *barco,* or hunting park, to what might be called a pleasure park I take to be a sixteenth-century phenomenon, with again distinctly new

and professionals in the graduate design schools of architecture and landscape architecture points to the high degree of usefulness of this kind of work—linked text and photographs, verbal and visual narratives about design components—for the world of professional landscape architects, who will be contributing ever more to the literature on Italian gardens in future.[75]

In the final third of this article I would like to place the recent historiography of Italian gardens in two comparative contexts, one interdisciplinary and the other international. First, it can be evaluated against the background of the remarkable and creative evolution of the field of early modern history in the 1970s and 1980s, because of the latter's potential usefulness for the historiography of Italian gardens and for the incipient effect it has had very recently and gradually on their study. Second, a comparative mention, even if very brief, of the recent historiographies of the French, English, and Italian gardens can illuminate the salient features of each.

Many, though by no means all, of the new forms of history writing that have become prominent in the last decades originated in France and in the work of French historians, such as Georges Duby, Emmanuel Le Roy Ladurie, François Furet, and Michel Vovelle, among the many who contributed to the making of what was called by the late 1970s "La Nouvelle Histoire" (The new history).[76] I stress the example set by this kind of history, because of its potential, barely if at all used so far, for the study of landscape architecture in general and Italian gardens in particular. This structural historical approach was the grandchild of the group of historians known as the "Annales" group, which emerged in the 1930s and was led by Lucien Febvre and Marc Bloch; later, Fernand Braudel would become one of the most well known exponents of this kind of history writing.[77] The work of the Annales group and their followers was interdisciplinary. In particular, geographical and anthropological structures were used as historical frameworks.[78] Frequently, landscape was a protagonist of their narratives, as in Bloch's *French Rural History* and Braudel's *The Mediterranean*.[79]

The interdisciplinary nature of the Annales enterprise allowed a new *histoire des mentalités* (a history of mental conceptions) to emerge, which could be applied to a large range of human activities, experiences, and environments. Categories, such as popular culture, gen-

---

notions of scale and design beginning somewhere between the end of the sixteenth and the early seventeenth centuries" (p. 3). My own studies of the Roman baroque villa parks rely on Lazzaro's definitions of the park.

[75] Although I have not taken a statistical survey of the reception-history of works like the one by Lazzaro, my own teaching and my sharing of teaching notes with other colleagues in design faculties at the University of Virginia, Cornell University, the University of Illinois at Urbana-Champaign, and elsewhere makes it very clear that Lazzaro writes about categories that are both apt and apprehensible for designers' interests.

[76] See, among the first publications, M. Vovelle et al., eds., *La nouvelle histoire,* Paris, 1979.

[77] F. Braudel, *The Mediterranean and the Mediterranean World in the Age of Philip II,* 2 vols., London, 1972.

[78] Many studies of the Annales group have been made. See, among others, P. Burke, *The French Historical Revolution: The "Annales" School, 1929–89,* London, 1990; and *Marc Bloch, Lucien Febvre et les Annales d'histoire economique et sociale: correspondence,* vol. 1: *1928–1933,* annot. B. Müller, Paris, 1994.

[79] M. Bloch, *Les caractères originaux de l'histoire rurale francaise,* Paris, 1931.

der, public and private spheres, childhood, the family, death, physical gestures, the body, the gaze, and the vernacular, to name but a few, entered the domain of serious and academic history writing.[80] As Peter Burke, a historian who has devoted considerable work to analysis of the Annales and of the discipline of history in the twentieth century, has noted recently, the writing of history has moved "towards a more anthropological definition of the field," and has come "to include virtually every human activity."[81] The value of these approaches was recognized by relatively few architectural historians until the last decade, and when it was recognized, it was mostly by those who studied France in the Old Regime, such as Anthony Vidler.[82] The importance of these approaches for the history of landscape architecture, which as an interdisciplinary enterprise has analogies with the multivalent structure of human life, has begun to be understood recently.[83]

During the 1980s, when the new French approaches were being exported to England and America,[84] a parallel historiographical phenomenon called *microstoria* developed in Italy, and it continues today. Among its most well-known exponents are Carlo Ginzburg, author of *The Cheese and the Worms,* and Giovanni Levi.[85] Using anthropological approaches similar to those of Clifford Geertz, historians of *microstoria* have explored the larger ramifications of the ordinary structures of society in early modern Italy.[86] Peter Burke has taken up several implications of this approach in *The Historical Anthropology of Early Modern Italy* in the course of studying the meanings of gestures, speech, dress, and rituals. Although such a development has not yet taken place in the historiography of Italian gardens, it is to this type of work and to the extensive foundations that it has laid that the current and next generations of scholars of Italian gardens will be looking.

[80] As this article was going to press, the author read the excellent essay by D. R. Wright, "Some Medici Gardens of the Florentine Renaissance: An Essay in Post-Aesthetic Interpretation," in *The Italian Garden*, ed. Hunt, 34–59, and could only conclude that Wright's study of the "conventions of utilisation and functional requirements in relation to physical infrastructure" (p. 35) in the Medici Renaissance gardens leads the field forward into the study of gestural and bodily movements in Italian gardens, hence, an application *à la lettre* of Peter Burke's anthropological type of history of gestures, of hygiene, etc., for which see note 81.

[81] P. Burke, *New Perspectives on History,* London and New York, 1990.

[82] A. Vidler, *The Writing of the Walls: Architectural Theory in the Late Enlightenment*, Princeton, 1987, 1–5; for example, p. 1, where the "radical revision" of traditional boundaries is discussed.

[83] For example, M. Beneš, "Teaching History in the School of Design," *GSD News* (Summer 1993), 25–26.

[84] In the process, they were further enriched, for example, in the Department of History at Princeton University, where the historians Natalie Zemon Davis and Richard Darnton taught graduate courses with the anthropologist Clifford Geertz, whose book, *The Interpretation of Cultures*, New York, 1973, had a profound impact on the discipline of history. Fruit of such exchanges between history and anthropology has been P. Burke's *The Historical Anthropology of Early Modern Italy: Essays on Perception and Communication*, Cambridge, 1987, in which see pp. 3–7.

[85] C. Ginzburg, *Il formaggio e i vermi,* Turin, 1975, and English trans., *The Cheese and the Worms*, London, 1981; and idem, "Microstoria: due o tre cose che so di lei," *Quaderni storici*, n.s. [anno 29] 86, 2 (August 1994), 510–39, in an issue titled *Costruire la parentela: Tre interventi sulla microstoria.* The issue includes discussions on the topic by Ginzburg, Edoardo Grendi, and Jacques Revel.

[86] Also see R. Agò, "Gli storici italiani e le fortune dell'antropologia: Il dibattito sulla storia sociale in Italia," in *Orientamenti Marxisti e studi antropologici*, ed. R. Agò et al., Milan, 1980, 223–29.

The study of Italian gardens has so far not been structurally affected by the developments described above. As well, unlike the recent historiography of the French garden, it has not been affected by the work of poststructuralist theorists and thinkers such as the psychoanalyst Jacques Lacan, the philosopher and historian Michel Foucault, the sociologist Pierre Bourdieu, and the critic and theorist of literature and culture Roland Barthes. One can fantasize at present, for example, about a Lacanian or Foucauldian interpretation of Italian gardens in terms of the ideologies of their visual representations, along the lines of Louis Marin's use of Lacan and Barthes in studying Versailles among the visual panegyrics of Louis XIV in *Portrait of the King*.[87] Or one can imagine the application of a sociology of garden spaces to the Italian situation, along the lines of Bourdieu's and his *équipe* of art historians' numerous articles in *Actes de la recherche en sciences sociales* over the years, especially during the 1970s and 1980s. After all, Bourdieu did deal with spatial qualities and architecture, as in his study of the architecture of the Kabyle house in North Africa.[88] The same could obtain for the analogical use of Foucault's theories of spatialization of power in studying the layout of Italian gardens. Or, what about a rigorous critique of Italian Renaissance gardens in terms of social distinction, modeled after Bourdieu's *La Distinction*.[89] Short of such histories, one must now ask the question: How has the historiography of Italian gardens been different, in the aspects raised above, from those of French or English gardens in the early modern period?

Perhaps the most useful way to understand how and why the historiography of Italian gardens has not engaged with the developments mentioned above (and, I stress to the reader, *only mentioned*) would be to develop an overview that points to the critical differences in the recent historiographies of the French, English, and Italian gardens. Such a comparative study, though much needed in garden history, is too large for the scope of this article. What follows is not at all an attempt to cover the separate historiographies of English and French gardens, and by no means should it be viewed as such. It is simply a footnote, necessarily very limited, to the larger historiography of these three areas.[90] How-

[87] L. Marin, *Le potrait du roi*, Paris, 1981; English trans., *Portrait of the King,* trans. M. Houle, Theory and History of Literature 57, Minneapolis, 1988.

[88] See P. Bourdieu in English translation, *Algeria 1960,* Cambridge, 1979, for the Kabyle house, also reprinted in P. Bourdieu, *The Logic of Practice,* Cambridge, 1990, 271–83.

[89] P. Bourdieu, *La Distinction,* Paris, 1980; English trans., *Distinction,* London, 1984. A good place to begin might be Bourdieu's *Les Règles de l'art*, Paris, 1992; English trans., *The Rules of Art: Genesis and Structure of the Literary Field,* Stanford, Calif., 1995. For scholars of Italian gardens simply to use the words "social distinction" and "expression of magnificence" when describing the gardens and their patrons does not constitute a structural analysis of social distinction per se; a proper knowledge of social history and theory must be deployed. An exception in the very recent literature, in its ability to translate the traditional iconographical approach of art history into issues of contemporary theory and materialist cultural history, is C. Lazzaro's "Animals as Cultural Signs: A Medici Menagerie in the Grotto at Castello," chap. 10 in *Reframing the Renaissance: Visual Culture in Europe and Latin America, 1450–1650*, ed. C Farago, New Haven and London, 1995, 197–227 and notes, 331–35. Here and there contemporary theories are aptly and discretely taken up, as Lazzaro refers to Mikhail Bakhtin's *Rabelais and His World*, trans. H. Iswolsky, Cambridge, Mass., 1968, 332 n. 25, and to Michel Foucault's *The Order of Things: An Archaeology of the Human Sciences,* New York, 1970, 333 n. 65.

[90] The following section would indeed appear very superficial in its coverage, if taken as a full historiographical coda, rather than a minor comparative note, to the larger body of this text.

ever, what emerges even from the following few examples of the English and French studies is the fact that, while English and French gardens came to be considered recently, in the last 10 to 15 years, also by those in fields *external* to the field of garden history and its parent field, art history, as well as by mainstream art historians, Italian gardens have been studied essentially from a viewpoint *internal* to garden history and art history. The Italian situation is just at the point of changing course, and I believe that we shall soon witness a development parallel to that which can be ascertained for England and France.

Let us begin by looking at the case of early modern French gardens, which are better known as "classic" French gardens or, with reference to the definition of these gardens as a type, "the French château garden" and "the French formal garden" of the sixteenth and seventeenth centuries.[91] Until about 1980, the historiography of French gardens was the domain of French art historians or else of the owners and milieux of the châteaux gardens themselves. The numerous works of the Marquis Ernest de Ganay are a case in point. This situation changed in 1981, when the literary critic and theorist Louis Marin published a study of the textual and visual structures of the imagery of Louis XIV, *Le portrait du roi*.

Marin's study of the royal presence in the self-representations of Louis XIV examined panegyric texts, the cartography of Paris, medals, and festivals, as well the château and gardens of Versailles.[92] His approach combined the intellectual legacies of French poststructuralist thinkers, including Foucault, Barthes, and Lacan. With this publication, Marin opened a new avenue for the study of French gardens, through the case of the gardens of Versailles, by doing something analogous to what both the history of *mentalités* and Foucault's work had done for the history of French architecture of the Old Regime, especially that of the eighteenth century, noted above in the case of Anthony Vidler. Vidler himself described this process in the following terms: "The history of ideas and the history of artistic styles have been subsumed under larger questions: the dissemination of knowledge, the distribution of power, and the representation of status ... architectural expression has been interpreted as part of a larger social discourse of signs."[93]

From 1981 until today, an extradisciplinary vein in French garden studies has continued, at first in relatively small proportion to the works produced by art historians. For example, the sociologist Michel Conan has become a specialist in French garden history

[91] For use of these terms, especially "the French formal garden," and the earlier literature, see E. B. MacDougall and F. H. Hazlehurst, eds., *The French Formal Garden*, Dumbarton Oaks Colloquium on the History of Landscape Architecture 3, Washington, D.C., 1974; Woodbridge, *Princely Gardens*, passim; and Scully, *Architecture*, 221–73 and 284–92 (chapters on Le Nôtre's gardens). In the most recent literature as well, written by a sociologist, the term "French formal garden" is maintained. See C. Mukerji, "Reading and Writing with Nature: A Materialist Approach to French Formal Gardens," in *Consumption and the World of Goods*, ed. J. Brewer and R. Porter, New York, 1993, 439–60; and idem, *Territorial Ambitions*, passim, e.g., 8, "French formal gardens as laboratories of power."

[92] Marin, *Le portrait du roi*, esp. 180–92.

[93] Vidler, *Writing of the Walls*, 1. A somewhat similar approach, which involves the recognition that gardens are part of a cultural and social framework larger than their own discipline, can be seen in the chapter "Perspective, Gardening, and Architectural Education," by A. Pérez-Gómez in his *Architecture and the Crisis of Modern Science*, Cambridge, Mass., 1983, chap. 5, 165–201.

and assumed the directorship of Studies in Landscape Architecture at Dumbarton Oaks in 1997; he has written on the seventeenth-century treatise of André Mollet, the meanings of Le Nôtre's Bosquet of the Labyrinth at Versailles, and since 1990, at least, on French and other vernacular gardens. The structure of French intellectual and academic life has long encouraged the interdisciplinary presence of philosophers, sociologists, and anthropologists who teach in the architecture and design departments of French universities. Inside France, Antoine Picon and Thierry Mariage, and outside France, Vincent J. Scully and Chandra Mukerji, have made their major contributions to the study of French gardens precisely from extra disciplinary viewpoints that consider technology, fortifications, and land uses.[94]

So far in Italian garden studies we do not find anything that is comparable to the fertile appropriation of the French garden as a subject by French social and cultural historians and theorists, who provide new insights into French gardens as part of social histories or histories of mental conceptions. Nor did the Italian historians of *microstoria* appropriate the subject of villa gardens or the social world of their patrons. The reason for this difference with the French scholarship may be that French gardens were so deeply tied to the historical issues of monarchy, royal imagery, and a unified national territory and state (since the seventeenth century), which have been at the core of early modern French historical studies.

Like that of French gardens, the historiography of English gardens has also been affected in recent decades by scholarship external to the amateur culture and the discipline of art history that together had initially produced it. Up to about 1980, it was mainly the purview of distinguished amateurs, gentlewomen and -men, scholars such as Amelia Amherst and Christopher Hussey and circles connected to *Country Life Magazine* and the National Trust in England. Thereafter, historians of literature and art changed the course of English garden history by drawing on approaches based in academic and professional museum training. Key among them have been John Dixon Hunt, Peter Willis, and Roy Strong.[95] However, the fertile tradition of English social and cultural history that had developed from the 1960s to the 1980s, in the work of E. P. Thompson, Keith Thomas, Lawrence Stone, and others, was not then being drawn on by the garden historians.[96] Neither was the meth-

[94] For Scully and Mukerji, see above, note 91. There are also the contribution of a philosopher, A. S. Weiss, *Mirrors of Infinity: The French Formal Garden and Seventeenth-Century Metaphysics,* New York, 1995, and the forthcoming doctoral dissertation of a historian, Elizabeth Hyde, on the cultural contexts of flowers in France. See her paper, "The Cultivation of a King, or the Flower Gardens of Louis XIV," given 28 February 1998, in the symposium "Tradition and Innovation in French Garden Art: Chapters of a New History," University of Pennsylvania.

[95] For the authors mentioned above, C. Hussey, *English Gardens and Landscapes, 1700–1750,* London, 1967; P. Willis, *Charles Bridgeman*, London, 1971; R. Strong, *The Renaissance Garden in England*, London, 1979; J. Dixon Hunt and P. Willis, *The Genius of the Place: The English Landscape Garden, 1620–1820,* New York, 1975; 2nd ed., 1988; Hunt, *Garden and Grove.*

[96] Relevant to garden history would be works such as K. Thomas, *Man and the Natural World: A History of the Modern Sensibility*, New York, 1983, used, however, by Lazzaro, *The Italian Renaissance Garden*; L. and J. C. Stone, *An Open Elite? England, 1540–1880,* Oxford, 1984; and M. Smuts, *Court Culture and the Origins of a Royalist Tradition in Early Stuart England,* Philadelphia, 1987. However, the situation has much changed in the

odologically groundbreaking study by Mark Girouard, *Life in the English Country House: A Social and Architectural History*,[97] which had no issue or impact in English garden studies for a decade and more after publication.

Meanwhile, also in the 1960s to the 1980s, the native English landscape and its rural life, which W. G. Hoskins had studied in a pioneering way in *The Making of the English Landscape* (1955) from the geographical and agricultural points of view, were taken up as subjects by literary critics and theorists, geographers, and art historians inspired by both those in criticism and geography. The seminal figure in this development was Raymond Williams, whose Marxist critiques of the sociology of culture and literature founded an approach that has had a vital lineage for the last two decades. Williams's study of the poetry of John Clare in *The Country and the City* (1973) was flanked by that of John Barrell in *The Idea of Landscape and the Sense of Place* (1972). Their followers and students branched off to study English landscape gardens and landscape painting in artistic and geographical forms. Most well known today are the studies of Humphry Repton's estate designs by the geographer Stephen Daniels and the interpretation of landscape painting by the art historian Ann Bermingham in *Landscape and Ideology: The English Rustic Tradition, 1740–1860*.[98]

As in the comparison with the historiography of French gardens, we see that for Italian gardens in the last 20 years there are no studies equivalent to the English ones. However, both the French and English cases can suggest a range of future directions for Italian garden studies. In particular, the approaches to the French gardens in terms of territorial structures and the approaches to the English gardens in terms of landowning and geography would be rich avenues to take up. An application of neo-Marxist critiques would be very fruitful, if rigorously done and with proper documentation. We need a Manfredo Tafuri for the Italian villas and gardens, and best would be the application of his methodologies in studying Renaissance architecture.[99] To do this kind of work, Emilio Sereni's

last years, and it is interesting to note that J. Dixon Hunt, editor of the *Journal of Garden History* (founded 1981), has had Sir Keith Thomas as a member of the journal's editorial board.

[97] M. Girouard, *Life in the English Country House: A Social and Architectural History*, New Haven and London, 1978. In his preface, Girouard stated of English country houses, "Most people know comparatively little about how they operated or what was expected of them when they were first built . . . about how families used the houses which architects and craftsmen built for them."

[98] For example, A. Bermingham, *Landscape and Ideology: The English Rustic Tradition*, Berkeley and Los Angeles, 1986, see esp. the introduction, 1–6, and chap. 1, "The State and Estate of Nature," 9–54; S. Daniels, "The Political Iconography of Woodland in Later Georgian England," in *The Iconography of Landscape: Essays on the Symbolic Representation, Design, and Use of Past Environments*, ed. D. Cosgrove and S. Daniels, Cambridge, 1988, 43–82; and idem, *Fields of Vision: Landscape Imagery and National Identity in England and the United States*, Princeton, 1993. Related to these social and geographical approaches, but also based in archaeology of the landscape, is the work of T. Williamson and L. Bellamy, *Property and Landscape: A Social History of Landownership and the English Countryside*, London, 1987, and recently T. Williamson, *Polite Landscapes: Gardens and Society in Eighteenth-Century England*, Baltimore, 1995.

[99] M. Tafuri's article on Roman Renaissance urbanism, a classic, would be a good model to use for Renaissance landscape architecture: " 'Roma instaurata': Strategie urbane e politiche pontificie nella Roma del primo Cinquecento," in *Raffaello Architetto*, ed. C. L. Frommel et al., Milan, 1984, 59–106. Further to this point, M. Tafuri, *Ricerca del Rinascimento: Principi, città, architetti*, Turin, 1992.

perspectives on the Italian agricultural landscape will need to be mined in detail. In general, the comparative, international approach to gardens is useful at the level of the gardens themselves, and it is interesting to note that cross-fertilization has taken place between English and Italian garden studies in a seminal book by John Dixon Hunt, *Garden and Grove,* which has become a classic.

In conclusion, I would like to ask: What are the perspectives one can have for the historiography of Italian gardens in the years to come? I would like to point out several significant ones, including those suggested by the latest studies to appear, and to discuss their implications.

First, the current generation of younger scholars is making increasing use of the rich foundation that the last two decades have produced for social and cultural histories of the Italian regions. A highly articulated social history of Italian gardens and landscapes will eventually result. A few refined models for the study of landscapes and societies already exist for other nations in which landscape was a major cultural focus in early modern Europe, and these could inspire research on Italy.

These models regard landscape painting in particular, of which a key example is Simon Schama's essay "Dutch Landscapes: Culture as Foreground." While art historians such as Josua Bruyn read "scriptural" messages in the paintings, the historian Schama takes a new approach in interpreting the revolutionary qualities that emerged in Dutch landscape painting in the 1620s.[100] Schama connects the patriotic and geographical meanings of land in Dutch landscapes with the historical moment of liberation of the Netherlands from Spanish rule and with the period of reclamation of thousands of acres of land from the sea.[101] This approach is analogous to that used by Scully, Mariage, and Mukerji for French gardens. We need more of the same for Italy. In fact, it is an index of the state of the field that in the most recent cultural study of landscapes—for example, the essays in *Landscape and Power* brought together by W. J. T. Mitchell, the editor of *Critical Inquiry,* who is best known for his work on textual iconography and ideology of images—Holland, England, and colonial territories are the subject, and Italy is absent.[102]

[100] S. Schama, "Dutch Landscapes: Culture as Foreground," in Peter C. Sutton, *Masters of Seventeenth-Century Dutch Landscape Painting*, exhibition catalogue, Boston, 1987, 64–83. Compare the essays by J. Bruyn, "Toward a Scriptural Reading of Seventeenth-Century Dutch Landscape Paintings," ibid., 84–103, and by Schama. For another example of Schama's cultural history of art, see his "Perishable Commodities: Dutch Still-life Paintings and the 'empire of things,'" in *Consumption and the World of Goods*, ed. J. Brewer and R. Porter, New York, 1993, 478–88. Schama, who in 1993 with this author projected the offering of a core undergraduate lecture course at Harvard University on the cultural construction of landscapes, has had a long-standing interest in the subject. Later, in 1994, Schama joined the faculty of History and History of Art and Archaeology at Columbia University, New York. See his recent *Landscape and Memory*, New York, 1995.

[101] Schama does not work alone in this field. Also see the essays in D. Freedberg and J. de Vries, eds., *Art in History, History in Art: Studies in Seventeenth-Century Dutch Culture,* Santa Monica, Calif., 1991. The co-editors of this splendid volume are an art historian and an economic historian of early modern Europe.

[102] There is as yet no synthetic cultural history of Italian landscape painting and representations. For Mitchell's works, see W. J. T. Mitchell, ed., *Landscape and Power,* Chicago, 1994. The volume is not about gardens, but can be methodologically useful for writing about them, and the essays concern landscape representations from the seventeenth century in Holland to nineteenth-century "territorial" photography. Mitchell

Within this first large framework of social and cultural history, there are subhistories that will need to be explored. Just one example is the relationship of vernacular culture to high art forms in the *longue durée,* a subject that has never been fully addressed for Italian gardens. But significant conceptual ground has already been broken by James S. Ackerman, writing on the architecture of Palladian villas, and by Claudia Lazzaro, who in "Rustic Country House to Refined Farmhouse" first studied the issue with respect to Italian farmhouses and their typological kin in the palace buildings of villas from the fifteenth to the nineteenth centuries.[103] A few years later, in *The Italian Renaissance Garden,* Lazzaro illuminated much about Renaissance conceptions of vernacular culture and fine art in garden plantings by her discussion of nature and culture, noting for example the long historical "transition from the concept of simples to that of ornamental plants."[104]

Second, disciplines external to traditional Italian garden history, such as geography, anthropology, and history of technology (e.g., surveying and farming instruments, hydrology, and astronomy) are likely to have an increasing impact. For example, the model work by Denis Cosgrove, *The Palladian Landscape: Geographical Change and Its Cultural Representations in Sixteenth-Century Italy,* structures the landscape conditions that are essential for any analysis of Veneto gardens.[105] We will likely see studies titled similarly to the chapter on perspective and French seventeenth-century gardens by Alberto Pérez-Gómez, "Perspective, Gardening, and Architectural Education," in his *Architecture and the Crisis of Modern Science.*[106]

Third, those contexts of gardens that are considered to be relevant today are more numerous than ever, and a new scholarly attention to them is in good part the result of

---

and the authors subscribe to the view that "landscapes can be deciphered as textual systems," and "ask not just what landscape 'is' or 'means' but what it *does,* how it works as a cultural practice" (p. 1).

[103] C. Lazzaro, "Rustic Country House to Refined Farmhouse: The Evolution and Migration of an Architectural Form," *Journal of the Society of Architectural Historians* 44, 4 (December 1985), 346–67. Ackerman succinctly summed up Lazzaro's contribution: "Claudia Lazzaro has demonstrated the widespread use of another villa type in Rome and Florence and their environs from the mid-sixteenth century on: a cubic block with a roof crowned by a smaller cube on a tripartite plan, as built by Vignola for the Villa Tusculana at [*sic:* Frascati] Tivoli, Villa Lante at Bagnaia, and the hunting lodge at Caprarola. She proposes that the design was typical of a class of rustic farmhouse, and that in the course of time some of these became villas and some villas reverted to their agricultural origins." *Distance Points*, 322.

[104] Lazzaro, *The Italian Renaissance Garden,* 13. She has also tracked a similar dialectic between high and low arts in the waters of the Villa Medici at Pratolino: "From the Rain to the Wash Water in the Medici Garden at Pratolino," in *Renaissance Studies in Honor of Craig Hugh Smyth,* ed. A. Morrogh, 2 vols., Florence, 1985, 2:317–26.

[105] Leicester and London, 1993. A decade of work precedes *The Palladian Landscape.* See D. Cosgrove, "The Myth and the Stones of Venice: The Historical Geography of a Symbolic Landscape," *Journal of Historical Geography* 8, 2 (1982), 145–69; idem, "Venice, the Veneto and Sixteenth-Century Landscape," in his *Social Formation and Symbolic Landscape,* Totowa, N.J., 1984, 102–41; idem, "Power and Place in the Venetian Territories," in *The Power of Place: Bringing Together Geographical and Sociological Imaginations*, ed. J. A. Agnew and J. S. Duncan, Boston and London, 1989, 104–23; and, among others, idem, "Mapping New Worlds: Culture and Cartography in Sixteenth-Century Venice," *Imago Mundi* 44 (1992), 1–25.

[106] Cambridge, Mass., 1983, chap. 5, 165–201.

massive archival campaigns, as well as of new methodologies. Archival work is more extensive than before (and supported by longer-term research fellowships at centers such as the Fondazione Benetton in Treviso, Harvard University's Villa I Tatti in Florence, the École française de Rome, the American Academy in Rome, etc.). It has unearthed inventories of everything in the gardens, from statuary and flower beds to grottoes, aviaries, and deer parks. All of these documents can be considered in both their diachronic and synchronic contexts.[107]

The interest in understanding Italian gardens in their multitude of relevant contexts is revealed by the recent monographic, yet multidimensional, approach taken by French and Italian teams of scholars in respect to single major sites.[108] In 1989–90 the Villa Medici in Rome and the Boboli gardens in Florence were the focus of an exhaustive and rich set of interpretations of all aspects of these gardens and their interrelationships with architecture, technology, hydrology, theater, patronage, and social uses, among other categories.[109] *La Villa Médicis* is a multivolume masterpiece of encyclopedic analysis of the villa's architecture, painted interiors, art collections, antiquities, and the gardens, from the latter's location on historical maps and their visual representations to typologies of garden fences, walls, avenues, and fountains. *Boboli 90,* authored by a very international team, reconstructed every aspect of the garden from its historical plantings to its cat population; the subtitle, *Atti del convegno internationale di studi per la salvaguardia e la valorizzazione del giardino,* draws attention to one of the driving forces that operated in both these documentary enterprises, for the Villa Medici as well as for Boboli, namely the interest in preservation and adaptation of the historical Italian garden for contemporary use. Architects and landscape architects were among the authors, notably Giorgio Galletti for the Boboli gardens.[110] Issues of preservation and modern uses of Italian gardens will continue to structure the historical research.

[107] Among other thoughts on the subject, see M. Koortbojian's review of E. Cropper et al., eds., *Documentary Culture,* in *Art History* 17, 1 (March 1994), 110: "What these examples allow us to recognize is that one and the same document may have a differing significance at different historical moments. Thus their substance must be grasped both synchronically and diachronically if we are to gauge their meaning with confidence." E. Cropper, G. Perini, and F. Solinas, eds., *Documentary Culture, Florence and Rome from Grand-Duke Ferdinand I to Pope Alexander VII: Papers from a Colloquium Held at the Villa Spelman, Florence, 1990,* Villa Spelman Colloquia 3, Bologna and Baltimore, 1992.

[108] This is a different approach from the kind of comprehensiveness used to understand Italian gardens of one region, such as Coffin's *Gardens and Gardening,* which however, is similar in dealing with all aspects of the Roman gardens, from horticulture to theater and classical statuary.

[109] *La Villa Médicis,* 5 vols., Rome, 1989–91. Of the projected five volumes, volumes 1–3 had appeared by 1991; volumes 4–5 are forthcoming. Vol. 1: B. Toulier, *Documentation et description*; vol. 2: G. Andres et al., *Études*; vol. 3: P. Morel, *Décors peints*; vol. 4: A. Cecchi and C. Gasparri, *Les collections du cardinal Ferdinand*; vol. 5: *Sources écrites et annexes,* which is the massive documentary appendix for all the preceding volumes. The comprehensive documentary approach to the gardens is exemplified in the article by Suzanne Butters, "Ferdinand et le jardin du Pincio," in vol. 2, *Études,* 350–411. For Boboli, see Acidini Luchinat and Garbero Zorzi, eds., *Boboli 90.*

[110] Also see another example of collaboration in research by a historian and a designer, C. Acidini Luchinat and G. Galletti, *Le ville e i giardini di castello e petraia a Firenze,* Pisa, 1992.

Fourth, individual components of garden making await richer study that will build on the major research of the previous generations of scholars. Primary among these components are the horticultural and botanical aspects and the technology and social uses of fountain art in Italian gardens. The pioneer for horticulture and botany was Georgina Masson in *Italian Gardens.* Her research of the 1950s to the 1970s was for a manuscript titled "Collectors and Connoisseurs of Renaissance and Baroque Garden Flowers"; its publication was cut short by her death in 1982. Masson's research was subsequently built upon by Paola Lanzaro, Elisabeth MacDougall, Claudia Lazzaro, and most recently Ada Segre.[111] Lucia Tongiorgi Tomasi of the University of Pisa separately has structured the field with a remarkable series of studies on Italian Renaissance botanical gardens and the floriculture of the Medici ducal court in Florence, in terms of both species and their painted representations.[112] It may not be a coincidence that the major scholars in this domain, from Masson, MacDougall, and Tongiorgi Tomasi to Lazzaro and Segre, have, like Jane Loudon and Gertrude Jekyll before them, been women.

This brings us to the issue of gender and Italian gardens. A fifth perspective on the study of the field will surely involve more work on women and men in the gardens and the landscapes that surround them (see figures in Figure 10). So far, the instances in which gender in Italian gardens has been addressed have been few, namely Lazzaro in respect to garden sculpture and Ackerman to male ecclesiastics as patrons of villas in Renaissance

[111] Masson, *Italian Gardens,* appendix, "Flowers Grown in Italian Gardens," 279–92, sowed the seeds for all subsequent research. Also see Masson, "Italian Flower Collectors' Gardens in Seventeenth-Century Italy," in *The Italian Garden,* ed. Coffin, 61–80. For her book "Collectors and Connoisseurs," Masson had been assembling archival materials and visual documents on European flower gardens. She had combed the Vatican Library, the Caetani and other family archives in Rome, and libraries from Brussels to Prague in search of original watercolors, prints, and documents. Her proposal for the book was ready in 1979, and she sent it that year to Victoria Newhouse of the Architectural History Foundation, Inc., where the manuscript was eagerly received, but her death unfortunately prevented completion. Masson's papers and research, for which (by request of the late Hubert Howard, head of the Fondazione Caetani) I made a hand-written catalogue in 1984, were bequeathed by her to the Archivio Caetani, Rome.

Recent studies include Lazzaro, *The Italian Renaissance Garden,* passim, and its appendix, "Common Trees and Plants in Italian Renaissance Gardens," 323–25; E. B. MacDougall, "A Cardinal's Bulb Garden," in *Fountains, Statues, and Flowers*; the many publications of L. Tongiorgi Tomasi; A. Segre, "Horticulture and the Emergence of the Flower Garden in Italy (1550–1660)," Ph.D. diss., York University, England, 1995; and A. Tagliolini and M. Azzi Visentini, eds., *Il giardino delle Esperidi: Gli agrumi nella storia, nella letteratura, e nell'arte,* Florence, 1996.

[112] See, among her other writings, L. Tongiorgi Tomasi, "L'immagine naturalistica a Firenze tra XVI e XVII secolo: Contributo al rapporto 'arte-natura' tra manierismo e prima età barocca," in *Immagini anatomiche e naturalistiche nei disegni degli Uffizi: Secc. XVI e XVII,* exhibition catalogue, ed. R. P. Ciardi and L. Tongiorgi Tomasi, Florence, 1980, 37–67. A comprehensive bibliography is in L. Tongiorgi Tomasi and F. Garbari, *Il giardiniere del Granduca: Storia e immagini del Codice Casabona,* Pisa, 1995. The large project, based at Windsor Castle, the Royal Library, to catalogue the drawings that belonged to the antiquarian Cassiano Dal Pozzo (1588–1657), including those of citrus fruits and plants, will publish its first volumes on citrus fruits in 1997. Preceding the Windsor publication, see D. Freedberg, "Cassiano Dal Pozzo's Drawings of Citrus Fruits," in *Il Museo Cartaceo di Cassiano dal Pozzo, Cassiano naturalista,* Quaderni puteani 1, Milan, 1989, 16–36; and idem, "From Hebrew and Gardens to Oranges and Lemons: Giovanni Battista Ferrari and Cassiano Dal Pozzo," in *Cassiano Dal Pozzo,* 37–72.

Rome and to gender in treatises on country life.[113] Such instances will multiply in the future, as the field of research on early modern Italian women, men, and gender issues is already wonderfully vast and is still growing rapidly.[114]

Erotic life in the garden, a related topic, has recently been surveyed by Michael Niedermeier in *Erotik in der Gartenkunst* for early modern European gardens.[115] As gardens were more private areas for erotic trysts, out of the earshot and eyesight of servants and others, than the more public spaces of palaces and houses, they were often used for both courtship and banished acts. The travel diary of the Marquis de Sade when in Rome in the late eighteenth century alludes to such activities in the Villa Medici, as do other such journals for other Italian gardens.[116] Perhaps a future investigation might involve judiciously applying the theories of Jürgen Habermas on public and private spheres to Italian garden spaces in the context of gender studies.

On a broader level for gender and Italian gardens, one can ask: How were gender and its social construction in early modern Italy relevant, or not, to the conceptualization, design, and uses of villa gardens? In Rome, for example, the papal court was historically unique in being a gendered court, in which ruler and courtiers were celibate male ecclesiastics. All the other Italian and European courts joined men and women together in shared court rituals, and, in fact, the presence of both sexes was essential to the very tradition of

[113] C. Lazzaro, "The Visual Language of Gender in Sixteenth-Century Garden Sculpture," in *Refiguring Woman: Perspectives on Gender and the Italian Renaissance,* ed. M. Miguel and J. Schiesari, Ithaca, N.Y., 1991, 71–113; Ackerman, review of Coffin, *Villa in the Life,* 242, for male celibacy and clerics as the main patrons of villas at the papal court in Rome; and J. S. Ackerman, *The Villa: Form and Ideology of Country Houses,* Princeton, 1990, for gender in Renaissance villa treatises and rural life.

[114] The kind of studies that the scholar can draw on from historical and art historical perspectives include, among others, the following for the Roman territory, as an example: G. Conti Odorisio, *Donna e società nel seicento: Lucrezia Marinelli e Arcangela Tarabotti,* Rome, 1979; R. Agò, "Maria Spada Veralli, la buona moglie," in *Barocco al Femminile,* ed. G. Calvi, Bari, 1992, 51–70; C. Valone, "Roman Matrons as Patrons: Various Views of the Cloister Wall," in *The Crannied Wall: Women, Religion, and the Arts in Early Modern Europe,* ed. C. A. Monson, Studies in Medieval and Early Modern Civilization, Ann Arbor, 1992, 49–72; and idem, "Women on the Quirinal Hill: Patronage in Rome, 1560–1630," *Art Bulletin* 76, 1 (March 1994), 129–46. For a recent view beyond the Roman region, see Geraldine A. Johnson and Sara F. Matthews Grieco, eds., *Picturing Women in Renaissance and Baroque Italy,* Cambridge and New York, 1997, with bibliography to date.

Not all scholars of gender in gardens and of early modern women are women; see, for example, the references in D. R. Coffin, *The English Garden: Meditation and Memorial,* Princeton, 1994, to the diaries of women to discuss their uses of the gardens for contemplation. This has also been noted by S. Bending, review of Coffin, *English Garden,* in *Journal of Garden History* 15, 3 (July–September 1995), 190–91: "Notably, many of the diaries he draws upon were written by women, and if landscape design has appeared in many histories as something made by and for men in this period, Coffin is one of the first writers to put women back into the garden. Most clearly in the seventeenth century, Coffin is able to show how women such as Anne Slingsby, Lady Anne Clifford, and Mary Rich, Countess of Warwick, made use of the garden as a site for meditation" (p. 190).

[115] M. Niedermeier, *Erotik in der Gartenkunst: Eine Kulturgeschichte der Liebesgarten,* Leipzig, 1995. For mention of this theme in Italian Renaissance gardens, see G. Masson, *Courtesans of the Italian Renaissance,* London, 1975. I thank Michel Conan for the latter reference.

[116] I am including a chapter on erotica in the garden in my *Landscape and Society,* where such diaries will be discussed.

court culture, which was based on the chivalrous couple of knight and lady (as indicated, for example, by the figures in Figures 5 and 6). Other questions beg research: How did the overlapping jurisdictions of the two worlds—the male celibate ecclesiastical one and the secular family one with both sexes—meet in the territory of the Roman villa and garden (Figs. 9, 10)? How does the Roman situation compare with that of the other Italian regions (Figs. 5, 6, 10)? Further research would then involve comparison of the answers to these questions with the situations of other international early modern cultures, such as England, France, the Netherlands, and the Ottoman Empire, to mention a few.

Sixth, interrelationships between the professional world of landscape architecture and the world of academic scholarship n Italian gardens have yielded new understanding of the processes of design and conceptualization of the gardens, and should be maintained.[117] Seventh, there will be a very strong contribution to the future scholarship on Italian gardens by Italians, both professional landscape architects and art historians. The new doctoral degree in art history (*dottorato di ricerca*) set up by the Italian government several years ago has stimulated a high degree of professionalization of that field in Italy. Italian garden history is becoming truly international. Eighth and last, interregional and international comparisons of early modern Italian gardens with French, English, Ottoman, Mughal, and other gardens should be pursued, as such comparative work reveals the deeper structures to which these garden designs make reference. In summation, I can state my belief that a very interesting and necessary future direction for studies of the Italian garden will grow from the kinds of social history and theoretical work that have been mentioned in the last third of this article. While several much overused current terms such as social and cultural "practices," borrowed from sociologists and critics, for example, Bourdieu, will surely be outdated for history writing within some years, when the fashion has changed, the strong intellectual legacy of their ideators will carry on and be the basis for future work. It will be interesting, too, to write a sociology of the field of historians of Italian gardens, as well of French and English ones. Who, in fact, will be the garden historians of the next generation?

I wish to thank Professor Francesca Santoro L'Hoir, fellow of the American Academy in Rome (1996–97), for reading a first draft. I am also very grateful to the institutions that have supported my research on Italian villa gardens over many years with precious grants: Studies in Landscape Architecture at Dumbarton Oaks, the American Association of University Women, American Academy in Rome, National Endowment for the Humanities, J. P. Getty Center for Art History and the Humanities, and most recently, the Graham Foundation for Advanced Studies in the Fine Arts. Their support has been simply invaluable.

[117] Several recent Ph.D. dissertations were written by scholars who also have either undergraduate or master's degrees in landscape architecture, for example, the late Donna Salzer (the villas of Galeazzo Alessi, Harvard University, 1992) and Dianne Harris (eighteenth-century Lombard villas, Berkeley, 1996); and the forthcoming dissertation by Joseph Disponzio at Columbia University on the theorist Morel and eighteenth-century French gardens.

Approaches (New and Old) to Garden History

John Dixon Hunt

I

Why do we need a history of gardens? One could simply borrow an answer from mountaineers who are asked why they climb Mount Everest: because it's there. We already have histories of luggage, furniture, clothes, and ice cream,[1] so we may surely allow ourselves the luxury of a history of gardens, since they have been and are so evidently *there*. But unlike at least Mount Everest, gardens exist as a direct result of human intention and deliberate manipulation of the organic and inorganic world. Moreover, unlike now luggage and ice cream, gardens constitute, in both their making and their consumption,[2] a significant and in many respects unique human action. And so they deserve their own history, every bit as much as religion, furniture, sport, and science.

But if that history is to yield insights that no other history does—a point to which the conclusion of this essay will return—its practitioners need to confront the assumptions, methods, and procedures they rely upon to write it. If we compare the history of landscape architecture to that of religion or science, examples of human activity that have acquired their own histories and historical methodologies[3]—let alone the more established histories of nations and institutions—we find that we do not always match their rigor, scope, and conceptual assumptions.[4]

[1] On luggage, see J. G. Links et al., *Bon Voyage: Designs for Travel*, New York, 1986, and the Brooklyn Museum's exhibition of handbags (purses) mounted in 1997; on furniture there is a large literature, but see items relevant to our concerns here, like Monique Eleb, *L'Invention de l'habitation moderne*, Paris, 1995, or Leora Auslander, *Taste and Power: Furnishing Modern France*, Berkeley and Los Angeles, 1997; on clothes, Emanuele Gallo, *Il valore sociale dell'abbigliamento*, Turin, 1914, and particularly Anne Hollander, *Seeing through Clothes*, New York, 1978; finally, Anne Cooper Funderburg, *Chocolate, Strawberry, and Vanilla: A History of American Ice Cream*, Bowling Green, Ohio, 1995.

[2] An awkward term, too contaminated by Marxism, but it will serve in the absence of another to indicate all human experiencing of gardens and other forms of landscape architecture.

[3] In the first, I would cite the fundamental work by Emile Durkheim, *The Elementary Forms of Religious Life*, 1915, reprinted New York, 1965, which incidentally provides a plausible model for exploring the role of the garden form as a site of special experience. (I am grateful to Michel Conan for urging this point upon me some years ago.) For an example of writings in the second, those by the late A. C. Crombie, notably *Augustine to Galileo: Mediaeval and Early Modern Science*, rev. ed., 2 vols., Cambridge, Mass., 1952, are equally exemplary.

[4] Students of our subject are often nervous about prosecuting their work rigorously. See the surely unconscious betrayal of this attitude in the British Garden History Society's *Newsletter* 49 (Spring 1997), 9, where "the serious garden historian" is identified as one who "wishes to explore a period *in some depth*" (emphasis added).

There is a cluster of significant reasons why this is so. The history of the garden has never been accorded its own status, sui generis, as a topic of study independent of those disciplines that have generally supplied its students. The modern term used to characterize the activity of making gardens and other designed landscapes—"landscape architecture," adopted by John Claudius Loudon in 1840[5]—gestures toward a dual or bifurcated activity that awkwardly draws its energies on the one hand from the older, more established and theoretically grounded discipline of architecture and on the other (given the derivation of the term "landscape")[6] from the fine art of painting. This is, however, to assume that modern landscape architecture is or needs anyway to be interested in its professional history, an assumption that it is not always possible to make.[7] Not surprisingly, therefore, serious approaches to the study of landscape architecture have come primarily from the historians of architecture and art. More recently, literary studies, geography, botanical history, sociology, anthropology, and cultural history—to name but a few disciplines—have each set its sights on the study of gardens.

Now this diversity, this interdisciplinarity of approach, is to be welcomed (and for reasons to be considered later). But in the academy especially it has been attended with the major disadvantage that every colonizing approach—whether from art history, literature, biohistory, geography, or sociology—tends to treat the garden as an interesting element, but usually a marginal element, of that discipline.[8] The politics of academe, including the pragmatics of establishing a career, do not readily encourage students to entertain gardens as the object of full-time study. As an object of historical study gardens therefore remain, with rare exceptions, on the margins of professional academic life and are therefore themselves perceived to be marginal.

Yet outside the academy gardens have never been this marginal. Think of how widely different cultural systems have invoked gardens in their sustaining narratives; how these

[5] For the title of his edition of *The Landscape Gardening and Landscape Architecture of the Late Humphry Repton*, London, 1840.

[6] I refer to its derivation from the Dutch *landschip*, signifying a painted representation of some territory. However, the involvement of painting as a model for especially landscape gardening, above all at the point when our current historiography was being determined, has also played its role in this dualistic labeling. See, for example, both William Shenstone's "I have used the word landscape gardener; because in pursuance to our present taste in gardening, every good painter of landscape appears to me the most proper designer" ("Unconnected Thoughts on Gardening," in *The Works in Verse and Prose, of William Shenstone, Esq.*, 2 vols., London, 1764, 2:129) and A. J. Downing's "Again and again has it been said, that Landscape Gardening and Painting are allied" (*A Treatise on the Theory and Practice of Landscape Gardening*, 4th ed., New York, 1850, 72).

[7] The role of history in professional schools of landscape architecture is, at best, an uneasy one. On the one hand, it appears to threaten the creative energies of practitioners, holding them prisoner to precedent (a fear that especially seizes insecure or less talented designers); on the other, when landscape architects do demonstrate a historical curiosity, their versions of the past have largely tended to sustain their own professional position.

[8] See, for instance, the wording used by David R. Coffin in introducing the studies that formed the first Dumbarton Oaks Colloquium publication: "The literary historian of pastoral poetry, the scholar of landscape painting, and the architectural historian concerned with the villa realize that the garden is essential *to their interests*." D. R. Coffin, ed., *The Italian Garden*, Washington, D.C., 1972, viii, emphasis added.

myths of garden creation and garden consumption have proliferated in human experience—they can be tracked so easily, though nobody has done it strenuously, through the arts of painting and poetry. So we need to argue more vigorously and rigorously for gardens as a central, essential expression of cultural and social life and therefore not a theme to be left to those who see them as peripheral, let alone charmingly peripheral, to some other activity.

It will be argued (correctly) that much work on gardens has come from outside the academy, from gardenists with the distinct advantage of not having had to defend their corner in academic life:[9] the pioneering work of Georgina Masson on Italian gardens or the still unduly neglected history of British gardens by Alicia Margaret Tyssen-Amherst would be good examples,[10] as would also the British Garden History Society and its publications. I personally would welcome this continuing extrainstitutional garden history more warmly if I felt that it proceeded by some larger vision of its subject and its future development. Such a principled projection of purpose in scholarly enquiry might arguably be sought from institutional resources; but sadly, the amateur seems to have been poorly served by the professional scholar in that regard. Whether by virtue of the *parti pris* of individual disciples or of the rebarbative effects of coterie jargon, *le patois du cénacle*, the professional example of such academic developments has pushed the amateur gardenist away, beyond useful contact with scholarly discourse.[11]

In this regard—the potential liaison or rapport between amateur and professional historians—we have to recognize that a significant segment of work in our field is produced through trade publishing in books and magazines. That is in itself an interesting aspect of the subject, the role of garden making in contemporary material culture. One consequence of the profusion of trade publishing is that the pragmatic nature of its products tends to distract from any concern with the conceptual, misleading even those who might otherwise be interested into confusing gardening with gardens. However, we need to bridge this divide. It is not enough within the academy for the biohistorian, say, to talk and even write with others like cultural historians;[12] what we need inside and outside the academy is an idea of the garden comprehensive enough to involve all elements of gardening, including the haptic, say, or the therapeutic role of making and caring for gardens within human culture.

[9] However, the *amateur* or *dilettante*, as the usage of those words implies, has lost much respect in a world of increased specialization. See Andrew Ballantyne, *Architecture, Landscape and Liberty: Richard Payne Knight and the Picturesque*, Cambridge, 1997, chap. 1.

[10] Masson's *Italian Gardens*, New York, 1961, is her central contribution; Tyssen-Amherst's *A History of Gardening in England* was published in London in 1895.

[11] The gardenist amateur often seems acutely dismayed and in fear of the professional scholar, as any survey of the publications of the British Garden History Society will serve to reveal. See, for example, the typical "trepidation" expressed by one of its reviewers in face of "books by American academics" (*Garden History* 24 [1996], 288). Whether this is simply an (understandable) insecurity that pervades any amateur activity, or something endemic to the study of gardens, is a question not to be addressed here.

[12] I'm not sure that Jack Goody's *The Culture of Flowers*, Cambridge, 1993, contributed much to, let alone drew significantly upon, garden history, but it was a brave attempt to initiate inquiry across disciplines.

The acknowledgment of a full range of human interests within garden history may be approached another way, through the kinds and levels of writing it elicits. James Elkins addressed this matter tentatively, even courteously, in the *Journal of Garden History* a few years back when he inquired why gardens were "mild soporifics" or why garden writing so often turns away from the analytical toward the sentimental, the heterogeneous (i.e., unfocused?), and the "conceptually scattered" or incoherent.[13] Elkins implied that the language of garden experience, inasmuch as it rarely seems in touch with (self-constituted) garden scholarship, nevertheless rehearsed a wider and more significant range of human concerns. In similar vein, Martin R. Dean, whose first novel was *Die verborgenen Garten* (Hidden gardens), has asked what functions a garden might have today beyond "a keep-fit trail or a dog toilet." His answer is one altogether liable to defeat due academic process: he writes that gardens provoke "an interest in things without obvious interest." His visits to Parisian gardens while writing that first novel discovered for him a pleasure

> in becoming aware of seeing and experiencing something without a specific purpose and which stimulated flashbacks of memory and a panoramic sequence of thoughts and associations. People out for a walk were transplanted from the main streets into other times and spaces—without violence and by a purely synaesthetic art of seduction. Gardens are much like the imaginary landscape of a metropolis. They link thoughts to preconscious conditions while you walk, and reflect actual thought processes on a pre-rational level in their tendency to grow densely and run wild at the wayside.[14]

This may recall the remarks by Louis Carrogis, called Carmontelle, in explanation of the scope and function of the experience of his Jardin de Monceau (Fig. 1): it was to be "un pays d'illusions" where the visitor would encounter "tous les temps & tous les lieux."[15] It is this aspect of the garden, a site (if you like) of virtual realities as well as real horticultural virtues, that authorizes the strain of "reverie" or "curious drifting" that Elkins and Dean are right to identify and other garden historians are slow to acknowledge.[16]

[13] James Elkins, "On the Conceptual Analysis of Gardens," *Journal of Garden History* 13 (1993), 189–98. An anxiety of excessive response has always lurked among gardenists. Compare Elkins's critique with Sir Henry Wotton's aside in *Elements of Architecture*, London, 1624, that he will not describe his experience of some "incomparable [Italian] garden" because that would be "poetical" (pp. 109–10).

[14] Martin R. Dean, "Nature as a Book—a Book as Nature," *Journal of Garden History* 17 (1997), 172–73.

[15] Carmontelle, *Jardin de Monceau*, Paris, 1779, 4. A translation of the passage reads in part: "If a picturesque garden can be made into a territory of illusions, why shouldn't we do it? Illusions provide only delight; if liberty guides them, let art direct them, and we'll never be far from nature. Nature varies according to climate; let us try through illusion to vary climates also, or rather to banish the memory of our own; let us carry into our gardens the scene-changes of the Opera; let us show, in a real situation, what the best painter might design as decor—all times and all places." For more on this passage, see my essay, "The Garden as Virtual Reality," in *Das künstliche Paradies: Gartenkunst im Spammungsfeld von Natur und Gesellschaft*, ed. Marcus Kohler (*Die Gartenkunst*, special issue, 1997).

[16] The phrases are Elkins's, "Conceptual Analysis," 189. His essay remains a refreshingly clear and sharp diagnosis of the nature of gardens and what writing about gardens might address, yet it is rarely invoked.

1. Jardin de Monceau

II

In part, I am lamenting that garden history, both amateur and professional in its different ways, proceeds with very little sense of what one might call its larger responsibilities. These are various. Some of them are responsibilities that pertain to any kind of history writing; and at some point we ought to situate our particular history writing within the larger inquiries into the discipline maintained over the past several decades, a consuming, not to say contentious, debate to which garden historians make virtually no reference.[17] But the more important topic for our purposes in this volume is to define the responsibilities of our history vis-à-vis its particular subject. It is the qualities endemic to gardens, their integrity and essence as objects of study, that must dictate the histories we write about them. This is where Elkins's and Dean's identification of the particular character of garden experience becomes important.

One responsibility that is incumbent upon any historian but often shirked by gardenists is to set their local work in context. There is currently, for example, a considerable activity of writing about and publishing on what is called the revival of formal gardening around 1900; every month it seems a new and potentially interesting garden designer is rescued from oblivion. Yet this new wine is poured into old-shaped bottles. We rarely explain these

[17] The literature on this is vast, exciting and contentious; those interested might begin (where I myself have started) with *A New Philosophy of History*, ed. Frank Ankersmit and Hans Kellner, London, 1995, with its bibliographical essay by one of the editors, and *Histories: French Constructions of the Past*, ed. Jacques Revel and Lynn Hunt, New York, 1995.

figures emerging from the shadows of the shrubbery in the light of either any narrative of garden making that might explain their significance over and beyond their mere presence on the scene, or any idea of the garden, to which they may or may not have contributed.[18]

In part this is a refusal to envisage clearly a *longue durée* of garden history. This brings me to a major aspect of my argument. We have not bothered to revise our narratives since the late eighteenth century. Astonishing as this claim must seem in a postmodernist world where every point of view is worth its weight in jargon, it is true that we continue to subsist as garden historians upon narrative assumptions and strategies set out by a group of historians with a very special interest—not to say bias—in constructing a narrative that privileges one particular kind of garden making.

As late as circa 1700, European gardening did not see any one mode of laying out grounds as superior to any other. Certain modes were undoubtedly preferred by given individuals, by given groups and societies, but such history as was offered at that time did not premise its narrative upon the triumph of one style over another. Above all, it did not pit "formal" against "informal"[19] and nation against nation—indeed, garden modes were often able to transcend European political rivalries with surprising ease. This is clear if we read carefully the remarks that Joseph Addison or Stephen Switzer published in praise of French garden art, and published at a moment when conventional garden history wants to argue that these two, among others, were setting up a British gardening in opposition to a continental one. What such a convention ignores is the chance to see André Le Nôtre, for example, as a far more complex figure, who clearly saw garden art as a means of representing (abstracting, epitomizing) nature through forms that could be regular and irregular; it is the latter mode that he invokes in his design for the Bosquet des Sources at the Trianon (Fig. 2). It is only our latter-day English histories that explain this proposal as "informal gardening,"[20] using such a gloss to show how even the great French master knew in his heart where all good design must lead—to the Elysian Fields of Stowe and the British heartlands of natural gardening. French histories have a contrary bias, as we shall see.

Le Nôtre left us no written theory by which to counter such analysis. But in England at the same period a devoted set of gardenists, among them John Evelyn and John Beale, collected written materials that reveal that they shared the (how shall we say?) tolerant, actually commonsensical, view of garden making: namely, that it required the adjudication of the different contributions of art and nature without seeing one or the other as inevitable or superior. As Evelyn put it in "Elysium Britannicum," "Art, though it contend with

[18] For instance, in publications like George C. Longest, *Genius in the Garden: Charles F. Gillette and Landscape Architecture in Virginia*, Richmond, Va., 1992, or Judith Tankard, *The Gardens of Ellen Biddle Shipman*, New York, 1992, their subjects might be made more interesting if we saw them presented within a different framework. Mac Griswold and Eleanor Weller, *The Golden Age of American Gardens*, New York, 1992, would be another instance of the recovery of garden materials without sufficient explanation of their historical, let alone historiographical, significance.

[19] It is an interesting question, too, whether the very need to provide historical accounts with sequential format, when it arose, did not force narratives into a teleological vein.

[20] See, for example, the entry on the Trianon in the *Oxford Companion to Gardens*, ed. Geoffrey Jellicoe et al., Oxford, 1986, 588, or Christopher Thacker, *The History of Gardens*, London, 1979, 157.

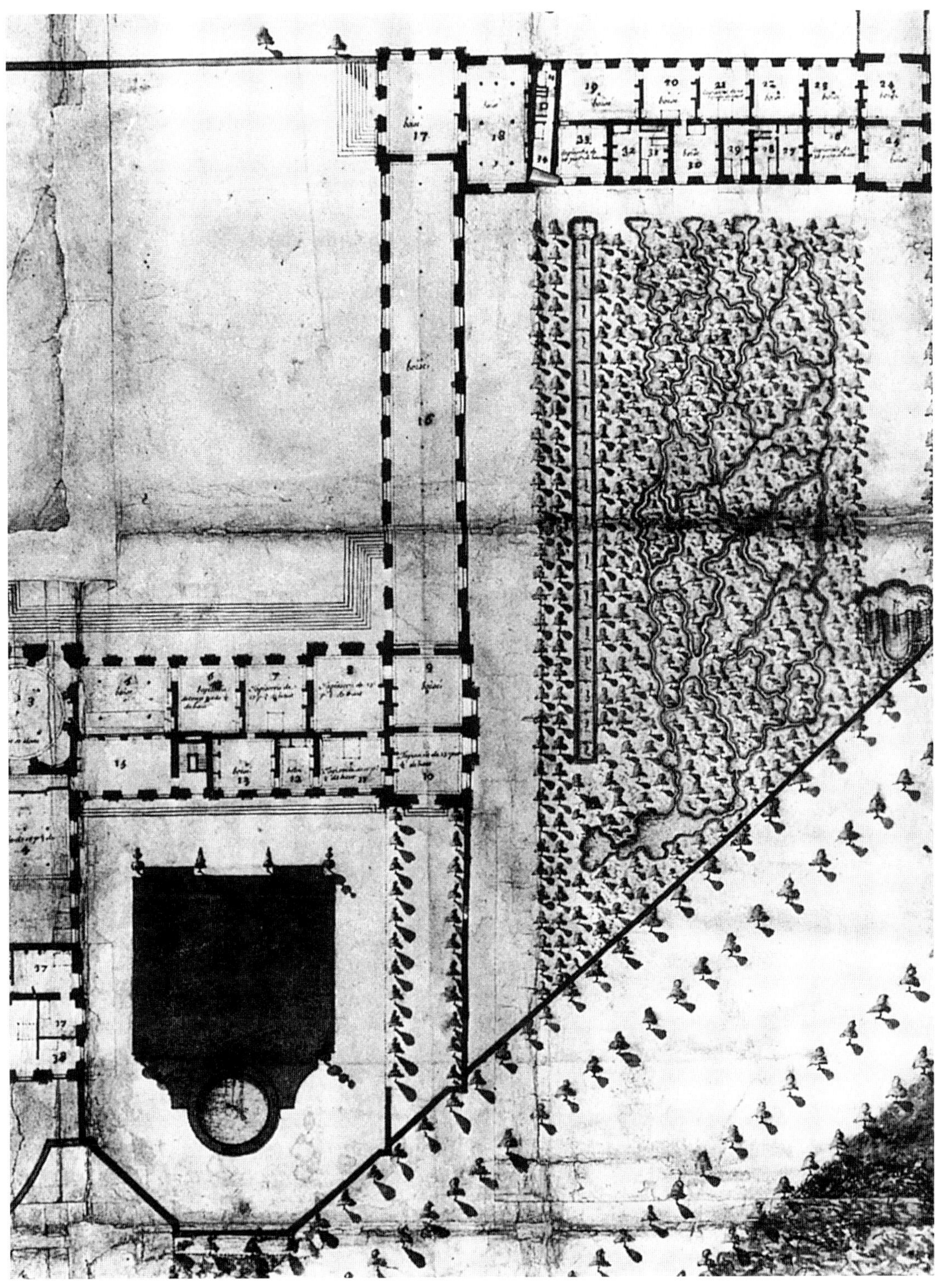

2. The Trianon de Marbre, Versailles, detail showing Le Nôtre's Bosquet des Sources. Engraving by Perelle, Bibliothèque Nationale (from Kenneth Woodbridge, Princely Gardens: The Origins and Development of the French Formal Style, *New York, 1986,* fig. 241)

Nature; yet might by no meanes justle it out"; Beale more particularly queried "in what points wee should disaffect the charges & cumber of Art, when the productions of Nature wilbe more proper."[21]

These perspectives had important historiographical consequences, but they would be lost to theory and practice (of both garden making and history writing) within a century. Those remarks by Evelyn or Beale are now simply read in the light of the succeeding and triumphant historiography that celebrates the English picturesque garden as the climax of design narrative and therefore wants to claim Beale as its champion *avant la lettre*.[22] Nobody seems to be in a hurry to object to such argumentation. Teleology rules okay![23]

During the early years of the eighteenth century, garden making and its historiography and theorizing continued to sustain this tolerant acceptance of different modes of garden making, even in the face of increasingly nationalist tendencies in England. But the end of both tolerance and common sense came by the 1760s with Horace Walpole and other exponents of the so-called English landscape garden, notably Thomas Whately.[24] From that point on, it became impossible to register the evenhandedness of remarks by Joseph Addison and Alexander Pope or the range of writings by Stephen Switzer as they addressed the different forms that garden layout might adopt. For Walpole, Whately, and their successors the "modern" garden had become at once "natural" and "British"; it was opposed to—and shown to have triumphed over—"foreign," "archaic," and "unnatural" or "artificial" styles. Since the main culprit here—for political as much as horticultural and architectural reasons—was France, this dreadful legacy was associated with the French. (The Dutch came in for strictures, too. However, since a Dutchman had been invited to the thrones of England and Scotland in 1688, it was not quite cricket to blame the Dutch as strongly as the French, so at least one early spokesman tried to limit the Dutch garden style to "town gardens.")[25]

Horace Walpole's *A History of the Modern Taste in Gardening* was particularly tendentious, resourceful, and, above all, horribly persuasive;[26] yet it also enshrined a fundamental contradiction. As Michael Leslie shows elsewhere in this volume, Walpole wished to claim

[21] John Evelyn, "Elysium Britannicum," fol. 117; Beale is from *Culture and Cultivation in Early Modern England*, ed. Michael Leslie and Timothy Raylor, Leicester, 1992, 229. I discuss these garden writers and practitioners, along with Switzer considered as their successor, in the "Historical Excursus" of my forthcoming volume, *The Greater Perfection: A Theory of Gardens*.

[22] See Peter Goodchild, " 'No phantasticall utopia, but a reall place': John Evelyn, John Beale and Backbury Hill, Herefordshire," *Garden History* 19 (1991), 106–27.

[23] But see Quentin Skinner, "Meaning and Understanding in the History of Ideas," *History and Theory* 8 (1969), 3–53.

[24] It would be interesting to examine more precisely why and how the English came to write a master narrative of gardening at this time—a provoking query that I owe to David Leatherbarrow. That a particularly nationalistic garden history coincided with the enlarged imperial (commercial and political) ambitions of Great Britain—including even such reversals or such challenges to its power and hegemony as the loss of the American colonies—points to one explanation. See, however, Michael Leslie's discussion of Walpole in this volume.

[25] See Stephen Switzer, *The Nobleman, Gentleman, and Gardener's Recreation*, London, 1715, xiii.

[26] The critical edition of Walpole's essay is *Horace Walpole, Gardenist: An Edition of Walpole's "The History of the Modern Taste in Gardening,"* ed. I. W. U. Chase, Princeton, N.J., 1943; but see also the Ursus Press edition,

that the English garden he championed had no historical rootedness and had been there all along, waiting for a William Kent and a Lancelot Brown. This position, however, is betrayed both by Walpole's teleological emphases—"more perfect perfection"—and by his otherwise shrewd point that all images of Eden are culturally produced, that is to say, historically rooted. His basic argument skillfully navigates between those contradictions. While foreigners, so his tale goes, had been misled since time immemorial into imposing themselves upon nature, the English had discovered the only true mode of gardening; since this constituted "more perfect perfection," it never needed to be altered ever again (a not unreasonable conclusion, if one accepts the logic of all the rest). Indeed, we could pass this ultimate sophistication on to those benighted French, Germans, Italians, and ex-colonials in America as England's supreme gift to the natural environment. Which is what we proceeded to do, with the active collaboration of those duped foreign nationals. Bemused and grateful, they in their turn started to write landscape histories as the narratives of how natural, modern, and "English" landscaping saved them from the old despotic geometrically designed gardens associated with the wicked French absolutism of the *ancien régime.*

It must have taken rare presence of mind as well as some political courage for anybody to challenge the hegemony of this progressive and naturalizing narrative of landscape architectural history, despite its proud anglocentrism. Yet from the late eighteenth century onward there were theorists ready and willing to challenge the prevailing historiography. In their different ways, Jean-Marie Morel and Alexandre-Louis Joseph de Laborde in France, C. C. L. Hirschfeld in northern Germany, Ercole Silva and others like Luigi Mabil in northern Italy, A. J. Downing somewhat later in North America—all tried to resist a narrative that (of course) left them and their own territories in the uncomfortable position of merely mimicking a style that the British had evolved and established once and for all, a style that had little relevance to their own social, geographical, and climatic conditions.

Interestingly, the theoretical writings of those figures have yet to receive anything like adequate discussion, though certain holders of Dumbarton Oaks fellowships have worked on Hirschfeld, Morel, and Downing over the last dozen years.[27] When Morel, Hirschfeld, Silva, and Downing do receive their wider due, Walpolean historiography will—hopefully—be rejected; we shall recognize how in their different ways these writers urged their readers to

---

with my introduction, New York, 1995. Walpole cannot, of course, be uniquely blamed for the teleology of his narrative. It was a topos of all cultural translation that new manifestations of old material would be better than the originals; add to this the whole notion of the "progress of the arts," and the Walpolean strategy cannot be singled out for blame. As concerns gardening, for example, John James dedicates his translation of D'Argenville's treatise to James Johnston by writing: "We may hope to see, ere long, our English Pleasure-Gardens in greater Perfection, than any the most renowned, in France, or Italy, since our Woods and Groves, our Grass and Gravel, which are the great subjects of this Work, are allowed to surpass in Verdure and natural Beauty, whatever is to be found in those Countries." *The Theory and Practice of Gardening . . .*, London, 1712, fol. A2r.

[27] Judith Major, *To Live in the New World: A. J. Downing and American Landscape Gardening*, Cambridge, Mass., 1997; Linda Parshall's work on Hirschfeld, including her translation and abridgment of his *Theörie der Gartenkunst*, forthcoming, with an introduction, in the Penn Studies in Landscape Architecture, and Joseph Disponzio's Columbia University Ph.D. diss. on Morel.

choose indifferently among modes of garden design and to use whichever were best suited to representing through the various forms of garden art the local or national culture and topography that gave landscaped sites their being.

This British historiography has not been the only one to generate bias, though it has been of international scope and is, arguably, the most conspicuously tendentious; its astonishing appeal to the historiographers of all European and American national garden cultures is what makes it worth remarking. But we could look, for instance, at a parallel conduct of history in France. Le Nôtre continues to be the acknowledged *maître*—and rightly so, he was a genius and a true artist of space. Yet the reluctance to accept alternative forms of design, even by Le Nôtre himself as at the Bosquet des Sources, has denied attention to what happened during the eighteenth century (let alone the nineteenth). In the early years of the twentieth century André Vera argued incessantly in print that the so-called picturesque garden style was no less than "an act of sabotage against the National Revolution."[28] The same spirit of reverence for the inherently geometric tradition of Le Nôtre presumably underlies the continuing failure to see the light of day of Ernest de Ganay's study of the so-called English or picturesque garden in France.[29] And witness the amusing strategies by which the French during the period de Ganay treats opted to deflect contributions to garden design from across the English Channel by calling them "anglois-chinois"—a signal of how early this French historiographical bias was initiated.

Yet despite the voices, like Hirschfeld's or Downing's, raised in explanation of how new territories had to reinvent garden making for their own cultural ends, the historiographical perspective that derived from Walpole remained virtually unchanged, with the French privileging of Le Nôtrean garden art sounding a minor and local counterpoint. The gravitational pull of the orthodoxy, coupled with and sustained by the almost stupefying acclaim of "naturalness" that ecological philosophies have also done much to endorse, infects all our popular narratives, often without their even being aware of bias. Thus the revival of so-called formal gardening around 1900 is accommodated, if at all, as an interlude, a footnote in garden history, an "unnatural" turn from which the Anglo-Saxon world has happily recovered. Or we fail to see that Prospect Park was just as contrived, just as factitious a mode of laying out grounds as Versailles had been; nor does it ever occur to any historian today that a restored wetland is every bit as constructed, is just as much a culturated value, as was topiary.[30]

The zeal with which the natural is celebrated as the be-all and end-all of landscape architectural evolution has distracted historical inquiries from tracking the relevance of

[28] See Dorothée Imbert, *The Modernist Garden in France*, New Haven, 1993, 53 n. 3.

[29] De Ganay's fully achieved two-volume manuscript lies, largely neglected, in the library of the Musée des Arts Decoratifs in Paris.

[30] This appears to be the thrust of a wonderful pamphlet in the collections at Dumbarton Oaks to which Michel Conan has drawn my attention. This anonymous *Lettre sur les jardins anglois*, Paris, 1775, wittily if subtly argues for the alterity of styles, though its final position (unclear through the nonchalance of its many ironies) may indeed simply reaffirm the Le Nôtrean position after all.

issues that were crucial to garden theory before the Walpolean hijacking. The most important of these are the idea of the garden as but one in a graded scale of natures, in its turn linked to the concept of representation in landscape architecture—not (if at all) mere mimesis, but rather the representation in garden forms of its society's whole "take" on the natural and cultural world around it.[31]

III

It remains to suggest where we should aim to go from here. This is obviously not the occasion on which to start writing an alternative history.[32] But what is possible is a series of guidelines or principles on which such a history—or histories (for I suspect that our pluralist and postmodernist age will require several)—will have to be constructed. They follow incrementally one from the other, and they grow out of this essay's arguments up to this point; each obviously requires an extended presentation, for which another occasion must be found.

1. Teleology is out, especially as a principle of judgment. Historians may explain Humphry Repton's design more clearly by seeing how he took over and responded to the earlier work of Capability Brown, and Brown himself may arguably be understood by how we see him in relation to his predecessor, William Kent; but we must not be fooled into the adjacent belief that what comes later or what is more natural is better. Teleology may have been in the air of the late eighteenth century, but it cannot be the oxygen that drives our analysis; indeed, Repton's return to new forms of regular layout, though extremely well documented of late, has not forced any reconfiguration of the narrative to include him and those who took up his ideas, J. C. Loudon and even A. J. Downing included. Indeed, the whole difficulty with the teleological bias of English historiography is what to do with the story that continues long after the supposed "end" except perhaps to map it as a battle of styles. At least the French can evade teleological narratives by seeing a *return* to geometrical designs during the nineteenth and twentieth centuries; but that in itself is insufficient.

2. Fresh narratives must stop pitting formal against informal, Le Nôtre against Brown, even gardens against ecology. These maneuvers are often unconscious, so let us get off automatic pilot.[33] Different garden styles are all modes of presenting, re-presenting, nature.

[31] I have written quite extensively recently on these themes and will not repeat those analyses here. See "Landscape, the Three Natures and Landscape Architecture," in *Artivisual Landscapes*, Amsterdam, 1992, 13–18; "Il giardino come territorio delle nature," in *Pensare il giardino*, ed. Paola Capone, Paola Lanzara, and Massimo Venturi Ferriolo, Milan, 1992, 35–39; and "The Idea of the Garden and the Three Natures," in *Zum Naturbegriff der Gegenwart*, ed. Joachim Wilke, 2 vols., Stuttgart-Bad Cannstatt, 1994, 1:305–25. These themes are recapitulated in my forthcoming book, *The Greater Perfection: A Theory of Gardens*.

[32] It gives pause to consider that the satiric summary of British history, *1066 and All That*, London, 1930, was written by authors R. J. Yeatman and W. C. Sellar, with Stephen Dowling as illustrator, who also produced an entertaining survey of our subject, *Garden Rubbish*, London, 1936. (I am indebted to the late Andrew Martindale for drawing my attention to this gem.)

[33] It is not as if we haven't been told this before. See, for instance, Henry Vincent Hubbard and Theodora Kimball, *An Introduction to the Study of Landscape Design*, New York, 1917, who wrote that "the two categories [formal, informal] have been the innocent cause of so much discussion and misapprehension" (pp. 33–34).

All design is "with nature," but all design is also "with culture"; indeed, sometimes the most "natural" theory or practice, as Raymond Williams and John Barrell among others have argued, has a cultural agenda or agendas at heart.[34] That the modes we lazily call "formal" and "informal" are the direct products of cultural contexts is not a big or surprising claim these days; however, it is one more honored in the breach of historical analysis than in the observance. All natures have been culturally constructed, and the garden historian must turn his/her attention to writing a history of those constructions particularly as they affect presentation and representation of landscape architecture.

3. It follows, too, that we must look sideways, not always dead ahead, in our narrative quest. We need to attend to smaller, non–"cutting edge" design, to other dynamics existing within a given culture: those between pleasure and profit,[35] those between vernacular gardens and those of various contemporary élites.[36] Just when we would expect the Walpolean party line to be paramount in England during the late eighteenth and early nineteenth century, the continuing vogue for geometrical gardens needs to be registered, as Tom Williamson has argued,[37] as well as the energies that were put into revising the parterre and wilderness into flower garden and shrubbery, as Mark Laird has also demonstrated.[38] But we should go further than both Williamson and Laird have been willing to do and ask what deep cultural needs this apparent refusal of the natural garden signified.

4. We must at one and the same time constitute garden history as independent of other histories and yet see its affinities with, particularly, social history and history of mentality.[39] For its independence, the garden must be acknowledged as "a site of contested meanings," as Craig Clunas puts it in his study of Chinese Ming gardening.[40] Yet if the garden is (Clunas again) "subject to the pull of a number of discursive fields," this in its turn requires what is loosely called interdisciplinarity, the ability to explore the various discourses drawn into the making and experiencing of gardens. In theory, such interdisciplinarity presup-

[34] Raymond Williams, *The Country and the City*, new ed., London, 1985; John Barrell, *The Dark Side of the Landscape*, Cambridge, 1980.

[35] See the useful work on this in Craig Clunas, *Fruitful Sites*, London, 1995, in particular 51 and 55.

[36] See the essay by Michel Conan in this volume, as well as his earlier argument in favor of the study of vernacular gardens, "The *Hortillonages*: Reflections on a Vanishing Gardeners' Culture," *The Vernacular Garden*, ed. John Dixon Hunt and Joachim Wolschke-Bulmahn, Washington, D.C., 1993, 19–46. See also, among other recent studies of this essential dimension of garden making, Gert Gröning and Joachim Wolschke-Bulmahn, *Studien zur Frankfurter Geschichte . . . Ein Jahrhundert Kleingartenkultur in Frankfurt am Main*, Frankfurt am Main, 1995; *Cent ans d'histoire des jardins ouvriers*, ed. Beatrice Cabedoce and Philippe Pierson, Grane, 1996; and Françoise Dubost, *Les jardins ordinaires*, Paris and Montréal, 1997 (first published in 1984 as *Côté Jardins*).

[37] In *Polite Landscapes*, Baltimore, Md., 1995, and, jointly with Anthea Taigel, in a special double issue of *Journal of Garden History* 11 (1991), 3–111.

[38] See M. Laird, *The Flowering of the English Garden: Ornamental Planting Design in English Pleasure Grounds, 1720–1800,* forthcoming in the Penn Studies in Landscape Architecture.

[39] See in this respect the arguments of Michel Conan at the conclusion of "The Conundrum of Le Nôtre's Labyrinthe," in *Garden History: Issues, Approaches, Methods*, ed. John Dixon Hunt, Washington, D.C., 1992, 145–50.

[40] Clunas, *Fruitful Sites*, 102 and (for the following phrase) 177.

poses a truly herculean familiarity with a wide range of materials and methodologies; in practice, it may require much more collaborative work. Historians, too, will need to take a wide trawl through materials with no obvious connection to gardening. This is partly because the materials and documents that will sustain garden history are not always the obvious ones (legal documents, for instance) and partly because in order to understand why gardens occupy such a privileged place in human discourse we need to understand all aspects of existence that might explain the garden's emergence, design, and use.

5. We need, above all, a history of the reception or consumption of gardens that acknowledges that they yield as much a dramatic as a discursive experience. There is a virtual dimension to the designed landscape: despite its palpable objectivity, it needs an addressee, as it were, to receive it—a spectator, visitor, or inhabitant, somebody to feel, to sense its existence and understand its qualities.[41] To use or to inhabit a landscape may be regarded as a response to its design, and to study such responses will bring us to a better understanding of design history. So we need to track how people have responded to sites in word and image. And especially since one of the essential features of a landscape architectural site is its fragility, its changefulness, even the unpredictability of natural elements notionally brought under the control of a designer, one way in which to capture this evanescent character is to plot the succeeding responses to it, or to understand by what different processes visitors of different kinds have accessed the garden experience under different conditions.[42] Further, this reception history will not be concerned, it will even be freed from the obligation, to ask whether a "reading" or experience of a garden is right or acceptable (this gets us out of the bind of reading our values into Le Nôtre or Brown); rather, we should seek to know how that reading process occurred and was conducted.[43]

6. To study the reception of or response to landscape architecture will, however, require more strenuous notions of exactly what is the object of that response or reception, in particular a better understanding of what a garden—the prototypical form of all landscape architecture—really is. How can we write adequate histories if we haven't seriously asked ourselves what on earth *is* the object of our narratives? Above all, historians must keep in mind that essential dialogue which gardens at their best always maintain between their palpable, physical existence and the fictive worlds into whose inventions, systems, and mytho-

[41] Paul Ricoeur calls this "reader, the protagonist forgotten by structuralism," in "Architecture and Narrative," *Identità differenze*, ed. P. Derossil, 19th Trienale di Milano, Milan, 1996, 71; the following sentence in the text is also adapted from Ricoeur's argument.

[42] I am thinking here especially of sites that were first private, then opened to public entry (Monceau, Stowe, Dumbarton Oaks). Reception study is not aimed, of course, at making the garden into a topos of the Berkeleian worldview: in other words, it doesn't exist only to be perceived; but it might probably exist best through perception. However, a reception study of gardens should allow, more than reception theory generally does, for the problematization of the phenomenalism of "reading" a site.

[43] Another way of explaining this strategy is to say that we should link a reception history to notions of semiosis (a term emphasized by C. S. Peirce), which shifts attention from the text of a semiotic message (such as a site) to the interpretative process whereby the listener or reader or viewer interprets it. See Michael O'Toole, *The Language of Displayed Art*, London, 1994, 215.

logical languages the garden visitor is seduced.[44] I realize that, if not inserting us in a vicious circle, this requirement does necessitate that we constantly adjust our ideas of the garden as we study further instances of its reception.

7. Finally, I return to the central claim made earlier. The garden is and has been a complex and central activity of humans, arguably a matrix of man's and woman's ambitions, instincts, and desires. The histories of it must therefore interrogate and narrate a cluster of concerns: how men and women represent themselves and their place in the world through the garden; what role the garden plays as a special site of beliefs, myths, fictions, illusions, and the melding of palpable (phenomena) with impalpable (noumena). The garden and by extension landscape architecture are key examples of what the French geographer Augustin Berque has designated *milieu* or, more precisely, *oecoumen,* places where human inhabitation marks and shapes the land for that purpose and where the earth is the condition that permits us to inhabit as humans.[45] Gardens can be considered a special case of this, because they focus the needs and the luxuries of that habitation in a concentrated mode. Even where the scale of such intervention becomes regional, it can be argued that the garden becomes a conceptual metaphor rather than, if at all, a formal design model.

The garden is unique among the arts in invoking living organic materials; it thereby offers historians the opportunity to track the role of both nature and culture, a prime dualism in the human condition itself that is mirrored by the gardens that men and women create (a unique activity among the animals). If I am right about this uniqueness of garden art and its place within the human conversation, then it will deliver—through the histories that we can write about it—a unique perspective. Garden history can and must tell us something that other histories don't. That's why we need it.

[44] I have studied this interaction somewhat more fully in my essay, "The Garden as Virtual Reality" (as above, note 15).

[45] These terms, art of *milieu* and *oecumen*, I have derived from the French geographer Augustin Berque. See his *Médiance: De milieux en paysages*, Montpellier, 1990, and *Être humains sur la terre*, Paris, 1996, respectively.

History and Historiography in the English Landscape Garden

Michael Leslie

I

"History in general," Horace Walpole said famously—sufficiently famously, at least, that he was content to cite himself repeatedly as a source—"is a Romance that is believed, and . . . Romance is a History that is not believed."[1] In considering the historiography of English gardens, and of the landscape garden in particular, we are inevitably taken back to Walpole and his little treatise, *The History of the Modern Taste in Gardening*.[2] The witty, epigrammatic statement that begins this paper should make us conscious that we are dealing with no naive, no ingenuous point of origin. Walpole would have had no difficulty in understanding the idea of the paradigm shift enunciated by Thomas S. Kuhn, the leading philosopher of the history of science, who asserts that that which passes for progress in science is less to do with the ultimate rightness of new ideas, and more to do with the way in which new stories of how the world works gain acceptance and displace old stories: to use Walpole's terms, how romances of science become accepted as histories, and how previously accepted histories become romances. As he composed his book, Walpole knew that he was in the powerful position of effectively initiating the historiography of what was already showing signs of becoming a peculiarly influential art form, not just in Britain but around the world. Because that art form looked likely to be so culturally pervasive, its first historiographers could aim to channel that burgeoning cultural authority in the service of their own cultural assumptions and imperatives.

My purpose in this paper is to stand back and look at this point of origination, to question what it was that Walpole was trying to achieve and what he very largely succeeded in achieving. For the sake of brevity, I include by implication only other influential members of Walpole's circle, particularly William Mason and Thomas Gray. My purpose is to ask what romance it was that they were hoping to induce us to believe and thus turn into history. What was the paradigm into which Walpole and his colleagues wanted to shift us?

[1] Letter to Robert Henry, 15 March 1783, *Correspondence of Horace Walpole*, vol . 10, ed. W. S. Lewis and Ralph S. Brown, Jr., New Haven, 1941, 173.

[2] All references to Walpole's text are to the edition by John Dixon Hunt, New York, 1995.

In trying to answer this question, I shall make three principal points. First, that the eighteenth century knew itself to be one of the great ages of historiography, and that, of all people, Horace Walpole was intensely conscious of this, given his personal contact with many of the great historians. This was a period that saw the publication of some of the preeminent monuments of history writing; but it also witnessed fascinating debates on the nature of history and fascinating expansions of the province of historiography. Walpole, again, was involved in all of these. Second, as well as the large philosophical debates on history, England witnessed a dirty, cutthroat struggle for possession of the historiographical field, and the chief protagonist was none other than Horace Walpole's father, Sir Robert, the first "prime minister." I shall argue that Horace Walpole's attitude toward historiography was heavily influenced by the historiographical battles of his youth, conducted in the period immediately before he began writing his *History*, and that his creation of the historiography of the English landscape garden was profoundly connected to them. I shall also argue that this connection was made in his mind because he recognized that the landscape gardens of the earlier eighteenth century were in fact not uncontroversial monuments to agreed virtues, but rather documents, polemical essays in the historiography of England, and that they themselves participated in those same battles for the control of historiography.

The focus of this paper is Walpole, but it is worth saying something briefly about the extraordinary conjunction of individuals and circumstances that contributed to the startling success of this occupation of the high ground of future historiography. Walpole was supremely well-connected, a figure whose impact on his culture is both maddening in its apparent dilettantism and virtually impossible to overrate. He was a political figure, one whose lifetime spanned the triumphs, disasters, and triumphs again of the new English empire;[3] who saw the frightening eruptions but also final disappearance of the challenge embodied in the heirs to the exiled Stuart dynasty to the constitutional settlement of 1688 (he was entering his thirties at the time of the Jacobite rebellion of 1745), only to live through the early years of the emergence of a very different threat in the form of the intellectual and popular democratic movements of the end of the eighteenth century and the French Revolution; and whose position and wealth depended on the survival of a particular sociopolitical system. Walpole's essay originally formed part of his larger work on the visual arts in England, *Anecdotes of Painting*, but the interpretation of his writings on landscape design must be integrated into an understanding not only of his other literary works, but also his wider and nonliterary activities, notably the creation of Strawberry Hill and the fostering of attitudes toward history, nation, and nationhood that that building participated in. Though brief and, in some important ways, incoherent, his *History* had immediate cultural access to the highest ranks, both during the period of its composition in manuscript from the early 1750s and once it was published in printed form to great interest and acclaim in 1780.[4]

[3] I call it "English" rather than "British" deliberately, to reflect the hegemony of England within the British Isles in all matters, political and cultural.

[4] It is a curious feature of the English discussions and histories of gardens that some of the most influential statements emerge only tentatively into the public realm, if at all. The prolonged gestation of

Walpole's friends, Thomas Gray and William Mason, came from more modest backgrounds, but both achieved remarkable influence. Gray's most famous poem, *Elegy in a Country Churchyard* (1751), is informed by many of Walpole's enthusiasms and fears; and that poem's immediate and lasting popularity, particularly in its illustrated form, promoted these concerns more widely.

Of the three, William Mason is a less well-known figure, and subject in our time to some ridicule. But *The English Garden*, his poem printed in 1771, anticipated the *History of the Modern Taste in Gardening* and was received with avidity by his contemporaries, and it clearly had an impact on the writing of other works on the history and interpretation of this art form. Mason exemplifies different features of the age from Walpole. He was not a man of high station or means, being from a minor middle-class family and raising himself through his professional exertions in the established Church of England. This in itself is significant. Mason achieved his authority as a member of the middle class: not an aristocrat, not even a member of the landed gentry, but one of the middling sort who for most of his life saw landscape gardening from the outside—in other words, not as someone engaged in the creation of landscapes himself, but as a visitor, an observer. Mason did eventually amass sufficient funds to create a modest estate for himself, and he certainly advised friends and patrons on the development of their estates. But the point remains valid: he is an outsider, an observer, even that currently fashionable term, a consumer. Mason's correspondence is eloquent of profound changes in English social life. His mobility is astounding: every year he embarked on peregrinations throughout the island, visiting friends and, more significantly, estates and gardens. Mason thus exemplifies two major features of the eighteenth century that are of crucial importance to the evolution of attitudes to landscape. First is the consolidation of a nonlanded class confronting the history of their country—one should really say creating the history of their country—and the history of their landscape, and devising ways of identifying with the tradition of garden and landscape making. Second, both essential to and dependent on the rapid economic development of Britain, is the change in the nature of communications: Mason is a tourist, one who visits but does not dwell. But while that implies a lack of proprietorship, there is a real sense in which the emergent middle class increasingly felt that it in some ways "owned" England as never before. Mason is also a political figure in two more traditional senses. Not only does his life unself-consciously exemplify the characteristics of this changing culture—he also engaged himself in political debate explicitly, not only through his involvement in the Yorkshire Association promoting parliamentary reform (the constitutional manifestation of that sense of "ownership") and in his contributions to attacks on the slave trade, but also in the ways in which his literary works address political topics (even if they are internally inconsistent, and occasionally incoherent). Mason's famous (but initially anonymous) *Heroic Epistle to Sir William Chambers* confirms, if confirmation were needed, that this group regarded the de-

---

Walpole's *History* resembles (but does not rival) John Evelyn's hestitation in completing and releasing his yet-unpublished "Elysium Britannicum."

signed landscape as a site for contests not only, maybe not even principally, over aesthetics, but over politics and the heart and soul of the nation. Walpole's correspondence is full of arch references to the quest for the authorship of Mason's satires on figures closely associated with the governments of George III; they betray both his delight in being thought the author himself, and his fear that should such an attribution become too widely held his political fortunes would suffer significant damage.

For the established political community of the aristocracy and the emerging political community of the middling sort, right reading of the landscape meant right reading of the past and vice versa. Walpole and his collaborators certainly recognized this. In a not-very-good sonnet, Mason descants on his homely garden path:

> Smooth, simple path! whose undulating line,
> With sidelong tufts of flowery fragrance crowned,
> "Plain, in its neatness," spans my garden ground;
> What, though two acres thy brief course confine,
> Yet sun and shade, and hill and dale are thine,
> And use with beauty here more surely found,
> Than where, to spread the picturesque around,
> Cart ruts and quarry holes their charms combine!
> Here, as thou leads't my step through lawn or grove,
> Liberal though limited, restrained though free,
> Fearless of dew, or dirt, or dust, I rove
> And own those comforts all derived from thee!
> Take then, smooth path, this tribute of my love,
> Thou emblem pure of legal liberty![5]

The last line, so lame in literary terms but so extraordinary in terms of the reading of garden paths, makes the point. But the key lies four lines earlier: Mason echoes that largely forgotten but hugely influential mid-seventeenth-century poem, Sir John Denham's *Coopers Hill.* Mason's "liberal though limited, restrained though free" is his homage with difference to Denham's paean to the Thames glimpsed in the English landscape, the emblem of true majesty and power:

> O could I flow like thee, and make thy stream
> My great example, as it is my theme!
> Though deep, yet clear, though gentle, yet not dull,
> Strong without rage, without ore-flowing full.[6]

[5] *The Oxford Book of Garden Verse,* ed. John Dixon Hunt, Oxford, 1993, 131.

[6] *Coopers Hill,* in *The Penguin Book of Renaissance Verse, 1509–1659,* selected with an introduction by David Norbrook, ed. Henry Woodhuysen, London, 1992, 158. The text of *Coopers Hill* is notoriously difficult to establish; see also Brendan O Hehir, *Expans'd Hieroglyphicks: A Critical Edition of Sir John Denham's "Coopers Hill,"* Berkeley, 1969.

"Liberal though limited, restrained though free"—Mason knew that Denham had read politics and history out of the landscape; he and his contemporaries read them and wrote them in designed landscapes and in landscape historiography. Richard Payne Knight, from the opposing camps in politics and landscape aesthetics, also looks back to Denham and imitates his use of the river and the topic of inundation, in *The Landscape*, his poem published in 1794, the year before Mason's sonnet, but certainly influenced by and in part modelled on Mason's *The English Garden*. Mason's deft appropriation of Denham, and Richard Payne Knight's of Denham and Mason, has all the sinewy self-awareness one would hope for in a modern spin doctor. Denham was deft and insidious, too, in his allusion to the simile of the uncontrolled river in the work of that master of political theory and rhetoric, Niccolò Machiavelli;[7] and it may be that Walpole, in an otherwise curious passage on "the inundation of luxuries,"[8] is consciously echoing this trope.

The analogy with spin doctors and the modern control of political interpretation is not random: both antiquarianism and the writing of landscape poetry were recognized as highly political from the sixteenth century on. Part of the urgency of the antiquarian movement came from the need to demonstrate the existence of an English history and culture separate from that of the Romans and the Roman Catholic Church, and the original Society of Antiquarians was formed by Matthew Parker, the archbishop of Canterbury, in 1572 while he was preparing his own work asserting the independence and antiquity of the new Anglican church. James I, fearful of the inconvenience of its constitutional researches, suppressed the Society, but in the period of the Civil Wars of the seventeenth century the leading antiquarians continued their work, believing that it contributed to the survival of an England threatened with destruction by the revolutionary forces. English identity and the English constitution were strongly contested concepts in the 1640s and again in the 1680s, and they were debated with vigor in the historical literature, as they were in the literature that took landscape for its theme.

The writers of the seventeenth and eighteenth centuries knew that it was the historiography, not the history, of English gardens that was their battleground. Their invention of English histories of landscape took place in a highly charged context of competing ideas and ideologies, in which the definition of the nation, the nation's origins, and an emerging national art form, clustered at the heart of a power struggle, ultimately less over the past than over the present and the future. In the *History of the Modern Taste in Gardening*, Walpole explicitly acknowledges that the definition of styles is a way of conditioning future developments, though he writes this with reference to Milton's descriptions of landscape in *Paradise Lost*, a poem more concerned to rewrite the past; but Walpole's correspondent George Hardinge immediately recognized that Walpole's praise of Milton applied at least as well to the author's own activities as a historian. He wrote on 10 November 1772, quoting (but also significantly adapting) Dryden's praise of Francis Bacon, in order to praise Walpole himself:

[7] *The Prince*, trans. George Bull, Harmondsworth, 1961, 130–31.

[8] Walpole, *History*, 24–25.

The world to Bacon doth not only owe
Its present knowledge, but the future too.

And Hardinge continues, "An idea which I have seen applied more happily to 'the prophetic eye of taste' in a certain little work just finished."[9] That phrase, "the prophetic eye of taste," is Walpole's praise of Milton; Hardinge here suggests that Walpole's History will itself condition the future of the landscape garden; and who can say he was wrong?

Walpole certainly recognized this polemic and hegemonic tendency in other contemporary historians, perhaps because he was so aware of it in himself. Abandoning discussion of politics on one occasion, he also asserts that he would not even believe contemporary historical accounts, saying that his contemporaries are "like Voltaire and David Hume [who] formed a story that would suit their opinions, and raise their characters as ingenious writers. For Voltaire with his *n'est-ce pas mieux comme cela?*, he avowed treating history like a wardrobe of ancient habits that he would cut and alter and turn into what dresses he pleased . . . "[10] Walpole's description of what he considered to be Voltaire's bad historiography is so close to being a description of his own architectural methods in the design of Strawberry Hill that one feels he must have recognized this as pertaining to his own practice in historiography as well.

II

Denham's *Coopers Hill*, a poem of political and philosophical reflections triggered by topography, is inconceivable without one of the developments in English historiography over the previous 150 years, the growth of English antiquarianism. English antiquarianism is very much a product of the Reformation and the seventeenth-century civil wars and the rapidly perceived danger of the loss of knowledge about England's past with the dissolution of the monasteries and other religious and civil institutions. Generations of heralds and scholars, William Camden and William Dugdale in particular, scurried furiously trying to acquire, record, and codify facts and artifacts from a disappearing past, and they did so in the way that heralds always had done: they chose a location, often defined by the valley of a major river, and traveled from its source to the sea recording everything historical that they encountered.[11] This method produced a profound sense of connection between the landscape and the nation's history, which was reflected in historiography, both national and local. Denham's poem is not historiography of the landscape, but it is an influential response to the growing desire—a particularly English desire—to "read" the landscape as the book not only of Nature or of God as in earlier times, but also as the book of history, the

[9] George Hardinge to Horace Walpole, 10 November 1772, *Correspondence*, vol. 35, ed. W. S. Lewis et al., New Haven, 1973, 569.

[10] Walpole to Lady Ossory, 8 December 1794, *Correspondence*, vol. 34, ed. W. S. Lewis et al., New Haven, 1965, 208–9.

[11] For a modern introduction to English antiquarianism, see Graham Parry, *The Trophies of Time: English Antiquarians of the Seventeenth Century*, Oxford, 1995.

nation's history. When the historiography of gardens, particularly the nationalistic historiography, came to be written a century later, the influence of the earlier example of the antiquarians and Denham's response to them is evident. Walpole and his associates are in some respects the tail end of the great antiquarian enterprise that had begun in England in the sixteenth century, the enterprise of Camden's *Britannia*, Dugdale's *Antiquities of Warwickshire*, and William Stukeley's *Abury and Stonehenge*, whereby the Englishness of the nation's history (in particular, political and religious) overwhelmed enthusiasm for a pan-European historical narrative that privileged the Roman and, still more unwelcome, the Roman Catholic. The antiquarians taught the presence of history within the landscape; Denham's poem is dependent on this heightened awareness of the legibility of the humanly designed and created environment.

Walpole was no stranger to the tradition of antiquarianism, and indeed his *History of the Modern Taste in Gardening* has an obvious connection with it, being appended as a coda to his edition of George Vertue's notebooks as the *Anecdotes of Painting*. The *Anecdotes* contains voluminous, well-documented scholarly information; it is a work of antiquarianism that has stood the test of time and, in its own way, conditioned English art historiography. But it is also profoundly unlike its coda, and Walpole cannot have been unconscious of the contrast.

This raises questions of the kinds of choices Walpole was making in composing his *History* of gardening. He was, as suggested at the outset, highly knowledgeable not just as a historian, but also as a student of historiography. Throughout his life, Walpole maintained a correspondence with other historians of various kinds, and this correspondence contains frequent commentary on the purposes of history writing and the different genres of historiography then available. One example must stand for many: his contact with one of the history writing titans of the Scottish Enlightenment, William Robertson. Robertson was a Presbyterian minister and principal of Edinburgh University for decades, as well as being Robert Adam's brother-in-law; he was the author of vivid histories of Scotland, of the emperor Charles V, famously of a history of America published with considerable acumen in 1777, and finally of the *Historical Disquisition concerning Ancient India* (1791). Walpole's correspondence with Robertson reveals his mastery of the current historical literature relating to a wide variety of subjects. On 30 May 1777 his compliments to Robertson on his recent volume include a confident *tour d'horizon*: "History has indeed arisen amongst us, while so many branches of literature have degenerated; and since your *America*, Mr. Gibbon's Roman history, and . . . [Robert Watson's] of Philip II have appeared within the space of eighteen months, the period must be allowed to be a shining one."[12]

His summary of modern French historiography that follows this comment shows how very self-deprecating he was when he claimed to have virtually no time to read. His often unflattering comments (including those on Robertson's work, in confidence to William Mason)[13] reveal not only his somewhat captious nature but also the sureness and

[12] Walpole to William Robertson, 30 May 1777, *Correspondence*, vol. 15, ed. W. S. Lewis et al., New Haven, 1951, 136.

[13] With which one compares his effusiveness to Robertson himself: "The chastity, the purity, the good

canniness of his judgement. He is skeptical of the philosophical histories of David Hume, on methodological grounds as well as on the grounds that Hume is a rather indolent historian with a cavalier attitude toward facts. Despite his sometimes derisive comments on Gibbon, there can be no doubt that Walpole understood the importance of the *Decline and Fall of the Roman Empire*. He distinguishes carefully and accurately among the different historiographical schools of his time, English, Scottish, and continental European, comparing them with past historiography, and he also distinguishes neatly between antiquaries and historians, giving more praise to the latter while obviously having a foot in both camps.[14] Throughout his correspondence and his own published works, Walpole reveals himself to be comprehensively abreast of both historiographical practice and contemporary debates concerning the nature of history.

Why then did he write this little volume as he did? At one point in the *History of the Modern Taste in Gardening* he asserts, "it is not my business to lay down rules for gardens, but to give a history of them."[15] The curiosity of this comment is that this is precisely what he did not do, as he himself seems eventually to acknowledge: "Though there have been only gleams of light and flashes of genius, rather than progressive improvements, or flourishing schools, the inequality and insufficience of the execution have flowed more from my own defects than from those of the subject." There are many things one could say about this extraordinary sentence, but what I want to stress here is its reflection on his historiographical method. The normal model for Enlightenment history writing is one that stresses a narrative, provides a sequence of causes and effects, a teleology; Walpole's own command of historical literature gave him plenty of examples. But he here acknowledges the essential discontinuity of his own account, his lack of interest in narrative; he acknowledges that he explains little, offering rather something much closer to a myth of origins with the intention of promoting an aesthetic rather than offering an account of its development. In this, and in his facetiousness about the possibility of determining the truth about the origin of things—what the more recent historian Marc Bloch called "the idol of origins," with similar distrust—his work resembles that of his close acquaintance, Jean-Jacques Rousseau. Rousseau, like Walpole, explicitly rejects the possibility of determining the origins of things, and Rousseau is entirely open, in his *Discourse on the Origin of Inequality* (1755), concerning his methods and the purposes of his myth: "Let us therefore begin by setting all the facts aside, for they do not affect the question. The Researches which can be undertaken concerning this Subject must not be taken for historical truths, but only for hypothetical and conditional reasonings better suited to clarify the Nature of things than to show their

---

sense and regularity of your manner, the unity you mention, and of which you are the greatest master, should not be led astray by the licentious frankness and (I hope honest) indignation of my way of thinking." Walpole to William Robertson, 4 March 1759, *Corrrespondence*, vol. 2, ed. W. S. Lewis and A. Doyle Wallace, New Haven, 1937, 204.

[14] "I have confessed to you that I am fond of local histories. It is the general execution of them that I condemn, and that I call *the worst kind of reading*." Walpole to William Cole, 13 March 1780, *Correspondence*, 2:204.

[15] Walpole, *History*, 51.

genuine origin, like those our Physicists make every day concerning the formation of the World."[16] Rousseau's object here is in part to release himself from the grip of scriptural authority that might constrict his scope for speculation and assertion, and Walpole does the same thing at the opening of the *History of the Modern Taste in Gardening*, with his less-than-reverential references to "the good man Noah" and the Garden of Eden. Discarding the scriptural references that had been *de rigueur* in virtually all garden history to his day, Walpole is, like Rousseau, able to emancipate himself from providential schemes of history, with their sequence of perfection, paradise lost, and the painful steps to its recovery or re-creation.[17] Nor are Walpole and Rousseau very interested in the normal Enlightenment narrative of humanity's upward progress. Both writers wittily, openly, and knowingly play games with historiography in order to achieve their aims. In fact, one needs to take seriously the nature of Walpole's title: "history of the modern taste in gardening." Whatever he may sometimes imply, this is not an overall history of gardening, not even of English gardening, but takes as its subject only "the modern taste in gardening." Walpole's gestures toward the standard narrative of origins onward are, like Rousseau's *Discourse on the Origin of Inequality*, acts of impersonation, designed to promote his aesthetic through the adoption and exploitation of a culturally favored rhetoric.

One might object that Walpole was writing a very different kind of work from that of the standard political historians, that the history of an art required a very different method. But he was writing at precisely the time when historiography had been fruitfully expanded to encompass this kind of topic. To use the example of William Robertson again, as well as the more standard works noted earlier, Robertson published, as a preface to his history of Charles V, his most remarkable work, the *View of the State of Society in the Middle Ages*. If Robertson and Hume in their principal works represented for Walpole the rationalizing political historiography of the Scottish Enlightenment, then Robertson's *View* offered him an example of an early form of sociological and cultural historiography, a history of manners, a combination of philosophy and history which, despite its shortcomings, remains impressive for its wide-ranging and open-minded attention to social, economic, and cultural phenomena. Robertson's example is significant, I think, not least because Walpole clearly understood his method.[18] Robertson wrote, "In pointing out and explaining these causes and events, it is not necessary to observe the order of time with a chronological accuracy; it is of more importance to keep in view their mutual connexion and dependence, and to show how the operation of one event or one cause prepared the way for another, and augmented its influence."[19] Walpole also appreciated the fineness of his per-

[16] *Discourse on the Origin of Inequality (Second Discourse)*, in *The Collected Writings of Rousseau*, vol. 3, ed. Roger D. Masters and Christopher Kelly, trans. Judith R. Bush et al., Hanover, N.H., 1992, 19.

[17] See John Prest, *The Garden of Eden: The Botanical Garden and the Re-creation of Paradise*, New Haven, 1981.

[18] On one occasion Walpole discloses to Robertson his hope of writing something in a similar vein: "There are two other subjects which I have sometimes had a mind to treat myself: though my very naming of one of them will tell you why *I* did not—it was *The History of Learning*." Walpole to William Robertson, 4 March 1759, *Correspondence*, 15:50.

[19] W. Robertson, *The History of the Reign of the Emperor Charles V*, vol. 1: *View of the State of Society in the Middle Ages*, London, 1769, 315.

ceptions, as did many others, including Voltaire, whose own histories and those of the authors of the French *Encyclopedié* stand as monuments of cultural historiography. Not for them the parochialism of J. R. Seely's epigram, "History is politics and politics is present history." Enlightenment writers took all human arts for their province, and felt that they could make histories and eloquent narratives from them all.

III

Why, then, in writing his history of the modern taste in gardening, did Horace Walpole avoid the models of Enlightenment historiography with which he was so familiar? There are several reasons, I think, but the one I want to emphasize is specific to English historiography and the evolution of the English landscape garden.

For Horace Walpole, and particularly in the matter of the taste in gardening, conflict over historiography had a specific resonance. He reached adulthood and the beginnings of his own political and scholarly career at just the moment when an already vigorous debate over historiography became truly explosive; and when his own father, Sir Robert Walpole, waged an intense campaign to control and manipulate the writing of history.[20] Ranged against the Walpole faction, which was entrenched in power, was the opposition, led in this respect by Henry St. John, Lord Bolingbroke. It was very much at the instigation of Bolingbroke, himself a philosopher of historiography, that this conflict took place, and it took place not least in garden art.

The principal point at issue was, not surprisingly, liberty, the subject later of Mason's garden path sonnet: liberty and its origins, and particularly the relationship between liberty and national history. The question of where liberty came from dominated attitudes toward the composition of histories in England for over a century. In the seventeenth century, those opposed to the Stuart monarchy and its desire to impose arbitrary government fostered a historiography designed to demonstrate that an Englishman's liberty did not derive from concessions by the monarch but from an ancient constitution, stretching back to the social and political organization of the Saxon tribes even before they invaded the islands. On the other side, before the Glorious Revolution of 1688, were historians who asserted the absolute powers of the monarchy, making it the donor of whatever liberties the subject enjoyed.

But the events of 1688 changed all that. Those previously opposed to the monarchy and its potentially excessive powers now installed their own kings, and they had secured much of the traditional power of the monarch and the state to themselves. There was a rapid reshuffling of positions, leaving the new Tory and Jacobite Opposition arguing *for* the

[20] In this discussion of the historiographical battles of the period of Sir Robert Walpole, I am much indebted to Isaac Kramnick, "Augustan Politics and English Historiography: The Debate on the English Past, 1730–1735," *History and Theory* 6 (1967), 33–56. Kramnick's interpretation has been criticized as overly accepting of Bolingbroke's self-presentation as the leader of the Opposition, in Alexander Pettit, *Illusory Consensus: Bolingbroke and the Polemical Response to Walpole, 1730–1737*, Newark, Del., 1997. See also, for the general cultural context, Christine Gerrard, *The Patriot Opposition to Walpole: Politics, Poetry, and National Myth, 1725–1742*, Oxford, 1994

Ancient Constitution, while its erstwhile supporters, and particularly the increasingly dominant Robert Walpole, now needed to assert that liberty had not existed in England at all until the old monarchy had been overthrown, and an entirely new constitutional dispensation had been invented by themselves, in a single, perfect action, owing nothing to earlier or foreign developments. Throughout the first four decades of Horace Walpole's life, a fierce contest for dominance in historiography was waged between these two camps, a battle for control of the past and its present and future meanings.

In the light of this debate, we can see that the earlier eighteenth-century gardens are not just places that contain passive memorials to historical figures and events. The greatest example must be that of the Temple of British Worthies in Lord Cobham's estate at Stowe. Here, the selection of historical figures to be memorialized—from the Saxon King Alfred from before the Norman Invasion, through the Elizabethan and Jacobean periods, to the Glorious Revolution of 1688 and contemporary England—does not merely celebrate individuals. Rather, it asserts historical continuity and progression from the origins of the English state to the present day, particularly in the fields of the Constitution and the establishment of English liberty. In other words, the sequence of national heroes asserts precisely that view of English history that Sir Robert Walpole's historiographers were determined to break.

The Temple was constructed in or around 1735. In that year, George Lyttleton's *Persian Letters* was published, and Lyttleton's fictional visitor to England makes the point, stressing the intensity of the debate over history going on at just this time: "Past Transactions are so variously related and with such a Mixture of Prejudice on both Sides, that it is as hard to know Truth from their Relations, as Religion from the Comments of the Divines."[21] The connection between Lyttleton and the Temple of British Worthies is well known: George Lyttleton was a member of the Temple family's cousinage, one of the "Boy Patriots," otherwise known as "Cobham's Cubs," and he is thought to have jointly written the inscriptions above the busts of the Temple. The Temple of British Worthies, then, is not just a monument, and not just history. It is a knowing intervention in historiography, self-conscious about the contested nature of its subject, and self-consciously writing into the historical narrative the pattern Cobham, Bolingbroke, and their friends wanted to see there, a physical structure and an intellectual pattern pitted diametrically against that championed by Horace Walpole's father. Stowe offers not just heroes but a paradigm for the interpretation of the past; it offers a pattern whereby not only history, but also the present and the future, are to be understood. The Elysian Fields at Stowe revivifies the dead metaphor of the physical patterns of history. The great landscape gardens of the earlier eighteenth century celebrated concepts such as liberty and piety, as has often been said. But they do so not as concepts floating outside time; rather, the gardens proposed and elaborated patterns of history at a time when such patterns were fiercely contested. They were thus, themselves, exercises in historiography. It was surely not just seeing the headless statue of his father presiding over the ruined Temple of Modern Virtue that led Horace Walpole to say that he

[21] *Letters from a Persian in England, to His Friend at Ispahan*, 2nd ed., London, 1735, no. 59, p. 179.

had "no patience at building or planting a satire," a comment he makes just as he is beginning to write his *History*; rather, the stance taken at Stowe and elsewhere on the crucial matter of historiography was one that he opposed and sought to suppress. Stowe's romance could not be permitted to become history.

The classic statement of the Oppositionist historical case appeared, we are not surprised to learn, at exactly the same time that the Temple of British Worthies was being built. On 5 July 1735, Bolingbroke's journal *The Craftsman* contained the following sentence: "From the earliest accounts of the time, our ancestors in Germany were a free people, and had a right to assent, or dissent to all laws; that right was exercised and preserved under the Saxon and Norman kings; even to our days; and may an uninterrupted exercise thereof, continue till time shall have no more." The Temple of Liberty (1744–48), now known as the Gothic Temple, drove home that Oppositionist historiographical assertion, that English liberty was not invented by the Glorious Revolution of 1688, as Robert Walpole needed to have believed in order to sustain his own power; but that English liberty had a long and distinguished history all the way back to the so-called Dark Ages and the societies of the Saxons, statues of whose gods originally surrounded the Temple, while the interior of the Temple was and is adorned with the entirely fictitious armorial bearings of Cobham's supposed Saxon ancestors. Anyone who knows the interior of Strawberry Hill will remember that there is a similarly placed armorial ceiling in the temple of the neo-Gothic; but there is nothing Saxon about it, the arms being those of the post-1066 kingdoms claimed by the Norman monarchs. The key temples at Stowe are knowing, deliberate interventions in historiography, created at the moment at which debate on the subject was most intense and central to the nation's idea of itself and to its political culture. This is especially true of the Gothic Temple, "a trumpet-call of Liberty, Enlightenment and the Constitution," which, as many visitors noted, stands proudly elevated over the estate, "domin[ant] presque sur tout le *Jardin*."[22]

IV

Horace Walpole approached the historiography of the English landscape garden with great knowledge of his culture's association of landscape and history; of the documentary historiography of the antiquarians; and of the dominant narrative styles and structures of the historians of the Enlightenment.[23] But he chose to follow none of these paths, I suspect because he feared that the patterns these historiographical models would impose would ultimately reveal weaknesses not only deep within the aesthetic, but also in political romances he was determined to promote.

Instead, under the guise of history he writes a kind of anti-history. It is highly important to Walpole that the English landscape garden should be seen as honored with antiquity

[22] J. De C., *Les charmes de Stow*, London, 1748, as reprinted in *Descriptions of Lord Cobham's Gardens at Stowe, 1700–1750*, ed. G. B. Clarke, Buckinghamshire Record Society 26 (1990), 171; see also John Martin Robinson, *Temples of Delight: Stowe Landscape Gardens*, Andover, 1990, 98–103.

[23] See Richard Quaintance, "Walpole's Whig Interpretation of Landscape History," *Studies in Eighteenth-Century Culture* 9 (1979), 285–300.

while possessing no inconvenient historical rootedness. In other words, he is determined to suggest that, like that other great English cultural icon, Shakespeare, the landscape garden should not be for an age, but for all time. Walpole will not, cannot, deny that the English landscape garden as he defines it has become the fashion only in his own lifetime; but he can read it out of, or into, all previous periods of English culture, as having lain there waiting for a William Kent and a "Capability" Brown to recognize. The aesthetic of the English landscape garden could not, for Walpole's purposes, be invented or discovered, for these verbs would fix it as a phenomenon bound by history; but if it patiently awaited repeated moments of recognition, for individuals and ages to perceive suddenly that all nature was a garden, then the correct hierarchy could be preserved: "We have discovered the point of perfection. We have given the true model of gardening to the world . . . original in its elegant simplicity."[24] Even though the history of English gardens reveals "such preposterous inconveniencies prevail[ing] from age to age, good sense in this country had perceived the want of something at once more grand and more natural."[25] Walpole's audacity here is breathtaking. He acknowledges that everything known "from age to age" disproves his case, only to assert that, despite all evidence, the undefined "good sense in this country" had always been conscious of "the true model of gardening."

The success of Walpole's dehistoricization can be seen in accounts of gardens, both real and imaginary, in the next couple of generations, and the best example is the famous response to the landscape at Donewell Abbey by the eponymous heroine of Emma. Walking through the pleasure grounds, Emma reaches a terminus:

> It led to nothing; nothing but a view at the end over a low stone wall with high pillars, which seemed intended, in their erection, to give the appearance of an approach to the house, which never had been there. Disputable, however, as might have been the taste of such a termination, it was in itself a charming walk, and the view which closed it extremely pretty.—The considerable slope, at nearly the foot of which the Abbey stood, gradually acquired a steeper form beyond its grounds; and at half a mile distant was a bank of considerable abruptness and grandeur, well clothed with wood;—and at the bottom of this bank, favourably placed and sheltered, rode the Abbey-Mill Farm, with meadows in front, and the river making a close and handsome curve around it.
>
> It was a sweet view—sweet to the eye and the mind. English verdure, English culture, English comfort, seen under a sun bright, without being oppressive.[26]

Passages such as this make one doubt whether one would have wished to have a prolongued conversation with Jane Austen, to have sat next to her at a dinner party to be filleted as neatly as the fish. That the whole topic of English landscape is political, openly acknowledged in that final word "oppressive," is present throughout the passage, and the construction of the gardens—with their denial of progress ("It led to nothing") and the

[24] Walpole, *History,* 55.

[25] Ibid., 28.

[26] Jane Austen, *The Novels of Jane Austen,* ed. R.W. Chapman, vol. 4: *Emma,* London, 1933, 361.

substitution of taste for substance—delicately and ruthlessly lays bare her society's, and her own, preference for a Walpolean reading of cultural geography. And yet the very names of the places—Abbey and Abbey-Mill Farm—cannot help but remind the reader of a history being suppressed, the history of the extortion of property from the Church at the time of the Reformation. The name of the owner, Mr. Knightly, might associate him with an unchanging ideal of chivalry, but his house equally constantly reminds us of his upward mobility. It is Done Well Abbey, in one of Jane Austen's deliberate and devastating lapses of taste, like those in one of her other great landscape descriptions, that of Sotherton in *Mansfield Park.* Austen writes Emma Woodhouse's response to her future husband's estate as that of a Walpolean; but she also reveals throughout that she knows that this is a comfortable fiction, controlling the present through historiography. Austen's conservatism and delight in the culture of the intelligent, benevolent country gentry are set against the knowledge that their apparent timelessness is illusory, that rather than really epitomizing an eternal "England," the assertion of such timelessness is a weapon in the struggle for control of a world undergoing profound and rapid change.

By asserting the ever presence of the aesthetic of the English landscape garden, Walpole can remove his ideal from the inconvenient associations of accounts based in time, process, and "progress." Rather than chart its evolution, he presents his ideal aesthetic as the result of a kind of parthenogenesis, sprung fully armed from the head of Nature, recognized fitfully and darkly throughout English history, and only clearly, face to face, in his own lifetime. By a bizarre coincidence, this strategy fitted exactly with the historiographical imperatives of his father's political party, which needed an ideal of liberty similarly free of the contamination of time, progress, and evolution. For Robert Walpole's party, liberty could not be created by slow and steady Saxon and English process; it had to exist perfect and whole from its beginning in the Big Bang of the Glorious Revolution of 1688. The fact that the Opposition to the Walpolean historiography of liberty was written powerfully in the earlier landscape gardens only made more urgent Horace Walpole's need to substitute his own ideal, and to control its future through his romance of the past.

There is an obvious paradox here: Walpole's version of the English landscape garden claimed that it had existed forever, that this aesthetic was one of the eternal verities; his father's historiography asserted for English liberty the very reverse, that it was utterly new. But the point lies in the concomitant claim that neither the (Horace) Walpolean aesthetic nor (Robert) Walpolean liberty was subject to development over time: both were absolutes, they were perfect as created, not subject to evolution. Neither could be traced back through earlier, less successful approaches, since to acknowledge evolution or connection would run the risk of acknowledging that all might be relative. Both Walpoles needed to assert that the excellence of the ideals they championed could not be exceeded. Horace Walpole shows himself conscious of the obvious challenges to his assertion when he satirizes the onward march of taste: "No succeeding generation in an opulent and luxurious country contents itself with the perfection established by its ancestors, more perfect perfection [being] still sought";[27] his solution is to take his own "point of perfection" out of history altogether.

[27] Ibid., 40–41.

Within the *History of the Modern Taste in Gardening* these ambitions produce other, local paradoxes. His garden historiography is an attempt to remove from the subject those things that we most frequently expect to find in histories: accounts of development and causal relationship. It is a strange history that asserts the irrelevance of time and process, yet in effect this is precisely what Walpole does. Tracing the way in which Horace Walpole persuades his readers of the rightness of his aesthetic can be frustrating. He achieves his aim, not by argument, logic, or demonstration, but by rhetorical means, principally by substituting at crucial moments his own writing persona for the key subject of his discussion, and then defying the reader to attack something as urbane, charming, and inconsequential as "Horace Walpole." But Walpole was no stranger to the deceptive strength of the insubstantial, as the wonderful illusions of Strawberry Hill's painted stone walls and papier-mâché fan vaulting make clear. These paper structures, the book and the house, are, however, only the physical vehicles of substantial, intensely directed mental power, with the strength of steel, and the steel belongs to a mind determined to seize control of the interpretation of the English garden, striking its blows under the cover of inconsequentiality. Viewing the extraordinary Gothicky confection of Strawberry Hill involved a complex interplay of responses, and these ensured that some of the more obvious grounds for adverse judgement were rejected. Just as one might draw oneself up to attack the affection for the neo-Gothic, or the highly selective and rather unscholarly forms of Gothic employed, just as one might move toward critical judgement . . . an awareness that this was all, literally, paper thin would reveal one's own rigor as a breach of good taste. Striking out at papier-mâché fan vaults is as offensive as breaking a butterfly upon a wheel.

Yet, just as those flimsy fan vaults were highly influential, so was the *History of the Modern Taste in Gardening*: Walpole's cultivation of a pose of stylistic inconsequence deflects attention from the penetrating and penetrative implications of his historiographical example. Walpole's contemporaries were well aware of the potential effects of historiography so elegantly written. Roger Schmidt sums up Dr. Johnson's strictures on certain strands of historiography in this way: "The polite historian's use of rhetoric . . . effaces the distinction between fiction and truth."[28] Walpole himself would change nothing in the phrase, but to replace the word "fiction" with "romance" and "truth" with "history." Suzanne Gearhart has seen this compromising of the generic boundaries as a characteristic of the age, titling her book on the works of the French Enlightenment *The Open Boundaries of History and Fiction*.[29]

The legacy to us as historians of the designed landscape has been profound. The linguistic phenomenon that is Walpole's little essay has in many ways delimited the way in which, to this day, English garden history is written. The landscape gardens of the later eighteenth century promoted by Walpole continue to be seen as in some way the apex of garden art, the fulfillment of the potential of English culture, not only in the artistic sense of

[28] Roger Schmidt, "Roger North's *Examen*: A Crisis in Historiography," *Eighteenth-Century Studies* 26 (1992), 74.

[29] Suzanne Gearhart, *The Open Boundaries of History and Fiction: A Critical Approach to the French Enlightenment*, Princeton, 1984.

the word, but in the wider sense of all English human activity (as in the quotation I used earlier from Jane Austen's Emma). And only that aesthetic is to be awarded the supreme accolade of being described as "English": the English landscape garden. Other periods in England produce Dutch gardens, or Anglo-Dutch, or French, or Italianate; or they are delimited by period or style: Renaissance, Mannerist, Victorian. But only this is described as "English," without a modifier defining its period. As the summit of human endeavor, the English landscape garden is also the closest that that endeavor can get to the perfection of creation itself, Walpole linking it to Milton's anglicization of Paradise, and thus Nature (untenable as this is, even within Britain, where the variety of landscapes is so extraordinary, let alone when nature's variety is considered more widely).

Even as we recognize the tendentiousness of the parameters set by Walpole and his contemporaries, we continue to work within them, often rewriting episodes but somehow failing to replace their master myth. But we need to recognize that Walpole's little essay is not the history of the ha! ha! Truly, it is ha! ha! historiography, designed to achieve the separation of one pristine idea, to prevent contact and contamination with a whole series of others, while concealing the fact that this has been done. And brilliantly successful it is. But it is time we emancipated ourselves from its magic, by leaping a different fence, and seeing that all historiography has a context.

Mughal Gardens: The Re-emergence of Comparative Possibilities and the Wavering of Practical Concern

James L. Wescoat Jr.

The history of Mughal gardens, a tradition that originated in Central Asia and extended into South Asia in the sixteenth through eighteenth centuries, faces intellectual and practical challenges that bear heavily upon its future, warrant a reappraisal of its past, and have relevance for other garden traditions as well (Figs. 1, 2). This paper identifies and addresses these challenges by setting Mughal garden history in a comparative context, first by assessing developments in related fields of Islamic garden studies, and second, by appraising the place of Mughal gardens in broader fields of historical and practical inquiry.

There has been more research on Mughal gardens in the past decade than in any other period of history. Numerous articles have appeared in journals of landscape architecture, geography, and art history, as well as South Asian and Islamic studies.[1] In 1996, the Smithsonian Mughal Gardens Project yielded two volumes published by Dumbarton Oaks and Ferozsons

[1] Catherine Asher, "Babur and the Timurid Char Bagh: Use and Meaning," *Environmental Design: Journal of the Islamic Environmental Design Research Centre* (1991), 46–55; Gauvin Bailey, "The Sweet-Smelling Notebook: An Unpublished Mughal Source on Garden Design," in *Gardens in the Time of the Great Muslim Empires: Theory and Design*, supplement to *Muqarnas* 7, ed. Attilio Petruccioli, Leiden, 1997, 129–39; James Dickie (Yaqub Zaki), "The Mughal Garden: Gateway to Paradise," *Muqarnas* 3 (1986), 128–37; Ebba Koch, "The Zahara Bagh (Bagh-i Jahanara) at Agra," *Environmental Design: Journal of the Environmental Design Research Centre* (1986), 30–37; idem, "The Mughal Waterfront Garden," in *Gardens in the Time of the Great Muslim Empires*, ed. Petruccioli, 140–60; idem, "Mughal Palace Gardens from Babur to Shah Jahan," *Muqarnas* 14 (1997), 143–65; *Marg* 26, 1, (special issue, *Landscape Architecture and Gardening of the Great Mughals*); Elizabeth B. Moynihan, "The Lotus Garden Palace of Zahir al-Din Muhammad Babur," *Muqarnas* 5 (1988), 134–52; Subhash Parihar, "Some Extinct Mughal Gardens in the Punjab and Haryana," *Islamic Culture* 58 (1984), 251–54; idem, "Hadironwala Bagh, Nakodar," *Oriental Art* 39 (1993), 39–46; idem, "A Little Known Garden in India: Aam Khas Bagh, Sirhind," *Oriental Art* 31 (1985/6), 421–32; Attilio Petruccioli, ed., *Il giardino islamico: Architettura, natura, paesaggio*, Milan, 1993; idem, *Gardens in the Time of the Great Muslim Empires*; Abdul Rehman, "Garden Types in Mughal Lahore according to Early-Seventeenth-Century Written and Visual Sources," in *Gardens in the Time of the Great Muslim Empires*, ed. Petruccioli, 161–72; D. Fairchild Ruggles, "Humayun's Tomb and Garden: Typologies and Visual Order," in *Gardens in the Time of the Great Muslim Empires*, ed. Petruccioli, 173–86; Philippa Vaughan, "The Mughal Garden at Hasan Abdal: A Unique Surviving Example of a 'Manzil' Bagh," *South Asia Research* 15 (1995), 241 ff.; James L. Wescoat Jr. and Joachim Wolschke-Bulmahn, "The Mughal Gardens of Lahore: History, Geography and Conservation Issues," *Die Gartenkunst* 6 (1994), 19–33; James L.

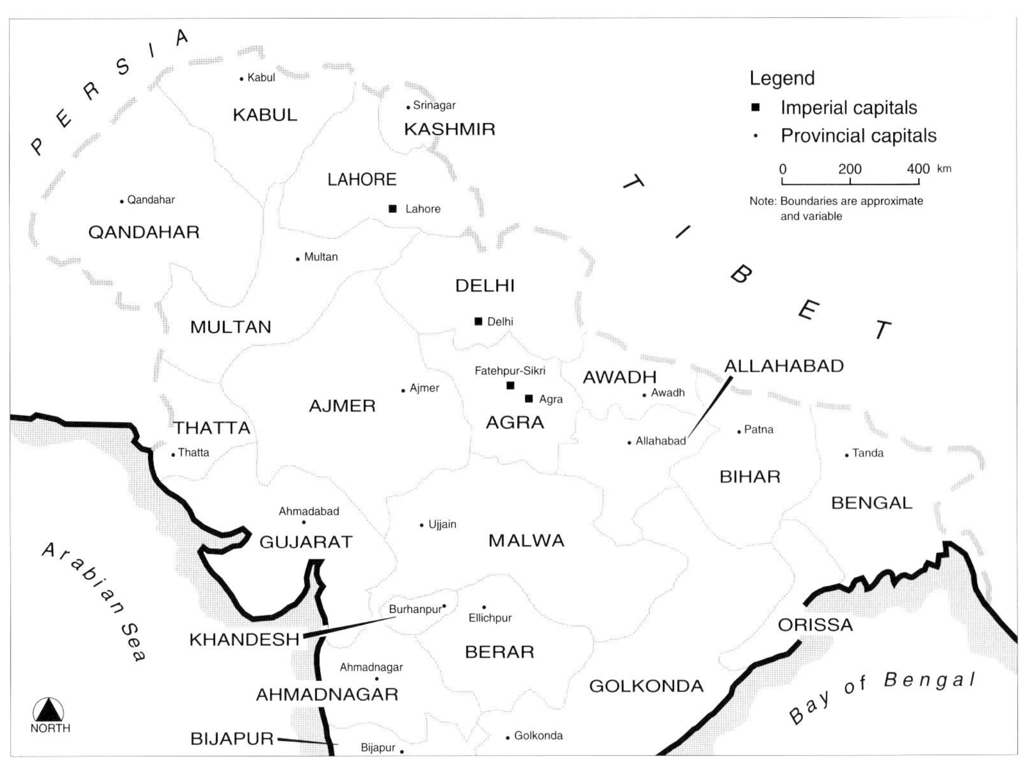

1. The Mughal Empire and its major provinces, ca. 1590

Publishers in Pakistan.[2] These works include historiographic perspectives that trace the field from Constance Mary Villiers-Stuart's *Gardens of the Great Mughals* (1913) to the Smithsonian Mughal Gardens Project.[3] Other essays examine the historiography of Mughal garden conservation and restoration, from the early surveys of Alexander Cunningham and

---

Wescoat Jr., "Mughal Gardens and Geographic Sciences, Then and Now," in *Gardens in the Time of the Great Muslim Empires*, ed. Petruccioli, 187–202; idem, "From the Gardens of the *Qur'an* to the Gardens of Lahore," *Landscape Research* 20 (1995), 19–29; idem, "The Scale(s) of Dynastic Representation: Monumental Tomb-Gardens in Mughal Lahore," *ECUMENE: Journal of Environment, Culture, and Meaning* 1 (1994), 324–48; idem, "Ritual Movement and Territoriality: A Study of Landscape Transformation during the Reign of Humayun," *Environmental Design: Journal of the Islamic Environmental Design Research Centre* (1993), 56–63; idem, "Gardens of Conquest and Transformation: Lessons from the Earliest Mughal Gardens in India," *Landscape Journal* 10, 2 (1991), 105–14; idem, "Gardens of Invention and Exile: The Precarious Context of Mughal Garden Design during the Reign of Humayun (1530–1556)," *Journal of Garden History* 10 (1990), 106–16; idem, "Picturing an Early Mughal Garden," *Asian Art* 2 (1989), 59–79; James L. Wescoat Jr., Michael Brand, and M. Naeem Mir, "The Shahdara Gardens of Lahore: Site Documentation and Spatial Analysis," *Pakistan Archaeology* 25 (1993), 333–66; and eidem, "Gardens, Roads, and Legendary Tunnels: The Underground Memory of Mughal Lahore," *Journal of Historical Geography* 17, 1 (1991), 1–17.

[2] Mahmood Hussain, Abdul Rehman, and James L. Wescoat Jr., eds., *The Mughal Garden: Interpretation, Conservation, Implications,* Lahore, 1996; James L. Wescoat Jr. and Joachim Wolschke-Bulmahn, eds., *Mughal Gardens: Sources, Places, Representations, and Prospects,* Washington, D.C., 1996.

[3] In addition to works already cited, benchmark studies include E. B. Havell, "Indian Gardens," *House and Gardens* 6 (1904), 213–20; Oscar Reuther, *Indische Palaste und Wohnhauser,* Berlin, 1925; Marie Luise Gothein,

2. *Waterworks on the middle terrace of Shalamar garden, Lahore, Pakistan*

Henry Cole to the current conservation projects by Indian and Pakistani archaeologists, architects, and landscape architects (Fig. 3).[4]

So it might reasonably be asked, what more can be said about the development of Mughal gardens research at present? Of course, compared with European garden research, there is enormous scope for additional research of every sort—archaeological, archival, interpretative—as well as for further commentary on earlier work. But cataloging those needs, and their relations to past research, is not the aim of this paper.

Instead, I want to show that as recent work on Mughal gardens was being completed, the situation changed in ways that warrant a reappraisal of the field. There was rapid devel-

Indische Garten, Munich, 1926; R. Jairazbhoy, "Early Garden-Palaces of the Great Mughals," *Oriental Art* 4 (1958), 68–75; Sylvia Crowe et al., *The Gardens of Mughal India*, London, 1972; Elizabeth B. Moynihan, *Paradise as a Garden in Persia and Mughal India*, New York, 1979; Saifur R. Dar, *Historical Gardens of Lahore*, Lahore, 1982; and Subhash Parihar, *Mughal Monuments in the Punjab and Haryana*, Delhi, 1985. Recent historiographic perspectives include James L. Wescoat Jr. and Joachim Wolschke-Bulmahn, "Sources, Places, Representations, Prospects: A Perspective of Mughal Gardens," 5–30, and Elizabeth B. Moynihan, "But What a Happiness to Have Known Babur," 95–126, both in *Mughal Gardens*, ed. Wescoat and Wolschke-Bulmahn; as well as James L. Wescoat Jr. , "The Mughal Gardens Project in Lahore," in *The Mughal Garden*, ed. Hussain, Rehman, and Wescoat, 9–22.

[4] Muhammad Yusuf Awan, "Conservation of Historic Buildings and Gardens in Lahore: Implications for a National Conservation Policy for Pakistan," 143 ff.; Michael Brand, "Surveying Shahdara," 123–29; Mahmood Hussain, "Conservation of Garden Sites and Urban Sprawl in Lahore," 165–72; Sajjad Kausar, "Shalamar Garden, Lahore," 133–42; and M. Rafique Mughal, "Theory and Practice in Garden Conservation," 111–14, all in *The Mughal Garden*, ed. Hussain, Rehman, and Wescoat.

Mughal Garden Research		Mughal Garden Conservation	
1995	Smithsonian Mughal Gardens Project, *Mughal Gardens* and *The Mughal Garden* Moynihan, "The Lotus Garden Palace" Parihar, *Mughal Monuments in Punjab*	1996	Mehtab Bagh, Agra; Kashmiri Gardens; Jahangir's Tomb-Garden, Lahore; Anjuman Mimaran, Pakistan
1980	Moynihan, *Paradise as a Garden*	1980	Pakistan Institute for Nuclear Science and Technology, "Leakage Investigation . . . Shalamar Garden, Lahore"
1970	Crowe et al., *The Gardens of Mughal India*	1970	International Council of Monuments and Sites Committee conference on Islamic gardens
1960	Jairazbhoy, "Early Garden-Palaces"	1960	
1950		1950	
			Independence of India and Pakistan leads to separate departments of archaeology
1940		1940	
1930		1930	
	Gothein, *Indische Garten* Reuther, *Indische Palaste*		
1920		1920	Marshall, *Conservation Manual*
1910	Villiers-Stuart, *Gardens of the Great Mughals*	1910	
1900	Havell, "Indian Gardens"	1900	
		1890	Archaeological Survey of India, *Annual Reports, Memoirs*
		1880	Cole, *Reports of the Curator of Ancient Monuments; Tomb of Jahangir*

3. Timeline of major writings on the history and conservation of Mughal gardens

opment of garden research in regions connected with the Mughal Empire, including Central Asia, Persia, Turkey, Egypt, Spain, and parts of Europe. Those works open up the prospect of regional comparison that could lead to new perspectives on Mughal gardens, that is, to a "re-emergence of comparative possibilities."[5] At the same time, there are growing concerns that these scholarly advances do not speak to the pressing problems of landscape conservation, experience, conflict, and design in South Asia today, hence the other half of my subtitle, "the wavering of practical concern." But first, highlights of the emerging situation of Mughal gardens research, beginning with garden research in regions related to the Mughal realm (Fig. 4).

The Emerging Situation

New Regional Research

Timurid Central Asia. It is well known that Mughal gardens descended from Timurid Central Asia, but in 1995 Maria Eva Subtelny showed just how that transmission occurred

[5] Over the past century of garden history, there have been several waves of literature comparing Mughal gardens with other realms of Islamic or Oriental garden design, as will be discussed in a later section of the paper. In the 1980s and early 1990s, in contrast, research focused on specifically Mughal places and developments.

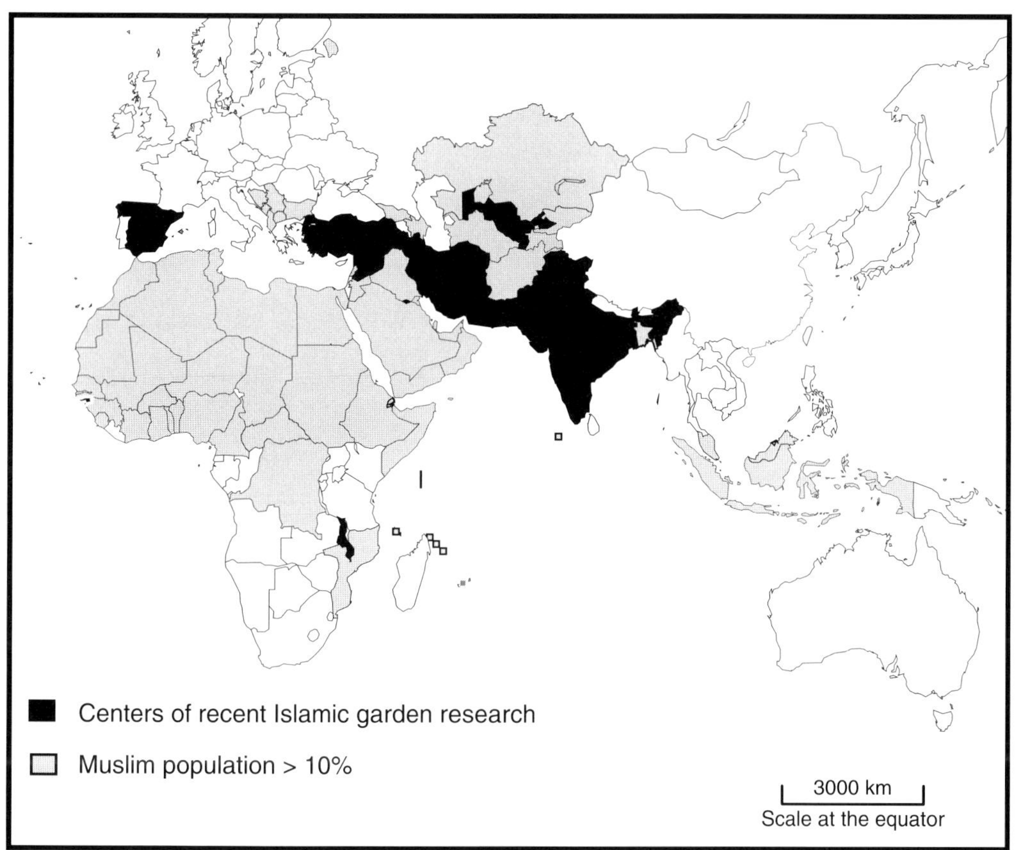

4. Regional centers of Indian and Islamic garden research

by reexamining a Timurid garden treatise, the *Irshad al-Zira'a.*[6] The author, patron, and family of that text had an enormous influence on the Timurid gardens of Herat, which the first Mughal ruler, Babur, saw at a formative moment in his career.[7] But Subtelny also revealed their influence on the earliest Mughal gardens in Agra and Delhi, including Humayun's tomb, thus establishing a historical connection between Timurid and Mughal landscape design.

Roya Marefat has shed new light on the Timurid antecedents of Mughal gardens at the Shah-i Zinda funerary complex in Uzbekistan, and Robert McChesney has linked

[6] Maria Eva Subtelny, "A Medieval Persian Agricultural Manual in Context: The Irshad al-Zira'a in Late Timurid and Early Safavid Khorasan," *Studia Iranica* 22 (1993), 167–217; idem, "Mirak-i Sayyid Ghiyas and the Timurid Tradition of Landscape Architecture," *Studia Iranica* 24 (1995), 19–60; idem, "Agriculture and the Timurid *Chaharbagh*: The Evidence from a Medieval Persian Agricultural Manual," in *Gardens in the Time of the Great Muslim Empires,* ed. Petruccioli, 110–28.

[7] Zahir ud Din Muhammad Babur, *Baburnama,* trans. W. Thackston, Washington, D.C., 1996; James L. Wescoat Jr., "Gardens vs. Citadels: The Territorial Context of Early Mughal Gardens," in *Garden History: Issues, Approaches, Methods,* ed. John Dixon Hunt, Washington, D.C., 1992, 331–58; and idem, "Gardens of Conquest."

gardens with land ownership and property transactions in Bukhara.[8] Lisa Golombek and Roya Marefat underscore the importance of Timurid garden patronage by and for women, a theme taken up by Ellison Findly and others in the context of Mughal India.[9]

Persia. Although garden history has slowed since the revolution in Iran in 1979, some important advances have occurred there. Bernard O'Kane shows how gardens mediated nomadic and urbane cultural traditions, effecting a transition "from tents to pavilions," though not a full resolution of the cultural tensions therein, which is in many respects analogous with Timurid and Mughal landscape history.[10] Mahvash Alemi raises new questions about European images, prints, and drawings of Persian gardens as a source of historical evidence.[11]

South Asia. In India, Sultanate gardens and waterworks have received detailed examination in relation to Mughal gardens.[12] Curiously, Hindu and Buddhist garden history remain separate, less-developed fields of inquiry. However, a substantial body of landscape evidence deals with Vijayanagar, a medieval Hindu kingdom in southern India roughly contemporary with the Timurid period, which undertook subtle processes of "Islamicization" in selected cultural forms.[13] The most substantial garden archaeology project in South Asia, however, is underway at Sigiriya, Sri Lanka. Built a millennium before the Mughal period, Sigiriya has striking similarities in layout and design which have yet to be formally compared with later Indian or Islamic gardens.[14] Brief notice also appeared in 1996 of a Mughal

[8] Roya Marefat, "Beyond the Architecture of Death: The Shrine of the Shah-i Zinda at Samarqand," Ph.D. diss., Harvard University, 1991; Robert D. McChesney, "Some Observations on 'Garden' and Its Meanings in the Property Transactions of the Juybari Family in Bukhara, 1544–77," in *Gardens in the Time of the Great Muslim Empires,* ed. Petruccioli, 97–109.

[9] Lisa Golombek, "The Gardens of Timur: New Perspectives," *Muqarnas* 12 (1995), 137–47; idem, "Timur's Gardens: The Feminine Perspective," in *The Mughal Garden,* ed. Hussain, Rehman, and Wescoat, 29–36; Roya Marefat, "Timurid Women: Patronage and Power," *Asian Art* (Spring 1993), 28–49; Ellison Findly, "Nur Jahan's Embroidery Trade and Flowers of the Taj Mahal," *Asian Art and Culture* 9 (1996), 7–25; idem, *Nur Jahan, Empress of Mughal India,* Oxford, 1993.

[10] Bernard O'Kane, "From Tents to Pavilions: Royal Mobility and Persian Palace Design," *Ars Orientalis* 23 (1993), 249–68.

[11] Mahvash Alemi, "The Royal Gardens of the Safavid Period: Types and Models," in *Gardens in the Time of the Great Muslim Empires,* ed. Petruccioli, 72–96.

[12] E.g., Anthony Welch, "Gardens that Babur Did Not Like: Landscape, Water, and Architecture for the Sultans of Delhi," in *Mughal Gardens,* ed. Wescoat and Wolschke-Bulmahn, 59-93; Yves Porter, "Jardins Pre-Moghols," in *Jardins d'Orient,* Res Orientales, Paris, 1991, 37–54. Unfortunately, Allen Thrasher's 1992 Dumbarton Oaks symposium paper on Sanskrit garden texts remains unpublished. A regional history that encompasses pre- and post-Mughal eras is Saifur Rehman Dar, "Whither the Historical Gardens of Punjab? Garden Traditions of Punjab," in *The Mughal Garden*, ed. Hussain, Rehman, and Wescoat, 37–54. Catherine Asher's work provides a highly nuanced treatment of Hindu and Muslim garden patronage during the Mughal period, e.g., "Gardens of the Nobility: Raja Man Singh and the Bagh-i Wah," in ibid., 61–72.

[13] George Michell, *Architecture and Art of Southern India: Vijayanagar and the Successor States,* Cambridge, 1995; Burton Stein, *Vijayanagar,* Cambridge, 1989; Philip B. Wagoner, " 'Sultan among Hindu Kings': Dress, Titles, and the Islamicization of Hindu Culture at Vijayanagar," *The Journal of Asian Studies* 55 (1996), 851–80.

[14] Seneca Bandaranayake, "Presentation on the Excavations and Ethnoarchaeology of Garden and Urban Design at Sigiriya," paper presented at East-West Center, Honolulu, 1991.

natural history manuscript titled *Farhang-i-Aurang-Shahi,* dating to the reign of Aurangzeb (1658–1707 C.E.).[15]

Syria and Iraq. The 1976 Dumbarton Oaks Colloquium volume *Islamic Gardens* noted a paucity of research on gardens in Arab and Turkish regions, but several recent developments shed light on their historical connections with and potential relevance for Mughal gardens. The early model of monumental Abbasid gardens along the Tigris River at Samarra, for example, may have diffused into eastern as well as western Islamic realms.[16] Yasser Tabbaa showed how the reduction in scale of courtyard-garden complexes at Aleppo, compared with earlier sites such as Samarra, was accompanied by increased refinement in the design of garden spaces and waterworks.[17]

Turkey. In Turkey, Scott Redford has excavated Seljuk garden sites at Alanya, pushing back the record of Islamic garden archaeology in that region to the thirteenth century, and demonstrating the importance of archaeological inquiry for Islamic garden research.[18] Redford also frames Seljuk garden sites in relation to antecedent Greek-speaking Christian cultures in a way that suggests lines of comparison between Muslim and Hindu garden landscapes in India. For the Ottoman period, Gulru Necipoglu has published on both interior courtyard gardens of the Topkapi Palace and the suburban garden landscapes of Istanbul.[19]

Al-Andalus (Spain). The most vigorous conceptual and methodological experiments in Islamic garden research are taking place in Spain. James Dickie has developed a typology of Moorish gardens that builds upon the Roman antecedents of the *hortus* (which becomes *rawda*), *vigna* (*manjara*), *domus urbana* (the palatine gardens of the Madinat al-Zahra and Alhambra), and *villa rustica* (such as those surrounding the Generalife).[20] The classical roots and pragmatic experimental character of Andalusion agronomy are boldly surveyed by Karl Butzer, who puts forward hypotheses about the evolution of Islamic agronomic sciences in relation to social and cultural history in ways that invite comparative inquiry with the Persianate realm.[21]

[15] James J. White, "A Seventeenth-Century Persian Manuscript in the Asiatic Society, Calcutta," *Huntia* 9, 2 (1996), 175–78.

[16] Alastair Northedge, "An Interpretation of the Palace of the Caliph at Samarra (Dar al-Khilafa or Jawsaq al-Khaqani)," *Ars Orientalis* 23 (1993), 143–70.

[17] Yasser Tabbaa, "Circles of Power: Palace, Citadel, and City in Ayubbid Aleppo," *Ars Orientalis* 23 (1993), 186–87.

[18] Scott Redford, "Thirteenth-Century Rum Seljuk Palaces and Palace Imagery," *Ars Orientalis* 23 (1993), 219–36.

[19] Gulru Necipoglu, "The Suburban Landscape of Sixteenth-Century Istanbul as a Mirror of Classical Ottoman Garden Culture," in *Gardens in the Time of the Great Muslim Empires,* ed. Petruccioli; idem, *Architecture, Ceremonial, and Power: The Topkapi Palace in the Fifteenth and Sixteenth Centuries*, Cambridge, Mass., 1991.

[20] James Dickie (Yaqub Zaki), "The Hispano-Arab Garden: Notes toward a Typology," in *The Legacy of Muslim Spain,* ed. S. K. Jayyusi, Leiden, 1992; idem, "Garden V(3)(iii), Islamic Spain," in *The Dictionary of Art,* ed. Jane Turner, vol. 12, New York, 1996.

[21] Karl Butzer, "The Islamic Traditions of Agroecology: Crosscultural Experience, Ideas, and Innovations," *ECUMENE: Journal of Environment, Culture, and Meaning* 1 (1994), 1–50. See also John Harvey, "Garden Plants of Moorish Spain," *Garden History* 3 (1975), 10–22; Andrew M. Watson, *Agricultural Innovation in the*

Most significant for garden research per se are D. Fairchild Ruggles's pioneering efforts to integrate different disciplinary perspectives, including those of agronomic, visual, poetic, and historical modes of garden analysis, in her research at the Madinat al-Zahra complex near Cordoba.[22] She examines how the garden was seen and used, to gaze upon peoples and places, and how those structures of vision were related to the social and spatial structure of power in Cordoban culture, a line of analysis she recently extended to Humayun's tomb-garden in Delhi.[23] Ruggles also retraces the diffusion of garden models from Samarra in Iraq to Spain and thence to Qala Bani Hammad in Algeria.

Most recently, Elizabeth Dean Hermann has presented a dissertation on urban landscape history under the Nasrids in fourteenth-century Granada, extending the scale of garden research to the city and its countryside, and linking it with processes of political control and disease ecology.[24] Hermann is the first professional landscape architect to write a dissertation on Islamic garden history. She and others at Harvard and the University of Pennsylvania are now examining the historical connections between Islamic and Italian gardens in Spain and Italy—which takes us to the theme of comparison, and to the second set of developments that are transforming the situation of Mughal garden studies.[25]

Comparative Research

The literature on Islamic gardens in the 1970s frequently compared (or juxtaposed) Mughal, Persian, and Moorish gardens.[26] During the 1980s greater emphasis was placed on regional garden research, as surveyed above, which paved the way for a new round of comparison (Fig. 5). The new comparisons take three geographic patterns: Mediterranean, pan-Islamic, and multiregional.

Early Islamic World: The Diffusion of Crops and Farming Techniques, 700–1100, Cambridge, 1983; Irfan Habib, "Notes on the Economic and Social Aspects of Mughal Gardens," in *Mughal Gardens,* ed. Wescoat and Wolschke-Bulmahn, 127–38; and note 6, above.

[22] D. Fairchild Ruggles, "Madinat al-Zahra's Constructed Landscape: A Case Study in Islamic Garden and Architectural History," Ph.D. diss., University of Pennsylvania, 1991; idem, "Vision and Power at the Qala Bani Hammad in Islamic North Africa," *Journal of Garden History* 14 (1994), 28–41; idem, "The Gardens of the Alhambra and the Concept of the Garden in Islamic Spain," in *Al-Andalus: The Art of Islamic Spain,* ed. Jerrilyn D. Dodds, New York, 1992, 163–72; idem, "The Mirador in Abassid and Hispano-Umayyad Garden Typology," *Muqarnas* 7 (1990), 73–82; idem, "Historiography and the Rediscovery of Madinat al-Zahra," *Islamic Studies* 30 (1990), 129–40; idem, "A Mythology of an Agrarian Ideal," *Environmental Design: Journal of the Islamic Environmental Design Research Centre* (1986), 24–27.

[23] Ruggles, "Humayun's Tomb and Garden."

[24] Elizabeth Dean Hermann, "Urban Formation and Landscape: Symbol and Agent of Social, Political, and Environmental Change in Fourteenth-Century Nasrid Granada," Ph.D. diss., Harvard University, 1996.

[25] I refer to seminars on "Mediterranean architecture" led by Mirka Beneš, Howard Burns, and Gulru Necipoglu as well as Hermann. See also Cammy Brothers, "The Renaissance Reception of the Alhambra: The Letters of Andrea Navagero and the Palace of Charles V, " *Muqarnas* 11 (1994), 79–102.

[26] *The Islamic Garden,* ed. Elisabeth B. MacDougall and Richard Ettinghausen, Washington, D.C., 1976, included a chapter on Mughal gardens, as did John Brookes, *Gardens of Paradise: The History and Design of the Great Islamic Gardens,* London, 1987; and Jonas Lehrman, *Earthly Paradise: Garden and Courtyard in Islam,* Berkeley, 1980.

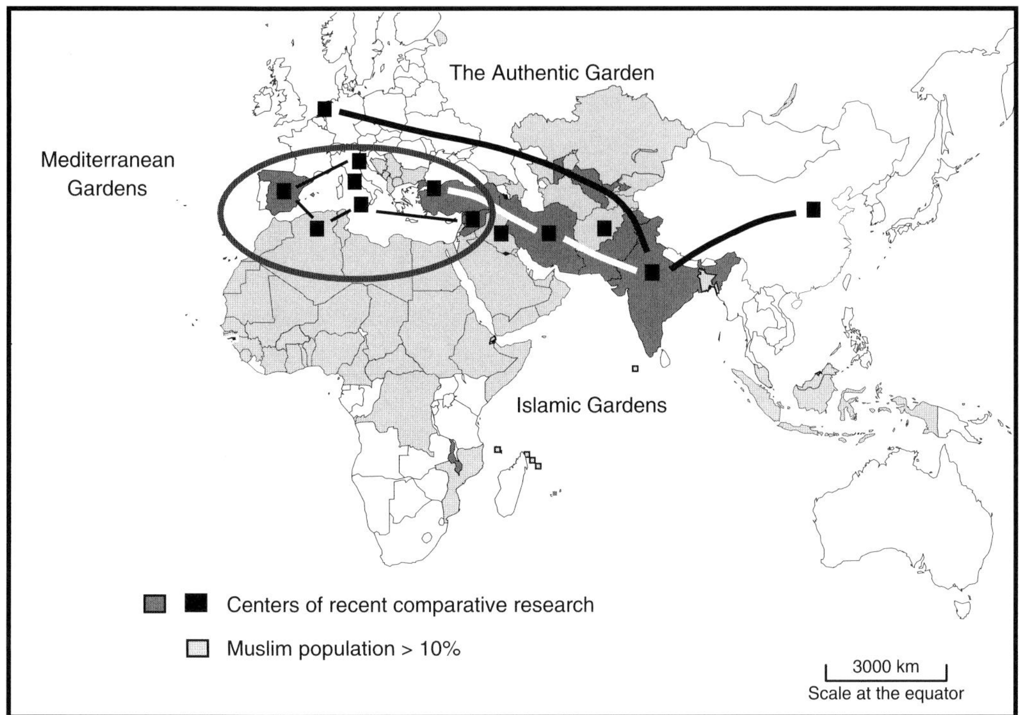

5. Areas of recent comparative garden research involving Indian and Islamic gardens

Mediterranean comparisons. Studies examining the Mediterranean concentrate on Spanish, Maghribi, Sicilian, and Italian gardens. Tabbaa and Ruggles retrace the historical links between gardens of the eastern Abbasid capitals at Samarra and Ghazna with those of the Umayyad west in Spain and Sicily although these gardens are not directly connected with Mughal realms to the east.[27] These Mediterranean studies focus on contact and transmission (i.e., genealogy) more than on similarities and differences in garden form, function, or meaning (i.e., comparison in a formal sense).

Pan-Islamic comparisons. Interest in genealogy and comparison converge in pan-Islamic garden histories spanning areas from Spain to India (usually omitting Southeast Asia). Although this genre has tended to simply juxtapose gardens from different regions to exemplify a common theme, such as paradise symbolism, several studies have begun to undertake more formal and societal comparisons.[28] Necipoglu's volume on pre-modern Islamic palaces, which includes numerous brief references to gardens, compares Ottoman,

[27] Yasser Tabbaa, "The Medieval Islamic Garden: Typology and Hydraulics," in *Garden History,* ed. Hunt, 303–29; Ruggles, "Vision and Power"; idem, "The Mirador in Abassid."

[28] Books on paradise gardens and chapters on the Islamic garden emphasize the similarities and historical connections over the differences and independent developments in different periods and realms of Muslim garden design. Most recently, see Hermann Forkl et al., eds., *Die Garten des Islam,* Stuttgart, 1993.

6. The jharoka *marble window in the Diwan-i Am pavilion in Lahore Fort, Pakistan*

Safavid, and Mughal palace architecture using the theoretical framework of the "gaze" to illuminate differences among the three dynasties and to counter monolithic representations of them and their architectures.[29]

It should be noted, however, that while Western scholars study the power and logic of the gaze, South Asian archaeologists show more interest in the *gaz,* i.e., the physical unit of measurement used to lay out gardens and other sites. They focus on the *gaz* to understand how gardens were physically constructed and spatially organized.[30] Analysis of the *gaz* reveals a logic of numbers in gardens that were decimally proportioned and points toward principles of proportion in Mughal garden layout. Analysis of the gaze, by contrast, concentrates on phenomena such as *jharoka* windows where kings appeared as much to be seen in ways that would maintain the symbolic order, stability, and beauty of their empire as to oversee their lands and peoples (Fig. 6). In Mughal times, *gaz* and gaze were closely related to one another. Gaps between them arose as colonial archaeological and art historical scholarship diverged in the nineteenth century, and later widened to serve more distant geo-

[29] Gulru Necipoglu, "An Outline of Shifting Paradigms in the Palatial Architecture of the Pre-Modern Islamic World," *Ars Orientalis* 23 (1993), 3–26; idem, "Framing the Gaze in Ottoman, Safavid, and Mughal Palaces," *Ars Orientalis* 23 (1993), 303–42.

[30] For elaborations of this point, see Wescoat, "The Mughal Gardens Project in Lahore"; and Wescoat, Brand, and Mir, "Shahdara Gardens."

graphic and cultural audiences in the post-colonial world. But the historiographical gap between *gaz* and gaze may be more easily bridged than the gulf between these scholarly perspectives and the unfathomed realms of popular garden experience, past and present, which pose challenges revisited later in this paper.

Attilio Petruccioli has pioneered pan-Islamic garden research in special issues of *Environmental Design* that deal with relationships between gardens and urbanism in Muslim societies.[31] Petruccioli has published an edited volume, *Il giardino islamico: Architettura, natura, paesaggio,* which explores the forms, contexts, and expressions of Islamic gardens. Most recently, he has edited a special issue of *Muqarnas* on what Italian scholars call "territory," the regional contexts of Islamic garden design.[32]

Multiregional comparisons. A probing comparative effort was published in a special issue of *Marg,* an Indian art and architecture magazine, on the patronage of the Mughals and Medicis. In that volume Ebba Koch explored the diffusion of *pietra dura* floral inlay work used in Michelangelo's chapel at the church of San Lorenzo in Florence and Shah Jahan's palace and tomb architecture in Delhi and Agra.[33] Although not writing about Mughal gardens per se, Jan Pieper compared the hanging gardens of Rajasthan with those of Renaissance Italy.[34]

Other long-distance comparisons include Tabbaa's and Ruggles's examinations of the influences of Samarra on palace-garden complexes in Syria and Spain; Findly's study of international trade and diplomatic gift-giving as they influenced floral ornament in Indian textiles; Vivian Rich's examination of European herbal images in Mughal floral painting; and botanical contacts between Europe and Asia, including a recent article on Mughal botanical illustration.[35] Ruggles has also adapted visual methods of analysis developed in Moorish gardens to a case study of visual experience at Humayun's tomb.[36]

More wide-ranging experiments pursue such themes as the authentic garden, which encompasses Dutch, Islamic, and Chinese gardens, and a collection of essays on gardens of the Orient, which ranges from ancient to modern southwest Asia.[37] Although somewhat unclear about their comparative aims and methods, these efforts challenge conventional categories of garden history in Europe and Asia.

[31] Attilio Petruccioli, ed., *Environmental Design: Journal of the Islamic Environmental Design Research Centre,* 1 and 2 (1986), special issues, *City as Garden* and *Garden as City*.

[32] See note 1.

[33] Ebba Koch, "Pietre Dure and Other Artistic Contacts between the Court of the Mughals and that of the Medici," in *Patrons of Art: The Mughals and the Medici*, ed. Dalu Jones, *Marg* 39 (1988), 29–56.

[34] Jan Pieper, "Hanging Gardens in the Princely Capitals of Rajasthan and in Renaissance Italy: Sacred Space, Earthly Paradise, Secular Ritual," *Marg* 39 (1988), 69–90.

[35] Tabbaa, "Medieval Islamic Garden"; Ruggles, "Humayun's Tomb and Garden"; Findly, "Nur Jahan's Embroidery Trade"; Vivian Rich, "The Development of Mughal Floral Painting with Particular Reference to the Sixteenth and Seventeenth Centuries," Ph.D. diss., School of Oriental and African Studies, London, 1981; R. Desmond, *The European Discovery of Indian Flora,* Oxford, 1991; White, "Seventeenth-Century Persian Manuscript."

[36] Ruggles, "Humayun's Tomb and Garden."

[37] L. Tjon Sie Fat et al., *The Authentic Garden: A Symposium on Gardens,* Leiden, 1991; Rika Gyselen, ed., *Jardins d'Orient*, Res Orientales, Paris, 1991. China poses especially promising comparisons with Persianate gardens; see, for example, Philippe Foret, "Making an Imperial Landscape in Chengde, Jehol," Ph.D. diss., University of Chicago, 1992.

7. Asaf Khan's tomb-garden, Lahore, which has received little conservation attention for its architecture or garden plantings

Practical Issues

These comparative perspectives on garden cultures, past and present, raise questions about the relationship between academic research and the practical concerns of communities who use, visit, and work in Mughal gardens. The investigations cited above focus primarily on garden patronage, political symbolism, and genealogy. As intellectually stimulating as these themes are for our understanding of Mughal gardens, they do not engage the social, spatial, or environmental problems at extant garden sites, nor do they consider what difference such inquiry makes for modern landscape conservation, experience, or design.

Even garden conservation has been neglected (Figs. 7, 8). The loss of garden plantings is often lamented, but to little effect. The Smithsonian Mughal Gardens Project did bring together essays by archaeologists, curators, and conservationists. But those essays documented how generally neglected, ill-prepared, antiquated, and inconsequential garden conservation and restoration research have been in the region.[38] Elizabeth Moynihan's work on the Lotus Garden at Dholpur was committed to conservation of the site, and identified some of the practical difficulties of linking excavation, inquiry, and long-term conservation. Non-

[38] See Hussain, Rehman, and Wescoat, eds., *The Mughal Garden,* and note 4, above, on conservation chapters. The work of the Anjuman Mimaran, an architectural heritage organization in Lahore, stands out for its conservation projects in the Walled City of Lahore and documentation projects in Punjab province.

8. Layers of partially documented conservation work on the plinth of Jahangir's tomb-garden, Lahore, Pakistan

governmental conservation organizations such as the Anjuman Mimaran in Lahore, Indian National Trust for Art and Cultural Heritage (INTACH) in Delhi, and the Aga Khan Trust for Culture have undertaken important cultural heritage conservation experiments, and they are now beginning to consider garden projects.[39]

The aims and methods of Mughal garden conservation have evolved but little over the present century, and do not speak to the experience, interests, or problems of modern South Asian societies. Those societies include an increasingly large and diverse middle class tourism sector, for example, but with the exception of a National Park Service study of the riverfront gardens at Agra, there has been little research on tourist experience, behavior, or problems at Mughal gardens.[40] Tourism represents one of the largest sources of foreign exchange in India, but it also seems to encourage damaging interventions in the form of *son et lumiere* shows, concessions, and hasty restoration projects in Mughal gardens.

[39] For projects in Lahore, see James L. Wescoat Jr., "Waterworks and Culture in Metropolitan Lahore," *Asian Art and Culture* (Spring/Summer 1995), 21–36; and Wescoat and Wolschke-Bulmahn, "Mughal Gardens of Lahore." For recent perspectives on urban heritage conservation, including gardens, see Santosh Ghosh, *Architectural and Urban Conservation,* Calcutta, 1996.

[40] National Park Service, *Agra Heritage Project,* New Delhi, 1994. The University of Illinois Department of Landscape Architecture and Varanasi Development Authority collaborated on a landscape planning experiment at Sarnath. See *Sarnath: Design Guidelines and Case Studies for Tourism Development,* New Delhi, 1990, and *Sarnath: A Master Plan for Tourism Development,* New Delhi, 1989.

9. The destruction of a Sikh gurudwara *in Lahore, Pakistan, following riots and destruction of the Babri* masjid *(Babur's mosque) in Ayodhya, India*

Recent history has revealed how culturally sensitive Mughal sites can be, as when riots occurred at the Ayodhya mosque, built by Babur over what was believed to be the birthplace of Rama. That multidecade controversy and lawsuit ended when a fundamentalist Hindu mob tore the mosque to the ground.[41] Waves of retribution and counter-retribution followed against temples, mosques, and Sikh *gurudwaras* in India and Pakistan (Fig. 9).

Research on landscape conflict has not extended to Mughal gardens despite a significant record of litigation over their ownership, use, and conservation.[42] The project Pluralism and Its Cultural Expressions, sponsored by the Rockefeller Foundation and Aga Khan Trust for Culture, offers a promising approach to constructive communication and conflict resolution.[43] A park project outside Tehran, the Bagh Shadi Jamshediyeh, also reveals that good landscape design can weave together traditional and modern

[41] Reinhard Bernbeck and Susan Pollack, "Ayodhya, Archaeology, and Identity," *Current Anthropology* 37, suppl. (1996), 138 ff.; Sarvepalli Gopal, *Anatomy of a Confrontation: The Babri Masjid-Ramjanmabhumi Issue,* New Delhi, 1991.

[42] Cf. Richard Smardon and James Karp, *The Legal Landscape,* New York, 1992.

[43] Hassan Uddin Khan and Clifford Chanin, *Pluralism and Its Cultural Expressions,* Geneva and New York, 1995.

garden design in ways that provide "space for freedom" even in contexts of political, economic, and cultural turmoil.[44]

The links between garden history and landscape design in South Asia are weaker than those between architectural history and practice, which reflects the importance of sustained institutional and financial commitment from organizations such as the Aga Khan Trust for Culture.[45] Individual designers such as Ravindra Bhan and Elizabeth Moynihan in India and Sajjad Kausar and Kamal Khan Mumtaz in Pakistan have drawn inspiration from historic gardens for modern landscape design projects in ways that speak to contemporary situations.[46] Several landscape architecture master's theses also address the relations between historic gardens, landscape conservation, and modern parks.[47] But these examples are few in a region of one billion people. In the absence of landscape architecture programs in Pakistan and their early stage of development in India, the problems of landscape design in and around Mughal gardens seem formidable.

Underlying these practical problems is a lack of basic research on the nature of experience at Mughal gardens. Surprisingly, there have been no detailed studies of aesthetic experience at Mughal gardens in any era, past or present. There have been no studies of garden workers (*mali*s) who are generally poor and of low status, garden visitors, or garden superintendents. Without such knowledge the odds of speaking to modern interests and concerns at Mughal gardens, or of influencing their conservation in any meaningful way, seem poor. Several decades ago, Marshall Hodgson wrote, "Perhaps such [cultural] traditions can be reduced to the status of museum pieces and local color for attracting tourists; or to eclectic sources of 'inspiration' for professional designers."[48] Tourism and eclectic inspiration are indeed evident at Mughal gardens today, but even they seem dimly understood. Thus, in addition to the gap between *gaz* and gaze mentioned earlier, we must also consider the widening gulf between historical research and the experiences of those who sit, walk, and work in these gardens (Figs. 10, 11). To date, there has been little probing research on what people actually experience or care about at Mughal gardens.

[44] Description of the Bagh Shadi Jamshediyeh, Tehran, Iran, presented by Dr. Mina Marefat on behalf of Gholam Reza Pasban Hazrat at the seminar "Sustainable Landscape Design in Arid Environments," Dumbarton Oaks, 7 December 1996.

[45] See, for example, Aga Khan Award for Architecture, *Toward an Architecture in the Spirit of Islam,* Proceedings of Seminar 1 in the series Architectural Transformations in the Islamic World, ed. Renata Holod, Aiglemont, Gouvieux, France, 1980; Aga Khan Award for Architecture, *Architecture for Islamic Societies Today*, ed. James Steele, London, 1994, especially on landscape design for the Diplomatic Quarter of Riyadh, Saudi Arabia; and Ismail Serageldin, ed., *Space for Freedom: The Search for Architectural Excellence in Muslim Societies,* London, 1989.

[46] See Hussain, Rehman, and Wescoat, eds., *The Mughal Garden*, 165 ff., for a brief treatment of their work. The Middle Eastern literature is more substantial. See Hesam Joma, "The Earth as a Mosque: Integration of the Traditional Islamic Environmental Planning Ethic with Agricultural and Water Development Policies in Saudi Arabia," Ph.D. diss., University of Pennsylvania, 1991; Timothy Cochrane and Jane Brown, eds., *Landscape Design for the Middle East,* London, 1978. A new Mughal garden design project underway at Lister Park in Bradford, England, speaks to the cultural interests of that community and is supported in part by the Heritage Lottery Fund. See http://www.bradford.gov.uk/art/mughal/mughal_frames.html.

[47] Saeeda Rasool, "From Private Gardens to Public Parks: A Study of Transformation in Landscape of Lahore, Pakistan," master's thesis, University of Illinois, Champaign, 1994; Najmus Saqib's master's project on Kamran's Baradari, Lahore, Department of Land, 1994.

[48] Marshall Hodgson, *The Venture of Islam*, vol. 3, Chicago, 1974, 430.

10. A local family posing in the Diwan-i Khas garden pavilion, Lahore Fort, Pakistan

11. Vendors in Shalamar garden, Lahore

12. The Mehtab Bagh project area across the Yamuna River from the Taj Mahal in Agra, India

13. Aerial view of Shalamar garden, Kashmir (photo: courtesy of Michael Brand)

Two new research projects have an opportunity to address this wavering of practical concern (Figs. 12, 13). The Mehtab Bagh project opposite the Taj Mahal on the Yamuna River in Agra is setting new archaeological standards for Mughal garden research. In addition to surface survey and historical documentation, it is using paleobotanical and excavation techniques. It also seeks to coordinate the interests of ministries of culture, tourism, and planning at multiple levels of government.[49] Another research project on the conservation of Mughal gardens in Kashmir also has an opportunity to speak to modern interests in garden history and conservation in that embattled region.[50]

Comparative Possibilities

On the one hand, the regional, comparative, and practical developments discussed above signal a reemergence of comparative opportunities for Mughal garden history. On the other hand, we still lack the basic conceptual, methodological, and practical apparati for comparative research. Mughal garden history depends upon comparative research in part because it fits so awkwardly within conventional categories of garden history—Indian, Islamic, medieval, and Persian.

Four fields of historical inquiry, however, have shaped the context and identity of Mughal gardens. They are Indo-Islamic garden history (a hybrid field), Indo-Islamic art and architectural history (another hybrid), world garden history, and world history at large. In each field, it is useful to ask the following questions: How are Mughal gardens defined? What is deemed to be significant about them? How significant have they been for the progress of that field? These questions entail large literatures ranging in scale from site to civilization, but several historiographic patterns may be sketched.

Perspectives from Indo-Islamic Garden History

Indo-Islamic garden history is a composite field that stands at the intersection of three broad cultural traditions: Indian, Islamic, and Timurid or Persianate (Fig. 14). In the early decades of this century, Mughal gardens were most often portrayed as "Indian gardens," constructed upon the ancient landscape foundations of Hindu and Buddhist civilization. Early garden historians such as Havell, Villiers-Stuart, and Gothein took this approach, stressing Hindu water, vegetation, and architectural symbolism.[51] Mughal gardens were envisioned as an adaptation of these older, more extensive traditions

[49] Elizabeth B. Moynihan, "Background on Proposal to Document the Mehtab Bagh," memo, 5 May 1996, copy on file with author. An ongoing lawsuit covering the larger Taj Trapezium region is one of the driving forces behind conservation efforts in the Agra metropolitan area. See *M. C. Mehta v. Union of India*, Supreme Court judgment, 30 December 1996, copy on file with author.

[50] Indian National Trust for Art and Cultural Heritage, personal communication, 10 April 1997.

[51] Havell, "Indian Gardens"; Gothein, *Indische Garten*; Reuther, *Indische Palaste und Wohnhauser*; Constance Mary Villiers-Stuart, *Gardens of the Great Mughals*, London, 1913. In her preface, Villiers-Stuart acknowledges the influences of Her Highness Maji Sahiba of Bharatpur, Her Highness Princess Bamba Duleep Singh, George Birdwood's treatise on the Christmas tree, and Havell (which reflect stronger Hindu than Muslim associations) (p. xi).

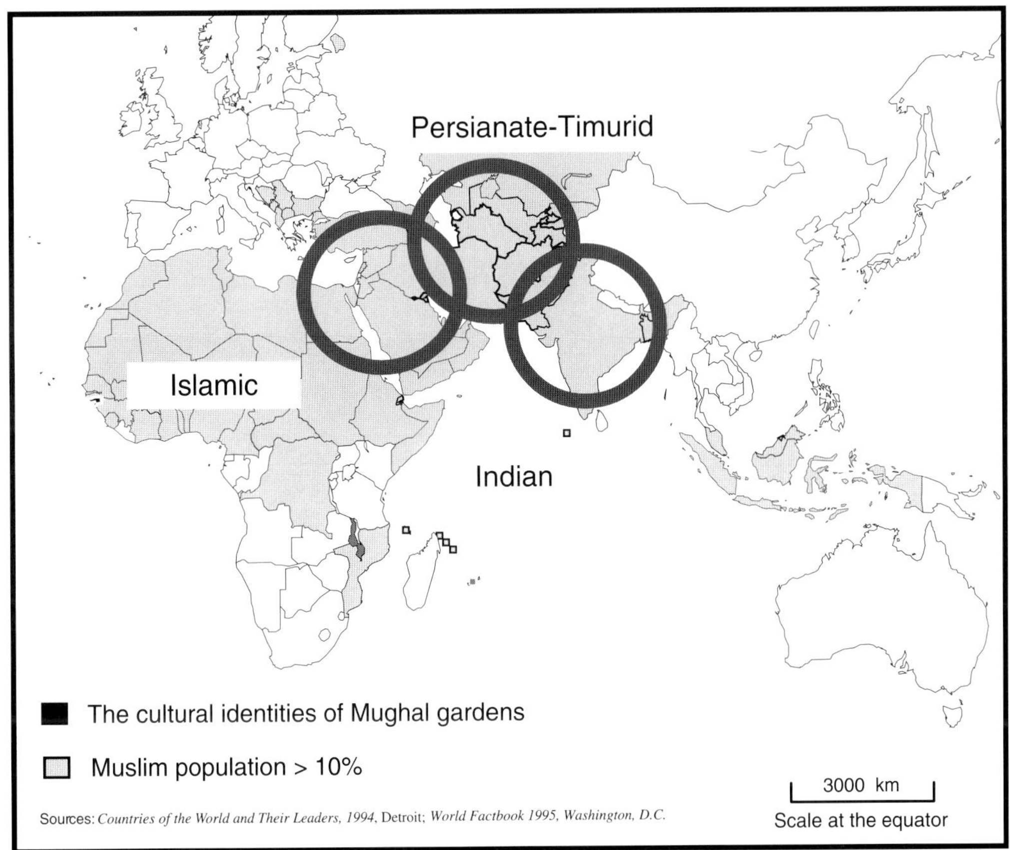

14. Centers of cultural identity relevant in Mughal garden history

more than as a foreign innovation or imposition upon a conquered land.[52] Recent examples of this approach include Saifur Rehman Dar on Punjabi gardens, Ali Akbar Hussain on Deccani gardens, and Catherine Asher on sub-imperial patronage. They shed light on the cultural continuities and relations among Hindu, Sikh, Muslim, and colonial garden traditions.[53] Asher, for example, shows how Hindu and Muslim iconographies of light and political authority were combined in the patronage of Raja Man Singh, a Hindu Rajput noble in Akbar's court.[54]

[52] Villiers-Stuart stressed the Hindu symbolism at Akbar's tomb at Sikandra. Cf. Dickie, "The Mughal Garden"; and Ram Nath, "Persian Inscriptions of the Upper Gallery of Akbar's Tomb at Sikandra, Agra: Contents and Raison d'Etre," *Journal of the Pakistan Historical Society* 34 (1986), 221–35.

[53] Dar, "Historical Gardens of Punjab"; Catherine Asher, "The Mughal Garden 'Wah' near Hasanabdal"; and Ali Akbar Hussain, "Qutb Shahi Garden Sites in Golconda and Hyderabad," all in *The Mughal Garden*, ed. Hussain, Rehman, and Wescoat.

[54] Catherine Asher, "Mughal Sub-Imperial Patronage: The Architecture of Raja Man Singh," in *Powers of Art: Patronage in Indian Culture*, ed. Barbara Stoler Miller, Delhi, 1992, 183–201; and idem, *The Architecture of Mughal India,* Cambridge, 1992.

Beginning at some point in the early 1970s, however, perhaps with the Dumbarton Oaks Colloquium "The Islamic Garden," Mughal gardens were increasingly viewed as a branch of Islamic garden history.[55] The Aga Khan architecture programs and the Islamic Environmental Design Research Centre in Rome encouraged inquiry in this direction. Greater attention was given to Qur'anic and Sufi sources of garden imagery and symbolism. Attilio Petruccioli's *Il giardino islamico,* is a recent example in this genre. Once Mughal gardens are viewed as a type of Islamic garden, a pattern of interpretation unfolds that illuminates the Muslim and partially eclipses the Hindu, Sikh, and European sources of Mughal garden history.

Elizabeth Moynihan's *Paradise as a Garden in Persia and Mughal India* effectively balances these Islamic and Indian perspectives on Mughal gardens with a third cultural tradition the "paradise garden" that originated in Persia and Central Asia.[56] Although the Persian connection had long been known, it was not effectively woven together with Indian and Islamic perspectives before Moynihan's book.[57] The Timurid-Persianate perspective is advancing in related fields of art and architectural history, and it now dominates but does not fully erase or subsume the other two approaches.[58]

These three categories of cultural identity were important for the Mughals themselves. The first Mughal ruler, Babur, sought to distinguish his gardens from antecedent Indian ones.[59] The third ruler, Akbar, although not a great garden builder, promoted syntheses of Hindu, Muslim, and Timurid traditions in art and architecture as well as constructive engagement with foreign cultures, including Jesuit missionaries and European ambassadors to his court.[60] Islamic theology, strictly construed, had less significance in garden design than in mosques, madrassahs, mazars, and public works.[61] As with other facets of Mughal culture, gardens acquired significance as political media for processes of "Islamicization" in Hindu and Rajput building, and vice versa.[62] In Mughal times, as at

[55] Although critical of the term "Islamic garden," I have retained much of its scope and implications, e.g., in James L. Wescoat Jr., "The Islamic Garden: Issues for Landscape Research," *Environmental Design: Journal of the Islamic Environmental Design Research Centre* (1986), and "Gardens of the *Qur'an*."

[56] Moynihan's *Paradise as a Garden* has a clear regional focus on the Persianate and Timurid realm. Other authors have invoked the term "paradise garden" to refer more broadly to Muslim garden traditions from Spain to India and pre-Islamic Persian antecedents, which conflates Persian and broader Muslim and classical conceptions of "paradise" and "garden."

[57] For a perspective on the Timurid-Persianate identity of the Mughals, see Hodgson, *The Venture of Islam,* 59 ff.

[58] Lisa Golombek and Donald Wilber, *The Timurid Architecture of Iran and Turan*, 2 vols., Princeton, 1988; Tom Lentz and Glenn Lowry, *Timur and the Princely Vision: Persian Art and Culture in the Fifteenth Century,* Washington, D.C., and Los Angeles, 1992.

[59] For various interpretations of Babur's attitudes, see Moynihan, "But What a Happiness"; Welch, "Gardens that Babur Did Not Like"; and Wescoat, "Gardens of Conquest."

[60] Asher, *Architecture of Mughal India*; Ebba Koch, *Mughal Architecture: An Outline of Its History and Development, 1526–1858,* Munich, 1991.

[61] On Babur's limited religious patronage, see Howard Crane, "The Patronage of Zahir al-Din Babur and the Origins of Mughal Architecture," *Bulletin of the Asia Institute* 1 (1987), 95–110. Cf. Wescoat, "Gardens of the *Qur'an*."

[62] See Wagoner, "Sultan among Hindu Kings." "Islamicization" builds upon Marshall Hodgson's theoretical framework for the diffusions and transformation of Muslim (vis-à-vis Islamic or religious) culture.

Ayodhya today, the identity politics of landscape design could reinforce the unifying, or differentiating, forces in society at large. Most modern garden historians take a syncretic approach to the cultural identity of Mughal gardens, an approach that fits the subject well but figures awkwardly with broader fields of historical inquiry, as the following perspectives indicate.

Perspectives from Indo-Islamic Art and Architectural History

Gardens receive little attention in surveys of Indian or Islamic art and architectural history.[63] Some works offer a couple of paragraphs and some indexing of gardens, but none devotes a chapter or significant portion of a chapter to gardens. On the one hand, this reflects a conceptual and spatial gap between chapters on buildings, which are treated like monuments or objects, and chapters on the historical and civilizational context of those monuments. The scales of landscape and garden—the mesoscales—fall between the rubrics of monument and city.[64] On the other hand, architectural surveys do employ other spatial categories that subsume gardens in various ways, e.g., as elements of a tomb complex, palace complex, and fortress complex. Under that approach, gardens become a secondary level of analysis contingent upon the primary function of the building complex. Against that approach, Ebba Koch has shown that Mughal funerary architecture has close affinities with both residential and palace architecture, which renders such functional classifications less useful than landscape approaches in which gardens would figure more prominently.[65]

Garden historians may still profit from analogies with Indian and Islamic architectural history. Architectural comparisons of Mughal, Safavid, Ottoman, and European architecture, for example, indicate promising avenues for comparative garden research.[66]

Perspectives from World Garden History

Mughal gardens receive greater attention in world garden histories, in which, how-

[63] There are few garden references, for example, in Sheila S. Blair and Jonathan M. Bloom, *The Art and Architecture of Islam, 1250–1800,* New Haven, 1994; Percy Brown, *Indian Architecture: The Islamic Period,* Bombay, 1942; Richard Ettinghausen and Oleg Grabar, *The Art and Architecture of Islam, 600–1250,* Hammondsworth, 1987; James Fergusson, *History of Indian and Eastern Architecture,* London, 1910; Ernest B. Havell, *A Handbook of Indian Art,* London, 1920; Robert Hillenbrand, *Islamic Architecture: Form, Function, and Meaning,* New York, 1994; John D. Hoag, *Islamic Architecture,* New York, 1975; Ernst Kuhnel, *Islamic Art and Architecture,* trans. K. Watson, London, 1966; George Michell, ed., *Architecture of the Islamic World: Its History and Social Meaning,* London, 1978; and Giovanni T. Rivoira, *Moslem Architecture: Its Origins and Development,* trans. G. N. Rushforth, London, 1918.

[64] Even the massive collection of articles on Islamic art in *The Dictionary of Art,* vol. 16, ed. Turner, New York, 1996, 94–560, omits gardens and landscape (consigning "gardens" to a separate entry). These omissions are surprising in light of Grabar's well-known chapter, "The Symbolic Appropriation of the Land," in *The Formation of Islamic Art,* New Haven, 1973. Golombek and Wilber, *Timurid Architecture,* include a short chapter on gardens.

[65] Koch, *Mughal Architecture;* also idem, "The Char Bagh Conquers the Citadel: An Outline of the Development of the Mughal Palace Garden," in *The Mughal Garden,* ed. Hussain, Rehman, and Wescoat, 55–60.

[66] See John Hoag, "The Tomb of Ulugh Beg and Abdu Razzaq at Ghazni: A Model for the Taj Mahal," *Journal of the Society of Architectural Historians* 4 (1968), 234–48; and Necipoglu, "Framing the Gaze."

ever, their identity problems become acute. A survey of world garden histories reveals four basic patterns of treatment: no mention, a chapter at the beginning, a chapter at the end, and multiple references.

Some histories omit Mughal gardens altogether.[67] Such lapses occurred in late nineteenth and early twentieth-century accounts that followed an "ancient-medieval-oriental" narrative in which Indian gardens were classified as ancient, Moorish gardens as medieval, and East Asian gardens as Oriental. Mughal gardens did not fit. Similar results obtained in "ancient-medieval-Renaissance" narratives that led from the ancient world, including India, to modern Europe, leaving seventeenth-century Asia out. The most surprising example of the first case occurred in Marie Luise Gothein's otherwise excellent *Geschichte der Gartenkunst*. She later wrote a full monograph, *Indische Garten*.[68]

Most twentieth-century garden histories include one or more chapters on Islamic gardens that contain a section on Mughal gardens.[69] Those sections are situated after the chapter on ancient or medieval gardens but always anachronistically before the Renaissance!

A small number of nineteenth-century garden histories, such as those of John Claudius Loudon and Marcel Fouquier, place "Oriental gardens," including Mughal gardens, at the end of a survey that begins with the ancient Mediterranean and proceeds to modern Europe or America.[70] In contrast to his otherwise detailed garden survey by regions, for example, Loudon crudely asserted that as there had been no historical development of non-European garden traditions, they are best described under the heading of the "present situation."[71] From that perspective, "Oriental gardens" have no history except insofar as they are studied, borrowed, or rejected in Europe.

Two recent works address these category problems by discussing Indo-Islamic gardens in more than one cultural context and as having antecedents and connections in different periods and places. Although somewhat awkward and impressionistic, Geoffrey Jellicoe's *Landscape of Man* discusses India in ancient, Islamic, and modern contexts.[72] *The Dictionary of Art* discusses Mughal gardens under its South Asia heading with a cross-reference to the Islamic section (though no reference in the section on Central Asia and Iran).[73]

[67] Derek P. Clifford, *A History of Garden Design,* London, 1962; Sylvia Crowe, *Garden Design,* London, 1958; Francesco Fariello, *Architettura dei giardini,* Rome, 1967; Georges Gromort, *L'art des jardins,* Paris, 1934; Arthur Mangin, *Histoire jardins anciens et modernes,* Tours, 1887; Georges Riat, *L'art des jardins*, Paris, 1900; Albert F. Sieveking, *The Praise of Gardens: An Epitome of the Literature of the Garden Art,* London, 1899.

[68] Marie Luise Gothein, *Geschichte der Gartenkunst*, 2 vols., Berlin, 1914; idem, *Indische Garten.*

[69] Alfred-Auguste Ernouf and Adolphe Alphard, *L'art des jardins*, Paris, 1886; Norman T. Newton, *Design on the Land: The Development of Landscape Architecture,* Cambridge, Mass., 1971; Christopher Thacker, *The History of Gardens,* London, 1979.

[70] E.g., Marcel Fouquier and A. Duchene, *Des divers styles de jardins*, Paris, 1914.

[71] John Claudius Loudon, *An Encyclopedia of Gardening,* new ed., London, 1860. For a critique of such views, see Eric Wolf, *Europe and the People without History,* Berkeley, 1982.

[72] Geoffrey A. Jellicoe, *The Landscape of Man: Shaping the Environment from Prehistory to the Present Day,* London, 1975.

[73] Vivian Rich, "Gardens: Indian Subcontinent," 72–76, and Yasser Tabbaa, "Islamic Lands," 76–85, both in *The Dictionary of Art,* ed. Turner.

Such problems are nothing new for scholars of European gardens who regularly deal with the international transmissions of English, French, Dutch, German, and Italian gardens. But they have not yet extended that subtlety of awareness and interpretation to Indic or Islamic contexts. Indeed, as transnational research unfolds and the number and complexity of traditions increase, it is hard to imagine how any of the prevailing frameworks of world garden history would accommodate the results. Progress in world garden history, it seems to me, depends more upon creative approaches to historical geography than upon further advances in historiography. On the subject of historiography, however, it is worth pausing to consider how South Asian and Muslim scholars might write about Mughal gardens in a global context. This treatment has not yet happened, but we may turn to the field of world history for a sense of some of the issues involved.

Perspectives from World History

If we ask how Mughal gardens fit within "world historical" writing, which is experiencing a revival these days associated with concerns about globalization and global change, the answer is humbling (Fig. 15). There are not many references to Mughal gardens in world histories! Even so, debates among world historians have relevance for Mughal garden historiography. In 1956, for example, the Islamicist Marshall Hodgson wrote "In the Center of the Map: Nations See Themselves at the Hub of History," in which he put forward the now familiar argument that the historian's position influences the geographic center of historical inquiry.[74] He deviated from colleagues past and present by positing a "center of the world map" around what is today Iran. If we take his argument seriously and ask, where are the centers of the map relevant for Mughal garden history, we obtain some interesting results.

Anglo-Imperial. The earliest Mughal garden historians, Villiers-Stuart and Havell, were servants of the British Empire.[75] By no means a monolithic category, such writers engaged in debates among utilitarians, geopoliticians, and liberal reformers (generally sympathizing with the latter). While deeply sympathetic with Indian gardens and gardeners, in contrast to nineteenth-century British horticulturalists who regarded Indian gardeners as "slaves of custom,"[76] they were nevertheless bound up with a regime of heritage management in the interests of empire—unity, stability, productivity, legitimacy and, above all, control. The import of this perspective becomes clear in the case study of Villiers-Stuart later in this chapter.

Eurocentric. European travelers from the Mughal period onward reported back to Eurocentric world historians who were prominent then, and are again influential in the

[74] Marshall Hodgson, "In the Center of the Map: Nations See Themselves at the Hub of History," *UNESCO Courier*, 1956, reprinted in Marshall Hodgson, *Rethinking World History: Essays on Europe, Islam and World History*, ed. Edmund Burke III, Cambridge, 1993.

[75] Villiers-Stuart, *Gardens of the Great Mughals*, preface; Havell, "Indian Gardens." See also Partha Mitter, *Much Maligned Monsters: A History of European Reactions to Indian Art*, Chicago, 1992, 270–77.

[76] The expression "slaves of custom" was used in the first volume of the Royal Agri-Horticultural Society in India in 1824.

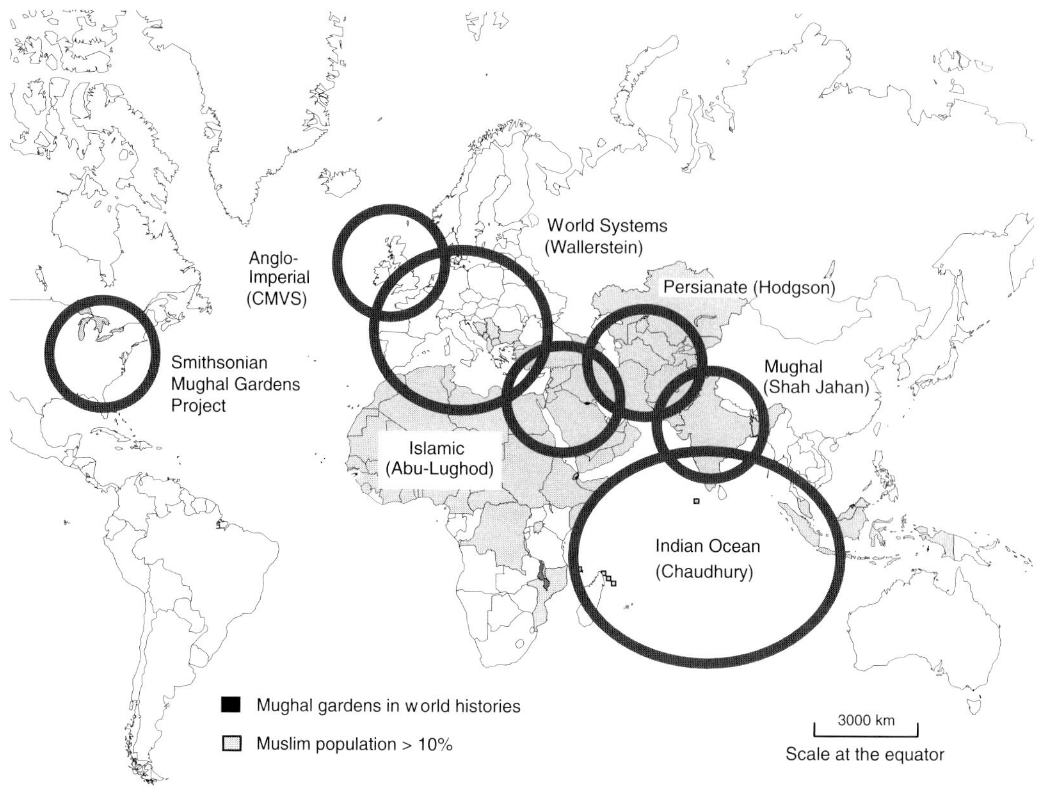

15. World history perspectives relevant to Mughal garden history

postcolonial era as nationalist perspectives yield to broader "Western" ones. World systems theorists such as Immanuel Wallerstein, for example, classify India and much of the Middle East as "semiperipheral," that is, outside the European "core" of world history from the sixteenth century on.[77]

Islamicate. Hodgson, by contrast, put Persia at the center of the world map from the ninth through sixteenth centuries. He termed this hub the Persianate-Islamicate realm, and by his account it exceeded Europe in institutional, economic, and cultural development.[78] It is sobering to recall that the center of the map in Timurid times lay in places such as Samarqand and Bukhara, where few gardens survive, and also in Herat, Kabul, and Ghazna, where in the wake of current conflicts precious little of anything may survive.

Indian. K. N. Chaudhuri offers a larger scale and more easterly worldview, based on the Indian Ocean, which puts India at the center of a map of world trade and cultural exchange through the eighteenth century.[79] The even broader, multivalent, geographic frame-

[77] Immanuel Wallerstein, *The Modern World-System: Capitalist Agriculture and the Origins of the European World-Economy in the Sixteenth Century,* vol. 1, New York, 1974.

[78] Hodgson, *The Venture of Islam.*

[79] K. N. Chaudhuri, *Asia before Europe: Economy and Civilization of the Indian Ocean from the Rise of Islam to 1750*, Cambridge, 1990.

work of Janet Abu-Lughod reminds world historians that multiple circuits existed in the thirteenth and fourteenth centuries in the world "before European hegemony," and that several of these were centered around Muslim societies and economies.[80]

As noted earlier, there are as yet no Mughal garden histories that reflect a self-consciously Islamicate or Indian perspective on the subject. Instead, the literature on Mughal gardens *from* South Asia tends to combine colonial archaeological methods—empirical, pragmatic, and conserving—with flashes of post-colonial critique, reflection, and concern, but little discussion of the literature emanating from Europe or America, which stands in striking contrast to the literatures of "subaltern studies" and post-colonial cultural and environmental debates.[81]

U.S. The United States constitutes another "center of the map." In contrast to the earlier Anglo-imperial garden historians, however, U.S. garden historians do not discuss their geopolitical situation or interests explicitly, which tends to obscure and displace (but not erase) their perspective. Our research in Pakistan, for example, coincided with the Soviet presence in Afghanistan, large U.S. programs in the region, and funding from the PL-480 Food for Peace program.[82] These historical circumstances had important consequences for Mughal garden history. Based in Pakistan, in a period of Islamicization, our research gave particular attention to hypotheses about "Islamic" dimensions of Mughal garden history.

Similarly, the opening of new Central Asian nations and the closing of Iran, Afghanistan, and other nations to U.S. scholars has deepened our understanding of Timurid vis-à-vis Safavid and other loci of Muslim garden history. If the impacts of "globalization" on cultural heritage, including gardens, are a concern, these American world historical and ideological perspectives and their critics deserve greater attention in the years ahead.

Practical Concern: Villiers-Stuart's *Gardens of the Great Mughals*

These regional and global perspectives underscore the importance of comparative inquiry for understanding Mughal gardens. They also indicate some of the "practical concerns" that are at work in garden history. The final section of this chapter returns to the practical concerns surrounding Mughal gardens—cultural identity, conflict, landscape development, conservation, and landscape design—that were surveyed at the beginning of the paper to show how Mughal garden history combines comparative and practical inquiry.

A full historiographic treatment of this theme lies beyond the scope of this chapter. My aim is to demonstrate that Mughal garden studies arose from the strong practical concerns of early historians, who used (and misused) comparative analysis to advance those concerns. An ideal case comes from the first book published on Mughal gardens, Constance

[80] Janet Abu-Lughod, *Before European Hegemony: The World System, A.D. 1250–1350,* Cambridge, 1989.

[81] Ranajit Guha, ed., *Subaltern Studies: Writings on South Asian History and Society,* New Delhi, 1982–, annual; see also the literature cited in James L. Wescoat Jr., David Faust, and Richa Nagar, "Social and Cultural Geography," in *Encyclopedia of Sociology and Social Anthropology,* New Delhi, in press.

[82] Hussain, Rehman, and Wescoat, eds., *The Mughal Garden.* Cf. Moynihan, *Paradise as a Garden.*

Mary Villiers-Stuart's *Gardens of the Great Mughals* (her subsequent book on Spanish gardens makes frequent comparisons with Mughal gardens).[83]

Like many pioneers of a new field, Villiers-Stuart made heavy use of comparisons and analogies to support her argument for greater attention to Mughal gardens.[84] To understand her uses of comparison, it is useful to sort and map them systematically (Fig. 16). The "raw data" run as follows: Villiers-Stuart dedicates her book to "all east and west who love their own gardens." She strives to write for English and Indian readers. In her preface she regrets that Mughal gardens have had limited appeal for English readers, and that gardens are neglected vis-à-vis other aspects of Indian art even though "the Mughal Paradise Garden supplied the leading motive in Mughal decorative art, and still underlies the whole artistic world of the Indian craftsman and builder" (p. viii). Her motive is to examine these cultural functions of gardens and to prepare her arguments in time to "illustrate the bearing of Indian garden-craft on the pressing problem of New Delhi as well as on the larger study of Indian handicrafts" (p. viii). The planning and design of New Delhi were well under way at the time she wrote but had given far less attention to the historical or environmental bases of landscape design than to architecture and urban design. She speaks to issues of climate, color, and symbolism that were being discussed in related building fields in New Delhi, and strives to correct misperceptions of Indian gardens, often by laying blame at the feet of English economic, cultural, and administrative policies that were undermining traditional crafts in India.

These functional concerns had their symbolic, even spiritual counterpart, in the first chapter of the book, where Villiers-Stuart asserted that art is more symbolic in the East than in Europe and that the spirit of Eastern gardens is water while that of Western gardens is plants (pp. 2–3). She found similarities between Mughal and Tudor gardens (the latter "swept away by the sham romanticism of the eighteenth century and . . . the once lauded landscape gardener 'Capability' Brown," p. 20). Mughal public gardens were compared with English almshouses, and contrasted with English parks. Villiers-Stuart decried the Anglo-Indian abandonment of Mughal garden symbolism for plant breeding and horticultural science. The decline of spirituality and advance of modernity in the West were external, but not insignificant, for her project.

Her comparative vision ranges further afield. New Delhi is compared with Isfahan. Kashmiri gardens seem like Italian Baroque gardens, albeit more neglected. "When these Italian gardens are so much admired, photographed, and visited, why are the Mughal baghs of the Indian foot-hills . . . ignored?" (p. 25). Even Chinese and Japanese gardens receive more attention. She draws analogies with French and Dutch garden history, always in an attempt to explain why Indian garden-craft is neglected and in decline (pp. 30–31). Like Havell, her explanations include increased movement via railroads, which enable

[83] Constance Mary Villiers-Stuart, *Spanish Gardens,* London, 1936.

[84] James L. Wescoat Jr., "Varieties of Geographic Comparison in *The Earth Transformed*," *Annals of the Association of American Geographers* 84 (1994), 721–25.

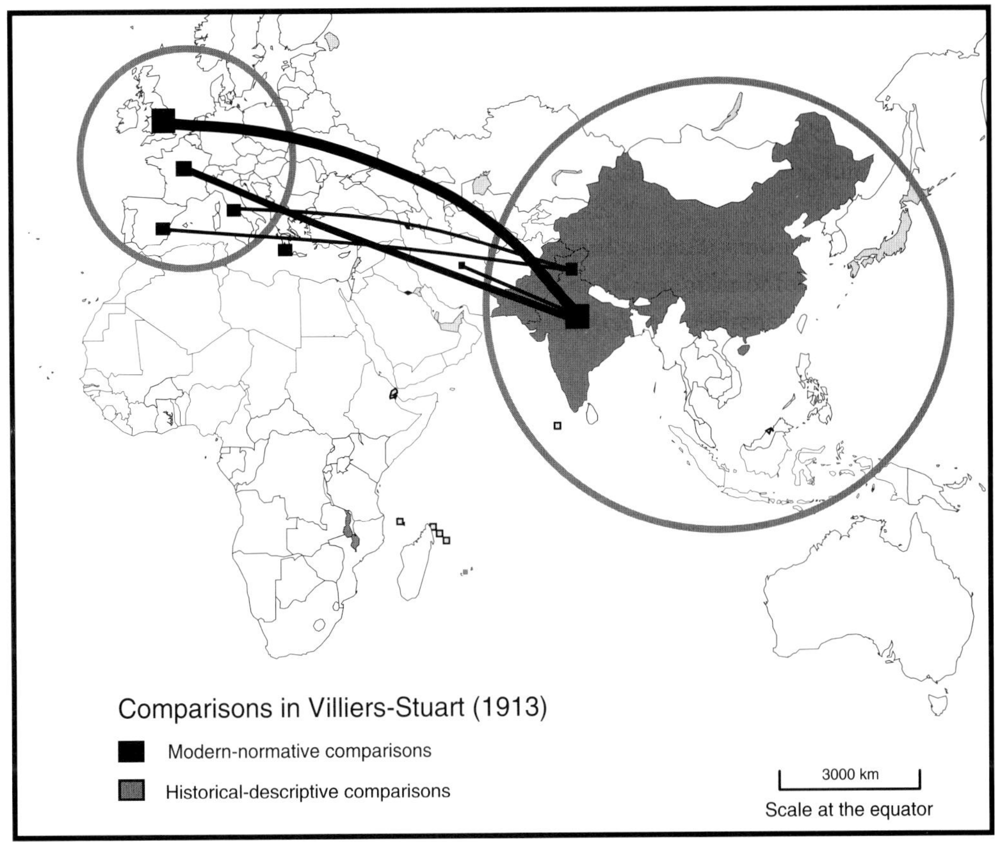

16. Areas of Villiers-Stuart's comparisons between Mughal gardens and other garden traditions

people to travel to climatologically favored hill-stations rather than to design places on the plains to be as favorable as possible. She laments Indian emulation of English garden tastes. And she blames the Mughal emperor Aurangzeb for "banishing Hindu craftsmen from the Moslem court" (p. 267).

Her remedy, indeed her "dream," articulated in chapter 12, is for British clubs, residences, and public grounds to combine English science with Indian symbolism, or rather, a peculiarly imperial conception of Indian symbolism. She believes that garden symbolism goes "to the very root of national life" and that "a love of nature generally, especially of flowers, is as much a national characteristic of the English as of Indians" (pp. 273–74). Her dream of national unity would be fulfilled at the "Delhi of King George," which indicates the importance she attached to gardens and garden history as expressions of the authority and ideology of empire.

She ardently believed that the spiritual meaning and beauty of gardens could foster loyalty among Indian subjects. It is worth quoting her argument at length:

17. Archaeologists, architects, and gardeners working on the restoration of the Wah garden tank, Pakistan

Ideas of "peaceful domination" or "dignified rule" are but a poor exchange for Indian religious feeling, for the deep traditional reverence of Indians for their Emperor.

The material advantages of our good government—peace, laws justly administered, education, sanitation, hospitals, even the fairyland of European science—leave the mass of India cold. . . . Here lies the great opportunity of New Delhi, for the motive that can really move and lead India must be a religious one. (pp. 275–76)

. . . .

If the palace at New Delhi could form part of a scheme with a great Imperial Indian garden, with its symbolic divisions, water-ways, avenues, fountains and walls, Indian art would receive a stimulus and Indian loyalty a lead which it would be impossible to overrate, although hard to believe in England, where the gardens, beautiful as they are, lack the practical use and deeper religious significance of Indian garden-craft. (pp. 279–80)

Those words close the book that launched the field of Mughal garden history. It comes as little surprise that scholars of the post-colonial era do not quote or mention them, and that they eschew such normative proposals for linking past and present, dominance and submission. Villiers-Stuart opened a Pandora's box of comparative themes, many of them misconceived on factual and other grounds, but some of them deserving critical and constructive attention.

Studies of Mughal gardens, undertaken by designers more often than by classically trained scholars, also emerge from practical and comparative interests. In recent decades those interests seem repressed, unvoiced, or underexamined (Fig. 17). A research project on Kashmiri gardens, for example, would no doubt harbor some hope, however modest, for conservation and conciliation in that embattled region of multiple cultural identities. How can such practical aims be envisioned, articulated, and pursued? As noted at the beginning of this chapter, we lack the theoretical and methodological apparati needed for comparative practical inquiry. Probing conservation projects, linked with further historiographic research on Mughal gardens—from Villiers-Stuart to the present—might illuminate some of the possibilities, and pitfalls, for comparative research, and thereby contribute to a constructive reweaving of scholarly and practical interest in the gardens of the world.

"Leaping the Property Line": Observations on Recent American Garden History

Kenneth Helphand

Just five years before the British Colonies declared their independence, Horace Walpole in the *History of the Modern Taste in Gardening*, in what is perhaps garden history's most famous phrase, pronounced that William Kent had leapt the garden fence and saw that all nature was a garden.[1]

When design professionals take on a project, they are given or assemble a set of plans, maps, and drawings to enable them to work on the site. Typically on these drawings there is a thick dashed boundary noting the limits of the project. This is the area they are accountable for, for which they gather data, for which they are contracted to produce a product or proposal. It's what the client cares about. For enlightened professionals one of the first rules and conceptual acts in any design process is to broaden the area of concern, to extend the boundary, to leap the property line. Not in this case to see that everything beyond the bounds is a garden—it may or may not be—but in recognition that to fully understand what is within the line, within the bounds, it is essential to look beyond. At the primary level this means first a study of the immediate environs to understand how they have given shape to the site, but this is only the first layer. Conceptually it is more than that; it is an extension of boundaries, drawing new lines in both time and space. Only by this expansion of context, by extending the field of vision and the range of concern, can one truly understand and appreciate what lies within. What is true for design is true for design history as well.

New lines have been drawn and others need to be extended and demarcated in studies of American garden history. The territory, both geographical and intellectual, is surely too grand. Our understanding of each and how each modifies the other—America, garden, and history—has been changing. Our concept of America, what we mean by garden, and how we study history, are all under intensive scrutiny.

Lines and boundaries divide inside from out. I want to look at influences and impacts from without, or what has been often seen beyond the bounds of garden history, largely from the world of American studies. The basic stories, the narratives of garden history, are

[1] H. Walpole, *History of the Modern Taste in Gardening (1771/1780),* in J. D. Hunt and P. Willis, *The Genius of the Place*, Cambridge, Mass., 1988, 313.

evolving. The content of the story has changed. Much of the American garden tale has been descriptive and often antiquarian. The descriptive story is still essential to establish a base data level of information of who, what, when, and where—especially since so little of the information existed. Garden scholars had neglected it or addressed other matters. Thus, recent work such as the *Pioneers of American Landscape Design* publication and database is critical, as is *The Catalog of Landscape Records in the United States* at Wave Hill and the establishment of various regional garden history associations and archives.[2] There has been a claiming of garden and landscape architecture's rightful historical place. There has been a making up for years of neglect when little was documented and less discussed. This was prompted by many forces, but it includes the pressure of responding to the immediacy of what rapidly disappears either through neglect or willful destruction. Gardens can quickly become invisible. The twentieth-century works of an Ellen Shipman, Jens Jensen, or even Tommy Church have disappeared or go unheralded. There is another critical aspect, a discovery of what was right before one's eyes, that where one was walking en route to see something else that was seemingly important, was in itself significant. The garden or landscape wasn't just the frame for a building. It is a fundamental perceptual shift. The ground becomes the figure.

The method of the tale is changing as well; it is more analytical and interpretative, and it has adopted and adapted techniques from diverse disciplines: art and architectural history, literature, folklore and geography. There is revisionism, where the old story is revised, as well as the writing of new stories, with new characters and new plotlines. In the world of historiography, the past 25 years has been an intensely active period. There have been successive waves of methodologies and areas of interest. The historical canon has been pried open in a struggle to do full justice to describing and understanding the nature of human experience. Extended boundaries have been drawn in terms of gender and sexuality, and the varieties of peoples that make up American culture and society are beginning to be given their historical due, as are the complexities of interactions among cultures and peoples. History, which was too often from the top down, is now more often looked at from the bottom up, and what was looked at from afar is looked at from within. The methods of historical evidence have kept pace and are of course much debated: quantifiers, structuralists, poststructuralists, semioticians. Perhaps most significant is the emergence of cultural studies where garden history's role should be self-evident but is only beginning to be explored. The garden is a ripe site for investigation as cultural studies engages the complexities and ambiguities of meaning, the intersections of ideology and creative activity, and questions of representation, through an expanded awareness of what constitutes evidence for intellectual inquiry.

Of great import to garden history has been the reassertion and the rediscovery for many (although obviously not for garden historians) that the material world, and not just

[2] C. Birnbaum and L. Crowder, eds., *Pioneers of American Landscape Design: An Annotated Bibliography*, Washington, D.C., 1993; C. Birnbaum and J. K. Fix, eds., *Pioneers of American Landscape Design*, II: *An Annotated Bibliography*, Washington, D.C., 1995; *Catalog of Landscape Records in the United States*, Bronx, N.Y., 1987–.

materialism, matters. Thus a concern for physical reality from the scale of artifact to landscape to the role of space in general has become paramount. Geography, no longer concerned with the stigma of being branded a prisoner of environmental determinism, reemerged to reassert its rightful position in understanding place. Environmental history, which lay moribund for much of this century, has returned. We are beginning to see historical studies that look first to the environment, and not just for maps to ground events in a basic geography. The impact of Fernand Braudel and the Ecole des Annales is fundamental in this context.[3] This new environment is not just a foundation to be covered in chapter one of a survey text; it is conceptualized as a continuing actor as a historical force. This is having a profound and subversive effect on historical studies. *Environmental Review*, now called *Environmental History*, the journal of the American Society for Environmental History, began publishing only in 1976.[4] It is significant to note that the *Journal of Garden History* begins five years later.

How do these developments impact the garden? A look at the literature of environmental history reveals that in this burgeoning realm, virtually all speak of landscape, but few speak of that most special and concentrated landscape, the garden. The return leap from the landscape back across the garden wall appears to be more difficult than the exit from the garden. It may be just a time lag. For example, one would expect the ideas of historian William Cronin on the development of Chicago, as exposed in *Nature's Metropolis: Chicago and the Great West*, and his theory on the connections of an urban environment to its hinterland to influence how we think about the prairie school or the development of the Chicago Park System.[5] Or those of Donald Worster, who has appropriated Wittfogel's concept of hydraulic civilization and imaginatively applied it to the American West, to modify the garden histories of the oasis cultures of that region.[6] I don't see this happening enough. Oddly, ecological thought or methodology has barely penetrated garden history. Cronin's edited volume, *Uncommon Ground*, and particularly Anne Spirn's contribution, "Constructing Nature: The Legacy of Frederick Law Olmsted," point in promising directions.[7]

Let us ask some questions of the garden under the rubric of American studies and the cultural context of the American garden. How do we understand that context, and how have designers responded to it? Landscape as idea and actuality is central to understanding American myth and culture. American visions are a litany of landscape ideas and ideals. The elusive American Dream—or better, dreams—has its manifestations in the landscape. The New World, the City on the Hill, the frontier, house and home, the west, the wilderness, the open road—all of these are landscape concepts (Fig. 1). These crystallizations of American experience have all undergone reexamination and revisionist critique in recent years.

[3] F. Braudel, *The Mediterranean World in the Age of Phillip II*, New York, 1966.

[4] *Environmental Review,* 1976–89; *Environmental History,* 1989–.

[5] W. Cronin, *Nature's Metropolis: Chicago and the Great West,* New York, 1991.

[6] D. Worster, *Rivers of Empire: Water, Aridity, and the Growth of the American West*, New York, 1985.

[7] A. Spirn, "Constructing Nature: The Legacy of Frederick Law Olmsted," in *Uncommon Ground: Toward Reinventing Nature*, ed. W. Cronin, New York, 1995, 91–113.

1. Typical American farmer's residence (from J. W. Goodspeed, The Master Spirits of the World and the American Citizen's Treasure House, *Chicago, 1872, 100)*

In the realm of ideas, nature itself has undergone critical evaluation. What was seemingly simple is no longer taken for granted, and what was often seen in bipolar terms is more complex. Thus there is a culture of nature and a nature of culture. At a more basic level, the cultural becomes "natural" and the natural, "cultural."[8] American "nature" is part of the nation's cultural identity, its ideology, even its religion.[9] How are we rethinking *American* "nature" (Fig. 2)? Despite, or perhaps because of, the profundity of this connection, too often "nature" in American history has been sold as an elixir, a patent medicine cure-all for what ails our civilization, an escape, an illusion, as opposed to a true remedy and a more traumatic cure for what ails us.

American idealism and American pragmatism unite and do battle in a landscape arena. This is so at all scales, the garden included. The garden's functions are complex. It is not only a retreat; it has a more assertive presence.[10] How are those dreams realized and actualized in garden design, in languages that are symbolic, spatial, material, and behavioral? Is the garden part of the American dream? If so, what kind or kinds of garden? Is it private or

[8] A. Wilson, *The Culture of Nature: North American Landscape from Disney to the Exxon Valdez,* Cambridge, Mass., 1992; Raymond Williams, *Keywords: A Vocabulary of Culture and Society*, New York, 1985.

[9] J. Conron, *The American Landscape: A Critical Landscape of Prose and Poetry,* New York, 1973; H. Huth, *Nature and the American: Three Centuries of Changing Attitudes,* Berkeley, 1957.

[10] K. Helphand, "Defiant Gardens," *Journal of Garden History* 17 (1997), 101–21.

Crystal Cascade.

2. Crystal Cascade (from Portland White Mountains Railroad Guide, *1853)*

public? At the domestic level, how does it connect to the house and home, which are so vitally tied to American individualistic ideals and expressions of self? Is it constant? Has it been a universal dream? How does it vary spatially and regionally? How has it evolved? Each of these questions deserves consideration. Here let us examine just three seminal concepts of the American experience and their application to garden history. Each offers an expanded context for understanding the American garden. The first, the machine in the garden, is conventional, but it needs updating and reexamination. The second, the everywhere community, suggests questions that remain consistently unaddressed and under-

3. General view of the Middle States (from S. G. Goodrich, A Pictorial Geography of the World, *Boston, 1849, 210)*

scores the need to examine unstated assumptions. The third, baby boomers, is more speculative in its possible application to garden studies.

The Machine in the Garden

Alexis de Tocqueville in 1831 noted that "No sooner do you set foot upon the American ground than you are stunned by a kind of tumult. A confused clamor is heard on every side, and a thousand simultaneous voices demand the satisfaction of their social wants. Everything is in motion"[11] (Fig. 3). His contemporary, Andrew Jackson Downing, an equally keen cultural observer, wrote, "We must look for a counterpoise to the great tendency toward constant change, the restless spirit of emigration, which form part of our national character.... One does not need to be much of a philosopher [referring to Tocqueville] to remark that one of the most striking of our national traits is one of a spirit of unrest."[12] Downing's concept of home, what kind of houses and gardens Americans could and should live in, was the counterpoise he was seeking, a rest for this restlessness. Domingo Sarmiento of Argentina observed, "If God were suddenly to call the world to judgment, He would

[11] A. de Tocqueville, *Democracy in America*, New York, 1841, 271.
[12] A. J. Downing, *Rural Essays*, New York, 1853, 13–15.

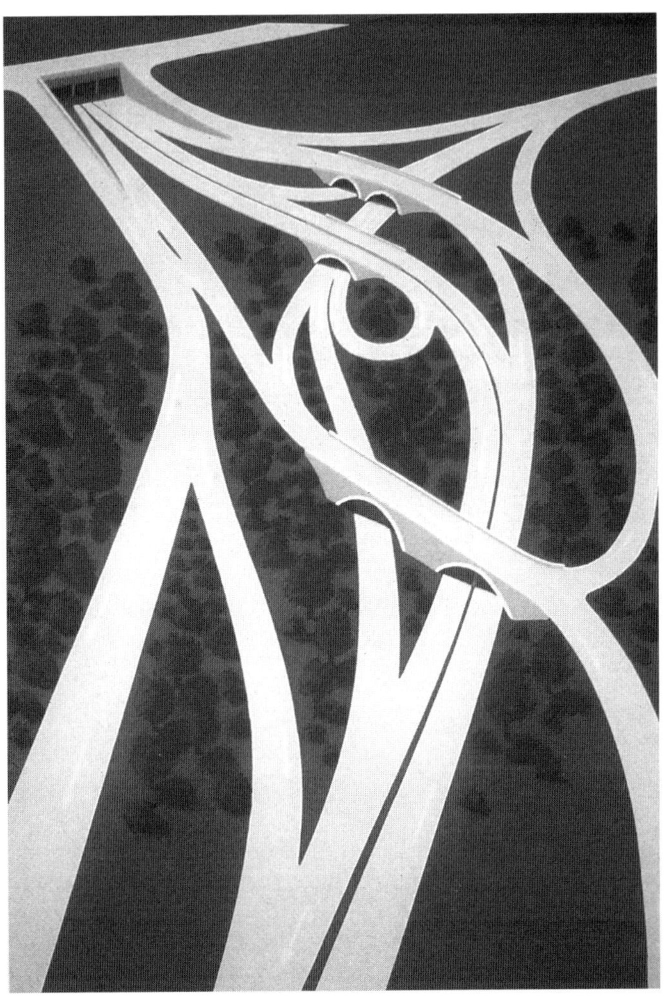

4. Hans J. Barschel, cover, Fortune Magazine, *June 1938*

surprise two-thirds of the population of the United States on the road like ants."[13] He could write this in 1847! American infatuation with mobility is a deep-seated cultural value that the automobile has only accentuated, not determined[14] (Fig. 4). Most American garden history deals with a period during and after the Industrial Revolution; therefore our gardens are almost all the products of a technological age. Are they just refuges, or is it a more complex and ambivalent relationship? The full set of connections of American garden and American machine needs more exploration.

The Machine in the Garden, Leo Marx's analysis of the pastoral in American life and literature, studied the impact of technology and industrialization on the traditional and rural society of nineteenth-century America.[15] Marx concluded that Americans have con-

[13] D. Sarmiento, *Travels in the United States in 1847,* trans. M. A. Rockland, Princeton, 1970, 133.
[14] W. Zelinsky, *The Cultural Geography of the United States,* Englewood Cliffs, N.J., 1973.
[15] L. Marx, *The Machine in the Garden*, New York, 1964.

5. Madisonville, Ohio, 1870s

sistently sought an idealized pastoral "middle landscape," a best of both worlds of city and country, machine and tradition, as a golden mean between these poles (Fig. 5). The ideology has certainly influenced the history of community design and especially the American suburb.[16] It is also surely visible in modern advertising as a marketing device, but one with profound cultural resonance.

Marx's analysis was grounded in actuality, but he emphasized the machine in the garden as metaphor. What of a more literal interpretation? What of the actual machine *in* the garden? The pair of house and garden has in this century been triangulated by the automobile and its associated spaces. Is not all twentieth-century garden and landscape design in some measure a response to the automobile? Does the car sit within the garden boundary or beyond? Should not our purview for the residence include the driveway and parking as a garden space? The car is certainly the twentieth century's machine in the garden. Does it destroy it? Does the sound of a horn, the hum of tires on pavement, the tons of steel and glass moving or at rest offer the same clarion call that Hawthorne's train whistle symbolized as a destruction of the pastoral illusion did for Leo Marx's analysis of nineteenth-century America? The implication I read in modern garden history is that it does. American gardens have been true to international twentieth-century modern garden de-

[16] C. Girling and K. Helphand, *Yard Street Park: The Design of Suburban Open Space*, New York, 1994; P. Rowe, *Making a Middle Landscape*, Cambridge, Mass., 1991.

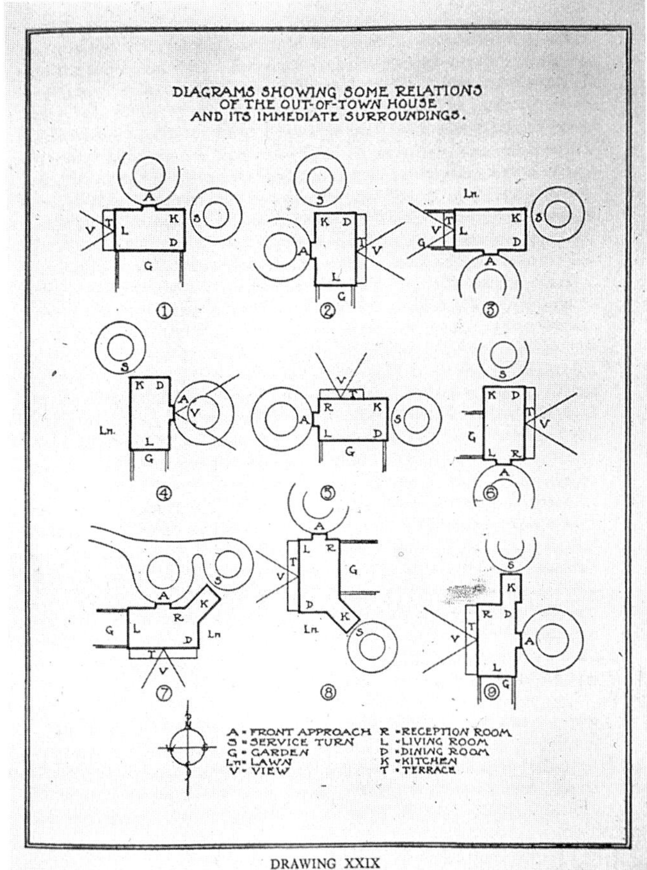

6. *"Diagrams showing some relations of the out-of-town house and its immediate surroundings" (from H. Hubbard and T. Kimball,* An Introduction to the Study of Landscape Design, *after 254)*

sign, which has hidden the car away or eliminated it from the garden frame, even when it sits squarely within its boundaries. It is a magnificent act of prestidigitation. Finding cars in images is often as difficult as finding people in architectural photography. This is the opposite of popular experience and much professional guidance. Family photo albums are filled with children posed in front of the new car, often with the house and garden in the background. Henry Hubbard and Theodora Kimball in their 1917 text, *An Introduction to the Study of Landscape Design,* showed designs for estate driveways (Fig. 6), and in 1922 Frank Waugh gave basic design advice for a new problem, the automobile turn.[17] Certainly Frank Lloyd Wright confronted the car. The drive at Fallingwater almost passes through the house, and Jens Jensen was the landscape architect for the Lincoln Highway Association. Contemporary designs like Peter Walker's work at IBM Solana in Westlake, Texas, include a serious exercise in parking lot design (Fig. 7)—one of the basic design problems of the twentieth century, like it or not.[18] There is virtually nothing in garden history that seriously deals with

[17] H. Hubbard and T. Kimball, *An Introduction to the Study of Landscape Design,* New York, 1917, 254 ff.; F. Waugh, *Textbook of Landscape Gardening*, New York, 1922, 63–65.

[18] P. Walker, *Minimalist Gardens*, Washington, D.C., 1997, 128–31.

7. *Peter Walker, parking lot, IBM Solana, Westlake, Texas*

these issues and places. Are we all heirs to Humphry Repton, in his fashion of screening out the unpleasant and undesired from the scene?

Tocqueville's, Downing's, and Sarmiento's observations have been echoed by many others. The poles of the stability of home, domesticity, responsibility, and community vie with the lure of the open road and the stimulation of mobility and change. The quest for that middle landscape is fundamentally the ideology that is the foundation of American community design from Olmsted's Riverside to Clarence Stein and Henry Wright's Radburn plan to Frank Lloyd Wright's Broadacre City to the New Urbanists' neotraditional designs.[19] Frank Lloyd Wright's observation about road designers, "there is no more important function looking toward the city of the future than to get the best architects in the world interested in road design," is not yet taken seriously either by designers or historians.[20] For example, it is impossible to understand or think of Frederick Law Olmsted without recognizing his profound accommodation to American mobility, from Central Park's circulation system to that great American invention, the parkway. The unique hybrid of parkway oscillates back and forth between the imperatives of "park" and "way" and their respective roles, meaning, and configuration in the American scene. The parkway was a model of the integration of road and open space, technology and

[19] Girling and Helphand, *Yard Street Park*.
[20] F. L. Wright, *The Disappearing City*, New York, 1932, 50.

8. Samuel Lancaster, Columbia River Highway, Oregon, 1914

nature. The struggle to find a compatibility of form and function that might accommodate modern mobility, its desires and technics, with the park, as a place of community and contact with nature has been a desire since its nineteenth-century formulation by Olmsted and has continued through its twentieth-century automotive variant. Designed linear landscapes like Oregon's Columbia River Highway designed by Samuel Lancaster (Fig. 8), Gilmore Clarke's Westchester parkways, or the Blue Ridge Parkway are the landscape monuments of their age. Fortunately parkway history has begun to be given its due in an annual conference on the subject. Christian Zapatka's *The American Landscape* insightfully discusses this most essential and oft-neglected aspect of American landscape architecture and engineering design.[21]

There are other places to look to inform our investigations. If the twentieth century is an automotive one, it is also the age of film. Both industries saw their beginning in this country in 1895, with the manufacture of cars by the Duryea Brothers and Thomas Edison's kinetoscope. As a medium of cultural expression film records landscapes both actual and imagined. Film is a telling indicator of landscape values and visions. It has also become a primary purveyor of landscape imagery and myth.

Dream has multiple meanings. It refers to sleep, a somnambulant state, but it is also a vision of possibility, an ideal. Dreams can be beneficent and comforting, but bad dreams can be nightmares. Looking at recent American film reveals two starkly contrasting realms. The boundaries of our landscape experience are marked by the pastoral and the apocalyptic—that is, the voluntary escape, the "wish landscape," and the condition imposed by circumstance, the world of fear and terror.[22] The pastoral is inhabited by escapists, the apocalyptic by survivors. These extremes are part of the emotional terrain of the contemporary world and our landscapes. However, most of us dwell at the center, seeking to avoid the perils of apocalyptic doom and death, only dreaming of the pastoral, the world of fantasy and escape. Many recent films—and American films dominate the theaters of the globe—have offered us visions of these polarized worlds. Their atmosphere is immediately identifiable, color-coded in a Technicolor, THX spectrum of emotions. The apocalyptic is dark, loud, fiery, rainy, with toxic air, water, and land as opposed to the bright quiet of the pastoral and the persistence of the greens, blues, yellows, and a nature that is bountiful, safe, and nurturing. One of the more striking recent machine in the garden images is in *Die Hard with a Vengeance,* the 1995 film in which Bruce Willis and Samuel Jackson commandeer a taxicab and drive *through* Central Park.[23] Traffic is tied up, so they avoid Olmsted's carriage roads and go overland with park patrons scattering before them. Their park journey concludes with an extraordinary leap over the garden wall, the southern boundary of Central Park—in a yellow cab.

Everywhere Community

An American garden? The elusive grail of defining our national characteristics in design form is and should be questioned in the light of how the very meanings of "American" are in flux. How does the garden and its history accommodate our immigrant tradition and the ongoing discussions of multiculturalism, regionalism, and diversity? Individualism, the characteristic of the American self that Tocqueville so brilliantly noted in his work over a century and a half ago, is easily readable in the landscape. As the

[21] C. Zapatka, *The American Landscape*, New York, 1995.

[22] K. Helphand, "Battlefields and Dreamfields: The Landscape of Recent American Film," *Oregon Humanities* (Winter 1990), 18–21.

[23] *Die Hard with a Vengeance*, 1995, directed by J. McTiernan.

geographer Wilbur Zelinsky notes, "faith in the absolute goodness of letting every individual do almost anything he wishes is writ large across the American landscape."[24] However, the population is not composed of atomistic persons. A central question in the American experience and landscape has been: How does one create community given that characterization of the American self? A distinct dialectic of individual and community has evolved, and it is triangulated, and perhaps paradoxically stabilized, with Americans' restless mobility, where the road is both release and connective tissue.

The American garden story has been told as the adaptation, assimilation, and accommodation and dispersion of predominantly European, but also Asian and African landscape forms, materials, and ideas to the American continent and its environment and peoples.[25] This is enacted at the national scale and then in its regional variants. It is logical that the region has structured most American garden studies.[26] Designers work within specific regions; the landscape frames the possibilities for design, acting as both constraint and opportunity. Some landscape architects have had national or even international practices, but virtually all of these individuals when working outside their home base speak of the distinctiveness of regional design and the imperative to respond to local characteristics. Kenneth Frampton's call for a critical regionalism should find a particularly receptive ear among garden and landscape historians.[27]

In our era there has been a broad concern for what is often described as a sense of place, a resurrection of the classical ideal of the genius loci. This has many parallels in the cultural and personal search for identity, for "roots," the investigation of home and hearth, a neoromanticism and neopastoralism, a deep nostalgia. All of these sentiments are embodied in a resurgence of interest in gardens, which are intertwined with these ideologies and emotions. Why have these concerns surfaced now? Some of it surely results from a feeling of loss, a perceived placelessness, a reaction to high and complex technologies. Garden, as an activity and place, is seen in contradistinction to these trends, as an assertion of place, a built or concretized nostalgia, and as a site in antithesis to technological forces, mass mobility, and social anomie.[28]

The critical regionalist perspective and the imperative of place are laudable and concerns I strongly endorse, but there is another side. An equally powerful story is less about the continuing differentiation of forms and places than about their homogenization, a dramatic contemporary phenomena, but one that history shows us is not new to the American experience. Many authors, such as John Kouwenhoven, David Lowenthal, Wilbur Zelinksy, Grady Clay, John Stilgoe, Robert Riley, and most notably J. B. Jackson have focused their attention on describing the "American" landscape, emphasizing national characteristics.[29] Individual

[24] Zelinsky, *Cultural Geography,* 16.

[25] D. Streatfield, *California Gardens: Creating a New Eden,* New York, 1994.

[26] T. O'Malley and M. Treib, eds., *Regional Garden Design in the United States,* Washington, D.C., 1995.

[27] K. Frampton, "Ten Points on an Architecture of Regionalism: A Provisional Polemic," *Center* 3 (1987), 20–27.

[28] E. Relph, *Place and Placelessness,* London, 1976.

[29] J. B. Jackson, *Landscape: Selected Writings of J. B. Jackson,* ed. E. Zube, Amherst, 1970; idem, *Discov-*

9. Subdivision, Denver, Colorado, 1996, aerial view

design is nested within the norms of local practice, set within the parameters of regional design and the grander framework of national patterns (Fig. 9). An understanding of the resonance and relationship between these physical and cultural scales is imperative for a full comprehension of any design.

As historian Daniel Boorstin writes in *The Americans: The Democratic Experience,*

> The first charm and virgin promise of America was that it was so different a place. But the fulfillment of modern America would be its power to level times and places, to erase differences between here and there, between now and then, and finally the uniqueness of America would prove to be its ability to erase uniqueness. Elsewhere democracy had meant forms of personal, political, economic, and social equality. In the United States, in addition, there would be a novel environmental democracy. Here, as never before, the world would witness the "equalizing" of times and places.[30]

---

ering the Vernacular Landscape, New Haven, 1984; idem, *A Sense of Place, A Sense of Time,* New Haven, 1994; J. Stilgoe, *The Common Landscape of America*, New Haven, 1982; J. Kouwenhoven, *The Beer Can by the Highway: Essays on What's American about America,* New York, 1961; D. Lowenthal, "American Landscape Tastes," *Geographical Review* 58 (1968), 285–96; R. Riley, "Speculations on the New American Landscape," *Landscape* 24 (1980), 1–9; G. Clay, *Real Places,* Chicago, 1994.

[30] D. Boorstin, *The Americans: The Democratic Experience*, New York, 1973, 307.

10. Instant homes, Bend, Oregon, 1983

Boorstin goes on to describe the characteristics of what he calls the "everywhere community," new forms of association not rooted in traditional values and places, but connected by looser and less conventional bonds of consumption and statistics. One of the seminal observations about the American character has profound landscape and garden implications.

How is the garden a setting within the "everywhere community"? What role does it have to play? If we accept Boorstin's analysis, what kinds of gardens do we create that respond to these seemingly contradictory poles of concepts of community? In traditional patterns of community, people are bound to specific places and locales for periods of long duration. Boorstin asserts that Americans desire to have that quality of community everywhere, easily accessible, available to all, and ideally instantly (Fig. 10). In the American experience there has always been this tension of mobility and stability, home and the open road. This is the dichotomy Downing wrote about. Our concern for this dilemma is heightened in our own era, but it is not new to American history and experiment. Paradoxically, change is one of our constants.

We can extend Boorstin's idea and ask, what is the everywhere garden? How does the garden fit in this equation as place and ideology? Is it a countervailing tendency, a stabilizing force, a balm for change—or is the American garden another "everywhere" phenomenon, like Sears, frozen food, or McDonald's (Fig. 11)? It may have both roles, but our studies have privileged the place specific and the regional. The everywhere community idea, or the everywhere garden, asks us to seriously address whether all virtue lies in con-

11. McDonald's parterre

sulting the genius loci in all. All value does not lie at one end of the place spectrum. Everything that is generic, national, or even multinational need not be the personification of evil. (I am not suggesting that this is all positive; only that we need to address both sides of a complex equation.) The desire for security and the comfort of the predictable, the expectation of certain forms, norms, materials, or spaces is to be respected. The theoretical insights of Kevin Lynch on urban imagery and the empirical studies of Rachel and Stephen Kaplan postulate that a combination of characteristics of coherence and legibility coupled with mystery and complexity in environments is crucial in the creation of satisfying and rich landscape experience.[31] Their insights can inform our attitudes toward landscape history.

Look at our national landscape designs and spaces in this light: the city park, main street, historic districts, freeways, shopping malls, house and garden. They are all, in J. B. Jackson's analysis, classic spaces: regular, predictable, comforting.[32] Gardens are literally rooted, but the American yard, its welcome entry, the signification of home as framed by spacious lawn and choker of foundation plantings, the driveway and its parked car, and the garden's appearance as a place of ease, leisure, family life, and as an expression of care, are everywhere

[31] K. Lynch, *The Image of the City*, Cambridge, Mass., 1960; R. and S. Kaplan, *The Experience of Nature: A Psychological Perspective,* Cambridge, 1989.

[32] Jackson, *Sense of Place.*

12. Residence of Sarah Willis, Mayfield, Santa Clara County, California (photo: from Thompson West, Historical Atlas Map of Santa Clara County, California, *San Francisco, 1876)*

phenomena. It is an identifiable national pattern that overrides most regional characteristics, which to a large degree are (and here I overstate the case) like decorator choices for the home (Fig. 12). The garden is then one forum where individualism, community, and mobility meet and all assert themselves.

Gardens are designed and made, but they are then remade. Suburban historian Barbara Kelly reported in *Levittown: Rebuilding the American Dream* that Levitt built the houses that the homeowners in that community literally rebuilt along with the landscape.[33] This is a commonplace garden event, yet largely unstudied. Gardens are sites that are personalized and, in the American vernacular, customized, much the same way as cars, an individualization of stock merchandise.[34] With gardens the opportunities are even greater, for the methods are more widely practiced, the technological expertise more common and the costs lower, but the motivation is similar.

Baby Boomers

We now live in the era of the baby boomers, that dramatic demographic bulge of postwar population explosion that has affected all aspects of modern American culture. Some reflection on the landscape experience and creations of the baby boomers and its

[33] B. Kelly, *Levittown: Rebuilding the American Dream,* Albany, N.Y., 1993.

[34] J. Raban, *Old Glory: An American Voyage,* New York, 1981.

13. Suburban "frontier," Eugene, Oregon

characteristics should form the context for an exploration of the postwar American landscape design of the past 50 years, almost a quarter of the life of the republic. The postwar landscape belongs to the baby boomers, their parents, and now their children. One can generalize from the particular: through environmental autobiographies the history of the landscape is revealed. These adults, most of us, know the measures of landscape change well, for memory acts as a gauge and guidepost. Many recall moving from city to a suburban fringe or frontier, an outpost of community bordered by woods, streams, range, or desert, only to later see favored and secret places of play and discovery subdivided, paved, and culverted.[35] These were places at a frontier, perhaps the most debated concept in American cultural history. The frontier and Frederick Jackson Turner's formulation of its impact on the American character, what Western historian Patricia Limerick calls the "F" word in American history, continues to exert its power. The frontier is a zone of contact, but what it means, where it is, and who occupies which side of its moving boundary has changed.[36] There are gardens on the frontier, but the garden can also be a frontier and there are frontier gardens[37] (Fig. 13). In frontier situations the garden has been an actual and symbolic agent of landscape change, an isobar of development and domesticity.

[35] K. Helphand, *Colorado: Visions of an American Landscape,* Niwot, Colo., 1992.

[36] P. Limerick, *The Legacy of Conquest,* New York, 1987.

[37] For garden histories that use the frontier idea, see D. Streatfield, "Western Expansion," in *Keeping*

14. Nick at Night, TV Land mural, Seattle, Washington, 1992

In the post–World War II decades technological invention and its subsequent democratization changed the landscape and our relationship to it. The fundamental verities of seasonal change, inside and outside, here and there, now and then, were called into question. Television brought people inside, yet was ironically a "window" on the world (Fig. 14).

Eden: A History of Gardening in America, ed. W. Punch, Boston, 1992, 97–117; and D. Harris, "Making Gardens in the Athens of the West: Bernard Maybeck and the San Francisco Bay Region Tradition in Landscape and Garden Design," in *Regional Garden Design,* ed. O'Malley and Treib, 13–68.

15. Brochure cover, Environmental Illusions, *Rock & Waterscape Systems, Irvine, California*

Jet travel brought the globe into home range and created an international touristic landscape, while space travel brought the whole earth into view. Air conditioning domesticated heat, brought activity indoors, changed the landscape of summer and the south, and made possible the sunbelt. A winter technology of ski lifts, skimobiles, and new equipment transformed mountain regions into boom (and bust) environments. Commonplace landscape sights and senses changed as transistors, then silicon chips, led to the miniaturization and mobility of sound, calculating, and message transmission. What was "natural" (i.e., a landscape product) was increasingly synthesized, including materials, foods, products, and places.

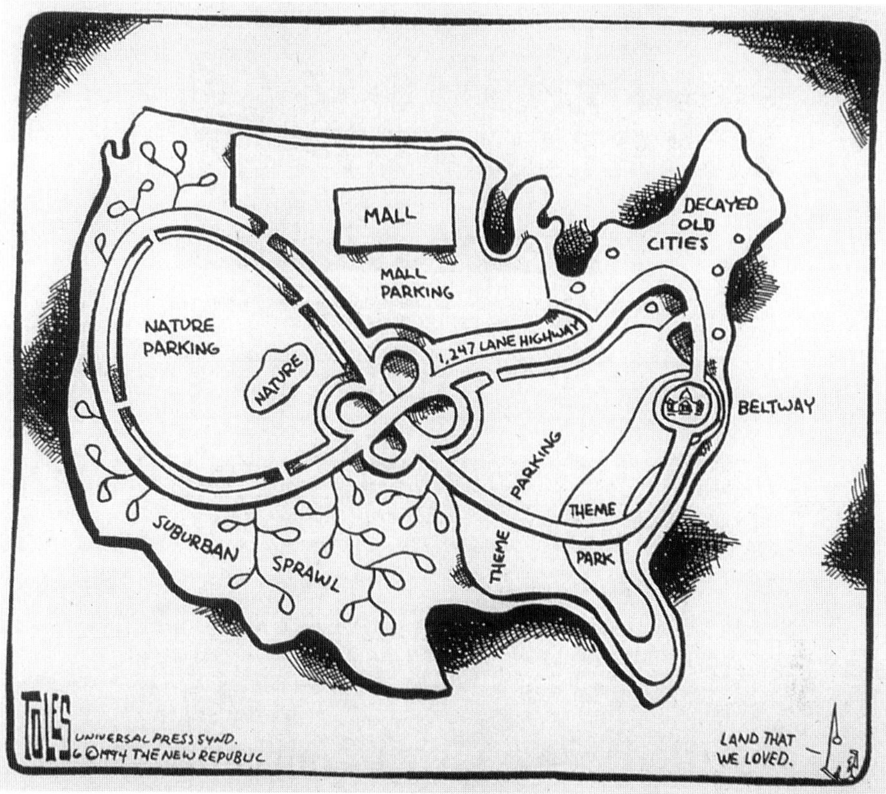

16. Toles ©1994 The Buffalo News (reprinted with permission of Universal Press Syndicate. All rights reserved)

Plants could be plastic, foods instant, places ersatz (Fig. 15). These developments are all part of the framework for understanding the postwar American garden, often as a counterpoise to these developments.

We return to the machine. In this era the automobile reached its ascendant stage, dominating city and countryside, culture and politics. A reaction to its ill effects also began, and freeway construction was halted in its tracks. More than any other factor, the car created a new metropolitan morphology. Finding, creating, and regulating places for automobiles was the governing concern of much land planning and design (Fig. 16). Baby boomers came of age with automotive malls, plazas, and communities, which now dominate commerce, leisure, and home life. The modern landscape complex of a dense core of structures and pedestrian activity ringed with parking emerged as the standard prototype. Popularized by Detroit architect Victor Gruen, his shopping center and downtown plans proved to be remarkably adaptable, and the same basic program is found in corporate headquarters, industrial parks, high schools, junior colleges, PUDs, airports, resorts, and expositions. All of these developments were projects undertaken by landscape architects. These are the villas and garden complexes of our time.[38]

[38] F. Koetter, "The Corporate Villa," *Design Quarterly* 135 (1987), 31–40.

The impact of these technologies has been simultaneously centrifugal and centripetal, spreading things and people apart and pulling them together, creating dispersed concentrations. Landscape design and planning often concentrated on balancing and modulating these opposing forces. New zones, districts, and vocabularies emerged: urban renewal, historic districts, gentrification, ring roads, gated communities, and theme parks. On the other hand, classic concepts and common wisdom were resurrected. It is no accident that the urban fountain environments of Lawrence Halprin emerge in this period. Oftentimes designs sought the solace of the traditional, such as markets, villages, or greens, while accommodating newer functions, but often in name only. Landscape architecture's fundamental axiom of seeking the genius loci, a sense of place, was revived as a counterforce to the impacts of ignoring its imperatives. But too often environmental design was a cosmetic styling change, where places were treated as products to be packaged[39] (Fig. 17).

Parks, along with the garden, the fundamental unit of landscape architecture, are an indicator of response to these changes. Many urban open spaces had been left to decay as urban populations shifted and land uses altered. To fulfill desires for adventure, inspiration, and recreation people sought nature far afield, in a quest for new landscape experiences. The traditional seashore vacation could mean a Hawaiian package tour, while for the affluent and adventurous mountain vacations could be Nepalese trekking. In the wild landscape, state and national parks slowly moved from a development ideology to dealing with the dilemmas of carrying capacity.

The 1960s saw a resurgence of park interest. At its best there was return to the solace, comfort, and trust in "nature" coupled with a sense of new and revived possibilities for the public park. The civic role of open space was reasserted in organized festivals, impromptu gatherings, theatrical presentations, counterculture "be-ins," and antiwar demonstrations. The resurgence of interest in Olmsted and nineteenth-century visions of the park as a civic meeting ground *and* a work of landscape artistry was no accident. Many new projects of the time were of reclamation and rediscovery. Riverfronts, ports, remnants of nature in the city, vacant, unused, leftover places like quarries, railyards, industrial relicts and artifacts, and historic sites became transformed from liabilities to opportunities. The reclamation and rediscovery spirit was a harbinger of recent concerns for the creation of a sustainable landscape. The baby boomers' sometimes indulgent pastoral nostalgia for lost places of childhood is more than sentimentalism; it is a recognition of the need to carefully modulate and design landscape change.

Conclusion

I have noted three concepts that might further inform American garden scholarship: the machine in the garden, the everywhere community, and baby boomers. In conclusion, let us return to the question of the narratives. One of the changes in recent historical studies has been a return to narrative history, which means not only telling the story but good storytelling. Our best historians are doing this. But what of the stories that we call

[39] Riley, "New American Landscape."

17. Temporary environmental landscaping—future site of Prestige Shopping, Miami, Florida, 1973

fiction, but which of course are often closer to truth? For garden history in other cultures, we accept the literary as fundamental evidence, be it *The Romance of the Rose* or *Paradise Lost.* There are of course classic American garden tales, such as Poe's "Garden of Arnheim." There are a few modern American literary examples: Chance's garden in Jerzy Kozinski's *Being There* or Alice Walker's ruminations in the essay "In Search of Our Mother's Gardens."[40] There are some wonderful popular works, such as Michael Pollan's *Second Nature,* grounded in autobiographical insights.[41] Literature can be not only another site we research for insight; it can, through its power, communicate history and theory in a profound way. There are too few literary attempts at garden history. Nature writing is enjoying a renaissance, but much of it is contaminated by an antiurban, antitechnological polemic, and few of these writers have leapt back from nature to garden. Perhaps they fear being impaled on the fence. I yearn for a garden tale that has the quality of W. D. Wetherwell's "The Man who Loved Levittown" which beautifully encapsulates postwar suburban history.[42] Let us encourage our writers—and that can be any of us—to write garden stories. We need more histories, of course, but we could also use some good stories.

[40] J. Kozinski, *Being There,* New York, 1972; A. Walker, *In Search of Our Mother's Gardens: Womanist Prose,* San Diego, 1983.

[41] M. Pollan, *Second Nature: A Gardener's Education*, New York, 1991.

[42] W. D. Wetherell, *The Man Who Loved Levittown*, Pittsburgh, 1985.

The Search for "Ecological Goodness" among Garden Historians

Joachim Wolschke-Bulmahn

Garden history is a more or less young discipline. Although intellectuals such as John Evelyn (1620–1705), Christian Cay Lorenz Hirschfeld (1742–92), and John Claudius Loudon (1783–1843) wrote about the history of gardens, garden history as a discipline is connected to the emergence of the profession of landscape architecture in the second half of the nineteenth century and established itself in the twentieth century.[1] Garden history and the various histories of gardens are affected by a variety of factors. Whether an art historian, a social scientist, a landscape architect, or a representative of another field investigates the history of gardens might affect the interpretation of garden history. The personal and group interests, as well as the social and cultural contexts of those who investigate and interpret gardens and their histories, are further influential factors. The same historic facts about garden design might be interpreted differently and result in a variety of ideas about garden history depending not only on the scholarly background of the scholar but also, for example, the sociopolitical ideas and ideals of the historians.

As societies change over time, traditional values might be called more and more into question and replaced by new values and ideals. For example, in the 1970s the first efforts were taken to investigate the impact of National Socialism on landscape architecture in Germany. Research suggested a reinterpretation of twentieth-century German garden and landscape history. In the 1980s and 1990s gender issues have become a topic for garden history. The role of women in such fields as landscape architecture and nature preservation remains largely unexplored, but the first attempts have been made to investigate whether there has been a particular impact of women on the field that perhaps could offer perspectives for the future. The broadening of the study of garden history to include not only

[1] An important step in the development of landscape architecture as a profession in the United States was the founding of the American Society of Landscape Architects (ASLA) almost a century ago, in 1899. The Verein deutscher Gartenkünstler (VdG) (Association of German Garden Artists), the first professional organization in Germany, was established in 1887. Gert Gröning and Joachim Wolschke-Bulmahn, *1887–1987: Deutsche Gesellschaft für Gartenkunst und Landschaftspflege e.V. (DGGL): Ein Rückblick auf 100 Jahre DGGL*, Schriftenreihe der Deutschen Gesellschaft für Gartenkunst und Landschaftspflege 10, Berlin, 1987, describes the history of the VdG in more detail.

gardens of the elite but also those of the middle class and so-called lower social groups, such as industrial workers and African Americans, is another phenomenon that indicates changing sociopolitical values in the second half of the twentieth century.

"Ecology" and the Study of Garden History

This interdependence between garden history and broader social, political, and cultural issues will be elucidated by examining a particular example, the perception and interpretation of various historic ideas about "natural" garden and landscape design by garden historians as proof for proper "ecological" behavior. Such terms as "ecology" and "nature" have time and again been used by landscape architects as if they conferred moral authority in order "to justify their designs or to evoke a sense of 'goodness,' but . . . they are generally ignorant of the ideological minefields they tread."[2] Using German and American examples, this article examines a specific aspect of recent developments in garden historical studies—the search of garden historians[3] for ecologically appropriate behavior, for "ecological goodness," in the history of landscape architecture. By using the phrase "search for ecological goodness," I want to point at a special approach to the study of garden history, one guided not so much by the interest in analyzing how our predecessors dealt with ecological issues and nature, but by the longing to prove that they behaved in an ecologically proper way and lived in harmony with nature. Various questions may be raised, for example, when did garden historians first start paying attention to ecological issues? What are their motives and what are they interested in when emphasizing "ecological goodness" in the history of gardens? Are there special political, social, or environmental developments that foster such special interests in garden history? Is the search for "ecological goodness" in the history of garden and landscape design a national phenomenon, or can we find it in various countries? And is it a phenomenon of the twentieth century with its apex perhaps in the second half of our century?

The term *Okologie* ("ecology") was coined in 1866 by the German zoologist Ernst Haeckel and defined more fully by the same scientist in 1870.[4] Early historical accounts of gardens in Germany and elsewhere do not use such terms as "ecology" and "ecological," e.g., Oskar Hüttig's *Geschichte des Gartenbaus* (History of horticulture) (Berlin, 1879), Carl Hampel's *Die deutsche Gartenkunst, ihre Entstehung und Einrichtung mit besonderer Berücksichtigung*

[2] Anne Whiston Spirn, "The Authority of Nature: Conflict and Confusion in Landscape Architecture," in *Nature and Ideology: Natural Garden Design in the Twentieth Century,* ed. Joachim Wolschke-Bulmahn, Dumbarton Oaks Colloquium on the History of Landscape Architecture 18, Washington, D.C., 1997, 253–54.

[3] The term "garden historian" in this paper does not refer exclusively to the relatively small number of scholars explicitly studying the international history of gardens and landscape architecture. Rather, it includes a broad number of scholars, landscape architects, and others who refer to garden history in a more general way.

[4] "By ecology we mean the body of knowledge concerning the economy of nature—the investigation of the total relations of the animal both to its inorganic and to its organic environment; including above all, its friendly and inimical relations with those animals and plants with which it comes directly or indirectly into contact—in a word, ecology is the study of all those complex interrelations referred to by Darwin as the conditions of the struggle for existence." Jonathan Bate, *Romantic Ecology: Wordsworth and the Environmental Tradition*, London and New York, 1991, 36.

der Ausführungsarbeiten und einer Geschichte der Gärten bei den verschiedenen Völkern (The German garden art, its origin and establishment with special consideration of its executional works and a history of gardens of the various people) (Leipzig, 1902), and Marie Luise Gothein's two-volume *Geschichte der Gartenkunst* (History of garden art) (Jena, 1914). In their treatise on landscape architecture and its history, *An Introduction to the Study of Landscape Design* (New York, 1917), Henry Vincent Hubbard and Theodora Kimball do not refer to "ecology," nor is the term found in their work's comprehensive index.[5]

In the 1970s historians began discussing ecology, particularly environmental problems and the rise of ecological movements in various Western nations. One main objective was to better understand today's environmental problems and ascertain how and why they evolved. Numerous treatises on the history of ecology, environmentalism, and what have been called early ecological movements were published. Among them are Roderick Frazier Nash's *Wilderness and the American Mind* (New Haven and London, 1967), the various editions of *American Environmentalism: Readings in Conservation History* by the same author (New York, 1976), Franz-Joseph Brüggemeier's and Thomas Rommelspacher's (eds.) *Besiegte Natur: Geschichte der Umwelt im 19. und 20. Jahrhundert* (Defeated nature: environmental history of the nineteenth and twentieth centuries) (Munich, 1987), Anne Bramwell's *Ecology in the Twentieth Century: A History* (New Haven and London, 1989), Jost Hermand's *Grüne Utopien in Deutschland: Zur Geschichte des ökologischen Bewußtseins* (Green utopias in Germany: about the history of ecological awareness) (Frankfurt am Main, 1991), and Jonathan Bate's *Romantic Ecology: Wordsworth and the Environmental Tradition* (London and New York, 1991).

Landscape architects and garden historians also took an interest in the role of ecology. They looked for the historic contribution of landscape architecture to environmental protection. Garden writers and landscape architects who had developed concepts of natural garden design were now seen as early ecologists. Thus, for example, Gillian Darley characterizes William Robinson as "a whole-hearted ecologist."[6] Ecological significance is attributed to his 1870 book, *The Wild Garden*: "Fragments and echoes of the specific ideas in *The Wild Garden* continued to resurface until the recent upsurge of interest in ecology suddenly gave them a new relevance. Robinson always was just as much an ecologist as he was a designer, a maker of artifacts."[7] Also, the American landscape architect Jens Jensen has recently been praised for his ecological significance. In the introduction to the 1990 reprint of Jensen's *Siftings* we read: "Jensen's view that we should make our designs harmonious with nature and its ecological processes was to become the preeminent theme of modern American landscape architecture practice."[8] And the German garden writer and landscape

[5] Nevertheless, references to ideas that later became discussed as ecological ones can be found in these and other contemporary publications. For example, Hampel defined gardens belonging to the "natural garden style" as "following nature and its laws and aiming at their idealization." C. Hampel, *Die deutsche Gartenkunst*, Leipzig, 1902, 2.

[6] G. Darley, review of *The Wild Garden*, by William Robinson, *Journal of Garden History* 4 (1984), 203.

[7] R. Mabey, introduction to *The Wild Garden*, by William Robinson, reprint of the 1870 edition, London, 1983, xix f.

[8] Charles E. Little, "Jens Jensen and the Soul of the Native Landscape," foreword to *Siftings*, by Jens Jensen, reprint of the 1939 edition, Baltimore and London, 1990, xiii.

architect Willy Lange, a contemporary of Jensen, is commended by an advocate of natural garden design as the garden architect "who laid the foundations of all of our nature gardens, including those of our times."[9]

The Search for "Ecological Goodness" in German Garden History

The search for "ecological goodness" in the history of gardens is not a new phenomenon. It is found already at the beginning of the twentieth century, although the term "ecology" was not yet popular. One of the garden architects whose writings reflect this search, and probably the first German garden architect who used the term "ecology" to describe his own ideas about garden design, was Willy Lange in his 1907 book, *Gartengestaltung der Neuzeit* (Garden design of modern times).[10] Lange and his followers assumed that the German people had a genetically based relationship to nature and were closely bound to particular landscapes. Natural garden and landscape design therefore was seen as a fundamental prerequisite for preserving the racial, and thus the cultural, strength of the German people.[11] The application of biology and ecology, which Lange understood as a subdivision of biology,[12] served to establish the proper plant associations for garden and landscape design.[13] According to Lange garden art had to derive its design criteria from "the ecology of plants, that is, from their relationship to their habitat."[14]

Elsewhere I have elaborated on Lange's ideas about natural garden design.[15] I now would like to discuss Lange's preoccupation with searching for "ecological goodness" in German garden history. Lange used a look back into the history of gardens, although a very biased one, to justify his argument for the future of a race-specific German garden art that

[9] Reinhard Witt, "Wiedereröffnung des Garten Eden," *Natur* (1986), 82.

[10] In *Gartengestaltung der Neuzeit,* Lange described ecology as "a new plant system, the ecology (the doctrine of the relationship of the place to the *Haushalt* of the plants)" (2nd ed., Leipzig, 1909, 171). In a later edition Lange wrote, "Only the newer botany notices the plant in relationship to its soil. The newer botany bases the doctrine of the social coexistence of whole groups of species strange to each other on the doctrine of ecology, i.e., the science of the place and *Haushalt* of the plant."

[11] Or, as the landscape architect Wiepking-Jürgensmann expressed in 1944, "Only the existence of a race-specific environment . . . produces within us the best creative forces." Heinrich Friedrich Wiepking-Jürgensmann, "Bilder und Gedanken zum Aufbau der deutschen Landschaft in den Ostgebieten," *Gartenbau im Reich* 1 (1944), 1.

In various publications Gert Gröning and I discuss the racist character of Lange's ideas about natural garden design, e.g., "Changes in the Philosophy of Garden Architecture in the Twentieth Century and Their Impact upon the Social and Spatial Environment," *Journal of Garden History* 9, 2 (1989), 53–70; eidem, "Some Notes on the Mania for Native Plants in Germany," *Landscape Journal* 11, 2 (1992), 116–26; and J. Wolschke-Bulmahn, "Nature and Ideology: The Search for Identity and Nationalism in Early Twentieth-Century German Landscape Architecture," *American Institute for Contemporary German Studies Seminar Papers* 17 (February 1996).

[12] "Die Lehre von den Lebensgemeinschaften ist der Naturkunde als ökologische Biologie heute geläufig." Lange, *Gartengestaltung der Neuzeit,* 171.

[13] Cf. Willy Lange, *Der Garten und seine Bepflanzung*, Stuttgart, 1913, 29.

[14] Willy Lange, "Die Pflanzung im Garten nach physiognomischen Gesetzen," *Die Gartenkunst* 6 (1904), 169.

[15] See, for example, Gröning and Wolschke-Bulmahn, "Changes in the Philosophy," and Wolschke-Bulmahn, "Nature and Ideology."

he saw in special concepts of natural garden design. For Lange the English landscape garden corresponded to what he believed were race characteristics of the Germans. He wrote in 1927 that in Europe "the Germanic spirit of race remembered its age-old relation to the forest nature with its sunny clearings and formed it into the 'English park,' according to an immediate feeling for home, into an art beauty, which did not imitate nature, but aggrandized it according to the 'ideas' of her own innate life."[16]

Lange's appreciation of the English landscape garden as in harmony with German race characteristics went hand in hand with the rejection of the regular or formal gardens as not appropriate for Nordic people. For Lange, the regular Italian and French garden were rooted in different race characteristics:

> The contrast between the "formal" French and the "informal" English garden style are much more deeply arising from different *Weltanschauungen,* and these again from the differences between the souls of the two races; because in the soul of the race all feelings, action, and nonaction are rooted. The French style garden is the garden expression of the south-alpine Mediterranean race; the English style germinates from the reawakened feeling for one's race of the north-alpine, the Nordic people. . . . In an unconscious way the nordic man "protested" in Pückler against the un-Nordic spirit in garden life.[17]

"In the architectonic garden," Lange continued, the Nordic man "perished in the swamps of races from the south."[18] The gardens of the Italian Renaissance therefore were, for Lange, evidence of "how deep the southern half of Europe stood against the northern half with regard to the execution of garden planting. . . . The gardens of the Italian Renaissance are 'built,' not 'planted' gardens."[19] And further, "Even the gardens of the Italian Renaissance deserve appreciation more as a building than as the gardener's art of planting. If we could see them with today's critical eyes at the time, when they came into being, they perhaps would be unbearable to us."[20] With the rise of National Socialism, Lange became more and more radical in his racist interpretation of the history of gardens. He published his ideas not only in professional journals, but also in volkish magazines, e.g., his article "Nordic Garden Art" in the magazine *Die Sonne* (The sun) and another article, "German Garden Art," in the National Socialist magazine *Deutsche Kulturwacht* (German culture guard).[21]

[16] Willy Lange, *Gartenpläne,* Leipzig, 1927, 82.

[17] Ibid., 5.

[18] Ibid., 6.

[19] Lange, *Garten und seine Bepflanzung,* 7:8.

[20] Lange, *Garten und seine Bepflanzung,* 19. Like Lange, Jens Jensen rejected formalism in garden design as not appropriate for the Nordic people. He wrote in 1938 in a paper for the International Horticultural Congress Berlin, "The Nordic, or if you please, Germanic mind, is not imbued with formalism of any kind. To him it is an affected thing. It does not speak the truth as the truth should be told by an intellectual people. To him it is foreign." Jens Jensen, "Park and Garden Planning," in *12. Internationaler Gartenbau Kongress Berlin 1938,* ed. Generalsekretär des Kongresses, Berlin, 1939, 1007.

[21] Willy Lange, "Nordische Gartenkunst," *Die Sonne* 6, 3 (1929), 118–26; idem, "Deutsche Gartenkunst," *Deutsche Kulturwacht* (1933), 7, 8–9.

The Search for "Ecological Goodness" during National Socialism

For historians in general, not only for garden historians, the period of National Socialism in Germany is of special interest. National Socialism offers extreme examples of the intermingling of scientific and political judgements. This relates also to ecology. With regard to landscape architecture and garden history we can learn how ideas about "ecology" that apparently lack political and ideological significance were seen as highly political and ideological. Some of them had fatal results for specific ethnic, religious, and other social groups, as they served to justify the expulsion and extermination of other people. Using National Socialism in Germany as a reference might help to better recognize the ambivalent character of similar ideas held at the same time in countries other than Nazi Germany.

During the period of National Socialism, Lange's biased interpretation of garden history was taken further by the acknowledged garden historian Franz Hallbaum. In 1935, two years after the takeover by the National Socialists, in his essay "Pückler und der Muskauer Park" (Pückler and the Muskau park), Hallbaum praised the new National Socialist interest in garden history in the following way:

> Until a few years ago the landscape way of design and with it the great historic creations in this style were not very popular, particularly among architects and garden architects. . . . The landscape garden was rejected as a romantic-sentimental gewgaw [*Spielerei*], as non-artful naturalism. We believe that today's time, which relates all branches of human activity to the questions of race, blood and soil will establish again the appreciation of the landscape garden style that it deserves, that it is really an "expression of our nature." Because the development of the landscape garden and the fight against the regular "French garden style" in the eighteenth century were deeply the expression of a race connected feeling for nature. The Nordic man with his pantheistic feeling for nature stands against the Mediterranean man and the Western people. He rejects the subjugation of nature, the cutting of shrub and tree. . . . The old Germanic love for trees revives again.[22]

Whether Hallbaum did believe in this kind of racial disposition for a specific garden style or whether he had other motives to promote this ideology is unclear. At least, garden historians were not forced to argue during National Socialism in this racist way. In the same volume in which his article was published, other authors discussed Pückler and his park design in Muskau and Branitz without references to a race-specific German feeling for nature. And a few years earlier, in his 1927 dissertation "Der Landschaftsgarten" (The landscape garden), Hallbaum himself did not interpret the landscape garden in such a racist way, although he already revealed a special preoccupation regarding a naive and arbitrary relation of southern people to nature.[23]

[22] Franz Hallbaum, "Pückler und der Muskauer Park," in *Fürst Hermann Pückler-Muskau*, ed. Paul Ortwin Rave, Breslau, 1935, 44 f.

[23] Cf. Franz Hallbaum, "Der Landschaftsgarten: Sein Entstehen und seine Einführung in Deutschland durch Friedrich Ludwig von Sckell, 1750–1823," Munich, 1927, 24.

The garden architect Hans Hasler might serve as another example of the search for a race-specific "ecological goodness" in German garden history. In his 1938 book, *Deutsche Gartenkunst* (German garden art), Hasler, a disciple of Lange, took this manipulative interpretation of garden history even further and tried to substantiate the racist idea of the close relationship of the Germans to nature and its reflection in the landscape garden and in natural garden design. He wrote,

> But as Germans we want to be proud of the fact that, besides England, it was Germany where the next higher stage of the evolution of gardens, the natural garden, was reached.—For centuries the race-specific Nordic idea of nature was buried for the design of gardens because of the domination of the formal garden. With the Renaissance southern ideas about design influenced not only the architecture, but also the gardens of the princely dynasties. . . . But that idea about design, which is characteristic of our race, forced its way and created, first in England and following in Germany, a fundamental change beginning in the middle of the seventeenth century.[24]

But the course of political events also affected this interpretation of garden history. With England as enemy in World War II, it was no longer considered suitable by some German garden historians to emphasize the common Nordic heritage and to acknowledge England as the creator of the landscape garden. Rather, they wanted to distinguish German garden traditions from English ones. The "ecological goodness" of the English landscape garden fell into discredit for some years. In 1940 garden architect Michael Mappes, editor of *Die Gartenkunst*, wrote "Schach dem 'Englischen Gartenstil'" (Give check to the English garden style).[25] With his article Mappes wanted to correct the "wrong idea that . . . the historic landscape style in garden design would be the indisputable achievement of progressive minds in England. . . . As with regard to other achievements of the British people, it is also time to evaluate with regard to garden art [*auf unserem Kultursektor*] particular ideas and, if necessary, to revise them."[26] Mappes then tried to offer garden historical evidence that the Germans revealed prior to the British "ecological goodness" and veneration of nature. He ended his article with the assertion that paintings of the fifteenth and sixteenth centuries would prove how much in Germany a parklike designed nature "long before the 'English garden style' was regarded and longed for as ideal."[27]

During the rule of National Socialism the interest in garden history and "ecological goodness" changed slightly. Professional landscape architecture strategies became closely connected to National Socialist ideology and politics. In accordance with the expansionism of the Nazis, landscape architects' interest in garden history moved away from the garden and toward the design of complete landscapes. They looked for historic evidence of ecologically proper design not so much of gardens but of whole landscapes, in order to find

[24] Hans Hasler, *Deutsche Gartenkunst,* Stuttgart, 1939, 90.

[25] Michael Mappes, "Schach dem 'Englischen Gartenstil,' " *Die Gartenkunst* 53, 4 (1940), 61–64.

[26] Ibid., 61.

[27] Ibid., 64.

models for reshaping the landscapes robbed from Poland in the fall of 1939. The land embellishment movement of the nineteenth century and its precursors became a focus of garden historical interest.[28]

According to the "blood and soil" ideology, the living space of the German people was a kind of volkish ecosystem. The ideal German people were seen as living in harmony and balance with their natural environment. Such a volkish concept of ecology gained special importance during World War II after the conquest of the Polish territories. A team of landscape architects, regional planners, architects, and others developed—under the leadership of Heinrich Himmler, Reichsleader SS and Reichs Commissioner for the strengthening of Germandom in the annexed east areas—concepts of how to redesign conquered Polish land into ideal German landscapes. According to the volkish idea of the "life community of people and landscape,"[29] the German farmers who should be settled there would need the appropriate landscape to feel at home in the newly conquered territory. Similarly Erhard Mäding, one of Himmler's planners, stated in his *Landespflege* (care of the land), "All organisms of a habitat, in the wider sense a landscape, depend on each other and condition themselves mutually. They are part of a biological life community [*Lebensgemeinschaft*]."[30] Mäding wrote in 1942 that the evaluation and the design "of today's landscape can only be related to the German people for whom it shall be a biological healthy living space, home for all future time."[31] Landscape architecture should provide support for a German identity and help suppress a Polish one.[32]

Two leading members of Heinrich Himmler's planning team, Erhard Mäding and Heinrich Friedrich Wiepking-Jürgensmann, advisor to Himmler for questions of landscape design, especially promoted ideas about an "ecological goodness" of German garden and landscape history in order to justify the conquest of the Polish territory, the expulsion of the Polish people, and the redesign of their landscapes into what they considered an ideal German environment. But the English landscape garden had lost its significance as a model for the volkish ecosystem that ought to be created. In 1942 Mäding published *Landespflege*; in the same year Wiepking published *Die Landschaftsfibel* (The landscape primer). Both authors referred time and again to garden history in order to substantiate their volkish concepts of environmental protection. Mäding rejected not only the Renaissance and Baroque gardens

[28] See, for example, Gert Gröning, "The Idea of Land Embellishment: As Exemplified in the Monatsblatt für Verbesserung des Landbauwesens und für zweckmäßige Verschönerung des baierischen Landes," *Journal of Garden History* 12, 3 (1992), 164–82.

[29] Erhard Mäding, *Landespflege: Die Gestaltung der Landschaft als Hoheitsrecht und Hoheitspflicht,* Berlin, 1942, 74.

[30] Ibid., 137.

[31] Ibid., 136.

[32] For further discussion of this aspect of the recent history of German landscape architecture, see, for example, Gert Gröning and Joachim Wolschke-Bulmahn, *Der Drang nach* Osten: *Zur Entwicklung der Landespflege im Nationalsozialismus und während des Zweiten Weltkrieges in den "eingegliederten Ostgebieten,"* Arbeiten zur sozialwissenschaftlich orientierten Freiraumplanung 9, ed. Gert Gröning and Ulfert Herlyn, Munich, 1987; eidem, "Politics, Planning and the Protection of Nature: Political Abuse of Early Ecological Ideas in Germany, 1933–45," *Planning Perspectives* 2 (1987), 127–48.

but also the English landscape garden as artificial and serving only aesthetic purposes:

> There were times when the garden design [*gärtnerische Gestaltung*] of the landscape and the natural forms served purely aesthetic purposes. . . . The landscape consciously was forced under fashionable rules [*wurde bewußt um modischer Regeln willen gezwungen*]. In most cases any usefulness [*Gebrauch*] was excluded, an artificial decorative landscape was created without any intention of producing an image of the free landscape, even in contrast to it. The garden of the Renaissance and the courtly park are good examples for this attitude. It is true that in the English garden the subjugation [*Pressung*] of the natural growth into the constructed form is loosened but the construction still remains. The idyllic and wild landscape is intended—not genuine—and the idea of its shape became the subject matter of the gardener's [*gärtnerische*] construction plan [*Bauplan*]. . . . Also the English garden is originally a decorative landscape determined by a particular class [*ständisch bedingt*].[33]

Mäding juxtaposed his biased interpretation of the English landscape garden with "the cultural landscape of the Goethe era," thus the heading of one of the chapters in his *Landespflege*. He glorified the so-called Goethe era as a time where the German people lived in biological balance with its environment: "The time from 1750 to 1830 is a period of the highest fertility of German life. It is literally and in the figurative sense a time of prosperity. A harmonic world view is gained, a beautiful living environment in house, garden and landscape is created, a state of biological balance is reached."[34] "The complete landscape," Mäding continued, "becomes finally interpreted as *Gesamtraumkunstwerk*. The land that satisfies heart and spirit is—as Novalis says—a German invention. The bounds of the parks are crossed. For the first time complete landscapes become designed, thus by Peter Joseph Lenné in the region of the Havel lakes between Potsdam and Charlottenburg, by Prince Pückler-Muskau and later by the disciple of Lenné, Johann Heinrich Gustav Meyer."[35]

In numerous publications Wiepking revealed a similarly biased perception of garden history, which gave Germany a unique role as the first nation ever to have reached a state of perfect harmony with its natural environment. Contemporary German landscape architecture stood, according to Wiepking, in the tradition of "the great designers around 1800 who liberated the German landscape and the German garden from the influence [*Ueberlagerung*] of foreign cultures."[36] Like Mäding he praised the contributions of Goethe, Sckell, Pückler, Lenné and others who had strengthened the "idea of the living space of a people as a *Gesamtkunstwerk* to be planned homogeneously."[37] Whereas Lange and others had seen the English landscape garden as an early expression of the alleged Nordic feeling

[33] Mäding, *Landespflege*, 202.

[34] Ibid., 94.

[35] Ibid., 96.

[36] Heinrich Friedrich Wiepking-Jürgensmann, "Der Beruf und die Aufgabe des Gartengestalters," *Die Gartenkunst* 48 (1935), 42.

[37] Heinrich Friedrich Wiepking-Jürgensmann, "Das Grün im Dorf und in der Feldmark," *Bauen, Siedeln, Wohnen* 20, 13 (1940), 442.

for close-to-nature design and as a rejection of the "southern" formal garden, Wiepking rejected at the height of World War II the landscape park as "an English invention," which would bear witness of the decline of the English people. In 1941 he criticized "the English park landscape of the purse, which is idolized by the whole world. The fruits of this 'Germanic' world of ideas, which has become decadent, are the slums of the industrial and harbor cities and the future loss of the Empire of old 'order.'"[38] Two years later Wiepking wrote, "A park is an English invention. In it the slums of the English industrial and harbor cities are looking at themselves. It is built on the ruins of countless farms. . . . The park of the propertied classes, who destroyed the people, is the symbol of the ruin of England and of the decay of the life community of the people. . . . Whereas the peasant's garden has a deep realistic meaning and is rooted in the people, the usual kind of park landscape became in many cases a senseless planting, an excessive waste and disregard of precious soil."[39] In this context Wiepking mentioned in an apologetic way that the German garden artist Peter Joseph Lenné, "as a child of his time," still would have been linked to this park design but that he was mainly interested in a sound and therefore beautiful cultural landscape.[40]

It is remarkable that Wiepking did not include in his criticism of excessively wasteful park design, for example, that of the German Prince Pückler who wasted his and his wife's fortune for the creation of the Muskau park landscape and who even, although still married, went to England to look for a new and wealthy wife in order to save the Muskau park.[41] It is also worth noting that Wiepking, at the height of National Socialism, did not mention any particular English garden artist. In 1966, however, 20 years after the fall of National Socialism, when the political situation in Germany had changed, he referred positively to the "garden revolution that started from England in the middle of the eighteenth century" as "in the light of intellectual and economical history an interesting development" and mentioned Repton in this context.[42] This

[38] Heinrich Friedrich Wiepking-Jürgensmann, "Raumordnung und Landschaftsgestaltung," *Raumforschung und Raumordnung* 5, 1 (1941), 19. The German text runs as follows: "Wer jedoch genauer hinsieht, erkennt die fast Ausrottung zu nennende Vernichtung der englischen Ackerwirtschaft auf der einen Seite, und auf der anderen die von aller Welt geradezu angehimmelte englische Parklandschaft des Geldbeutels. Die Früchte dieser dekadent gewordenen 'germanischen' Vorstellungswelt sind die Eledensquartiere der englischen Handels- und Industriestädte und der kommende Verlust des Empires alter 'Ordnung.' "

[39] Heinrich Friedrich Wiepking-Jürgensmann, "Der Landschaftsgedanke," *Neues Bauerntum* 35, 1 (1943), 6. The original text runs as follows: "Ein Park ist eine englische Erfindung. In ihm bespiegeln sich die Slums der englischen Industrie- und Hafenstädte. Er ist auf den Trümmern unzähliger Bauernhöfe errichtet worden. . . . Das Sinnbild des englischen Untergangs, des Verfalls der Lebensgemeinschaft des Volkes, ist der Park der besitzenden Klassen, die das Volk vernichteten. . . . Hat der bäuerliche Baumgarten einen tiefen lebensnahen und volksverankerten Sinn, so ist die Parklandschaft üblicher Art vielfach zu einer sinnlosen Pflanzerei, zu einer maßlosen Vergeudung und Mißachtung wertvollen Bodengutes geworden."

[40] Wiepking-Jürgensmann, "Raumordnung und Landschaftsgestaltung," 22: "Gewiß war er [P. J. Lenné] als Kind seiner Zeit noch durchaus parkverbunden, aber seine 1820 für das Gut Reichenbach in Pommern gegebenen Richtlinien enthalten schon das Grundsätzliche der gesunden und daher schönen Kulturlandschaft."

[41] On Pückler's search for a wealthy wife in England, see, for example, *Briefwechsel des Fürsten Hermann von Pückler-Muskau, herausgegeben von Ludmilla Assing,* Bern, 1971, reprint of the edition by Hoffmann and Campe, Hamburg, 1873, particularly vol. 7, 43–70, 231–33.

[42] Heinrich Friedrich Wiepking-Jürgensmann, *Geordnete Umwelt, Fruchtbares Land, Menschliche Wohlfahrt: Peter Joseph Lenné zum Gedächtnis,* Deutsche Gartenbau-Gesellschaft Schriftenreihe 18, Hiltrup, 1966, 5 f.

gives evidence of how Wiepking adjusted his interpretation of garden history to the political situation.

Numerous other examples could be presented here of the manipulation of garden history in order to prove the "ecological goodness" of German garden designers and the German people in general of the late eighteenth and early nineteenth century. These few references may suffice to demonstrate how the study and interpretation of garden history in Germany was influenced during the early twentieth century by ideology and political interests.

National Socialism as a Topic for Garden Historical Research

National Socialism itself and its relationship to landscape architecture in Germany became the focus of garden historical interest in the 1970s. The first works were published beginning in 1980[43] and initiated a still-ongoing debate among garden historians and landscape architects. The issues of National Socialism, blood and soil ideology, and volkish concepts of ecology and related aspects have been presented since then in numerous publications. The various authors interpreted garden history, of course, from different positions and with different interests. An interesting phenomenon in this debate has been the different assessments of possible connections between ideas about ecology, environmental protection, and National Socialist ideology.

Many a historian seems to have a longing for "ecological goodness" in garden history and tends to ignore the racist and ideological character of some historic concepts of ecologically proper garden and landscape design. This cannot be discussed in detail here but will hopefully be an object of future research on the historiography of garden history. A few references may suffice. One example is Jost Hermand's *Grüne Utopien in Deutschland*, in which, for example, he downplays the role of one of the leading Nazis, Rudolf Hess, the deputy of Adolf Hitler, as a "life reformer."[44] Similarly, Hermand ignores racism and reactionary ideas as an integral part of Rudolf Steiner's doctrine of anthroposophy and his concept of biodynamical agriculture.[45]

William Rollins, a student of Hermand, attempts with his 1995 article, "Whose Landscape? Technology, Fascism, and Environmentalism on the National Socialist *Autobahn*,"[46]

[43] Gert Gröning and Joachim Wolschke-Bulmahn, "Naturschutz und Ökologie im Nationalsozialismus," *Die alte Stadt* 10, 1 (1983), 1–17; eidem, "Regionalistische Freiraumplanung als Ausdruck autoritären Gesellschaftsverständnisses? Ein historischer Versuch," *Kritische Berichte* 12, 1 (1984), 5–47; eidem, *Natur in Bewegung: Zur Bedeutung natur- und freiraumorientierter Bewegungen der ersten Hälfte des 20. Jahrhunderts für die Entwicklung der Freiraumplanung*, Arbeiten zur sozialwissenschaftlich orientierten Freiraumplanung 7, ed. Gert Gröning and Ulfert Herlyn, Munich, 1986; eidem, *Der Drang nach* Osten.

[44] Jost Hermand, *Grüne Utopien in Deutschland: Zur Geschichte des ökologischen Bewußtseins*, Frankfurt am Main, 1991, 114.

[45] I discuss the ambivalent character of Steiner's concept of biodynamic agriculture in "Biodynamischer Gartenbau, Landschaftsarchitektur und Nationalsozialismus," *Das Gartenamt* 42, 9 (1993), 590–95; ibid., 42, 10 (1993), 638–42.

[46] William H. Rollins, "Whose Landscape? Technology, Fascism, and Environmentalism on the National Socialist *Autobahn*," *Annals of the Association of American Geographers* 85, 3 (1995), 494–520.

to prove the "ecological goodness" of Alwin Seifert, one of the leading Nazi landscape architects and a convinced racist. Rollins claims,

> Alwin Seifert and his fellow landscapers may have been Nazis, but it is also clear that, as garden architects, they were infused with an eighteenth-century philosophy of integrating nature and culture. The immediate origins of their *Autobahn* aesthetic, moreover, lay in the turn-of-the-century *Heimatschutz* movement. The *bodenständige* aesthetic which Seifert and his fellow gardeners subsequently applied to the *Autobahnen* was devoted to the idea of conservation; indeed, the *Landschaftsanwälte* tried as best they could to use the highway project as a platform for systematic ecological reform.[47]

It is important to note that Rollins ignores the inseparability of Seifert's and others' ideas about "conservation," for example, and their ideas about "purity of race" as in accord with "purity of landscape." Seifert was the garden architect who most clearly and openly articulated the political dimension of his ideas about natural garden and landscape design or, as he called it, *bodenständiges* (rooted in the soil) design. He wrote, for example, a few years before the takeover of the Nazis, that he introduced the category of rootedness in the soil consciously into the art of garden design: "I wanted to bring garden art into the struggle in all living spaces which has broken out in our days between "rootedness in the soil" and "supra-nationality."[48] According to Seifert, this struggle was "a fight between two opposing *Weltanschauungen:* on one side the striving for supranationality, for equalization of huge areas, and on the other the elaboration of the peculiarities of small living spaces, the emphasis of which is rooted in the soil."[49]

The "turn-of-the-century *Heimatschutz* movement" that Rollins referred to was a very ambivalent movement with a dominant volkish and reactionary wing.[50] Many members of this Heimatschutz movement became ardent followers of National Socialism because, among others, of the similarity of their ideas about blood and soil. Long before 1933 elements of National Socialist ideology were part of Heimatschutz ideas about the German people and German landscapes. To argue that the Heimatschutz movement originated in the late nineteenth century does not necessarily separate it from National Socialism. On the contrary, it calls for a careful investigation of nineteenth-century ideas in Germany about people, nature, and landscape.

Like Hermand and Rollins, Raymond Dominick tries to separate ecology and politics in his 1992 study, *The Environmental Movement in Germany.* He argues, for example, "To summarize, it would seem that only one kind of conservation, the völkisch variety of *Naturschutz,* was centrally and durably aligned with Nazism. . . . But other varieties of

[47] Ibid., 512.

[48] Alwin Seifert, "Randbemerkungen zum Aufsatz 'Von bodenständiger Gartenkunst,' " *Die Gartenkunst* 43 (1930), 166.

[49] Alwin Seifert, "Bodenständige Gartenkunst," *Die Gartenkunst* 43 (1930), 162 f.

[50] See in more detail Uwe Puschner, Walter Schmitz, and Justus H. Ulbricht, eds., *Handbuch zur "Völkischen Bewegung," 1871–1918*, Munich, 1996.

conservation thinking, for example those grounded in the science of ecology or in pantheism, persisted, and they lacked any intrinsic intellectual tie to Nazism."[51] Again, this statement ignores that different ideas about "ecology" have been in existence since Ernst Haeckel defined this term in 1866 and that some—of course, not all of them—were based on very reactionary ideas. In his study *Ernst Haeckel and the German Monist League: The Volkish Origins of National Socialism* (New York, 1971), Daniel Gasman illustrates how closely particular "ecological" ideas have been related to racism and other reactionary concepts of the relationship between humans and nature. He presents how those ideas later became an inherent part of the Nazi blood and soil ideology. Dominick stated that the group around Seifert "had no prior organizational and only weak ideological connections to the Nazi cause,"[52] and that "to protect himself . . . Seifert couched his arguments in National Socialist terminology."[53] Dominick ignores, for example, Seifert's close ties to Rudolf Hess and other leading National Socialists such as Fritz Todt and Albert Speer. He also ignores that Seifert announced his ideas about natural garden design as a conscious political statement, as elucidated above.

"Ecological Goodness" and the Study of American Garden History

During the past years the discussion of the relationship of German landscape architecture to National Socialism that Gert Gröning and I initiated has evoked numerous responses among scholars and landscape architects. As long as our discussion was confined to the period of National Socialism, most of the responses did not reflect indignation and anger. But when we pointed, for example, to similarities between professional ideas about natural garden design, the use of so-called native plants, and the rejection of so-called exotic plants during National Socialism and in the 1980s and 1990s, and therefore called for a scholarly analysis of recent trends in German landscape architecture, the value of any comparison between the time of National Socialism and recent developments in German landscape architecture was frequently denied. Similarly, American colleagues time and again criticized heavily our discussion, beginning in 1993, of similarities between racist ideas about natural garden design articulated by German landscape architects during National Socialism and ideas published by, for example, one of their American contemporaries, the landscape architect Jens Jensen. This criticism proceeded from deep misunderstandings.

By starting this discussion we intended neither to disqualify the use of so-called native plants nor to characterize proponents of natural garden design as authoritarian, Fascist, or neo-Fascist. Nor did we intend to equate National Socialism and the United States by presenting German and American examples and by pointing out similarities in a racist or nativist argumentation for natural garden design. The point of our parallel studies is elsewhere.

[51] Raymond H. Dominick, *The Environmental Movement in Germany: Prophets and Pioneers, 1871–1971*, Bloomington and Indianapolis, Ind., 1992, 114.

[52] Ibid., 222.

[53] Ibid., 110.

Examples taken from National Socialist landscape architecture might help to elucidate how ideas about society and humans can be connected to ideas about nature. Or perhaps in a more precise way, how ideas about society can be subsumed under ideas about nature. No modern society besides German society during National Socialism articulated any comparable radical and extreme ideas about relationships between people and nature, with fatal consequences for millions of humans. A careful analysis of the recent history of German landscape architecture might help, for example, to understand how ideas about nature translate into ideas about society and vice versa and how, perhaps unwittingly, racist and antidemocratic ideas can become reactivated even in democratic societies.

In the United States, ideas about ecology also played a role in early twentieth-century landscape architecture. Frank A. Waugh, Wilhelm Miller, Elsa Rehmann, and Jens Jensen are only four names that come to mind. The term "ecology" was more commonly used among landscape architects in the United States than in Germany at that time. Frank Albert Waugh (1869–1943) had studied under Willy Lange for several months in Berlin in 1910.[54] Waugh was fascinated by Lange's writing about natural garden design. In his 1910 article, "German Landscape Gardening," he stated,

> The best recent book on landscape gardening written in any language (and I cannot conscientiously except my own) is by a German. This man is Willy Lange, a landscape gardener in the suburbs of Berlin and a teacher in the Horticultural School in Dahlem. . . . Herr Lange believes in what we in America call the natural style of gardening. In actual practice his work comes nearest to that of Mr. Warren H. Manning of Boston of any in our country. He has a method, fully worked out on scientific lines, in thoroughgoing German fashion. He calls it the biological-physiognomical method; but it would fit better to our use of language to call it the ecological method. Very roughly stated, this theory asserts that plants should be assembled in a garden in their natural relationship—placing together those plants which associate with one another in nature, placing such plant society in its proper soil and on its proper geologic formation. The complete development of this theory forms an interesting study, and whether one is willing or not to make this the whole controlling principle in garden planting, one cannot help seeing that it is a very useful idea.[55]

Waugh, for example, wrote numerous books and articles in which he applied ideas about ecology to landscape architecture. For example, he referred to Lange in *The Natural Style in Landscape Gardening* as follows: "This ecological principle is the one most clearly

[54] For biographical information about Waugh, see Frederick R. Steiner, "Frank Albert Waugh," in *American Landscape Architecture: Designers and Places,* ed. William H. Tishler, Washington, D.C., 1989, 100–103. Regarding Waugh's studies under Lange, see Frank A. Waugh, "A Horticultural School," *Country Gentleman*, 23 June 1910, 604. I am indebted to Christopher Vernon for placing a copy of this and other articles published in the *Country Gentleman* at my disposal.

[55] Frank A. Waugh, "German Landscape Gardening," *Country Gentleman,* 25 August 1910, 790.

elucidated by Willy Lange in his important work, *Die Gartengestaltung der Neuzeit.*"[56] In 1931 Waugh published an article, "Ecology of the Roadside," followed five years later by "Roadside Ecology—California Notes."[57] It is important to notice that Waugh's and others' ideas about natural landscape design were also connected to particular ideas about races and nations and their relationship to the landscape. Waugh, for example, followed Lange's idea that in landscape gardening "styles are national—perhaps, more strictly speaking, racial."[58]

Elsa Rehmann also contributed to the introduction of ecology into landscape architecture with the book she wrote with Edith A. Roberts, *American Plants for American Gardens*, and such articles as "An Ecological Approach," published in 1933 in *Landscape Architecture.* Rehmann and Roberts wanted "to show the use of ecology in selecting American plant material for American grounds and gardens."[59] Warren H. Manning developed comprehensive ideas about natural or wild gardens, as has been discussed recently by Robin Karson.[60] It is remarkable that Waugh's, Rehmann's, Manning's and others' contributions to ecological or natural garden and landscape design have, compared to those of Jensen or, in England, William Robinson, not yet found adequate scholarly interest among garden historians. Perhaps the subtitle of Karson's essay about Manning, "Pragmatist in the Wild Garden," offers an explanation.

In particular, Jens Jensen has been glorified by garden historians as an ecological hero. In the dedication of the 1956 edition of his *Sifting,* the book is called a "classic of our times," and Jensen is named "the Thoreau of the twentieth century." Garden historians have ignored until recently the racist character of his ideas about an alleged relationship of a people to nature as an important basis for his ideas about regional landscape design. Neither in short biographical statements on Jensen, such as Stephen Christy's contribution to the 1989 publication *American Landscape Architecture: Designer and Places,*[61] nor in more extensive monographs, such as Robert Grese's *Jens Jensen: Maker of Natural Parks and Gardens* (Baltimore, Md., 1992), is the close relation between Jensen's ideas about so-called races, particularly the Nordic people, and his ideas about regional and ecological garden and landscape design discussed.[62] A striking example is Leonard K. Eaton's *Landscape Artist in America: The Life and Work of Jens Jensen* (Chicago, 1964). At the end of his book, on page 231 (out of 240 pages), Eaton states, "Like a good many Scandinavians, Jensen at first had an open mind about the Nazis. Their doctrines stressing the importance of home and family and the

[56] Frank A. Waugh, *The Natural Style in Landscape Gardening,* Boston, 1917, 52.

[57] Frank A. Waugh, "Ecology of the Roadside," *Landscape Architecture* 21, 2 (1931), 81–92; idem, "Roadside Ecology—California Notes," *Landscape Architecture* 26, 3 (1936), 119–27.

[58] Waugh, *Natural Style*, 52.

[59] Edith A. Roberts and Elsa Rehmann, *American Plants for American Gardens: Plant Ecology. The Study of Plants in Relation to Their Environment,* New York, 1929, 3.

[60] Robin Karson, "Warren H. Manning: Pragmatist in the Wild Garden," in *Nature and Ideology,* ed. Wolschke-Bulmahn, 113–30.

[61] Stephen Christy, "Jens Jensen," in *American Landscape Architecture,* ed. Tishler, 78–83.

[62] Grese ignores the racism as reflected in Jensen's *Siftings,* as discussed in Wolschke-Bulmahn, "Nature and Ideology."

superiority of the Nordic race had a certain appeal for him." Eaton at least refers to Jensen as a racist, although he ignores any relevance of his racism for his ideas about garden design.

Robert Grese's 1995 "Prairie Gardens of O. C. Simonds and Jens Jensen" may serve as another example of the biased longing for "ecological goodness" also among American garden historians that apparently leads them to ignore the political and ideological dimension such ideas often had in the recent history of gardens. Grese added to the final version of his essay a footnote that runs as follows: "Jensen clearly struggled with questions of race and environment. Like some other Northern Europeans of this period, Jensen felt that 'northern' races were superior. In a letter to Henry Ford's general secretary, E. G. Liebold, Jensen expressed concern over the practice of importing workers from Southern Europe and from the southern portions of the United States. He suggested that a mixing of races would reduce 'vitality and intellect.' "[63] On the one hand, this addition to the paper can be interpreted as progress in garden historical research. It at least acknowledges Jensen's racist ideas. On the other hand, it might make things worse. In Eaton's book Jensen's racism is mentioned in passing at the end of the book. Here it is done away with in a footnote as if it would be of no relevance for his ideas about landscape design.

Garden History, "Ecological Goodness," and the Recent "Mania for Native Plants" Debate

In the United States the discussion of this specific ideological dimension of ideas about ecology and natural landscape design started in the early 1990s; Gert Gröning and I discussed related issues in several publications.[64] Knowledge of German garden history, including the interdependence between National Socialism and the rise of concepts of natural garden and landscape design and their political function for National Socialist politics, made it easier to address such issues.

When comparing trends in German landscape architecture during National Socialism to recent trends in Germany or to contemporary trends in American landscape architecture, one should be aware of a variety of problems that call for careful further analysis. What, for example, were the political conditions for the landscape architecture profession in Germany and the United States in the 1930s? What were perhaps the particular circumstances in German society that encouraged landscape architects more than in other countries to develop and express racist ideas about garden design? Why could similar ideas about humans, nature, and gardens have different effects in different societies? Further questions

[63] Jensen, 1920, quoted in Robert E. Grese, "The Prairie Gardens of O. C. Simonds and Jens Jensen," in *Regional Garden Design in the United States,* ed. Therese O'Malley and Marc Treib, Dumbarton Oaks Colloquium on the History of Landscape Architecture 15, Washington, D.C., 118.

[64] Gröning and Wolschke-Bulmahn, "Mania for Native Plants"; Joachim Wolschke-Bulmahn, "The 'Peculiar Garden': The Advent and the Destruction of Modernism in German Garden Design," in *The Modern Garden in Europe and the United States,* ed. Robin Karson, Masters of American Garden Design, vol. 3, Cold Spring, N.Y., 1994, 17–30; idem, "Political Landscapes and Technology: Nazi Germany and the Landscape Design of the Reichsautobahnen (Reich Motor Highways)," *Nature and Technology: Selected CELA Annual Conference Papers* 7, Washington, D.C., 1996; idem, "Nature and Ideology."

can be raised for a scholarly analysis of the recent history of garden design in Germany and elsewhere, but the uniqueness of National Socialism in its fatal consequences for other people cannot serve as an argument to defer such comparative analyses and to renounce learning from this part of our recent history.

However, the use of National Socialism as an example to learn about ecology sometimes provokes vehement reaction. An episode that illustrates this is a series of papers and letters published in the *Landscape Journal,* that began with an article by Gert Gröning and myself, "Some Notes on the Mania for Native Plants in Germany." As the title indicates, the paper focused on German examples taken from the early twentieth century and especially from the period of National Socialism. Nevertheless, we related "the phenomenon [of the mania for native plants] to more contemporary events" and argued that recently "some authors use words like 'ecology' and 'ecological' as if they conferred moral authority."[65] Among others, we referred to the search for "ecological goodness" and "authority" as reflected in a resolution passed by the Twenty-first Congress of the International Federation of Landscape Architects in 1983, which wanted "nature to become the law." Paragraph 3 of the resolution reads: "All humans need to be instructed that they are part of nature without mercy and without a chance for escape, and above all are subject to her [i.e., nature's] laws. Human laws beginning with human constitutions and ending with special norms of law and norms of other subjects rank behind; to respect these [human laws] can only be requested if they are in compliance with the laws of nature."[66]

This attempt to call into question the idea of "ecological goodness" among landscape architects and garden historians was the starting point for a heated debate in *Landscape Journal,* which lasted for several years. The title of one of the responses may indicate the trend: "Natives and Nazis: An Imaginary Conspiracy in Ecological Design." The author, Kim Sorvig, professor of natural systems in the School of Architecture and Planning at the University of New Mexico, began his response in the following way: "Rhododendrons in the gas chambers! Kristallnacht against Kudzu! Gert Groening and Joachim Wolschke-Bulmahn attempt to link native-plant advocates with Nazism."[67] It created particular excitement that we expanded, based on German examples from the period of National Socialism that were difficult to call into question, the discussion in our response to Sorvig's letter, and that we included the example of Jens Jensen.[68] Sorvig, for example, complained in his second letter to *Landscape Journal* that we would "restate but fail to *substantiate* Nazism charges against Willy Lange, and add Jens Jensen to the hit-list."[69]

[65] Gröning and Wolschke-Bulmahn, "Mania for Native Plants," 124, 116.

[66] International Federation of Landscape Architects, "Resolution," *Das Gartenamt* 32, 11 (1983), 675.

[67] Kim Sorvig, "Natives and Nazis: An Imaginary Conspiracy in Ecological Design. Commentary on G. Groening and J. Wolschke-Bulmahn's 'Some Notes on the Mania for Native Plants in Germany, " *Landscape Journal* 13, 1 (1994), 58.

[68] G. Groening and J. Wolschke-Bulmahn, "Response: If the Shoe Fits, Wear It!" *Landscape Journal* 13, 1 (1994), 62 f.

[69] Kim Sorvig, letter to the editor, *Landscape Journal* 13, 2 (1994), 194.

It may only be added here that the most recent research done by Gert Gröning in the Sterling Morton Library, Morton Arboretum, sheds new light on the ambivalent role Jensen apparently played in American garden history. Even such a politician as Harold LeClaire Ickes, secretary of the interior, reproached Jensen with being anti-Semitic. Documents in the Morton Arboretum suggest a somewhat ambivalent position of Jensen between anti-Semitism and democratic values.[70]

In 1994 an article by Michael Pollan was published in the *New York Times Magazine*, titled "Against Nativism," in which Pollan discussed natural garden design in the United States but also referred to trends in German landscape architecture during National Socialism.[71] Pollan's article also became the target of highly emotional attacks. In June 1995 the Brooklyn Botanic Garden organized a symposium on the native plant issue, where Pollan's piece was subject to a highly emotional debate. Shortly before the Brooklyn Botanic Garden symposium, William R. Jordan III had published a response to Pollan titled "The Nazi Connection." He opened it with:

> Several times in the past few years I have been brought up short by the suggestion that ecological restoration is a form of nativism—the ecological version of the sort of racist policies espoused by the Nazis or the Ku Klux Klan. Like the Nazis and the Klan, restorationists espouse the exclusion and removal of immigrants, and even a program to ensure genetic purity of stock in order to protect the integrity of the native, the true-born, the Blut und Boden. Hence restoration offers a disturbing resemblance in the ecological sphere to policies of nativism, racism, and sexism in the social sphere—so the argument goes."[72]

A similar and, at best, sloppy use of language and careless way of dealing with this aspect of history is demonstrated by another participant in the debate for and against so-called native and exotic plants, Neill Diboll. In his contribution to the Brooklyn Botanic Garden symposium "Native Plants: Toward a Twenty-first-Century Garden," Dieboll likened native plants to the Jews and Gypsies of the Nazi era, and called invasive non-natives 'stormtrooper plants that are blitzkrieging across the landscape.' "[73]

[70] I am indebted to Gert Gröning for placing copies of these documents at my disposal. Ickes wrote, e. g., on 11 February 1994, to Jensen, "But I emphatically do not agree with you about Henry Ford. I can see nothing patriotic about a man who openly flouts the law. I do not care for a man who refused a government contract because it meant supplying airplane motors to England. I despise a man who continues to treasure a nazi decoration after Hitler has been exposed as a devil incarnate. It would seem from your letter that you share Mr. Ford's anti-semitism. If you do, I am sorry, because I would like to continue to respect you." Jensen himself rejected in letters to Ickes the reproach of being anti-Semitic and declared himself for democratic ideals.

[71] Michael Pollan, "Against Nativism," *New York Times Magazine*, 15 May 1994, 52–55.

[72] William R. Jordan III, "The Nazi Connection," *Restoration and Management Notes* (Winter 1994), 113 f.

[73] Quoted in Janet Marinelli, "Native or Not? Debating the Link between Fascism and Native-Plant Gardening, as Highlighted in BBG's Symposium on the Future of the Garden," *Plants and Garden News* 10, 3 (1995), 14.

Janet Marinelli, the organizer of the Brooklyn Botanic Garden symposium, also responded a year after Pollan's article had been published:

> The controversy came to a head last year in an article in *The New York Times Magazine.* . . .As a journalist, I was less than impressed by Pollan's article. He made superficial (and rather sensational) connections between Nazi garden designers and natural landscapers in the U.S. today. And he blithely dismissed the scientific credibility of ecological restoration and natural landscaping, its domesticated form—without talking to a single scientist. But I had to allow that, given our current anti-immigrant political climate, Pollan's charges merit some serious consideration.[74]

The paper that I presented at the Brooklyn symposium I later made available for publication in *Concrete Jungle* under the title "Native Plant Enthusiasm—Ecological Panacea or Xenophobia?" This title apparently did not satisfy the editors. They changed the title—without ever having contacted me—to a more dramatic one, "The Mania for Native Plants in Nazi Germany," although half of the paper discussed American examples. But perhaps this change caused *Harper's Magazine* to become interested in the paper and to publish excerpts from it.[75]

Conclusion

I have pointed out how the longing for "ecological goodness" has affected the perception of garden history of many a garden historian and landscape architect. Further research on these issues is necessary. It will be a task for the future study of garden history to further investigate how, perhaps, particular ideas about nature, nativeness, and ecology have contributed to antidemocratic political developments in various countries in order to better deal with ecological issues in the future. This discussion has recently broadened. I am referring, for example, to Anne Whiston Spirn's "The Authority of Nature: Conflict and Confusion in Landscape Architecture."[76] Similarly critically, Charles Lewis in his 1996 book, *Green Nature—Human Nature*, refers to the recent German garden and landscape history and urges that we should be aware of the ideological character of the native plant debate: "Concerns about the well-being of plant communities can become strong political issues. Many of the green movements in the United States and in Europe evolved in protest to environmental degradation and its effect on all life. But this positive desire to protect native or indigenous plants can have unexpected ominous overtones, as was evidenced in Germany." And later, "Environmentalism and protection of natural habitats, currently strong themes in world politics, are susceptible to being co-opted by groups whose intentions may not reflect the benevolent concerns of the majority of their follow-

[74] Marinelli, "Native or Not?" 1.

[75] In M. Dion and A. Rockman, eds., *Concrete Jungle: A Pop Media Investigation of Death and Survival in Urban Ecosystems*, New York, 1996, 65–69; *Harper's Magazine,* February 1997, 21 f.

[76] Spirn, "Authority of Nature," 249–65.

ers. . . . It is important that we take nothing at face value but try to learn who is speaking, what they stand to gain or lose, and what they really are saying."[77]

The longing for "ecological goodness" in the history of gardens, the search for historic examples that can show perspectives for the future and might offer hope, is an understandable and legitimate phenomenon but should not let us leave the ground of scholarship. Ecology and nature, concepts of native and exotic plants, are ideas. They are human concepts developed to better understand our environment. The notion of native plants "encompasses," as Gould stated, "a remarkable mixture of sound biology, invalid ideas, false extensions, ethical implications, and political usage both intended and unanticipated."[78] To better understand the goals behind such concepts and the underlying ideologies, to understand the "strengths and fallacies" behind the search for "ecological goodness" in landscape architecture, should be a goal of the future study of garden history.

[77] Charles Lewis, *Green Nature—Human Nature: The Meaning of Plants in Our Lives,* Urbana and Chicago, 1996, 124 f.

[78] Stephen Jay Gould, "An Evolutionary Perspective on Strengths, Fallacies, and Confusions in the Concept of Native Plants," in *Nature and Ideology,* ed. Wolschke-Bulmahn, 11.

From Vernacular Gardens to a Social Anthropology of Gardening

Michel Conan

Introduction

An interesting philosophical puzzle was introduced by Arthur Danto when asking in the manner of Wittgenstein, "What is left over when we subtract the arm from the motion produced when an arm is lifted?"[1] Danto had noted that Giotto figured Christ on the north wall of the Arena chapel at Padua, raising his arms in six different scenes, but that each of these gestures introduces a different meaning: admonition, magic, acceptance, commanding, blessing, and expelling. It suggests that only the intention remains when subtracting the arm. Two paintings, one by Titian, showing the Bacchanalia at Andros, and the other one done by Rubens after the painting by Titian, provide another example. They are showing almost exactly the same characters, the same things, and the same natural features of the landscape, yet it takes only a glance to see that they are totally different, allowing the design styles of the two artists to become conspicuous. Here, the question I shall raise is: What is left for the study of gardens when garden design is taken away?

This intriguing question was put to scholars at a conference at Dumbarton Oaks in 1990.[2] It was introduced by John Dixon Hunt in an attempt to broaden the field of garden studies in the same way that architectural history had broadened its field when acknowledging vernacular architecture as a legitimate object for architectural studies.[3] The word "vernacular" had been used for local languages as opposed to the dominant language of colonial invaders. It translated into an interest in architecture that was made according to folk practices and beliefs as opposed to the dominant practice of building design brought about by the ever larger division of labor in modern societies since the Renaissance. So the word "vernacular" was calling attention to works of architecture without architects, designs without designers, and cultural differences between custom-bound people and their so-

[1] A. C. Danto, *Analytical Philosophy of Actions,* Cambridge, 1973, ix.

[2] See J. D. Hunt and J. Wolschke-Bulmahn, eds., *The Vernacular Garden*, Dumbarton Oaks Colloquium on the History of Landscape Architecture 14, Washington, D.C., 1993.

[3] B. Rudolfsky, *Architecture without Architects*, New York, 1964.

phisticated rulers. The simple question was: What can architects learn from folk design that designers ignore? The same perspective could be adopted with regard to gardens. A large crop of new ideas could be expected since gardens studies had been mostly given to the study of design in self-consciously designed gardens.

There are many pieces of research that are centrally concerned with such gardens. They have been carried out for a variety of reasons, and very few offer a historical perspective. Social anthropologists have, for a long time, studied gardens in horticultural societies out of an interest in their economy, and more recently to test the explanatory power of ecological conditions with respect to their economic practices. I shall mention only two of them, a study of Samoan gardeners by Bronislaw Malinowski and a study of Jivaro Indians and their gardens by Philippe Descola. We shall then turn to the gardens of two dominated groups, a society of gardeners cultivating vegetables for sale in the city of Amiens, France, who lived under the powerful control of first the Church and then local merchants from the thirteenth century until the beginning of the twentieth century, and the gardens of African Americans in the United States today. A special group of marginalized gardeners in contemporary societies has received considerable attention. They have been called naive or visionary artists and *habitants-paysagistes* by Bernard Lassus, whose work will be reviewed briefly. Then I shall turn to allotments of working-class gardens, which have received much attention in several countries, and I shall limit my comments to Swedish research on these gardens. Even though there are not many studies of middle-class gardens, I should mention at least one study that was presented at a conference at Dumbarton Oaks by Todd Longstaffe-Gowan.

There is no tradition of "vernacular garden studies." This recent wording simply stands as an umbrella for studies of extremely different gardens. It is useful to review several types of vernacular gardens in order to show that there is no unity of form, content, or use that cuts across all of these different gardens. There is no concept of the vernacular garden that would apply to all of them, beyond the general idea of a garden. Nevertheless, many studies address similar issues, because relationships between gardeners and their gardens stand as a common focus. All of these gardens are expressions of dominated cultures and are created and maintained by groups subjected to social inequalities of some sort, and there are more of these than could be accommodated here. Gardens created by two of these groups, socially dominated groups and "visionary" folk artists in mass-consumption society, were presented at the 1990 symposium on vernacular gardens at Dumbarton Oaks. On the other hand, neither gardens of horticultural societies nor working-class allotment gardens have been discussed at Dumbarton Oaks, and most of the examples to be used are not available in English at present. Hence it was necessary to provide more background information for these two types of vernacular gardens. Yet each of these types has been analyzed from three perspectives: structure, order, and agency. These abstract terms will be introduced and illustrated empirically in each of our four studies. They will enable us to propose a common framework of theoretical analysis that could be used for studies of vernacular gardens as well as many others without ever suggesting that any two of these categories of gardens are similar. Actually, this attempt at discovering a common vantage point for the study of gardens, whether characterized or not by their design, leads from the history of period gardens to a social anthropology of gardening. From this perspective, there is no essence of a garden to be found in form, enclosure, or etymology. Gardens are simply places where a social group engages in gardening. This makes the definition of gardens contingent on economy, environment, and culture of any group of gardeners.

Horticultural Societies

Studies of native societies in several archipelagos of the Pacific Ocean and in South America have provided very detailed descriptions of gardens. The first of these was published in 1935 by Bronislaw Malinowski.[4] It was followed by several others, such as a study of Tikopians by Raymond Firth in 1939,[5] and more recently by Leopold Popisil in 1963 on the Papuans,[6] Maurice Godelier on the Baruyas of New Guinea,[7] and Philippe Descola on the Jivaro Indians of the Amazonian forest in 1986.[8] Most of these studies were concerned with the economy of native societies, and they paid attention to both ecology and cultural practices. More recently a large body of ecological studies of Indian economies in the Amazonian forest, which calls for detailed analysis of gardens and of gardening, has developed.[9]

The questions raised and methods applied in these studies have undergone significant changes within half a century. We shall avail ourselves of these changes to show how garden studies are deeply affected by choices of theoretical perspective and to introduce our own perspective. Hopefully it may be useful for research and lend itself to critique. Let me contrast briefly questions raised about gardens in the study of coral gardens by Malinowski, and in the Amazon basin by Descola. It may help to review similarities in order to introduce differences between the two studies. Malinowski and Descola both aimed at understanding the economic system of the people they visited, and both were struck by the importance of gardens. These gardens were cultivated in order to provide households with food and plants for different uses (this is mostly documented by Descola, who shows how the Achuar produce beer, poisons, medicine, and fibers) so that gardening certainly contributed to the general economy (even though circulation of goods reaped in the gardens were quite different in both societies). In neither case would ecological conditions suffice to account for gardening practices, and moreover it is quite striking that aesthetic pursuits were of utmost importance in both cases.

Let me elaborate on the evidence for aesthetic pursuits. Both studies were carried out by professional anthropologists committed to avoidance of cultural judgment passed upon

4 B. Malinowski, *Coral Gardens and Their Magic*, Bloomington, Ind., 1935.

5 R. Firth, *Primitive Polynesian Economy*, London, 1939.

6 L. Popisil, *Kapauku Papuan Economy*, New Haven, 1963.

7 M. Godelier, *L'idéel et le materiel: Pensée, economie, sociétés*, Paris, 1984.

8 P. Descola, *La nature domestique*, Paris, 1986; idem, *Les lances du crépuscule*, Paris, 1993.

9 R. Carneiro, "Subsistence and Social Structure: An Ecological Study of the Kuikuru Indians," Ph.D. diss., University of Michigan, 1957.

deeds or beliefs of native culture.[10] And yet, somewhat surprisingly, in front of the gardens both make comparisons with gardens from their own countries. Descola compares the orderly rows of cassava plants to an alley in a French garden and the thoroughly cleaned ground to a carefully tended parterre. "Its smooth and slightly sandy soil, studded here and there by the stalks of cassava plants, recalls the perfectly raked alley of a garden in the French style."[11] Malinowski is lyrical: "The gardens are certainly the more attractive part of the landscape. . . . We traverse a yam garden in full development, reminiscent somewhat of a Kentish hop-field and unquestionably more attractive. The exuberant vines climb round tall stout poles, their full shady garlands of foliage rising like fountains of green, or spilling downwards; producing the effect of abundance and darkness so often referred to in native spells."[12] Actually, they follow the same didactic approach: they describe their own aesthetic response to these gardens in order to introduce an account of aesthetic experience from a native perspective. This effort to put aesthetic judgment in anthropological perspective leads to two questions of method: Which are the objects of aesthetic experience? And under which description of this experience can we describe aesthetic appreciation?

For us, when discussing landscape, design and scenery would be an answer to the first question; disinterested contemplation of beauty, the sublime, or the picturesque an answer to the second. How should we account for the two natives' perspectives? Let us start with a description of aesthetic experience in Kiriwinian gardens in the Trobriands. In his first book, *Argonauts of the Western Pacific*, Malinowski already noted how important gardens were for natives:

> Half of the native's working life is spent in the garden and around it centers perhaps more than half of his interests and ambitions. In gardening the natives produce much more than they actually require, and in any average year they harvest perhaps twice as much as they can eat. . . . Again they produce this surplus in a manner which entails much more work than is strictly necessary for obtaining the crops. Much time and labour is given to aesthetic purposes.[13]

And when paying much attention to this aspect of their work, since it could not be accounted for by economic necessity, he would attempt to describe it from their own perspective, as he does in *Coral Gardens*: "The gardens are, in a way, a work of art [Fig. 1]. Exactly as a native will take an artist's delight in constructing a canoe or a house, perfect in shape, decoration and finish, and the whole community will glory in such an achievement, exactly thus will he go about the laying out and developing of his garden."[14] This aesthetic

[10] Malinowski explains that sons of a Kiriwinian family have to take care of their dead parents and that they should in particular taste their flesh; Descola explains how, as an honored family guest, one should eat living larvae of insects as big as a thumb by shearing the head from the body with one's teeth and by sucking slowly the greasy body afterwards. Neither one expresses a value judgment or even a word of personal comment.

[11] Descola, *La nature domestique*, 216.

[12] Malinowski, *Coral Gardens,* 57, 58.

[13] B. Malinowski, *Argonauts of the Western Pacific*, London, 1922, 58, 59.

[14] Malinowski, *Coral Gardens,* 80.

1. Waiting for a magic ceremony in a Trobriand garden (from Malinowski, Coral Gardens, *fig. 103)*

attention is expressed in the care and attention which is put into making visible the excellence of gardening practices to a native eye:

> A considerable amount of energy is spent on purely aesthetic effects, to make the garden look clean, showy and dainty. The ground before planting is cleared of stones, sticks and debris, with a meticulousness far beyond what would be strictly necessary on purely technical grounds. The cleared soil is divided into neat rectangles about 4 to 10 meters long, and 2 to 5 meters broad by means of sticks laid on the ground. These rectangles have little practical purpose, but much value is attached to the proportions and quality of the sticks which mark their boundaries. . . . . Pride is taken in selecting strong, stout and straight poles as supports for the yam vine. During all the successive stages of the work, visits are exchanged and mutual admiration and appreciation of the aesthetic qualities of the gardens are a constant feature of village life.
>
> A considerable amount of pleasure in well-accomplished work and the social pressure embodied in the imperative: "It is the right, honourable and enviable thing to have fine-looking gardens and rich crops"—these are the psychological elements which we shall find expressed in many features of gardening, harvesting and of the general economic condition.[15]

[15] Ibid., 80, 81.

But however important the aesthetic pleasure derived from enclosing the garden, cleaning the soil of stones and debris, and providing strong yam poles, the greater pleasure taken by all members of the community in the gardens is at harvest time. This is the time when all the villagers rush to the gardens, and when crops are brought back to the village in large baskets among much chatter and frolic.

Let us turn now to an account of aesthetic appreciation. Malinowski notes that the natives' sense of beauty cannot be divorced from a sense of material pleasure, and he writes somewhat bluntly,

> It was at that time that I received the first inkling that the Trobriander is above all a gardener, who digs with pleasure and collects with pride, to whom accumulated food gives the sense of safety and pleasure in achievement, to whom the rich foliage of yam-vines or taro leaves is a direct expression of beauty. In this, as in many other matters, the Trobriander would agree with Stendahl's definition of beauty as the promise of bliss, rather than with Kant's emasculated statement about disinterested contemplation as the essence of aesthetic enjoyment.[16]

He shows through a large number of detailed examples how unnecessary care is lavished upon practical activities, and how much public attention it receives, establishing the reputation of the gardener, and how it is used to appreciate the quality and quantity of the crop itself. He mentions the "almost pedantic perfection"[17] of the clearing of the ground on some special plots, the *leywota*, as well as the extra care and neatness lavished upon the laying of the boundary poles, the *tula*, and he goes on to show how aesthetic pleasure and economic activities are entwined: "There is no doubt that the *tula* add to the elegance of a garden plot. At first sight, however, it is difficult to see how they influence that economic or technical side of gardening, but there is no doubt that they fulfill indirectly such a function."[18]

The *tula* help to set up the squares in which each woman is going to work, and they take pride in having their square cleaned or planted better than that of their neighbor, claiming, "When the *tula* are there the work goes quickly, it is pleasant to do it; when no *tula* are there, or when they lie crooked, work goes slowly, we do not want to work."[19] Admiration begets envy, and it is no surprise to learn that Kiriwinian gardeners can be criticized for their laziness and for their lack of care when gardening, as much as they can be admired for the beauty of their gardens, since "good gardens are a virtue in themselves, a duty towards relatives-in-law and a duty towards the chief."[20] Thus this pursuit of beauty turns out to be a show of civic quality. Yet there is a limit that each member of local society must not exceed in this display of gardening excellence, since "a man may be attacked because his gardens are too good. He can then be accused of emulating his betters, of not

[16] Ibid., 10.

[17] Ibid., 120.

[18] Ibid., 121.

[19] Quoted in ibid., 122.

[20] Ibid., 175.

giving a fair proportion of his crops to the chief and to his relatives by marriage, and thus of acting disloyally and pandering to his own vanity and greed."[21] And when a man dies, an occurrence always attributed to sorcery, it is often believed that it happened because of his good gardens. In summary, for Kiriwinian gardeners aesthetic experience is derived from making care in all gardening operations visible for other villagers, and aesthetic appreciation entails the promise of plenty, of admiration by other villagers, and of good reputation among family members.

Let us now turn to the Jivaro gardens. Like Malinowski, Descola describes aesthetic concerns of Achuar gardeners. The beauty of a garden brings praise to the woman who is in charge of it. Beauty emanates from the sheer size of the garden, its careful weeding, and the variety of plants it holds. "It would be rather dishonorable for a woman to allow weeds to proliferate in her garden. . . . For the sake of the honor of a household a small garden carefully tended is to be preferred to a large garden a half of which lies fallow."[22] In Achuar society only women are in charge of gardening, whereas men are mostly responsible for hunting, building the house, and clearing the forest in order to establish the gardens. Yet the beauty of the gardens held by the different wives is a tribute to the virtue of the whole family. It is as actively sought as in the Trobriands: "The maniac meticulousness that presides over this activity [of gardening] goes far beyond sheer horticultural necessity. A beautiful garden can actually be characterized mostly by the gardener's ability to scrap nature's intervention that it displays. . . . Neither a twig, nor a turf should spoil the beauty of this polished place that asserts itself, undoubtedly to a greater extent than the house, as a pole opposite to the forest."[23] Descola also notes, "Being able to have a large variety of plants is a way for a woman to display her abilities as a gardener and all new plants are immediately adopted even though they only play a small role in the daily alimentation."[24]

Just as the criticism of a garden could lead a Kiriwinian gardener to suicide or incite tribal war, criticism of an Achuar gardener may incite jealousy and sorcery. This consists of special prayers, known only by women, that bring about the rotting or the drying of some garden plants. A woman whose garden is touched by such a plague searches her memory to remember all the other women who have visited her garden. The one who has lavished the most enthusiasm at the beauty of the garden is immediately known to be the culprit, since her excess of praise betrayed her jealousy.[25]

Malinowski shows that pride and self-esteem can be gained through gardening, and that aesthetic appreciation of gardens and their fruits is closely linked to the anticipated pleasures of social praise for good behavior in the ensuing exchanges of gifts between family members. Descola points to a similar relationship between aesthetic pleasure taken in tending a garden and its rewards in terms of family pride and social status for both the gardener and her household.

[21] Ibid.

[22] Descola, *La nature domestique*, 188.

[23] Ibid., 216.

[24] Ibid., 208.

[25] Ibid., 261.

Of course the relationships are not identical in both cases since different social structures are distributing status and creating social obligations that may beget self-esteem and social praise in different ways. So we ought to be aware of large differences despite broad similarities. In each case differences in social structure create different aesthetic experiences and different forms of aesthetic appreciation. This may invite students of landscape architecture to wonder how aesthetic judgment might be dependent on social structures.

There is another aspect of life in Kiriwinian gardens that Bronislaw Malinowski relates to aesthetics. In *Argonauts of the Western Pacific* he wrote, "There can be no doubt that the natives push their conscientiousness far beyond the limits of the purely necessary. The non-utilitarian element in their garden work is still more clearly perceptible in the various tasks which they carry out entirely for the sake of ornamentation, in connection with magical ceremonies and in obedience to tribal usage."[26] This implies only that magic may give rise to an aesthetic activity, and it gives a further twist to our ideas about aesthetics. Garden magic in the Trobriands is a public service that is performed in the name of the community by one of its most eminent leaders, the magician of gardens. "Magic and practical work are, in native ideas, inseparable from each other, though they are not confused. Garden magic and garden work run in one intertwined series of consecutive efforts, form one continuous story, and must be the subject of one narrative. To the natives, magic is as indispensable to the success of gardens as competent and effective husbandry. It is essential to the fertility of the soil: 'The garden magician utters magic by mouth; the magical virtue enters the soil.' Magic is to them an almost natural element in the growth of the garden."[27]

This raises a simple question. If Kiriwinian gardeners consider that garden skills and toil are responsible for the growth of their gardens and that the quality of the crop and the beauty of the garden can be put to the credit of the gardener, why do they pay so much attention to magic, and why do they practice it at all? Malinowski's answer, in a nutshell, is that gardening is an uncertain activity and that many hazards may reduce the gardeners' efforts to nought. Natives know very well how much careful work is necessary in order to prepare a good crop, but they know as well that no amount of work will prevent plagues or misfortunes, such as visits to the garden by wild animals, a drought, or a storm. They also know that crops may be abundant beyond all expectations. Magic explains away all aspects of chance. Natives ascribe happy results to magic, and misfortunes to black magic, or to flaws in the accomplishment of garden rituals.[28] "The belief that only sorcery lets loose the

[26] Malinowski, *Argonauts of the Western Pacific*, 58, 59.

[27] Malinowski, *Coral Gardens*, 62.

[28] "To the natives, . . . the aims of magic are different from the aims of work. They know quite well what effects can be produced by careful tilling of the soil and these effects they try to produce by competent and industrious labour. They equally know that certain evils, such as pests, blights, bush-pigs, drought or rain, cannot be overcome by human work however hard and consistent. They see also that, at times and in a mysterious way, gardens thrive in spite of all anticipations to the contrary, or else that, in a fairly good season favoured by good work, the gardens do not give the results they should. Any unaccountable good luck over and above what is due the natives attribute to magic; exactly as they attribute unexpected and undeserved bad luck to black magic or to some deficiency in the carrying out of their own magic." Ibid., 77.

2. Two women in an Achuar garden, drawn by Philippe Munch after a document by Philippe Descola (from Descola, Les lances du crépuscule, *119)*

pests and plagues which torment man is very deeply rooted. It has got a significant parallel in the belief that sorcery and sorcery alone is the ultimate cause of all which threatens human health and welfare and produces the accidents to human life. Neither crocodiles nor a falling tree nor death by drowning ever come of themselves, they are always induced by black magic."[29] Thus natives see magic as an activity that fulfills an important purpose; it reduces anxiety in the face of life's hazards, and it restores hope at times of distress. Care lavished upon magical aspects of gardening allows them to expect bountiful crops, and for that reason gives rise to aesthetic appreciation. This is a functionalist interpretation—magic and aesthetic each contributing to the maintenance of social order.

Descola, a student of Levi-Strauss, has traveled another intellectual path. Magic is as important in the Achuar gardens, but it follows a totally different pattern. Magic is part of the secret life that a woman gardener shares with the plants she raises in her garden. Natives consider these plants to be literally her children. Actually, both cultivars of plants and magic

[29] Ibid., 119.

spells to raise them are passed down from mother to daughter (Fig. 2). They are the source of women's power, their efficiency and their prestige in society. Descola has studied very carefully a number of Achuar gardens in different places, and he has measured their productivity and their sustainability in ecological, biological, and economic terms. His conclusion strikes a blow at Malinowski's theory of magic: there is no uncertainty in Achuar gardening, and there are sites that are used sometimes, but not always, by the Achuar where gardens may last indefinitely. Hence garden magic cannot be explained by a need for metaphysical reassurance in an uncertain world. Instead of studying gardens in and of themselves, he attempts to place both garden activities and garden lore in a broad relationship to other activities and other lore entertained by the household.

In order to achieve this, Descola adopts a structural method of inquiry, and this might be of interest for other kinds of garden studies. He looks for pervasive oppositions between concepts the Achuar people hold that they express in their behavior, use of space, myths, and accounts of events in their lifeworld. An opposition between culture and nature can be expected, but it craves comprehensive knowledge of natives' categories and an understanding of their mutual relationships. For instance, Achuar people think of wild animals, as well as of some supernatural spirits, as almost human because they have a family life, while they think of some tame animals, such as dogs, and some wild animals, such as the howler monkey, as non-human because they are incestuous. Moreover, there are other conceptual oppositions, which are striking, such as contrasts between forest, garden, and house, oppositions between roles of men and women, oppositions between roles of household members and roles of outsiders. Gardens, for instance, are almost exclusively a woman's domain, and the plants that she grows are her children whom she fosters with her work and magic.[30] The forest, in contrast, is almost exclusively the men's domain, and the animals that they hunt are thought of as parents through alliance whom they coax with their magic. In both cases danger is present. Hunting is physically dangerous, and any hunter can be killed by forest animals if he displeases some of the supernatural beings who look after forest animals. Gardens are also dangerous in their own way, for purely magical reasons, so that men avoid entering them. Cassava plants are believed to be thirsty for human blood, and men usually go across gardens walking on the top of very large fallen trees that enable them to escape their greedy leaves. This is also a source of danger for children, and their mothers spend a lot of energy pacifying through recitation of magic spells the bloodthirsty plants that they cultivate.

Many anthropologists working in the Amazon Basin have been struck by the resemblance between gardens and the forest. Fifteen months after the forest has been cleared, Achuar gardens have reached their grown-up appearance, and their three-tiered levels of

[30] This stands in strong contrast to the role of Kirwinian women in gardening. Let me quote again from Malinowski: "A woman never gardens in her own right. She is never styled 'owner of a garden' or 'owner of a plot.' She never works independently, but must always have a male for whom and with whom she works the soil, and this refers also to women of the highest rank whose husbands are necessarily of a lower rank than themselves." Ibid., 79.

foliage reproduce on a smaller scale and in a rather orderly fashion the surrounding forest. Larger-leafed banana trees and papaya trees provide the top cover, cassava plants contribute the larger part of the second cover that prevents the earth from being washed out by rain, and different vegetables and smaller plants provide the ground cover. Thus gardens appear as a cultural imitation of the natural forest. One of the most arresting results of the method used by Descola is that it enables him to show that this is only true to the eye of a Western observer. Actually, for the Achuar, the forest is just another garden that is cared for by spirits who are almost human (they take care of the wild animals as humans do their own tame animals, and they hunt them in order to eat them as humans do their poultry). He has shown that nature is organized according to social relations that are identical to social relations within the household.[31] Nature is perceived along a pattern derived from household life in Achuar society. It turns out that social relationships within their society provide the models for describing nature, rather than nature providing the model for social relationships and artifacts as we would have it. Women and garden plants are thought of on the model of parental relationships, while men and forest animals are thought of on the model of alliances between brothers-in-law. Thus social structure offers the model for a representation of the relationship between garden and forest, or one could say, between garden and the larger landscape. This division of space allows women to have a place of their own in the gardens where men are exposed to supernatural dangers from which they are protected by their magic. Thanks to these dangers women are not subjected to the will and the wrath of men everywhere, and they may enjoy a relative autonomy in the gardens. This is how we may come to assess the importance of gardens for the Achuar; beyond the resources that they provide, they embody a fundamental condition for the reproduction of family life and their social structure. Strangely enough, a structuralist method leads to a functionalist interpretation.

This confrontation of two great studies of horticultural societies shows as well, and most importantly, how interest in gardens changes over time under the mutual influence of new theoretical ideas such as structuralism, and new social movements of our times such as feminism and ecology. In short, gardening in horticultural societies results in a system of meanings that allow natives to create highly specific places set apart from the environment by their visual aspects, physical settings, ecology, and meanings. Relations between these places and their environment are predicated upon a small number of dyadic relationships between opposite categories of thought, such as nature and culture, metaphysics and physics, aesthetics and economics, and inside and outside. They offer the sight of visually ordered places, but a knowledge of gardening activities reveals an even more striking ecological order. All of this stresses social or cultural conformity and it can only yield limited opportunities to individuals for creative activities. Since gardening appears as an expression of social structures, we should expect a conceptual diversity of gardens among diverse horticultural societies.

[31] Descola, *La nature domestique*, 398.

Gardens of Socially Dominated Groups

Gardens of native peoples are undoubtedly created, tilled, and maintained according to folk habits and practices that are quite different from gardening habits of the Westernized members of the neighboring societies on which they are usually dependent at least for the supply of iron tools and firearms. So we ought to consider all of these economies as vernacular economies rather than genuinely native, insofar as they are dependent on a larger market economy. There are a few studies of gardening practices that were presented at the symposium on vernacular gardens at Dumbarton Oaks, which dealt with gardens raised by members of a socially dominated group. One was concerned with a society of gardeners growing vegetables on small artificial garden islands in the riverbed of the Somme, near Amiens, France, between the thirteenth century and the early twentieth century. This closed group was under the political and economic control of local merchants. The other was concerned with gardening practices among African Americans in the southern United States.[32] Both studies call attention to the search for variety and to the display of personal taste and invention among gardeners; they also point to the kinds of social games that gardens make possible, games not always confined within the limits of the garden itself, as was made very clear with the boat races between proud gardeners rowing at night toward the market at Amiens. Neither type of garden was designed in a formal sense, and yet they evince a sense of order that can be appreciated only by a visitor who shares to a large extent the gardener's culture. Other people will fail to notice qualities and defects in garden care and layout, or they will misjudge them. Hence it may not be a surprise to learn that these gardeners were deriving a sense of cultural identity from the care and development of their gardens.

It is quite remarkable, however, that in both cases the gardeners' communities seem to uphold some values that had been defended by the dominant group even after it has abandoned them. The gardeners in the Somme River remained staunch supporters of the monarchy after the French Revolution, and African American gardeners seem to uphold many American agrarian values, such as resourcefulness, hard work, common sense, distrust of city life, and self-reliance, all of which were characteristic of white American rural owners' culture; moreover, gardening practices, choices of cultivars, horticultural techniques, and layout may have been symbolically expressive of a deeper cultural resistance. This raises very intriguing issues about the dynamics of cultural change in garden practices and garden design. Could we say that dominated groups tend to stick to traditional gardens while groups gaining access to power are more likely to look for new garden environments? Whether the question is well-formulated or not, these studies of vernacular gardens invite efforts at unraveling the social dynamics of the spreading of garden styles, or gardening techniques or garden uses.

[32] M. Conan, "The *Hortillonnages*: Reflections on a Vanishing Gardener's Culture," and R. Westmacott, "The Gardens of African-Americans in the Rural South," both in *The Vernacular Garden*, ed. Hunt and Wolschke-Bulmahn.

3. A rocaille garden in Marseilles. Grottoes by Gaspard Gardini, allée Nicolas (from M. Racine, Architecture rustique des rocailleurs, *Paris, 1981, 83)*

In short, gardening by socially dominated groups is an activity that enables a sense of community to be maintained, setting the group apart from a somewhat hostile social environment. It is expressed through rituals of interaction among gardeners and through social exchanges. These gardens offer a visual order that may escape a culturally blind visitor but which is exacting for the gardening community. It may give rise to the reuse of discarded items of the surrounding society that demonstrate a capacity for figurative creation without any specific meaning, as a way of inviting outsiders' curiosity. Otherwise gardening activities seem to be very socially constrained and to offer little opportunity for creation of altogether new meanings.

Gardens of Visionaries

There is a growing number of studies of gardens made by untrained artists. Many of these studies were stimulated by an interest in naive creations, and they give more attention to objects created in a place than to the features that made such a place into an invented garden. Actually, the same attitude is found in many contemporary gardens of sculpture designed by artists for their own work.[33] Yet several of these monographs provide a stimulating insight into the process of cultural change. Michel Racine in his study of rocaille gardens in the Marseilles region has shown how a group of immigrants with new technical abilities in rusticated masonry were able not only to introduce new garden features, but, even further, to bring a new vision and to change ways of appreciating private gardens among well-established garden owners (Fig. 3). They were not transmitting Italian garden

[33] Carl Milles's garden in Stockholm; Ian Hamilton Finlay's garden in Scotland; and Vigeland in Oslo.

patterns; they just happened to invent a way of using their know-how in gardens of well-to-do Marseilles owners in order to make a living. These changes were growing out of fresh approaches to garden layout in the most unexpected and unplanned way. This may be one of the reasons for the importance of visionaries, creators who can be acknowledged as such by members of their own social group because their production in some features breaks away from its cultural habitus. They may unwittingly stimulate the common development of new cultural patterns. It is commonly accepted that cultural developments in the arts follow a pattern described as the "trickle-down process," according to which new artistic ideas are supported by a social elite and are imitated and passed down the social hierarchy, becoming more adulterated the further it trickles down. This theory denies the lower classes any capacity for cultural influence on the creative process of artistic forms. This is probably an implicit assumption in many of our current garden studies.

An interesting study carried out by Bernard Lassus in the early 1970s supports a contradictory assumption. Lassus, then a young professor at the Beaux Arts in Paris who had been trained as a painter by Fernand Léger, was intrigued by the very careful developments of gardens in front of their houses by working-class people living in industrial suburbs. He chose to look at them with the same curiosity he would lavish on contemporary exhibits of the visual arts. He attempted to unravel the design problems that they were setting for themselves, paying more attention to their handling of spatial relationships than to the narrative or figurative aspect of their work. This led to three striking discoveries. First, he has shown that despite the seemingly unique aspect of each garden and the variety of sources from which design elements had been borrowed, they proceeded from a small number of specific tenets that he has characterized. Second, and most striking, these tenets of a working-class aesthetic turned out to be strictly opposed to the aesthetic tenets of modernist architecture, without the creators themselves being aware of this. Since these people were scattered in the north and east of France and in the Paris region, he suggested that they were expressing in their own way a popular culture common to their social group (Fig. 4). Third, he was able to show that a few of them who had pursued their creation over a longer period of time had achieved in their environmental creation a personal solution to metaphysical questions about time, man, and nature. These garden creations could be seen as testimonies to the quest for a comprehensive meaning of life that both traditional religious beliefs and modernist visions of the good society fail to offer. This development could be taken as idiosyncratic and very personal to each garden creator; conversely, it can be seen as a symptom of changes in popular cultures, linking together more visionaries. Following the same lines of reasoning as Lassus, this observation might suggest that in Western societies people who do not share in the excitement of social changes may find solace and support for their identities in gardens (nature adorned and transformed by landscape architecture), while public powers are trying to establish civic symbols through grand architectural designs with no attention to the creation of meaningful and playful landscapes. If this interpretation were shown to have some truth, it might call for renewed attention to so-called visionary artists and for public building policies as a source of cultural identity.

4. Suburban visitors viewing a garden near Nantes in France (photo: Bernard Lassus)

In short, gardening by visionaries is a way of asserting individual expression by offering an infinite variety of garden elements. In that sense it stands in opposition to gardening by socially dominated groups. However, it also enables these gardeners to redeem their self-esteem and to reclaim a social identity that their social environment is denying them, and to bring order to their own world. They are very often poor at expressing themselves through articulated speech, a disability many articulate outsiders capitalize on to depreciate their work while ignoring their creative use of figurative language. Creative gardening amounts to a public assertion by visionaries of their right to develop figurative systems without a semantic content. Of course, to critics who believe that there is no humanity outside discourse, both creations and creators are objects of contempt. These gardeners always create highly distinctive places that contrast vividly with their environments. Such relations between place and environment call into play a number of opposite categories that invite a structural analysis, such as habit and invention; class or neighborhood and individual; and, most importantly, sign and figure. These last two categories belong to two different realms of communication systems among humans: discourse and figurative language, of which they are the elementary forms. Signs command meanings, and meanings are always attributes attached to signs within some systemic order. Signs are decipherable. Figures, however, are not bound to a specific meaning; they always call upon the observer to imbue them with sense. Figures demand interpretation.[34]

Family Garden Allotments

Garden allotments (Fig. 5) offer an interesting example of public policies by local authorities meant to foster development of workers' gardens. They have received some attention during the last two decades. These policies started in earnest at the turn of the last century. Their objects went by different names in each country, such as workers' gardens, family gardens, community gardens, and even colony gardens in Scandinavia. They were issued in the name of improving the living conditions and the way of life of workers' families by well-to-do citizens, and they have been very often taken as a proof that workers "needed" gardens. Isn't it a common belief that economic demand results from primary or secondary needs, that is, from psychological cravings? So their success might be taken as proof that they fulfilled real needs felt by the workers. Nevertheless, these policies were opposed by trade-unionist leaders who feared that gardening would alienate the political will of the workers by engaging them in the pursuit of individual interests in a garden of their own, and that it would foster a false consciousness of their needs. They were right to a certain extent since these gardens were clearly intended to help workers' families develop frugal and peaceful habits of their own will.[35] The allotments were designed as a whole, but

[34] Yet figures can be inscribed with signs so that they introduce language into non-rhetorical usage. This is the case of emblems used in gardens in the eighteenth century, for instance. Conversely, some signs can be used according to rhetorical figures that allow poetic or symbolic communication of thought. This is the case in garden poetry, which La Fontaine claimed to be superior to gardens themselves. These remarks simply stress the importance of considering these two distinctive forms of human communication when considering any system of expression, because human expression always takes advantage of a dialectic of discursive and figurative language, albeit in a different way for each mode of expression.

[35] Anna Lindhagen, who was one of the major proponents of such policies in Sweden, wrote in her first book on the topic in a chapter devoted to the usefulness of garden allotments: "For the family the plot of land is a uniting bond, where all family members can meet in shared work and leisure. The family father, tired with the cramped space at home, may rejoice in taking care of his family in the open air, and feel responsible if the little plot of earth bestows a very special interest upon life." A. Lindhagen, *Koloniträdgårdar och planterade gårdar,* Stockholm, 1916.

5. Garden allotments at Thiais in the Paris suburbs in 1989 (from O. Cena, Les jardins de la sociale, *Paris, 1992, fig. 79)*

the gardens offered for rent were not subject to any design, thus inviting the initiative of their users, and pressuring them into a process of self-discipline. They seem to offer a perfect example of a power technique to which Michel Foucault has called attention in *Surveiller et punir*, as it was used by the bourgeoisie to curb the revolutionary impulses of the working class.[36]

A number of studies of these garden allotments have been carried out in Sweden and Denmark. Historical studies of their development support neither the view that these gardens would express essential cravings of the working class, nor the view that they were only the alienating outcome of a disciplinary project[37] carried out by bourgeois elites trying to weaken workers' movements. They show that the first users of these gardens belonged to the upper social groups of the working class,[38] and that their development has been the most successful when people felt the urge to grow food for survival, between 1914 and 1918, and after the economic slump in the early 1930s when 10 percent of all garden products in Sweden were grown in the 130,000 garden allotments in the country.[39] At the same time, allotment gardens offered possibilities for aesthetic pursuits and for a social life proceeding from these gardening practices to develop even long after the gardens had lost any real economic significance. This makes a study of contemporary uses of these gardens most interesting as part of a general study of the sense of garden experience in mass society.

Different methods have been used offering slightly different perspectives. Social aspects of allotment gardening have been stressed by some authors, such as Lena Jarlov. In her book *Boende och skaparglädje* (Dwelling and the joy of creation),[40] she shows how garden life has been sought deliberately by many Swedish renters in order to feel free, to achieve something by themselves, and to engage in neighborly relationships with other gardeners, often at the cost of worsening their housing accommodations because they had to move to get close enough to a garden allotment. An American social anthropologist, E. N. Anderson, has carried out a survey of popular gardens in the United States.[41] He provides a totally different interpretation of gardening practices, as conspicuous consumption allowing gar-

[36] According to an oral tradition, Anna Lindhagen was a social-democratic leader and is said to have met Lenin when he came to Sweden and to have taken him on a tour of garden allotments without winning his approval. This folk legend is interesting as a myth capturing a central contradiction of this policy for the workers' movement.

[37] A Danish worker recalling debates about garden allotments at the beginning of the century is quoted as saying, "It was something of a myth that people in the allotment garden had no other interest than the allotment. Even in the political propaganda one could notice a slightly demeaning attitude. For example, allotment gardeners were always made responsible for an unsatisfactory demonstration or parade meeting on the first of May." I. Tølstrup, *Kolonihaven,* Copenhagen, 1978, as cited by S. B. Ehn, *Kolonins sista strid,* Göteborg, 1990, 25.

[38] In 1904–5, in one of the very first allotment gardens, there were 42 percent workers, 27 percent craftsmen, and 21 percent salaried employees. See Ehn, *Kolonins sista strid,* 28.

[39] G. Englund and S. Hallgren, *Koloniträdgårdar,* Stockholm, 1974, 44–51.

[40] L. Jarlov, *Boende och skaparglädje. Människors behov av skapande verksamhet—en försummad dimension i samhällsplaneringen*, Göteborg, 1982.

[41] E. N. Anderson Jr., "Att anlägga en trädgård: en folkkonst," in *Folklig och Kommersiell konst: En antologi,* ed. Bengt Jacobsson, Varnamo, 1980.

den owners to display signs of their social position in the hierarchy of social classes. His research suggests that there are significant differences between upper-class and middle-class gardens, and that working-class gardens fail to exhibit a similar pattern, due to economic differences between their users and efforts to keep up with members of higher classes. He has also noted that all of these gardens are clearly raised so as to look different from the surrounding natural environment, which confirms that they can be looked at as man-made signs. A German student of gardens, Werner Nohl, points to the sense of appropriation of things and places that grows out of personal involvement in their making. His research claims that a major difference can be observed between upper- and middle-class gardens, which are mere status symbols and thus they lack personal significance, and working-class gardens, such as allotment gardens, which can give rise to a sense of appropriation when creativity is not hampered by excessively constraining collective rules. Thus Anderson and Nohl offer complementary interpretations of the class-related significance of gardens, stemming from totally different perspectives. Yet this is far from satisfactory. Both of them have proceeded from their own observations alone in order to support their interpretations, claiming implicitly an objective stand. Magnus Bergquist, following in the steps of Mark Francis, who had chosen to interview gardeners themselves to learn from them why they were gardening, went much further in his inquiries. He made in-depth studies of a few gardens in Sweden,[42] of the everyday life in the gardens and its experience by the gardeners, and he took pains to collect brief life histories of these gardeners in order to understand under what circumstances they became gardeners. From a methodological point of view this is a bold departure from most garden studies. It confronts the actual garden and its user's perspective, it explores everyday life in the garden and its social environment, and moreover it demands that attention be given to the life history of the gardener. It provides a fascinating insight into the relationships between vernacular gardens and developments of contemporary myths.

Nowadays these gardens offer their Swedish users the possibility to experience independence, a sense of ownership, and a sense of individual achievement,[43] as well as to indulge at the same time in flights of fancy that take them back into the good Swedish rural society of mythical times. Let us delve a little into this aspect of life offered by the allotment gardens since we are not used to thinking that modern men, who are supposed to be all too rational, could still be creators of mythical discourse. Both the association of gardeners and the garden allotment itself offer a miniature image of an enchanted rural society. Thus one may see these gardens as providing an anchoring of personal development and national identity to their users.

This slightly surprising mythical significance seems to be invented anew in each allotment thanks to independent initiatives by most of the gardeners. Of course this is the stuff

[42] M. Bergquist, *Trädgårdens betydelser för folk i flerfamiljshus*, Göteborg, 1980.

[43] The same idea was noted by Englund and Hallgren: "At present it does not pay any longer to cultivate one's vegetables and berries, say most allotment gardeners, but it is not so much the economy but rather the pleasure to have cultivated by oneself one's products that one seeks." See Englund and Hallgren, *Koloniträdgårdar,* 96.

that myths are made of—independent variations invented by natives along some common patterns. Here are some of the most salient traits of this image of rural society: the division of labor and authority along traditional lines between men and women, which has been changing so much in Swedish families over the last forty years, is very common and some conflicts even arise when "ladies' associations" start expressing too many ideas about the management of the allotment; self-government gives an image of old-time cooperation between free owners in agricultural hamlets;[44] a community spirit of mutual help and care prevails between neighbors; easygoing social relationships with neighbors take place over a glass of beer or a plate of herring with baked potatoes or a relish of *surströmming*,[45] which is unheard-of in housing areas; the community gathers around the maypole and organizes dances and drinks on the long midsummer day; all parents pay close attention to children's pleasures and teach them the joys of gardening; on almost every plot is built a small cottage surrounded by flowers and fruit-bearing bushes or fruit trees in the garden.[46] All of these features, which convey images of the good rural life in olden times, are given shape in a personal way, and constantly re-invented by the users of these allotments. This is a myth that expresses itself as the plot of a drama whose actors are the gardeners. In a sense the myth comes true through a series of rituals of everyday life. It is not the whole life any more than a feast at Versailles. This is but a temporary social gathering, a series of ritual encounters, that bring together people whose lives remain separate (they very seldom see each other at home during the winter, or at any other time during the year, and they do not engage in shared social events outside the gardens themselves). Hence we may look at these gardens and at the social practices that they foster as a whole, as social rituals that contribute to the maintenance of shared beliefs about the good society, and about the mythical past that they are supposed to emulate. In that respect these vernacular gardens do not seem so fundamentally different from the native gardens we described earlier.

A recent development documented by Gunilla Englund and Sören Hallgren is even more evocative of some unexpected beliefs attached to some of these gardens.[47] There is a bulging group of allotment gardeners who want to grow their own food according to so-called biologic or biodynamic principles. Discussions of food poisoning by chemicals in the mass media have given them a recent impetus. These gardeners are critical of applied science, so they avoid any uses of chemical fertilizers and pesticides. They also entertain a view of nature and of man's correct relationship to nature that implies some ideas about the "true forces" at work in nature that resemble mystical beliefs in a supernatural nature. Kjell Arman,

[44] "Work in the allotment gardens reminds [one] a little of the old peasant society," write Englund and Hallgren in a few pages where they describe at some length the features of life in the allotment gardens. See Englund and Hallgren, *Koloniträdgårdar,* 80, 83.

[45] Surströmming is a small Baltic Sea herring that is allowed to rot in a tin box before it is eaten. It is a pure relish for many Swedes, and a source of disgust for most foreigners.

[46] "A garden cabin may have a variety of origins. . . . But it is most common that garden cabins call to mind the [Swedish dream of a] little red cabin with white corners, a veranda decorated with joinery, and in front of the cabin a small flagpole with a flag flying at its top, surrounded with a resplendent flower parterre." Englund and Hallgren, *Koloniträdgårdar,* 118.

[47] Ibid., 105 ff.

one of their spiritual guides, advocates in slightly bombastic prose a new approach to nature: "If we use the laws of dead matter for the living things we shall eradicate life, but if we learn to acknowledge life as a force, and if we learn how to use it, we can make life out of matter—we can make bread out of stones."[48] He develops the old idea common in the eighteenth century that life is movement and that stillness is death. According to this notion, blowing wind and running waters bring health, while still air or waters are deadly. Hence biodynamic texts recommend a practice called *utrörning*, a new Swedish word meaning "stirring out," in order to give a new start to living forces. It calls upon stirring any manure that has been prepared for the garden into water, so that the living forces residing in the waters may penetrate into it. In order to make planting successful, the preparation should be spread on the earth within a few hours afterward, since the water cannot hold the "liberated forces" for a longer time. It is advisable to do this by moonlight.[49] The result of these practices is debatable, since unhealthy plants may produce counterpoisons of their own that may be more detrimental to human health than plants that have been sprayed with chemicals or pesticides. Nevertheless, the point is that, even at present, there are some gardeners who claim a positivistic view of nature, while others believe in a supernature and resort to magical practices when gardening. We need not travel to the Pacific Islands or to the rainforest in the Amazon to be confronted with magic in gardens.

These studies do not yield, as yet, a comprehensive picture of all developments and their dynamics. But they show how life in these gardens may have been important, how rituals of family or community life have taken place there, and how freedom of initiative has been conducive to large investment in aesthetic pursuits. Ironically, these aesthetic inventions have been (and still are) coming under attack by local authorities and by watchdogs of good taste. Of course, garden policies have not been produced for the sole benefit of the working class, and at different times other social groups have been targeted. Todd Longstaffe-Gowan has studied gardens of naval officers in Great Britain; others are interested in gardens of the middle class, for whom garden-cities have been designed in many countries since the end of the nineteenth century. All of these gardens seem to share a few features that were clearly shown by Longstaffe-Gowan; they are places where people could integrate into the established social order while indulging in individualistic shows of affluence. Several studies have been made in France of home and garden life in these suburban developments. In contrast to the developments of aesthetic invention and display of individual tastes and skills exhibited by the working class, one sees among the middle-class or upper-middle-class owners of these suburban homes and gardens the development of disciplinary attitudes imposing a strict limit upon the range of individual variation in the personal design of the garden and of the home environment. This observation echoes the work by Anderson. The meaning of gardens seems to be even more baffling than the relationship between magic and horticulture. We are led to wonder whether aesthetic con-

[48] K. Arman, *Jord och Bröd*, 1921, quoted by Englund and Hallgren, *Koloniträdgårdar*, 106. This book has been republished recently by the Rudolf Steiner anthroposophical press.

[49] Englund and Hallgren, *Koloniträdgårdar*, 106.

formism may be a self-imposed discipline of the middle class, which comprises people who revere common values of autonomy, initiative, and personal achievement at work and in leisure activities, while working-class people hold the reverse of these values.

In short, gardening in family garden allotments constitutes a system of expression that imposes strong constraints on the choice and organization of place, on behavior, and on family and group organization. Nonetheless, it allows individuals to develop personal expressions and to achieve a sense of empowerment and self-achievement that they cannot reach in ordinary city life. These garden allotments are always clearly distinct from their surroundings. They are very often established in derelict spaces that the gardeners have turned into highly civilized places. The relationships people entertain with nature can be captured under a number of dialectical categories, such as nature and culture; work and leisure; metaphysics and physics; aesthetics and economy; and social class and individual. These gardening communities are very orderly. They usually display a sense of ecological order, and the organization of space follows a twofold order: a step-wise scale of privacy between public and intimate places, and a semantic order allowing each garden to stand for a symbol of the good society somewhere between nostalgia and utopia. Rituals of interaction among gardeners and rituals of visit follow an orderly pattern of events, and colors, tastes, and fragrance in the garden contribute to patterns of spatial composition.

Conclusion

What have we learned that would be useful for studies in landscape architecture? Let us start from a simple remark. Visits to vernacular gardens have led to fascinating questions about the gardeners' roles in social reproduction and about gardening's contribution to cultural production. Gardening has turned out to be a system of expression, very much like language, music, painting, or dancing. It results from the development of some distinctive human capacities that can enable people to create all sorts of works, out of which only a few count as high art, understood as all forms of art entertained and enjoyed by socially dominant groups as symbols of social distinction.[50] This is why it invites a study of all corresponding human performances. Studies of vernacular gardens suggest a tentative definition for this domain. A social anthropology of gardening would be the study of an art that turns environments into places encapsulating intentions and representations about man's relationship to nature. Culture and social structure impinge upon such a relationship, so that a study of this art cannot limit itself to a study of its output. We should reach, as well, for an understanding of gardening as a creative process that contributes to cultural and historical change and is constrained in its practice and in its development by the existing cultural and social orders. Thus gardening appears as a system of expression that includes landscape architecture and much else in the creation of some very special places where people entertain a continuous relationship with living nature.

[50] In multi-layered societies, where there is not one single socially dominant group, the definition of high art is, not very surprisingly, a contentious issue.

The studies of vernacular gardens seem to suggest a broad methodological outline that could be applied in empirical studies of any kind of garden. Drawing upon the results of this survey, a social anthropology of gardening would rest upon four levels of analysis, dealing with the elements of gardening, structural organization of these elements, characteristic order and composition of figures and events within a place, and the domain of creative action it affords to individuals. Each of these levels can be discovered in vernacular gardens as well as in period gardens, even though many of the questions that they raise have not been studied until now, and some of them may be out of reach because of a lack of archival materials.

Elements of gardening comprise a description of *characteristic activities,* the *social organization* of each of them, *objects* or *forms* they help create, and the main *uses, emotions,* and *meanings* that each of these activities entails.[51]

Structural organization of gardening rests upon an acknowledgment of the *embeddedness of gardening culture* within the broader culture. This is an aspect of gardening that has been very seldom covered in studies of historical gardens and thus calls for a renewed effort. It would be especially valuable in order to avoid projecting contemporary western cultural perspectives onto gardens of other civilizations such as the Roman, Arabic, Persian, Japanese, and Chinese. In each case it would demand an assessment of intentions and representations of man's relationship to living nature when gardening with respect to cultural orientations of persons engaged in the gardening activities under scrutiny. We have seen that some couples of opposite categories, which can be mutually exclusive or dialectical, follow distinctive patterns in a given culture. Whenever they are significant for a gardening activity they may help us to understand how gardening relates to social action or to culture in general.[52]

Order and composition of figures have been at the center of studies in landscape architecture until now. Visual order has been given much attention. Nevertheless, the field suggested by studies of vernacular gardens is broader: *semantic order* deserves as much scrutiny, as does *ecological order,* which is very seldom studied. In addition, one may look at orderly organizations of cues or events that proceed from gardening activities such as *organizations of sensuous experiences* of sounds, odors, tastes, and motions. Each order may be expressed through a *figurative composition,* the principles of which should be discovered.

The study of *creative action* introduces a totally new field. It might allow a structural analysis of culture and praxis to come to grips with the history of social change. Let us note simply that both vernacular gardens and period gardens result from gardening practices that are socially and culturally constrained. Nevertheless, gardening activities have always al-

[51] Deforesting, planting, sweeping a yard, and visiting a historical garden are examples of elementary gardening activities, the knowledge of which would provide the building blocks for studies of the art of gardening.

[52] Among possible dyadic categories that we have already encountered are nature and culture; work and leisure; metaphysics and physics; aesthetics and economy; inside and outside; class and individual; consumption and action; social distinction and personal appropriation; habit and invention. Of course, these dyads may be combined in different ways, offering different structures of thought within which the art of gardens may be developed.

lowed some room for personal initiative and for unconstrained activities. We are interested, thus, in registering all actions that may introduce new elements or meanings in gardening or new experiences in gardens in order to understand their conditions of existence and to account for their impact on social and cultural change.

This falls short of providing a theoretical outline for a social anthropology of gardening. Much additional research will be required to create such an outline. Yet one may hope that, alongside art history of gardens and cultural geography of landscape, a social anthropology of gardening might open new vistas for research that would benefit from past scholarly achievements in studies of landscape architecture, and that would provide new sources of excitement. Theories in social anthropology of gardening can help us understand relations between a society and its gardens in a synchronic perspective or in a short-term perspective of change. It cannot replace historical studies. On the contrary, it might stimulate them by offering new insights to start with.

Longing and Belonging in Chinese Garden History

Stanislaus Fung

The modern historiography of Chinese gardens is something less than 70 years old, but its story is both complex and much neglected. In common with much of garden history in general, the modern study of Chinese gardens has proceeded in the absence of an overall unifying paradigm, so that generalizations about fundamentals in scholarly approach are hazardous. Scholars from a wide variety of disciplinary backgrounds have made contributions to Chinese garden history, but the development of this domain of work has had a noncumulative character. It is not uncommon for important work in Chinese publications to be substantially overlooked for decades in subsequent publications in both Chinese and other languages.[1] Without attributing a false coherence to a multifarious bibliography, the present essay is an attempt to articulate a sense of the basic aspects and prospects of the historiography of Chinese gardens by adopting a twofold strategy: (1) Exemplars. The essay focuses on exemplary works both in modern scholarship and in traditional literature as the fundamental units of understanding. From the numerous publications that have appeared on Chinese gardens and the many traditional works that have been brought into the light of modern scholarship, the essay will gather a handful as examples. As Giorgio Agamben explains, "Neither particular nor universal, the example is a singular object that presents itself as such. . . . These pure singularities communicate only in the empty space of the example, without being tied by any common property, by any identity."[2] The logic of the example is therefore very useful in illuminating a multifarious situation without a unifying paradigm, and in dealing with diversity in sources without reductive abstraction. (2) The

I would like to thank Professors Roger T. Ames, Michel Conan, and David L. Hall, as well as two anonymous reviewers, for their valuable comments on an earlier version of this essay. Chinese and Japanese proper names are given in the traditional order: surnames first. Chinese names, terms, and titles are transliterated in standard pinyin. Where a modern Chinese author's name is known in a different form of transliteration, I have followed the author's preferred form and given the pinyin version in brackets where possible.

[1] The study of Chinese garden designers, or more correctly, designers of rockeries, is a conspicuous case in point. See my "Guide to Secondary Sources on Chinese Gardens," *Studies in the History of Gardens and Designed Landscapes*, forthcoming, section 1.5.

[2] The idea is taken from G. Agamben, *The Coming Community*, trans. M. Hardt, Minneapolis, 1993, 10–11.

admixture of history and historiography. This essay emphasizes a sense of new prospects in the study of Chinese gardens by juxtaposing traditional sources and modern writings. The citation of modern studies of Chinese gardens and the discussion of traditional Chinese sources in a common space of examples has the effect of blurring the historical study of Chinese gardens and the modern historiography of Chinese gardens. This is because emerging possibilities for further research are often discovered in considering modern historiography in retrospect; this sense of possibilities can also inform our understanding of the significance of certain traditional writings, and a new understanding of the traditional writings can then offer a new understanding of the nature and specific assumptions of modern works of scholarship. In the midst of what one might call a feedback to and fro, one is often assaying a new thought on a given topic as much as reporting on established scholarship on that topic.

With these strategic remarks in mind, I would like to begin by offering readers unfamiliar with the study of Chinese gardens a simple sketch of three waves of scholarship that can be thought of as bursts of scholarly activity, focusing on works that offered comprehensive surveys of Chinese garden history. Starting in the 1930s with the early systematizing work of the Japanese scholar Oka Oji, *Shina tei'en ron* (On the gardens of China), and Sugimura Yûzo's *Chûgoku no niwa* (Gardens of China), we have the first attempts at the comprehensive narrative of historical developments and trends in Chinese garden history.[3] Japanese interest in Chinese gardens has had a long history, and after the reforms of the Meiji period, it certainly became a significant source of influence for Chinese academic developments.[4] Oka Oji's work is the most comprehensive chronological work on Chinese gardens of its time, but due to the limited circulation of Japanese books in China for several decades after its publication, it would be misleading to suggest that later Chinese research built on its findings.[5] In what might be considered a second wave, starting only in the mid-1980s, the early Japanese studies were superseded by Chinese works of comparable scope and detail. Zhang Jiaji's *Zhongguo zaoyuan shi* (History of Chinese gardens) and Zhou

[3] Oka Oji, *Shina tei'en ron,* Tokyo, 1934; Chinese trans., *Zhongguo gongyuan yuanlin shi kao,* trans. Chang Yingsheng, Beijing, 1988; Sugimura Yûzo, *Chûgoku no niwa,* Tokyo, 1966. Cf. Gotô Asatarô, *Shina no fûkei to tei'en,* Tokyo, 1928; idem, *Shina tei'en,* Tokyo, 1934.

[4] See Chen Zhi, "Zhongguo wenhua yishu dui Riben gudai tingyuan fengge de yingxiang," in *Chen Zhi zaoyuan wenji,* Beijing, 1988, 214–22.

[5] It is tempting to consider whether the writings of Japanese scholars on Chinese architecture and gardens were connected to Japanese imperialism or whether the Japanese were a vehicle of the cultural imperialism of Western visual literacy. These questions have not, to the best of my knowledge, been addressed by contemporary scholars, and detailed answers are not available without a much more detailed knowledge of the modern Japanese context of scholarly production. For suggestive remarks on Gotô Asatarô, see J. A. Fogel, *The Literature of Travel in the Japanese Rediscovery of China, 1862–1945,* Stanford, Calif., 1996, 200–209. My sense is that it would not be appropriate to address the issues in terms of Japan's cultural domination of China. The urgent question, to my mind, is not "Who dominated whom?" or "What were the effects of cultural imperialism?" but rather "What, in view of the importation of Western visual literacy to modern China, can the present possiblities for cross-cultural exchange be?" Or, borrowing the words of Fred Dallmayr, we can ask, how can one "salvage a nondomineering cultural potential under the debris of Eurocentricism and traditional Orientalism"? F. Dallmayr, *Beyond Orientalism: Essays on Cross-Cultural Encounter,* Albany, N.Y., 1996, xix.

Weiquan's *Zhongguo gudian yuanlin shi* (History of classical Chinese gardens) are works by senior scholars that come readily to mind among a large body of publications.[6] Then there is a third wave of scholarship, to which I belong, and from which perhaps the most important work is that of Wang Yi, a scholar of the Chinese Academy of Social Sciences in Beijing and the author of *Yuanlin yu Zhongguo wenhua* (Gardens and Chinese culture).[7] With this rough characterization of three waves of scholarly studies, one can point out that the categories "architecture" and "landscape architecture" in Chinese usage are modern categories and in fact came from post-Meiji Japan as *kenchiku* and *zôen*. Because the traditional Chinese order of knowledge did not include separate categories for what we now take for granted as disciplines or fields of academic study, we can see that there has been a sea change in the sorting and re-sorting of traditional writings pertinent to modern academic interest. This has been one of the major tasks, inventive as it was, that the early scholars such as Oka Oji and Chen Zhi have accomplished as their legacy. The current generation of scholars now face the task of dealing with the conceptual and theoretical issues that arise when Chinese garden history is discussed in a comparative way across different cultures. Of course, in a sense, this has been the case ever since the modern historiography of Chinese gardens began in the 1930s.

It is important to bear in mind that generations of scholars have worked under arduous conditions of war and of the Cultural Revolution, and however much it might be necessary to continue, extend, and revise the tasks and findings of one's academic predecessors, it would be indecent to overlook the personal, bodily commitment often required to broach certain traditional issues or to espouse certain values. Further, although the modern historiography of Chinese gardens has a history of only seven decades, its cultural trajectory and significance has to be understood against a broader and more complex time frame of the last 200 years. China has been going through momentous cultural and social changes as a result of its encounter with the West since the nineteenth century and is now entering a period when, for the first time, it seems to have found some way of dealing with the West.[8] The historiography of Chinese gardens and its prospects are very much part of a larger story of Westernization and modernization. Through the pioneering research of Chu-joe Hsia,[9] scholars have come to understand how much modern scholarship on Chinese architecture and gardens owes to the Beaux Arts tradition in assumptions, method, and approach.[10] When Chinese scholars identified traditional construction manuals as

[6] Zhang Jiaji, *Zhongguo zaoyuan shi*, Hei'erbin, 1986; Zhou Weiquan, *Zhongguo gudian yuanlin shi*, Beijing, 1990.

[7] Wang Yi, *Yuanlin yu Zhongguo wenhua*, Shanghai, 1990.

[8] R. Huang, *China: A Macro History*, Turn of the Century ed., Armonk, N.Y., 1997; Chinese version published as Huang Renyu, *Zhongguo da lishi*, Taibei, 1993.

[9] Chu-joe Hsia [Xia Zhujiu] is a professor of the Graduate Institute of Building and Planning at the National Taiwan University. A student of Manuel Castells at Berkeley, he has made conspicuous efforts at presenting modern urban theory to Chinese readers. He is founding editor of the refereed journal *Chengshi yu sheji/Cities and Design*.

[10] Chu-joe Hsia, "Yingzao xueshe—Liang Sicheng jianzhushi lunshu gouzao zhi lilun fenxi," in *Kongjian, lishi yu shehui—lunwen xuan, 1987–1992*, Taiwan shehui yenjiu congkan 3, Taibei, 1993, 1–40.

counterparts to the European tradition of architectural treatises, when they affirmed the value of traditional timber architecture as something consonant with Pugin's idea of structural rationalism, when they considered the "bracket system" as the Chinese counterpart to the classical orders in Western architecture—thanks to Chu-joe Hsia's work, we can now see these as instances that betoken a revolution in historical perspective as the Chinese world became China in the world. A form of traditionalistic thought emerged in the course of this process, taking hold of studies of Chinese architecture and gardens as it did other domains of cultural life, "insisting that the Chinese culture of the past still contained value in an entirely new cultural historic epoch."[11] Longing for tradition, for what is one's own, and longing for overcoming the problems of the past, and for the sense of belonging that marks allegiance to tradition or an international world of scholarship: these are considerations that have commonly occasioned difficulty when tradition and modernity are conceived as mutually exclusive and opposed. It is beyond the scope of this essay to offer a full treatment of these cultural issues. My main object here is to offer a sense of the opportunities for intercultural exchange in the domain of landscape architecture that our historical juncture seems to make available.

Visual Economy

One of the most conspicuous ways in which the study of Chinese gardens has been caught up in twentieth-century developments is the sea change in how the gardens are imaged in visual media. Western techniques of orthogonal drawing and spatial analysis, and the use of photography, have helped to produce our modern understanding of Chinese gardens. The study of the role of visual images in the historiography of Chinese gardens is a much neglected topic, and I can only indicate a few of basic considerations here.

The use of Western photography has offered viewers an impression of Chinese gardens from the nineteenth century onward. The use of Western techniques of architectural drawing to depict Chinese gardens has a longer history, and this usage became commonplace in the twentieth century.[12] Images of extant gardens are often used anachronistically to refer to a historically nonspecific "traditional" past.[13] Very rarely are sets of images used to document historical changes in gardens. An understanding of the processual nature of gardens is often sacrificed. The use of Western architectural drawing techniques has allowed modern notions of empty, isotopic space to be introduced to the study of Chinese gardens. The use of photography has broadened the range of visual images in the study of

[11] B. I. Schwartz, "History and Culture in Levenson's Thought," in *The Mozartian Historian: Essays on the Works of Joseph R. Levenson*, ed. M. Meisner and R. Murphey, Berkeley, 1976, 103.

[12] See for example, Liu Dunzhen, *Suzhou gudian yuanlin*, Beijing, 1979, and English trans., Liu Dunzhen, *Chinese Classical Gardens of Suzhou*, trans. Chen Lixian, ed. J. C. Wang, New York, 1993; Qian Yun, ed., *Classical Chinese Gardens*, Hong Kong, 1982; Zhongguo meishu quanji bianji weiyuanhui, ed., *Zhongguo meishu quanji, jianzhu yishu bian, san, yuanlin jianzhu*, Beijing, 1988.

[13] The problematic nature of this practice has been underlined implicitly by the recent work of Tanaka Tan, who compared textual records with extant gardens in order to show their differences. See Tanaka Tan, "Zhongguo zaoqi yuanlin fengge yu Jiangnan yuanlin shili," *Chengshi yu sheji* 1 (June 1997), 17–49.

Chinese gardens. When Chinese paintings, woodblock engravings, rubbings, and art objects of various kinds are used in conjunction with photographs and Western architectural drawings, the diversity of visual media involved in this visual economy is really considerable, but this became naturalized, so that most scholars have overlooked the specificity of the visual media involved. It would seem that the assumed referentiality of images—the idea that they allow viewers access to Chinese gardens as a visual reality—is a powerful and effective disincentive to probe into the function of representation.

It is a commonplace among students of the visual arts that photographs do not permit an unmediated access to "external reality." And we might wonder what readers do encounter in a work such as Florence Lee Powell's *In the Chinese Garden: A Photographic Tour of the Complete Chinese Garden, with Text Explaining Its Symbolism, as Seen in the Liu Yüan (the Liu Garden) and the Shih Tzu Lin (the Forest of Lions), Two Famous Chinese Gardens in the City of Soochow, Kiangsu Province, China.*[14] However, it is not necessary to choose between affirming the truth of photographs and denouncing them for their "fictitious" nature and dreadful "inauthenticity" as a mode of representation in the study of Chinese gardens. Recent work in comparative philosophy has given scholars good reason to reconsider the notions of image and representation involved here. Roger T. Ames writes,

> In our tradition, image in the vernacular combines the notions of perception and imagination, where the mimetic, representative, figurative, and fictive connotations of image are derived from the ontological disparity between a transcendentally "real" world and the concrete world of experience. The absence of such ontological disparity in the Confucian model will mean that image is the presentation rather than the representation of a configured world at concrete, literal, and historical level. . . . The meaning resident in the image as established is the act of establishing the image itself. Contrary to one's own naive expectations . . . what one finally "sees" in a work of art is the creative act that produced it. The creative process, not the object, is the repository of meaning. What is imaged is the process.[15]

Can we imagine the role of photography or of orthogonal drawings as eventful "presentation," in Ames's sense, in the imaging of Chinese gardens? Here, I would like to propose that two exemplary modern works on Chinese gardens are indicative of future possibilities of exploration.

In Chen Congzhou's study of Suzhou gardens, first published in 1956, black and white photographs are juxtaposed with quotations from Song dynasty song lyrics. One photograph, taken during daytime, is paired with the line, "The courtyard deserted, the

[14] F. L. Powell, *In the Chinese Garden: A Photographic Tour of the Complete Chinese Garden, with Text Explaining Its Symbolism, as Seen in the Liu Yüan (the Liu Garden) and the Shih Tzu Lin (the Forest of Lions), Two Famous Chinese Gardens in the City of Soochow, Kiangsu Province, China*, New York, 1943. As an earlier example, see also E. L. Howard, *Chinese Garden Architecture: A Collection of Photographs of Minor Chinese Buildings*, New York, 1931.

[15] R. T. Ames, "Meaning as Imaging: Prolegomena to a Confucian Epistemology," in *Culture and Modernity: East-West Philosophical Perspectives*, ed. E. Deutsch, Honolulu, 1991, 228–29.

1. The downstairs studio in the Storied Pavilion of Inverted Reflections in the Garden of the Unsuccessful Politician (from Chen, Suzhou yuanlin, *95)*

moon rises over the steps—shadows of the balustrade all over the ground" (Fig. 1). Here a sunlit scene is used to evoke a moment of quiet drama in the evening.[16] With another photograph, following the poetic allusion of a bridge named "Little Rainbow," Chen Congzhou juxtaposed it against the lines, "Walking with one's reflection along the brook, the sky lies under the clear brook / In the sky above are passing clouds; one seems to be in the passing clouds"[17] (Fig. 2). The force of poetic evocation takes us beyond Peng Yigang's

[16] One is reminded of Hervé Guibert's *Ghost Image*, trans. R. Bononno, Los Angeles, 1996.
[17] Chen Congzhou, *Suzhou yuanlin*, Shanghai, 1956; Japanese trans., Tokyo, 1982.

2. The view looking north from Little Surging Waves in the Garden of the Unsuccessful Politician (from Chen, Suzhou yuanlin, *80)*

more prosaic observation that the bridge serves as a dividing element that sets up a sense of spatial layering in the garden[18] (Fig. 3). Professor Chen commented on his own book by referring to notions of the empty and the full derived from theories of Chinese painting and poetics:[19]

> After accumulating materials for several years, I began writing by using what I had seen and thought about. My reflections were not baseless. I was seeking the empty

[18] Peng Yigang, *Zhongguo gudian yuanlin fenxi*, Beijing, 1986, analysis sheet 64.

[19] See F. Cheng, *Empty and Full: The Language of Chinese Painting*, trans. M. H. Kohn, Boston, 1994.

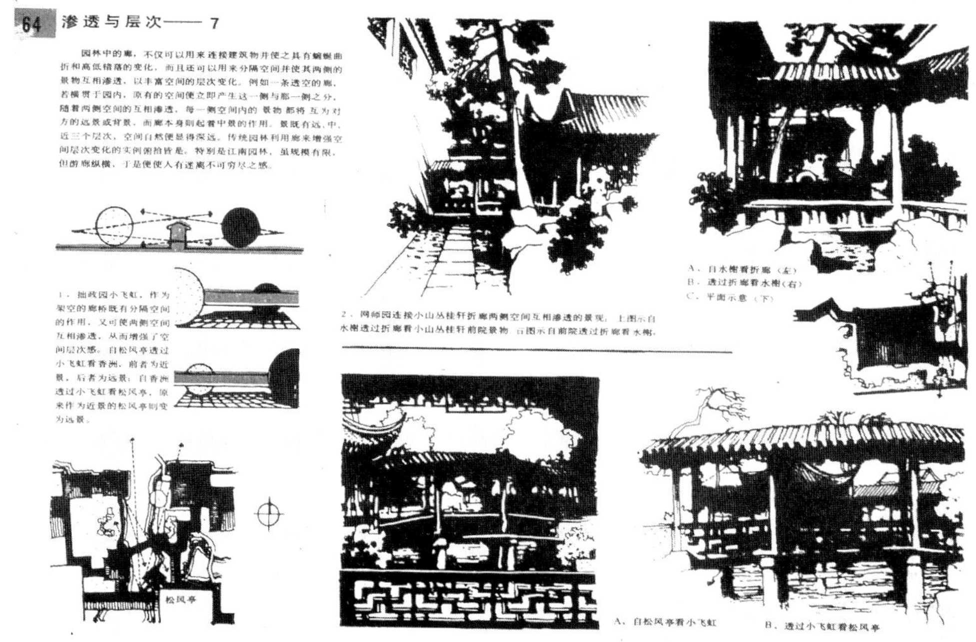

3. Analysis Sheet 64, on spatial layering and sequencing (from Peng, Zhongguo gudian yuanlin fenxi*)*

> in the full, thinking that there would be some kind of basis. Sentiments are stimulated by touring. Originally, these Chinese gardens were the gardens of literati, and had as their guiding thoughts poetic sentiments and painterly ideas. For this reason, my photographs connected naturally with the poetic works of writers that I had read before. I therefore appended lines from Song dynasty song lyrics to each photograph. . . . But in 1958, I was criticized for this, and was accused of having a strong sense of traditional literati consciousness. I could only lower my head and admit my failing—that my thinking had not been reformed properly. Now, thirty years later . . . my "preposterous act" of former times is again praised by readers.[20]

Returning to Ames's remarks, we can see that the meaning of the photographs becomes linked to the creative act of placing them next to the song lyrics. This process of making linkages is the repository of meaning, not the gardens themselves as landscape objects. The introduction of photography had the effect of transforming Chinese gardens from one kind of objects of pleasure (with implied acculturation of those who experience the gardens and so on) into another (with quite differently acculturized viewers). Professor Chen's juxtapositions dislocate the realistic effect of photographs and the visual drive to get a fix

[20] Chen Congzhou, "Wo de di yi ben shu—Suzhou yuanlin," in *Lien qing ji*, Shanghai, 1987, 123.

on an external reality by reopening the images to speculation. The juxtapositions stimulate the viewer to look and to look *again*, to do a double take, and take in the juxtapositions as a cultural practice.

With the benefit of hindsight, we can imagine two other ways of understanding the significance of Chen Congzhou's practice. On the one hand, following Ames's contrast of presentation and representation, we can turn to Michel Foucault's discussion of Magritte's *Ceci n'est pas une pipe*, where he contrasted Magritte's practice with *trompe l'oeil*: "We are farthest from *trompe-l'oeil*. The latter seeks to support the weightiest burden of affirmation by the ruse of a convincing resemblance."[21] If the photography of Chinese gardens constantly affirms before us, "This is a Chinese garden," by a ruse of a resemblance, Professor Chen's poetic quotations have the effect of teasing apart the regime of representation that rules over resemblance. The photographs are liberated from the duty of making a full and thorough documentation of an external reality into an open-ended series of juxtapositions of text and image.

On the other hand, following recent work on Chinese historical thinking, we can relate Professor Chen's practice to the notions of *xing* and *bi*, which characterize the "logic" or modus operandi of Chinese historical thinking. "*Xing* means to arise, to arouse—to be aroused by the past events to realize something; *bi* means to analogize, to 'metaphor,' from the far historical known to the novel uncertain present."[22] In this sense, the use of song lyrics in conjunction with photography "arouses" our attention and incites a serendipitous finding. At the same time, an analogy between the scene of the song lyric and the immediate scene of the photograph is established, metaphoring or ferrying us from the one to the other. By force of repetition as one encounters many juxtapositions of text and image, one gets a vague and rich sense of the sensibility that Professor Chen brings to the experience of Chinese gardens.

Peng Yigang's own *Zhongguo gudian yuanlin fenxi* (Analysis of classical Chinese gardens) is in appearance very different to Chen Congzhou's work. Peng's book is the most complete account of the spatial analysis of Chinese gardens, and uses Western techniques of architectural drawing extensively. However, Peng's spatial analysis is structured overall by headings such as introvert-extrovert, sequestration and exposition—counterparts and counterpoints that help maintain a sense of the reciprocity of ways of looking, along the lines of yin and yang. Peng's work seems to suggest a way of using Western techniques of architectural drawing in a way that cannot be identified as a simple appropriation. There is a large domain of research, yet to be explored by contemporary scholars, that would entail a study of how hazardous the transmission of modern Western techniques of architectural drawing to twentieth-century China has been, and how cultural differences might have been involved as techniques of drawing traveled to China. We can locate here an interesting possibility of "mutual regard" in diverse fields of contemporary scholarship

[21] M. Foucault, *This Is Not a Pipe*, trans. and ed. J. Harkness, Berkeley, 1983, 43.

[22] Chun-chieh Huang [Huang Junjie], "Historical Thinking in Classical Confucianism," in *Time and Space in Chinese Culture*, ed. Chun-chieh Huang and E. Zürcher, Leiden, 1995, 77.

in landscape architecture. If the modern Chinese have been rushing to import orthogonal drawing techniques in the study of landscape, the same techniques that contemporary scholars like James Corner are attempting to displace by developing them into newly sophisticated modes of landscape notation, it might be interesting for Professor Corner to see how traditional Western modes of drawing might be deployed in an unconventional manner, and for Chinese scholars to see how the conceptual foundations of orthogonal drawing are being challenged and new modes of notation explored.[23]

To be sure, these two works by Chen Congzhou and Peng Yigang are not typical of twentieth-century scholarship on Chinese gardens, but they suggest a way of thinking about it. Modernization and Westernization as they are involved in the production of knowledge of Chinese gardens do not amount to a kind of *telos*, an end accomplished and finished in simple and dreadful inauthenticity. Rather, for those interested in historiographical prospects, it seems more fruitful to compare what *appears* to have been installed in the course of Westernization with what has happened *in spite of* it.

Garden History

If we turn from twentieth-century writings to traditional writings on Chinese gardens, there is a significant "blackout." The use of visual means to record gardens takes a clear second place; the primacy of the word is conspicuous. However, the term for garden history, literally *yuan shi*, is scarcely to be found at all. In more than 2000 years of recorded history, there is, to the best of my knowledge, only one instance of the usage of the term *yuan shi*. In a late Ming anthology *Bing xue xie* (Portable ice and snow), offering literary "ice and snow" that bring a refreshing chill to "fiery households" and help readers ward off the world of vulgarity,[24] there is an essay titled "Yuan shi xu" (Preface to a garden history) by the great literatus Chen Jiru (1558–1639). The text begins,

> I once said that there are four difficulties with gardens: it is difficult to have fine mountains and waters; it is difficult to have old trees; it is difficult to plan; and it is difficult to assign names. Then there are three easy things: the powerful can easily seize the garden; in time, it can easily become unkempt; and with an uncultivated owner, it easily becomes vulgar. Nowadays, there are many famous gardens in Jiangnan. I often pass by them and rest my eyes on them. However, when I next visit them, they might still have bright flowers and shaded ferns, but the owner would not have the leisure to be there, or even if he could be there, he would fling his arm around and depart like a courier; or he would diminish the plans of his forebears, altering them abruptly each summer so that the garden would not be

[23] J. Corner, "Representation and Landscape: Drawing and Making in the Landscape Medium," *Word and Image* 8, 3 (July–September 1992), 243–75. Also relevant is T. Davis, "Photography and Landscape Studies," *Landscape Journal* 8, 1 (Spring 1989), 1–12.

[24] Chen Jiru, "Yuan shi xu," in *Bing xue xie*, comp. Wei Yong, Guo xue zhen ben wen ku [di yi ji, di si zhong], Shanghai, 1935, 1:1–2.

> completely renovated when his bones would already have decayed; or in the twinkling of an eye, he would sell it to another family, and then if a huge plaque does not label the entrance, a strong lock would bolt the door shut; or trees would be cut down to make mortars, and rocks would be pulled down to make plinths. The fallen beams and ruined walls would be like a house abandoned during a drought. Even if the eaves, rafters and shingles are maintained well, and the pines and chrysanthemums are the same as before, the owner of the garden could be an old wine-drinking and meat-eating reprobate, and every fern and every tree, every word and every sentence would cause the viewers to belch and feel like vomiting. They would stop their noses, cover their faces, and could not remain there for another moment. Having it would be a cause for regret; how could this compare to the pleasure of being rid of it?[25]

Chen Jiru's preface turns out to be written for his friend Fei Yuanlu, the owner of the Garden of Daily Visits (*Ri she yuan*), who was something of a reclusive writer. Chen says that Fei Yuanlu "was always writing prolifically, and in this he was in no way inferior to the ancients. Occasionally, he made use of his leisure to be a poet and engaged in elegant affairs. He composed verses in appreciation of things, and extending his delight, he continued by recording them, thereby forming a school of garden history."[26]

It would appear, therefore, that this "garden history" is basically a poetic record of experiences in a particular garden, by no means a comprehensive historical narrative, with "garden" as an overarching category, detailing historical developments, trends, and changes in Chinese garden making over various dynasties. This latter kind of history did not become available until the twentieth century, when Oka Oji produced his work. Traditional Chinese writings on gardens are focused on concrete particulars, and there is an enduring reluctance to operate at the level of treatises on general principles. We are in the context of a substantial philosophical problem here, for discussions of the foundations of historiography in the Western tradition, as I understand it, are closely related to notions of space and time in Kant and Hegel. For Kant, time and space are *a priori* theoretical forms of intuition, prior to thinking. Recent work in comparative philosophy has shown how Chinese notions of space and time are concrete. There is no sense of time as *a priori* form, or an abstract temporal corridor, in which events occur.[27] The traditional writings narrate particular gardens with a temporal field that each garden subtends. The distinctions that I am making here have tended to be obfuscated in the first two waves of modern scholarship. It is therefore the task of the current wave of scholarly studies to reconsider fundamental questions.

At a broader level of consideration, the focus of narration in traditional writings does

[25] Ibid., 1:1.

[26] Ibid., 1:2.

[27] See Huang and Zürcher, eds., *Time and Space in Chinese Culture*, Leiden, 1995. For a broader discussion of space-time in the context of Chinese garden history, see the important essay by D. L. Hall and R. T. Ames, "The Cosmological Setting of Chinese Gardens," *Studies in the History of Gardens and Designed Landscapes*, forthcoming.

not shift from particularity toward generalization and abstraction, but broadens to show how gardens were part of the transformation of dynastic fortunes. In this regard, Li Gefei's "Luoyang mingyuan ji" (Record of the celebrated gardens of Luoyang) (1095) is particularly illuminating.[28] Unlike many "records" (*ji*) that deal with an individual garden, the focus of this text on the gardens of an imperial capital seems a promising location for generalized description. Instead, the text offers nineteen sections, each dealing with an individual garden, to which is appended the following "discourse" (*lun*):

> Luoyang is situated in the centre of the world, commanding the [easterly entrance to the] pass between Xiao and Mian, fronting onto the throat and collar of Qin and Long [in the west], and is the nexus of thoroughfare in Zhao and Wei. Hence it is a place contested from the four directions. Everything is quiet when there are no incidents in the empire, but whenever trouble arises, Luoyang is the first to endure troops. I therefore once said the rise and fall of Luoyang is a sign of the empire's order or chaos. In the times of Jingguan and Kaiyuan (617–741), dukes and ministers and imperial relatives established residences and set out mansions in the Eastern Capital, said to be over 1000 in number. When it came to the time of disorder and rebellion which was followed by the violence of the Five Dynasties. The pools and ponds, bamboos and trees [of these places] were trampled by troops and fell into ruins, hillocks and wastelands. Tall pavilions and grand trees were consumed in smoke and fire, and transformed into ashes. They came to an end together with the Tang dynasty, passing away with it, with few places remaining. I therefore once said, "The prosperity and decline of gardens are signs of the rise and fall of Luoyang." Since the order and disorder of the empire is indexed by the rise and fall of Luoyang, and the rise and fall of Luoyang is indexed by the prosperity of gardens, how could the composition of records of celebrated gardens be in vain?[29]

This famous discussion of the historical rise and fall of gardens has two important features. The point of departure for articulating a sense of historical process is not the changes in positive characteristics of gardens summarized and narrated and accounted for. Rather, it is the *ephemerality* of gardens that offers the springboard for historical reflections that relate gardens to a broad picture of historical change.[30] At this broader level, the sense of the unfoldment of history is traditionally understood as the propensity of things.[31] Propensity resides in concrete situations simply as a function of the configuration of forces, and when the force of a tendency is exhausted, there is a moment of reversal, inaugurating a new and counter tendency in the unfoldment of events.

There is a sea change in the narratival employment of historical material in the twen-

[28] Li Gefei, "Luoyang mingyuan ji," in *Zhongguo lidai mingyuanji xuan zhu*, ed. Chen Zhi and Zhang Gongshi, Hefei, 1983, 38–55.

[29] Ibid., 54.

[30] See my "The Imaginary Garden of Liu Shilong," *Terra Nova* (Cambridge, Mass.) 2, 4 (Fall 1997), 14–21.

[31] F. Jullien, *The Propensity of Things: Toward a History of Efficacy in China*, trans. Janet Lloyd, New York, 1995.

tieth century, in a way that parallels the situation in the discussion of visual imagery above. In narrating Chinese garden history, some scholars overlay modern notions of linear chronological development and of progress onto a traditional dynastic framework of historical understanding. Historical perspectivism is the outcome. Bai Juyi's Thatched Hut in Mount Lu, for instance, is the first example of Chinese gardens in the literati tradition, according to Sugimura.[32] Other writers place it as an instance of the first *mature* fruits of the Chinese tradition of garden design. Wang Yi, however, considers the High Tang period as a pivotal point in the history of Chinese gardens. Before this time, Chinese gardens emphasized the experience of outdoor spaces; after this time, they were increasingly concerned with elaborating the relationship between interior spaces and outdoor areas.[33] I would argue that this is a suggestive view that might reward further study, for it allows us to think of Chinese garden history without recourse to a teleology, a generalized view of unilinear development, something that began and, later on, came to maturity, then to overelaboration, and finally went into decline. My sense is that just as Hayden White and the earlier work of Dominick LaCapra have taught us that historiographical employment of sources and historical facts is a constructive act that confers particular meanings, we might come to understand how changes in the sense and drift of the history of Chinese gardens are as significant as the sea change in imaging Chinese gardens.[34] In this regard, historians of Chinese gardens might well share with historians of gardens in other cultures a dissatisfaction with teleological explanations and an interest in issues of landscape and temporality.[35]

Textual Study

The Chinese tradition is very rich in the quantity and quality of writings on gardens. Indeed, Chen Congzhou recommends that "the study of Chinese gardens should *begin* with the study of Chinese literature."[36] This is not only because the ephemerality of gardens has meant that, as Stephen Owen might put it, "the form of survival becomes the content of what survives."[37] Rather, as I have argued elsewhere, garden writing and garden making can be considered mutually generating activities in Chinese culture, each calling forth the other.[38] It is therefore a matter of some regret that there is as yet no comprehensive guide to classical Chinese writings relevant to the study of gardens. In recent years, important efforts have been made to broaden the range of historical sources that inform our understanding

[32] Sugimura, *Chûgoku no niwa*, 44.

[33] Wang, *Yuanlin yu Zhongguo wenhua.*

[34] H. White, *Tropics of Discourse: Essays in Cultural Criticism*, Baltimore, Md., 1978; D. LaCapra, *Rethinking Intellectual History: Texts, Contexts, Language*, Ithaca, 1983.

[35] See J. D. Hunt, "Approaches (New and Old) to Garden History," in this volume.

[36] Chen Congzhou, "Zhongguo shiwen yu Zhongguo yuanlin yishu," in *Lian qing ji*, Shanghai, 1987, 8 (my emphasis).

[37] S. Owen, *Remembrances: The Experience of the Past in Classical Chinese Literature*, Cambridge, Mass., and London, 1986, 19.

[38] See my "Word and Garden in Chinese Essays of the Ming Dynasty: Notes on Matters of Approach," *Interfaces: Image, texte, language* 11–12 (June 1997), 77–90.

of Chinese gardens. Craig Clunas's study on Ming gardens as property from a materialist perspective draws on agronomic texts as well as essays and historical notebooks of the period.[39] A recently published index of the contents of the personal literary collections in the Imperial Library (*Si ku quan shu*) allows easy identification and location of about 6500 sources on architecture and gardens in the genre of "records" (*ji*).[40] Although only a very small fraction of these essays have been studied in modern scholarship, a detailed view of the history of Chinese gardens will emerge in time from their study and allow us to uphold new quantitative criteria for the use of evidence. Future scholars can also build on the valuable efforts of Chen Zhi and others who have edited and annotated some of the more important Chinese writings on gardens, among which the seventeenth-century treatise *Yuan ye* is perhaps the most prominent today.[41]

There is a significant problem arising from the preoccupation with annotation and translation of classical Chinese sources when an understandable focus on matters of semantic content diverts attention from considerations of a cross-cultural nature. *Yuan ye* is very much a case in point. Published in, or shortly after, 1635, it was hardly discussed in traditional writings, but in this century, thanks to Japanese scholars who thought that the reference to *zao yuan* in one of its prefaces made it the source of the Chinese and Japanese term for the modern profession of "landscape architecture," it has become an almost indispensable text to modern scholarship. This sea change in status is, in fact, no less dramatic than those of visual economy and historical sensibility that have been highlighted above. In this instance, a preoccupation with matters of semantic content can easily fall into the trap of naive assimilation of terms from one cultural context to another in order to satisfy professional interests. The fact that *Yuan ye* extolled the importance of master designers of gardens made it easily assimilable to modern understandings of the central role of professional designers. And much of the twentieth-century reception of this text has simply used a very sketchy understanding of it to provide the voice of the Chinese garden designer as an intentional subject.

By drawing on recent scholarship in architectural theory, landscape theory, and comparative philosophy, I have tried to show elsewhere that a new reading of *Yuan ye* can be generated. Following Augustin Berque's observation that the Chinese tradition has developed within a non-dualist cosmology and has not entertained "the subject/object opposition,"[42] I articulated the ramifications of this worldview by a close reading of certain key terms characterizing the importance of the master designer in *Yuan ye*.[43] Here too, it is necessary to emphasize the relevance of a discussion of landscape design without recourse to the binary opposition of subject and object, which has been much criticized in contem-

[39] C. Clunas, *Fruitful Sites: Garden Culture in Ming Dynasty China*, London, 1996.

[40] *Si ku quan shu wenji pianmu fenlei suoyin*, Taibei, 1989.

[41] Ji Cheng, *Yuan ye zhu shi*, 2nd rev. ed., ed. Chen Zhi, Beijing, 1988; Zhang Jiaji, *Yuan ye quan shi*, Taiyuan, 1993; English trans., Ji Cheng, *The Craft of Gardens*, trans. A. Hardie, New Haven, 1989; and French trans., Ji Cheng, *Yuanye: Le traité du jardin*, trans. C. B. Chiu [Qiu Zhiping], Besançon, 1997.

[42] A. Berque, "Beyond the Modern Landscape," *AA Files* 25 (Summer 1993), 33.

[43] S. Fung and M. Jackson, "Dualism and Polarism: Structures of Architectural and Landscape Architec-

porary scholarship in landscape architecture. In this way, the interests of translation, close reading, and cross-cultural discussion are seen to be closely interwined.

Conclusion

By way of conclusion, I would like to offer some supplementary comments on the approach that I have sketched out for thinking about Chinese garden history and its prospects. The basic impetus of my thinking has been the trope of reversal. Where one might have been inclined to attend solely to the positive and general characteristics of studies of Chinese gardens that can be obtained from generalization and abstraction, I pursued the opposite direction of thinking toward particularity and exemplarity. Where the importation of Western modes of representation might have prompted a simple narrative of Westernization in which Chinese studies of gardens would share the same scholarly procedures and concerns as Western scholars, I pursued the significance of the incompleteness of Westernization. Where one might begin by assuming, as most modern scholars had assumed, that historical sensibility and narration are transhistorical constants in the context of Chinese garden history, I have called attention to primary and contemporary sources that suggest a contrary interpretation. Finally, where modern scholars have isolated problems of translation from problems of analysis, and Chinese concerns from cross-cultural concerns, I have pointed to the significance of research that relates these problems and concerns to each other.

In relating Chinese concerns to cross-cultural frameworks of discussion, I think there is an important avenue of overcoming one aspect of Eurocentricism: I have in mind here the conception of culture that is based on the modern European notion of the autonomous and self-sufficient nation-state, according to which one would study French gardens and Japanese gardens as distinct domains of research. The critique of Eurocentricism involves not only the simplistic broadening of scholarly interests to the history of non-Western gardens, but must question the assumption that nation-states with national languages are the only possible cultural formations that produce "gardens," an assumption that underwrites an introvert specialization called Chinese garden history. When Chen Congzhou's photographs and song lyrics are scrutinized, or when the cross-cultural trafficking of techniques of visual analysis in garden history is studied closely, we find intimations of how "Westernized" Chinese historiography can contribute to new developments in a more general understanding of the prospects of garden history as an academic study. The Eurocentric assumption that the "flow" of scholarly proprieties has been "one-way" can, if one follows these intimations, give way to dialogic exchange.

---

tural Discourse in China and the West," *Interstices* (Auckland) 4 (1996); S. Fung, "Body and Appropriateness in *Yuan ye*," *Intersight* 4 (1997), 84–91.

Contributors

Mirka Beneš is associate professor of the history of landscape architecture at Harvard University, where she also lectures on Baroque architecture and urbanism. Her research includes Baroque Rome, early modern urban-suburban development, and modernism in landscape design. Her forthcoming book is on the Pamphilj and Borghese villa gardens and land ownership in Rome. She is also writing a book on landscape and society in Baroque Rome.

David R. Coffin is a former professor at Princeton University whose teaching and scholarship have centered on Renaissance architecture. He is the author of *The Villa d'Este at Tivoli* (1960), *The Villa in the Life of Renaissance Rome* (1979), *Gardens and Gardening in Papal Rome* (1991), and *The English Garden* (1994). In 1971 he organized and chaired the first Dumbarton Oaks Colloquium, "The Italian Garden."

Michel Conan is a sociologist and former head of the social science department at the National Center for Building Research in Paris. He has taught design thinking at Paris Val-de-Marne and research methods for garden history in a joint program of Paris La-Villette and Ecole des Hautes Etudes en Sciences Sociales. He has been instrumental in bringing a renewal of interest in garden history to France, where he has published and commented on reprints of rare garden books. In addition to having articles published on garden history, he has written several books on design processes. His most recent books are *L'invention des lieux* (1997), on how design may imbue a place with meaning, and *Dictionaire historique de l'art des jardins* (1997), a dictionary of historical terms in garden art. He is currently director of Studies in Landscape Architecture at Dumbarton Oaks.

Stanislaus Fung is deputy director of the Centre for Asian and Middle Eastern Architecture and senior lecturer in history and theories of architecture at the University of Adelaide, Australia. He taught in the School of Architecture at the University of New South Wales before joining the University of Adelaide in 1989. He is founding co-editor of *Fabrications: The Journal of the Society of Architectural Historians, Australia and New Zealand*. He is also consulting editor of the Penn Studies in Landscape Architecture series of the University of Pennsylvania Press and serves as a member of the editorial boards of *Architectural Theory Review* and the *Journal of Garden History*. Among his publications are entries in Macmillan's *Dictionary of Art* (1996) and papers in journals such as *Architectural Research Quarterly*.

Kenneth I. Helphand is professor of landscape architecture at the University of Oregon. He is the author of numerous articles and reviews on landscape history and theory and has a particular interest in the contemporary American landscape. His works include *Colorado: Visions of an American Landscape* (1991) and, with Cynthia Girling, *Yard Street Park: The Design of Suburban Open Space* (1994). Helphand serves as co-editor of *Landscape Journal*, is a fellow of the American Society of Landscape Architects, and is currently writing a book on landscape architecture in Israel.

John Dixon Hunt is chairman and professor in the Department of Landscape Architecture and Regional Planning at the University of Pennsylvania. He is a former director of Studies in Landscape Architecture at Dumbarton Oaks and academic advisor to the Oak Spring Garden Library Foundation, Upperville, Va. He is the author of *The Figure in the Landscape* (1976), *Garden and Grove* (1986), and *William Kent: Landscape Garden Designer* (1987); he has edited, among other volumes, the *Oxford Book of Garden Verse* (1993) and, with Peter Willis, *The Genius of the Place: The English Landscape Garden, 1620–1820* (1975). He is the founding editor of the *Journal of Garden History* and *Word and Image*.

Michael Leslie is professor of English at Rhodes College, Memphis, having previously been senior lecturer in English literature at Sheffield University in England. He has written widely on Renaissance literature and on the relationships between literature and landscape and the visual and verbal arts in the Middle Ages and the Renaissance, and edited the extensive papers of Samuel Hartlib. He is a founding editor of the *Journal of Garden History* and *Word and Image*. He is a senior fellow for Studies in Landscape Architecture at Dumbarton Oaks.

Elisabeth Blair MacDougall is a former director of Studies in Landscape Architecture at Dumbarton Oaks and associate professor in the Faculty of Arts and Sciences at Harvard University. She was promoted to full professor in 1976 and retired in 1988 as proffessor of th eHistory of Landscape Architecture Emerita. She has written numerous articles on the history of Italian Renaissance and Baroque gardens, which were re-published, along with several new essays, in *Fountains, Statues, and Flowers: Studies in Italian Gardens of the Sixteenth and Seventeenth Centuries* (1994). Since 1975 she has been a member of the Executive Committee of the International Federation of Landscape Architects–International Council of Monuments and Sites' Committee of Historic Gardens and Sites, a specialized division of ICOMOS. In addition, she served on the Executive Committee of the American National Committee of ICOMOS. Since 1968 she has served the Society of Architectural Historians in various positions, including director, president, and editor of the *Journal of the Society of Architectural Historians*.

James L. Wescoat Jr. is associate professor of geography at the University of Colorado at Boulder. He recently completed a ten-year program of research with the Arthur M. Sackler Gallery on Mughal gardens, which culminated in the publication of *Mughal Gar-*

dens: Sources, Places, Representations, and Prospects (1997), edited with Joachim Wolschke-Bulmahn, and *The Mughal Garden: Interpretation, Conservation, Implications* (1996), edited with Mahmood Hussain and Abdul Rehman.

Joachim Wolschke-Bulmahn is a former director of Studies in Landscape Architecture at Dumbarton Oaks and is currently professor of garden history at the Institute for Open Space Planning and Garden Architecture, University of Hannover. He has published widely on the history of landscape architecture and garden culture. A current focus of his work is the recent history of garden culture in Germany, on which he is collaborating with Gert Gröning of the University of Fine Arts, Berlin.

	MacDougall	Coffin	Beneš	Hunt	Leslie	Wescoat	Helphand	Wolschke-Bulmahn	Conan	Fung
Abstraction									X	X
Anthropological			X						X	
Archaeological						X				
Architectural		X	X	X		X	X		X	
Art		X	X	X	X	X	X		X	
Authority					X	X		X		
Colloquium		X	X			X				
Comparative			X			X				X
Context			X	X	X	X	X			
Cultural			X		X	X	X	X	X	
Culture		X	X	X			X		X	
Dehistoricization					X					
Design / process	X	X	X	X		X	X	X	X	
Design / project	X	X	X	X		X	X	X	X	
Design / realization	X	X	X	X		X	X	X	X	
Discipline		X	X	X			X	X		X
Ecological			X	X			X	X	X	
Environmental			X				X	X	X	
Experience			X	X		X	X		X	X
Explain				X	X				X	
Fellowship	X		X							
Function			X	X		X	X	X	X	X
Generalization										X
Historiography		X	X	X	X	X	X			X
Iconographical		X	X							
Idea			X	X			X	X	X	
Identity			X		X	X	X	X	X	
Ideology			X			X	X	X		
Image				X		X			X	X
Interest		X	X			X	X	X	X	X
Method	X		X	X	X	X	X	X	X	X
Nation		X	X	X	X	X	X	X	X	
Naturalize										X
Nature			X	X			X	X	X	
Paradigm					X					
Particular			X	X				X		X
Political		X	X	X	X	X		X	X	
Presentation				X						X
Professional			X	X			X		X	X
Public			X				X			
Reception			X	X						X
Reconstruction		X	X							
Regional		X	X			X	X			
Representation			X	X					X	X
Restoration		X	X			X				
Revise				X			X			X
Social		X	X		X	X		X	X	
Source		X	X			X			X	X
Teleology				X	X					X
Theoretical			X			X	X		X	X
Tourist			X		X	X				
Vernacular			X	X					X	X
Visual			X		X	X			X	X

Index

The table opposite displays the distribution of key words in the various articles. In the index, a vertical slash divides the page numbers by article to aid in finding relevant groups of entries.